# Fundamentals of
# Object-Oriented Design in UML

# The Addison-Wesley Object Technology Series

Grady Booch, Ivar Jacobson, and James Rumbaugh, Series Editors
For more information check out the series web site [http://www.awl.com /cseng/otseries/].

Armour/Miller, *Advanced Use Case Modeling, Volume 1*

Binder, *Testing Object-Oriented Systems: Models, Patterns, and Tools*

Blakley, *CORBA Security: An Introduction to Safe Computing with Objects*

Booch, *Object Solutions: Managing the Object-Oriented Project*

Booch, *Object-Oriented Analysis and Design with Applications, Second Edition*

Booch/Rumbaugh/Jacobson, *The Unified Modeling Language User Guide*

Box, *Essential COM*

Box/Brown/Ewald/Sells, *Effective COM: 50 Ways to Improve Your COM and MTS-based Applications*

Cockburn, *Surviving Object-Oriented Projects: A Manager's Guide*

Collins, *Designing Object-Oriented User Interfaces*

Conallen, *Building Web Applications with UML*

D'Souza/Wills, *Objects, Components, and Frameworks with UML: The Catalysis Approach*

Douglass, *Doing Hard Time: Developing Real-Time Systems with UML, Objects, Frameworks, and Patterns*

Douglass, *Real-Time UML, Second Edition: Developing Efficient Objects for Embedded Systems*

Fowler, *Analysis Patterns: Reusable Object Models*

Fowler/Beck/Brant/Opdyke/Roberts, *Refactoring: Improving the Design of Existing Code*

Fowler/Scott, *UML Distilled, Second Edition: A Brief Guide to the Standard Object Modeling Language*

Gomaa, *Designing Concurrent, Distributed, and Real-Time Applications with UML*

Gorton, *Enterprise Transaction Processing Systems: Putting the CORBA OTS, Encina++ and Orbix OTM to Work*

Graham, *Object-Oriented Methods, Third Edition: Principles and Practice*

Heinckiens, *Building Scalable Database Applications: Object-Oriented Design, Architectures, and Implementations*

Hofmeister/Nord/Dilip, *Applied Software Architecture*

Jacobson/Booch/Rumbaugh, *The Unified Software Development Process*

Jacobson/Christerson/Jonsson/Overgaard, *Object-Oriented Software Engineering: A Use Case Driven Approach*

Jacobson/Ericsson/Jacobson, *The Object Advantage: Business Process Reengineering with Object Technology*

Jacobson/Griss/Jonsson, *Software Reuse: Architecture, Process and Organization for Business Success*

Jordan, *C++ Object Databases: Programming with the ODMG Standard*

Kruchten, *The Rational Unified Process, An Introduction, Second Edition*

Lau, *The Art of Objects: Object-Oriented Design and Architecture*

Leffingwell/Widrig, *Managing Software Requirements: A Unified Approach*

Marshall, *Enterprise Modeling with UML: Designing Successful Software through Business Analysis*

Mowbray/Ruh, *Inside CORBA: Distributed Object Standards and Applications*

Oestereich, *Developing Software with UML: Object-Oriented Analysis and Design in Practice*

Page-Jones, *Fundamentals of Object-Oriented Design in UML*

Pohl, *Object-Oriented Programming Using C++, Second Edition*

Pooley/Stevens, *Using UML: Software Engineering with Objects and Components*

Quatrani, *Visual Modeling with Rational Rose 2000 and UML*

Rector/Sells, *ATL Internals*

Reed, *Developing Applications with Visual Basic and UML*

Rosenberg/Scott, *Use Case Driven Object Modeling with UML: A Practical Approach*

Royce, *Software Project Management: A Unified Framework*

Ruh/Herron/Klinker, *IIOP Complete: Understanding CORBA and Middleware Interoperability*

Rumbaugh/Jacobson/Booch, *The Unified Modeling Language Reference Manual*

Schneider/Winters, *Applying Use Cases: A Practical Guide*

Shan/Earle, *Enterprise Computing with Objects: From Client/Server Environments to the Internet*

Warmer/Kleppe, *The Object Constraint Language: Precise Modeling with UML*

White, *Software Configuration Management Strategies and Rational ClearCase: A Practical Introduction*

# Component-Based Development Series

Clemens Szyperski, Series Editor
For more information check out the series web site [http://www.awl.com /cseng/cbdseries/].

Allen, *Realizing eBusiness with Components*

Cheesman/Daniel, *UML Components: A Simple Process for Specifying Component-Based Software*

# Fundamentals of
# Object-Oriented Design in UML

## Meilir Page-Jones

foreword by Larry Constantine

## DORSET HOUSE PUBLISHING

New York, New York

## ADDISON–WESLEY

Boston • San Francisco • New York • Toronto • Montreal
London • Munich • Paris • Madrid
Capetown • Sidney • Tokyo • Singapore • Mexico City

The publisher offers discounts on this book when ordered in quantity for special sales. For more information, please contact:

Pearson Education Corporate Sales Division
One Lake Street
Upper Saddle River, NJ 07458
(800) 382-3419
corpsales@pearsontechgroup.com

Visit AW on the Web: www.awl.com/cseng/

*Library of Congress Cataloging-in-Publication Data*
Page-Jones, Meilir.
    Fundamentals of Object-Oriented Design in UML / Meilir Page-Jones.
        p. cm.—(Addison-Wesley object technology series)
    Includes bibliographical references and index.
    ISBN 0-201-69946-X (alk. paper)
    1. Object-oriented programming (Computer science)  2. Object-oriented analysis and design (Computer science) 3. UML (Computer science) I. Title.
    QA78.64.Q38 2000
    005.1′17—dc21
                                                     99–45825
                                                    CIP

ADDISON–WESLEY
Executive Editor: J. Carter Shanklin
Editorial Assistant: Kristin Erickson
Cover Design: Simone Payment

DORSET HOUSE PUBLISHING
Executive Editor: Wendy Eakin
Senior Editor: David McClintock
Assistant Editor: Michael Lumelsky
Editorial Assistants: Nuno Andrade,
                    Michael Richter

Text printed on recycled and acid-free paper.

ISBN 020169946X

4  5  6  7  8  9  MA   03 02 01 00

4th  Printing     September 2000

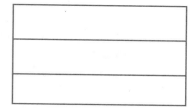

# Acknowledgments

If I were explicitly to acknowledge all the people that I should, the credits would still be rolling on page 94. So, instead, I offer a blanket "thank you" to the large group of colleagues who've inspired me, taught me, and set me straight over the years. But some folks deserve special thanks:

- The experts who offered their reviews and feedback on either the first or second edition of this book: Jim Beaver, Bob Binder, Ken Boyer, Tom Bragg, Tom Bruce, Martin Fowler, Alan Hecht, Mike Frankel, Cris Kobryn, Jim Odell, Tim Ottinger, Angel Rodriguez, Ben Sano, Mike Silves, Jess Thompson, Lynwood Wilson, and Becky Winant. Their suggestions were usually helpful, often thought-provoking, and sometimes hilarious. Thanks to their reviews, I avoided more than a dozen foolish errors and made dozens more significant enhancements. Thanks to their encouragement, I kept working to improve the book.

- Kendall Scott, for his exceptional work on the manuscript.

- Steve Weiss, who (along with Walter Beck) convinced me to branch out into object orientation, long before object orientation was fashionable. Without Steve, I would never have embarked on this book.

- Larry Constantine, who hit the first home run in software-design principles.

- Stan Kelly-Bootle, raconteur, wag of many tales, *bon vivant*, crafty linguist, creator of the *Shameless Chutzpah* column, and author of *Ni Fydd Mamog Arall Byth* (*There'll Never Be Another You*, among other Welsh historical romances), for lending me his support. (Stan, I'll return your support very soon.)

- Bert Weedon, who remarkably has enriched the art of music as much as he has the science of computational astrophysics.

- Ed Yourdon and Tim Lister, for their early faith in me.

- Bertrand Meyer, who remains a continual source of inspiration.

- Paul Becker, for his encouragement over the years.

- Roland Racko, for sharing his many insights.

- The ninety-seven authors of the object-oriented works that sit, partially read, on my bookshelf.

- The "Jolt Panel" of Miller Freeman, Inc.'s *Software Development* magazine, who honored me in 1996 with a Productivity Award for Dorset House's first edition of this book.

- Nuno Andrade, Michael Richter, Michael Lumelsky, David McClintock, Wendy Eakin, and the rest of the staff at Dorset House Publishing, high-quality prosemasters and bibliophiles, who work with great diligence and the latest technology. Their taking the not-inconsiderable trouble to completely remove syllepses, litotes, split infinitives, obscure words, unwieldy sentences beginning with gerunds that run on far too long, gratuitous self-references (such as this one), parenthetical and tangential (even distracting) digressions, inconsistent tenses, and really, like, superfluous extraneous adjectives that weren't needed created a professional work from an inchoate manuscript. Heroic and excellent work once again, folks!

- Carter Shanklin and the staff of Addison Wesley Longman for their part in bringing this edition of the book to market.

- My consulting clients and seminar students around the world, who shared their experiences with me and did their best to keep me honest.

- My family, who have retained their patience while living with a book-scribbling troglodyte.

Finally, no acknowledgment can be complete without recognition of two people who have long walked without peer through our industry:

- Professor Sid Dijkstra, whose contribution to software engineering is impossible to measure.

- Kedney Dogstar, the Legendary Coding Cowboy and inventor of eXtreme Debugging, who cuts more lines in a lunchtime at Bramston Capra Consulting than most of us do in a lifetime.

---

AUTHOR'S NOTE:
No methodologists were harmed in the making of this book.

---

DEDICATION

*To my family*

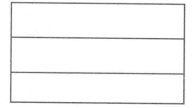

# Contents

# Foreword

Objects have become the ubiquitous building blocks of modern software, and object orientation is the pervasive paradigm of contemporary software-engineering practice. Books on object-oriented this or object-oriented that are discounted by the dozen, but when *What Every Programmer Should Know About Object-Oriented Design*, the first edition of this book, was published, it was immediately recognized as an original, insightful, and valuable contribution from one of the most consistently lucid thinkers and readable authors in software development today.

This newly revised and retitled second edition extends the foundation, expands the material, and updates the notation to create a reference of both immediate and lasting value. It is filled with fresh insights on object-oriented development, from the uses and abuses of inheritance, to how to model problematic data relationships in object classes. It is vintage Page-Jones, meaning up-to-the-minute and unflaggingly intelligent.

The author has been in the front-line trenches as a consultant and designer for decades, and the hard-won lessons show on every page of this book. I have been in the trenches with him, most recently collaborating on a very large-scale project with an initial use-case model of more than 340 use cases! He is, as the reader will learn, above all else, a pragmatist whose attention to fundamentals and detail is reflected in his analysis and design work as well as in his writing.

The truth is, Meilir is a gifted teacher who has a knack for taking complex and often misunderstood ideas and casting a conceptual light on them that makes them stand out in sharp relief from the confusing shadows. He can take a barrow-load of problems and wrap them up in a single archetypal example that makes it all seem so obvious that the rest of us are left wondering how we could ever have failed to see. What do you do when milking time arrives in the object-oriented dairy farm? Do you send a message to the **Cow** object to milk itself or a message to the **Milk** to un-cow itself? A moment's reflection and the need for an event manager to coordinate the milking becomes crystal clear. His clarifying examples, such as this one from a conference panel presentation or the "**Person** owns **Dog**" conundrum, have become part of the essential folklore of object orientation.

Indeed, this book aptly demonstrates how the long-established principles of sound design already in wide use by practicing professionals can carry over into and be adapted for developing object-oriented systems in the most advanced new languages and challenging contexts. Building on such fundamentals, the book maintains a relentlessly pragmatic focus based on real-world experience, distilling the essence of that experience into compact examples that will guide the developer, whether novice or old hand, toward better object-oriented software solutions.

Meilir draws on extensive experience with object-oriented development, as a consultant, as a teacher, and as a methodologist. He was codeveloper of the Synthesis method, one of the early systematic approaches to object-oriented analysis and design, and we were collaborators on the creation of the influential Uniform Object Notation, whose features can be found today reflected and incorporated into numerous object-oriented methods and notations. The legacy of our work can even be recognized in the Unified Modeling Language (UML) that has been adopted as a de facto industry standard and is used to illustrate and clarify examples throughout this book.

Here you will find everything you need to begin to master the fundamentals of object-oriented design. Not only are the basic techniques for designing and building with objects explained with exceptional clarity, but they are illustrated with abundant examples, and elaborated with discussions of the do's and don'ts of good object-oriented systems. The rest is up to you.

*September 1999*
*Rowley, Massachusetts*

Larry Constantine
Coauthor of *Software for Use:*
*A Practical Guide to the Models and*
*Methods of Usage-Centered Design*
(Reading, Mass.: Addison-Wesley, 1999)

"You say you want some evolution.
Well, you know, I'm doing what I can."

—Charles Darwin, *On the Origin of Species*

# Preface

People who reviewed this book in its draft form had several questions for me, questions that perhaps you share. Let me address some of them.

### I'm a programmer. Why should I care about design?

Everyone who writes code also *designs* code—either well or badly, either consciously or unconsciously. My goal in writing this book is to encourage O.O. professionals—and their number increases annually—to create good object-oriented designs consciously and prior to coding. To this end, I introduce notation, principles, and terminology that you and your colleagues can use to evaluate your designs and to discuss them meaningfully with one another.

### Will this book teach me an O.O. programming language?

No. Although I occasionally swoop down close to code, this isn't a book on object-oriented programming.

### But if I'm learning an object-oriented language, will this book help?

Yes, it will. If you don't currently know an object-oriented programming language, you can begin your object-oriented knowledge with Chapter 1. Knowing the key concepts of object orientation will speed your learning an object-oriented language and, I hope, boost your morale as you move into unfamiliar territory. The later chapters of the book, on sound design, will also help you in getting your early programs to work successfully.

On the other hand, if you're already an experienced object-oriented programmer, you can use Parts II and III of the book to enhance the design skills that are vital to your being a rounded, professional software designer or programmer.

### Why aren't the code examples in this book in C++?

I've written the code in this book in a language of my own devising, which is a blend of four popular languages: C++, Eiffel, Java, and Smalltalk. I did this because there are two kinds of programmers: those who are fluent in C++ and those who aren't. If you're a C++ aficionado, then you'll find the code a breeze to translate into C++. If you're not familiar with C++, then you might have found the language's arcane syntax distracting. Some examples are given in Java because it's more accessible to a non-Java programmer than C++ is to a non-C++ programmer. I'd like you to feel welcome in this book whatever your programming language might be.

### Why isn't this book devoted to the design of windows, icons, and menus?

There are two reasons: First, I don't believe that object orientation is useful only for the design of graphical user interfaces. Second, there are many books on the market devoted solely to the topic of object-oriented window design. I want this book to cover topics that are not well covered by other object-oriented books. However, in Chapter 7, I offer some notation for window-navigation design.

### Is this book about a methodology?

No. As you know, a development methodology contains much more than design. For example, there's requirements analysis, library management, and so on. Also, a true methodology needs to explain how the various development activities fit together. A lot of stuff!

So, instead of turning out a book as diffuse as many other books on object orientation, I decided to focus on a single topic: object-oriented design.

### You've said a lot about what this book isn't about. What **is** it about?

It's about the fundamental ideas, notation, terminology, criteria, and principles of object-oriented software design. Object-oriented software is software that comprises objects and the classes to which they belong. An object is a software construct in which operations (which are like functions or procedures) are organized around a set of variables (which are like data). A class implements a type that defines the group of objects belonging to that class.

The above modest sentences hold some surprising implications for software designers and programmers, implications that arise from the design concepts of inheritance, polymorphism, and second-order design. But, since you asked a specific question, let me give you a specific answer.

Part I of the book (Chapters 1 and 2) provides an introduction to object orientation. Chapter 1 summarizes the key concepts and demystifies "polymorphism," "genericity," and all the other O.O. jargon. Chapter 2 sets object orientation into the framework of previous developments in software. If you're already familiar with object orientation (perhaps by having programmed in an object-oriented language), then you can skip or skim Part I.

Part II (Chapters 3 to 7) covers Unified Modeling Language (UML), which has become the *de facto* standard notation for depicting object-oriented design. In passing, Part II also illustrates many of the structures that you find in object-oriented systems. Chapter 3 introduces UML for depicting classes, along with their attributes and operations. Chapter 4 covers UML for associations, aggregate and composite objects, and hierarchies of subclasses and superclasses. Chapter 5 sets out UML for messages (both sequential and asynchronous), while Chapter 6 covers UML for state diagrams. Chapter 7 reviews UML for system architecture and the windows that form a human interface.

Part III (Chapters 8 to 14) covers object-oriented design principles in some depth. Chapter 8 sets the scene with the crucial notions of connascence and level-2 encapsulation. Chapter 9 explores the various domains that "classes come from" and describes different degrees of class cohesion. Chapters 10 and 11 are the central pillars of Part III, applying the concepts of state-space and behavior to assess when a class hierarchy is both sound and extendable.

Chapter 12 offers some light relief, as it examines designs taken from real projects, including both the subtle and the absurd. (Chapter 12 is really about the dangers of abusing inheritance and polymorphism.) Chapter 13 looks at some ways of organizing operations within a given class, and it explains design techniques, such as mix-in classes and operation rings, that will improve class reusability and maintainability.

Chapter 14 takes a stab at the old question: "What makes a *good* class?" In answering this question, Chapter 14 describes the various kinds of class interface, ranging from the horrid to the sublime. A class with an exemplary interface will be a worthy implementation of an abstract data-type. If the class also obeys the fundamental principles laid out in earlier chapters, then it will be as robust, reliable, extensible, reusable, and maintainable as a class can ever be.

Chapter 15 rounds off the book by examining the characteristics, together with the advantages and disadvantages, of software components. In tracing the development of an object-oriented component for a business application, I recall some of the object-oriented principles of the previous chapters.

Although I've added plenty of examples, diagrams, and exercises to reinforce what I say in the main text, I must admit that the material in Part III gets tough at times. Nevertheless, I decided not to trivialize or dilute important issues. Some aspects of object-oriented design *are* difficult and to suggest otherwise would be misleading.

### Does this book cover everything in object-oriented design?

I very much doubt it. Each day, I learn more about object orientation, and I'm sure you do, too. Indeed, it would be a dull world if a single book could tell us everything about object-oriented design and leave us with nothing more to learn. And not everything in this book may be completely true! I certainly changed my mind about one or two things after writing my previous books, as I became older and wiser—well older, anyway.

So, although I think that I've covered many important design principles in this book, if you're serious about object orientation you should continue to read as much as you can and always challenge what you read.

### *Do you offer courses on object-oriented design?*

Yes. My firm, Wayland Systems, offers several courses on object-oriented topics. Our curriculum continually changes, so check out **www.waysys.com** for our latest offerings.

### *Bottom-line, as they say: Is this book for me?*

What kind of question is that? You expect me to say, "No!"? But seriously, folks, this book's for you if you are—or are about to become—a programmer, designer, systems engineer, or technical manager on a project using object-oriented techniques. Even if you're a beginner to object orientation, you can glean a lot from this book by reading Part I, practicing some object-oriented programming, and then returning to Parts II and III.

You should also read this book if you're a university student or professional programmer who has mastered the techniques of standard procedural programming and is looking for wider horizons. Much of the book's material is suitable for a final-year computer-science or software-engineering course in object orientation.

But, whatever your role in life, I hope that you enjoy this book and find it useful. Good luck!

*September 1999*                                                     Meilir Page-Jones
*Bellevue, Washington*
meilir@waysys.com

"All feel an habitual gratitude, and something of an honourable bigotry, for the objects which have long continued to please them."

—William Wordsworth, *Lyrical Ballads*

# Part I: Introduction

The term "object oriented" is intrinsically meaningless. "Object" is about the most general word in the English language. Look it up in a dictionary and you'll find a definition such as

> *Object:* A thing presented to or capable of being presented to the senses.

In other words, an object is just about anything!

The word "oriented" isn't of much help either. Defined as "directed toward," it usually plays the role of casting the term "object oriented" into an adjective. Thus, we have

> *Object oriented:* Directed toward just about anything you can think of.

No wonder the software industry historically had trouble in coming up with an agreed definition of "object-oriented." No wonder that this lack of clarity once allowed any peddler of soft wares to claim that his shrink-wrapped miracles were "object oriented." And no wonder that so many training courses on "object-oriented whatnot" have turned out to be either warmed-over old stuff or just plain claptrap.

When I first entered the realm of O.O., I decided to settle the definition of "object orientation" once and for all. I grabbed a dozen doyens of the object-oriented world and locked them in a room without food or water. I told them that they'd be allowed out only after they'd agreed on a definition that I could publish to a yearning software world.

An hour of screaming and banging within the room was followed by silence. Fearing the worst, I gingerly unlocked the door and peered in at the potentially gory sight. The gurus were alive, but were sitting apart and no longer speaking to one another.

Apparently, each guru began the session by trying to establish a definition of object orientation using the time-honored scientific practice of loud and repeated assertion. When that led nowhere, each of them agreed to list the properties of an object-oriented environment that he or she considered indispensable. Each one created a list of about six-to-ten vital properties.

At this point, they presumably had two options: They could create one long list that was the union of their individual lists; or, they could create a briefer list that was the intersection of their lists. They chose the latter option and produced a short list of the properties that were on all the individual lists.

The list was very short indeed. It was the word "encapsulation."

So the large-number-of-gurus-in-a-brawl approach to defining object orientation didn't yield much fruit. The problem is that the term "object oriented" is devoid of inherent meaning, and so its definition is totally arbitrary. Nevertheless, in Chapter 1, I take the plunge and give you *my* list of the software properties that constitute object orientation. You can either trust me that this is the "right" list, or you can take heart that it happens to contain the nine most popular properties selected by the twelve captive celebrities.

In Chapter 2, I identify some of the originators of object orientation. Following that, I analyze some prevailing social or cultural attitudes toward object orientation and counterpoint that with a discussion of object orientation from an engineering point of view. I conclude Chapter 2 with a brief account of object orientation's benefits to a software-development shop during each phase of software development.

# What Does It Mean to Be Object Oriented, Anyway?

As I mentioned earlier, I've unilaterally nominated nine software concepts that I find central to object orientation. Here they are:

Encapsulation
Information/implementation hiding
State retention
Object identity
Messages
Classes
Inheritance
Polymorphism
Genericity

The best way to illuminate the meaning behind these terms is to use a small example of object-oriented code. As I discuss this code during the chapter, you'll discover that the polysyllabic jargon of object orientation is less fierce in meaning than in appearance. Indeed, you're probably already familiar with many object-oriented notions—albeit under different names—from your previous software experience.[1] Three notes are in order before we begin.

First, the code that I present is a portion of a very simple object-oriented application. The application is a display of a miniature hominoid moving around a grid on a screen (the kind of thing that you might see in a video game). Although object orientation is certainly not limited to screen applications, such an application provides an excellent opening example.

Second, since I don't dwell much on the code's syntax or semantics, don't worry if the code doesn't make perfect sense at first. As I explain object-oriented terminology, I'll also explain the details of the code itself. I wrote the algorithm in an object-oriented pseudocode, the syntax of which is an average of the syntax of several mainstream object-oriented languages, such as C++, Java, Eiffel, and Smalltalk. (Incidentally, the **repeat...until...endrepeat** construct has nothing to do with object orientation. It's pure structured programming—a loop with the test in the middle.[2])

Third, although the two classes are not perfectly designed, they're good enough for our purposes in this chapter. But if you have any complaints about, say, the class **Hominoid**, stay tuned until Chapter 9, where I cover its design deficiency. (The deficiency is called "mixed-domain cohesion.")

Now, let's look at the application by dropping in on a memo from the software-team manager to the team itself.

**MEMORANDUM**

**From:**      **Alinah Koad, Software-Development Manager**

**To:**         **The Hominoid Software Team**

**Subject:**   **Hominoid-Controlling Software (V1.0)**

I just got word from the moguls in the oak offices that we've won the contract to control the hominoid hardware. We need to do a good job this time, folks, to make up for the fiasco of the seeing-eye robot that walked under a steamroller. In fact, the clients want us

---

[1] If you're curious about how object-oriented terminology varies from programming language to programming language, please take a look at the Blitz Guide to Object-Oriented Terminology at the end of the book.

[2] Where I quote code or pseudocode in the body of the text, I use **a font like this** to highlight it.

to demonstrate our software on a display screen before they let us turn it loose on their hardware. They've scheduled the demo of our software for next Monday.

In Version 1 of the software, the hominoid will simply have to navigate a bent linear path like the one shown below. You can think of it as consisting of square blocks placed in such a way as to yield a path one block wide, running from a START square (S) to a FINISH square (F). Each turn along the path will be a right angle, as in Fig. 1.1.

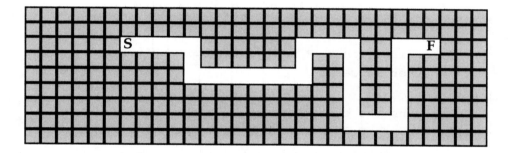

*Fig. 1.1: A path through the hominoid's grid.*

A single advancement by the hominoid carries it exactly one square forward (in the direction of its nose). It's important that the hominoid visit every square on the path from START to FINISH. It's even more important that the hominoid does not hit a wall, because then we'll look stupid and they won't let us install the software in the actual hardware hominoid.

Fortunately, we already have two classes written and stored in our object-oriented library. These are **Grid** and **Hominoid** itself. So, all you have to do by Monday is write the object-oriented code that uses the operations of these classes.

If you have any questions, you can contact me at my usual cabin in the Julius Marx Country Club. Have a nice weekend!

P.S. I enclose brief specifications for the two classes (**Hominoid** and **Grid**) that we have in the library.

Class External-Interface Specifications
(of the classes in the library)

Hominoid

New: Hominoid
// creates and returns a new instance of Hominoid

turnLeft
// turns the hominoid counterclockwise by 90°

turnRight
// turns the hominoid clockwise by 90°

advance (noOfSquares: Integer, **out** advanceOK: Boolean)
// moves the hominoid a certain number of squares along
// the direction that it's facing and returns
// whether successful

location: Square
// returns the current square that the hominoid is on

facingWall: Boolean
// returns whether the hominoid is at a wall of the grid

display
// shows the hominoid as an icon on the screen

Grid

New: Grid
// creates and returns a new instance of Grid with
// a random pattern

start: Square
// returns the square that is the designated start of
// the path through the grid

finish: Square
// returns the square that is the designated finish
// of the path through the grid

insertHominoid (hom: Hominoid, location: Square, **out** insertOK: Boolean)
// places the hominoid in the specified grid at the specified
// location and returns whether successful

display
// shows the grid as a pattern on the screen

---

## *Key*

| *Example* | *Meaning* |
|---|---|
| **advance** | Words beginning with a lowercase letter denote objects, instance operations, and instance attributes |
| **Hominoid** | Words beginning with an uppercase letter denote classes, class operations, and class attributes |
| **insertHominoid (hom: Hominoid, startSquare: Square, out insertOK: Boolean)** | Denotes an operation that takes an object of class **Hominoid** and an object of class **Square**, and returns an object of class **Boolean** (where **out** separates input from output arguments) |
| := | Assignment operator |
| **var** insertOK | Denotes a programming variable **insertOK** |

---

After their lost weekend, the team turned in the following object-oriented code.  In the remainder of this chapter, I often refer to this code to provide examples of the object-oriented abstractions that I describe.

```
var grid: Grid := Grid.New;           // creates new instances of Grid ...
var hom1: Hominoid := Hominoid.New;   // ... and Hominoid
                    // (The new instance of Hominoid will be pointed to by hom1)
var insertOK: Boolean;
var advanceOK: Boolean;
var startSquare: Square;
const oneSquare = 1;

startSquare := grid.start;
grid.insertHominoid (hom1, startSquare, out insertOK);

if not insertOK
then abort everything !;
endif;

    // set the hominoid in the right direction:
repeat 4 times max or until not hom1.facingWall
   hom1.turnLeft;
endrepeat;

grid.display;
hom1.display;

repeat until hom1.location = grid.finish

   if hom1.facingWall
   then hom1.turnLeft;
      if hom1.facingWall
      then hom1.turnRight; hom1.turnRight;
      endif;
   endif;

   hom1.advance (oneSquare, out advanceOK);
   hom1.display;

endrepeat
    // hominoid is at finish—success !
```

Using the hominoid code for illustration, let's turn again to the nine properties of object orientation that I nominated earlier. And the first winner is . . . the property on every one of the grappling gurus' lists: encapsulation.

## 1.1 Encapsulation

> *Encapsulation* is the grouping of related ideas into one unit, which can thereafter be referred to by a single name.

Software encapsulation is a concept that's almost as old as software itself. As early as the 1940s, programmers noticed that the same pattern of instructions would appear several times within the same program. People (such as Maurice Wilkes and his colleagues at Cambridge University) soon realized that such a repeating pattern could be hived away to a corner of the program and invoked by a single name from several different points in the main program.[3]

Thus was born the subroutine, as this encapsulation of instructions was termed. The subroutine was clearly a good way to save computer memory—a very precious commodity in those days. However, people subsequently realized that the subroutine also saved human memory: It represented a conceptual chunk that a person could (at one level, at least) consider and manipulate as a single idea.

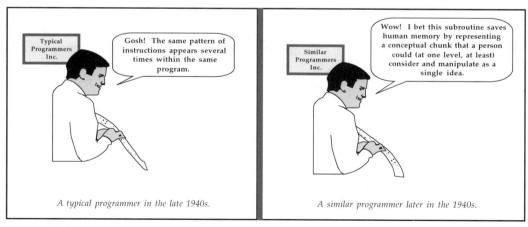

For an example, see Fig. 1.2, which shows a subroutine from a loan application.

---

[3] See [Wilkes et al., 1951].

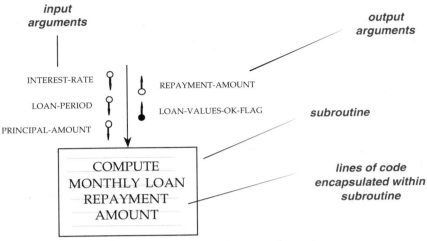

*Fig. 1.2: A subroutine.*

Encapsulation in object orientation has a purpose similar to that of the subroutine. But encapsulation is structurally more sophisticated.

> *Object-oriented encapsulation* is the packaging of operations and attributes representing state into an object type so that state is accessible or modifiable only via the interface provided by the encapsulation.[4]

An object consists of a set of operations and a set of attributes, as shown in Fig. 1.3. For example, an object such as the one pointed to by **hom1** has operations such as

>**turnLeft**, which turns the hominoid object to the left by 90 degrees,
>     and
>**advance**, which moves the hominoid forward

Each operation is a procedure or function that's normally visible to other objects, which means that it can be called upon by other objects.

Attributes represent the information that an object remembers.[5] Attributes are accessed and updated only via an object's operations. In other words, no other object can access an attribute by directly grabbing the underlying variable(s) that

---

[4] In other words, it's the encapsulation of state within the procedural mechanisms for accessing and modifying that state.

[5] You can think of these attributes as containing data. However, as we'll see later, attributes usually point to other objects, rather than to plain old data.

implement the attribute. Another object that needs the information held by an attribute can access the information only by appeal to one of the object's operations.

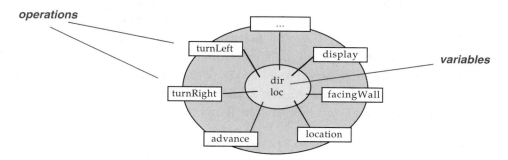

*Fig. 1.3: The operations and attributes of a hominoid object.*

Since only the object's operations may read and update the object's attributes, these operations form a protective ring around the central core of variables implemented within the object. For example, the operation **location** (probably implemented as a function, by the way) provides the objects outside the hominoid with the hominoid's location (presumably as a pair of x,y coordinates). We cannot directly access any variable implemented within the object (such as **xLoc** and **yLoc**) to get this information directly.

An object's structure therefore resembles a medieval European city, which would typically be surrounded by a protective wall. Well-defined and well-guarded gates through the wall regulated ingress to and egress from the city. In Fig. 1.4, I show a walled city with gates named after the hominoid's operation names.

*Fig. 1.4: A walled city with gates named by object operations.*

On a typical medieval day, staunch, honest yeopersons would enter the city via the gates. They would buy their pigs in the marketplace and then leave through a gate. Only the most villainous villeins and scrofulous scallywags would dare to scale the wall, swipe a swine, and steal away over the parapets.

In the interest of accuracy, I should point out that many object-oriented languages allow programmers to designate each attribute and operation as *public* (visible to other objects) or *private* (visible only within the object). Unless I state otherwise, I use *operation* to mean the typical, publicly visible operation and *attribute* to mean the typical, publicly visible attribute.

## 1.2 Information/Implementation Hiding

You may view an encapsulated unit from the outside (the "public view") or from the inside (the "private view"). The payoff of good encapsulation is the suppression in the public view of the myriad details to be seen in the private view. This suppression takes two forms: information hiding and implementation hiding.

The term "information hiding" implies that information within the unit cannot be perceived outside the unit. The term "implementation hiding" implies that implementation details within the unit cannot be perceived from outside.

> *Information/implementation hiding* is the use of encapsulation to restrict from external visibility certain information or implementation decisions that are internal to the encapsulation structure.

The hominoid object exemplifies the information-hiding property in that it contains some private information that's inaccessible from outside. An example is the direction in which the hominoid is pointing. From outside the object, we can change this information (through **turnLeft,** perhaps), but we cannot find its value—except, I suppose, by getting the hominoid to display itself and noticing which way its nose points.

However, the term "information hiding" addresses only part of what a good encapsulation may hide. Encapsulation often reveals information but hides implementation. This aspect is vital to object orientation: The variable inside an object that remembers the information provided by an attribute does not need to be implemented the same way as the attribute itself, which is available to other objects.

For example, although the hominoid object will tell us what its location is (via the operation **location**), we don't know how the object stores its location internally. It could be as (**xCoord**, **yCoord**) or (**yCoord**, **xCoord**) or polar coordinates or some magnificent scheme that its designer dreamed up at 1 a.m. So long as the object exports its location to us in a way acceptable to us as its clients, we don't care *how* it remembers its location.

Thus, **Hominoid**'s direction is an example of both information hiding and implementation hiding. For example, we don't know whether the direction information is held within the object as a numerical angle (with values of 0 to 359 degrees), as a single character (with values of **N**, **E**, **S**, and **W**), or as **percentDirection**, which expresses the direction that the hominoid is facing as a percentage of a full circle from 0 to 99.999.

In a future redesign, we might decide to reveal the direction information and to provide an operation to export the **direction** attribute to other objects. But even then, we'd retain implementation hiding because we still wouldn't need to know whether the implementation within the object was the same as that of the public information.

For example, we may decide that the object should hold **direction** internally in character form and—after converting it—export it publicly in angle form. In other words, the operation that provides the value of this attribute could convert it from an idiosyncratic internal representation to a numerical angle that most people would want to see as the attribute **direction**.

Information/implementation hiding is a powerful technique for taming software complexity. It means that an object appears as a black box to an external observer. In other words, the external observer has full knowledge of *what* the object can do, but has no knowledge of *how* the object may do it or of *how* the object is constructed internally. I show this schematically in Fig. 1.5.

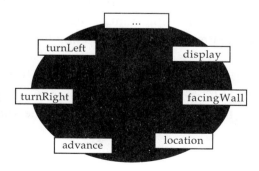

*Fig. 1.5: The Hominoid object seen as a "black box."*

Information/implementation hiding has two major benefits:

1. It localizes design decisions. Private design decisions (those within an object) have little or no impact on the rest of the system. Therefore, such local decisions can be made and changed with minimal impact upon the system as a whole. This limits the "ripple of change" effect.

2. It decouples the content of information from its form of representation. Thus, no user of information who is external to an object can become tied to any particular internal information format. This prevents external users of an object (other programmers, for instance) from meddling within it. It also prevents rogue programmers from introducing unstable connections to an object that depend on tricks and accidents of format. (I know that *you* wouldn't do such a thing, but you may have run across the software libertines of whom I speak at some time in your software career.)

## 1.3 State Retention

The third abstraction of object orientation pertains to an object's ability to retain state. When a traditional procedural module (function, subprogram, procedure, and so on) returns to its caller without any side effects, the module dies, leaving only its result as its legacy. When the same module is called on again, it's as if it were born for the first time. The module has no memory of anything that happened in its previous lives; indeed, like humans, it has no idea that it even had a previous existence.

But an object, such as the hominoid, *is* aware of its past. It retains information inside itself for an indefinite length of time. For example, a "caller" of an object may give it a piece of information and that caller—or another one—may later ask the object to offer up that information again. In other words, an object doesn't die when it's finished executing: It stands by faithfully, ready to leap into action again.

Technically speaking, an object retains state.[6] (*State* means, in effect, the set of values that an object holds. I discuss this further in Chapter 10.) For example, the hominoid retains indefinitely its knowledge of the square that it's on and

---

[6] If you're familiar with structured design, you may recognize this concept as *state memory*, as exemplified by an *information cluster*. See [Page-Jones, 1988], for example.

the direction that it's facing. However, we saw in Sections 1.1 and 1.2 that *how* the object chooses to retain that knowledge is its own internal business.

Object-oriented encapsulation, information/implementation hiding, and state retention are at the core of object orientation. But they're not new ideas. Dedicated, hard-working computer-science professors, huddled for countless years around whiteboards all over the world, have studied these ideas under the term *abstract data-type* (ADT).[7] However, object orientation goes well beyond the ADT, as the next six properties of object orientation (in Sections 1.4 to 1.9) reveal.

## 1.4 Object Identity

The first property of object orientation that transcends the concept of the ADT is a crucial property: Every object has its own identity.

> *Object identity* is the property by which each object (regardless of its class or current state) can be identified and treated as a distinct software entity.

There's something unique about a given object that distinguishes it from all its fellow objects. This "something unique" is provided by the *object-handle* mechanism,[8] which I'll explain by dissecting one line of the hominoid code:

**var** hom1: Hominoid := Hominoid.New;

The right-hand side of this line creates a new object (of class **Hominoid**), which I show in Fig. 1.6. Notice the object's handle, which for the object in the figure is the number 602237. The handle is an identifier attached to an object when it's created.

---

[7] An ADT is a data-type that provides a set of values and a set of interrelated operations each of whose external definition (as seen by outside users of that data-type) is independent of their internal representation or implementation. See [Liskov et al., 1981], for example.

[8] People who regard the term object handle as too informal use the term *object reference* instead.

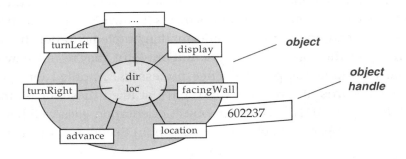

*Fig. 1.6: An object with its handle.*

Two rules apply to handles:

1. The same handle remains with the object for its entire life, regardless of what may befall the object during that time.

2. No two objects can have the same handle. Whenever the system creates a new object at run-time, the system assigns to the object a handle that's different from all other—past, present, and future—handles.[9] Therefore, you can always tell two objects apart, even if they're identical in structure and in the information they hold. They will have different handles.

The left-hand side of the line of code is the declaration **var hom1: Hominoid**. This is a normal program declaration that gives a programmer-meaningful name (in this case, **hom1**) to, say, a word of memory that can hold a value. The term **Hominoid** here is the name of **hom1**'s class, a topic that I discuss in Section 1.6.

As you may have guessed, the assignment (**:=**, which you read as "now points to" or "now refers to") causes the variable **hom1** to hold the handle of the object created on the right-hand side of the assignment statement.[10]

No one (programmer, user, anyone) will ever actually *see* the handle of the new object (602237), unless they root through memory with a debugger. Instead, the

---

[9] The handle is known formally as the *object identifier* (OID). Most object-oriented environments create this unique OID automatically. Also, most environments are not quite as pure as I suggest here. For example, they may recycle old handles from dead objects, taking care to preserve handle uniqueness only among the throng of *presently existing* objects.

[10] I use "points to" (and, later on, "pointer") in a general sense. Under the umbrella term "pointer," I include C++ *pointers*, C++ *references*, Eiffel *entities*, Smalltalk and Java *variables*, and so on.

programmer will access the object via the variable **hom1**, which was named by the programmer. In other words, **hom1** points to the object whose handle is 602237, as shown in Fig. 1.7.

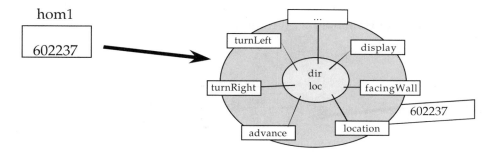

*Fig. 1.7:* **hom1** *points at the object whose handle is 602237.*

Some object-oriented environments use the physical memory address of the object as its handle. This is simple, but it can turn ugly if the object is moved in memory or gets swapped out to disk. It's better for a handle to be a meaningless, random, but unique number (though, of course, since we're not compiler designers, we have no control over how the computer conjures up handle values).

Let's say that we were now to execute another, similar, line of code:

**var** hom2: Hominoid := Hominoid.New;

This line will create another object (also of class **Hominoid**) with a handle of, say, 142857, and then will store that handle in the variable **hom2**. (See Fig. 1.8.)

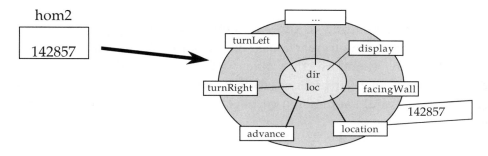

*Fig. 1.8:* **hom2** *points at the object whose handle is 142857.*

To make a point, I'll write another assignment statement:

   hom2 := hom1

Now the variables **hom1** and **hom2** both point to the same object (the first one we created, the instance of **Hominoid** with the handle 602237). See Fig. 1.9.

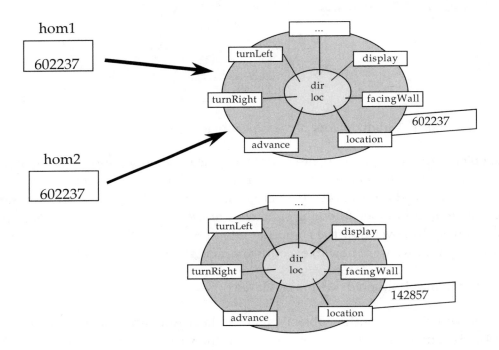

Fig. 1.9:   *Now both* **hom1** *and* **hom2** *point at the same object and the other object is no longer reachable.*

Having two variables pointing to the same object is not typically useful. But worse, we now have no way to reach the second object (the one whose handle is 142857). Effectively, therefore, that object has disappeared—just as if it had fallen down a black hole! In practice, it really does disappear. Most object-oriented environments would summon a garbage collector at this juncture to remove the object from memory.[11]

---

[11] A garbage collector in this context is a service of the operating environment, not that big loud smelly truck that rumbles down your cul-de-sac each Friday morning. Automated garbage-collection is well implemented in Java and Eiffel, but not—at this writing—in C++ environments.

The idea of giving every object its own identity by means of a handle seems innocuous in the extreme. Surprisingly, however, this simple idea causes a profound change in the way that we design and build object-oriented software. And that change is coming up in the next section. Stay tuned!

## 1.5 Messages

An object requests another object to carry out an activity via a *message*. Many messages also convey some information from one object to another. Most of the gurus included messages on their lists of vital object-oriented properties.

> A *message* is the vehicle by which a sender object **obj1** conveys to a target object **obj2** a demand for object **obj2** to apply one of its methods.[12]

In this section, I describe the anatomy of a message, the characteristics of message arguments, the role of an object sending a message, the role of an object receiving a message, and the three types of message.

### 1.5.1 Message structure

A message comprises several syntactic pieces, each of which is important in its own right in object-oriented design. Indeed, we'll return to each piece of a message many times throughout the book.

In order for object **obj1** to send a sensible message to object **obj2**, object **obj1** must know three things:

1.  The handle of **obj2**. (Obviously, when you send a message you should know to whom it's going.) **obj1** will normally store **obj2**'s handle in one of its variables.

---

[12] Object **obj1** and object **obj2** may be the same object. Hence, as I discuss in Chapter 5, an object may send a message to itself.

2. The name of the operation of **obj2** that **obj1** wishes to execute.

3. Any supplementary information (*arguments*) that **obj2** will require in the execution of its operation.

The object sending the message (**obj1** in the above) is called the *sender* and the object receiving the message (**obj2**) is called the *target*.[13]

The hominoid software offers several examples of messages.[14] One is this:

> hom1.turnRight;

Here, **hom1** points to (contains the handle of) the target object of the message. (If you recall, the handle was assigned to **hom1** by the assignment **var hom1 := Hominoid.New**.) **turnRight** is the name of the operation (belonging to the target object) that's to be executed. (This message doesn't need any arguments: **turnRight** always turns $90^O$.)

Sending a message is like calling a traditional function or procedure. For instance, in a "pre-O.O." language, we might have said,

> **call** turnRight (hom1);

But notice the inversion. With traditional software techniques, we appeal to a procedural unit and supply it with the object upon which to act; in object orientation, we appeal to an object, which then executes one of its procedural units.

At this stage of the book, such a distinction seems only syntactic—or at best philosophical. However, when I discuss polymorphism, overloading, and dynamic binding in Section 1.8, we'll see that this emphasis on "object first, procedure second" leads to an important practical difference between object-oriented structure and traditional structure. This is because different classes of objects may use the same operation name for operations that carry out different, class-specific behaviors or that carry out similar behavior but by different means.

---

[13] Other terms used for sender and target are *client* and *server* (or *service*), respectively.

[14] The code in the example earlier in this chapter is code within a sender object that I didn't specify.

### 1.5.2 Message arguments

Like the old-fashioned subroutine, most messages pass arguments back and forth. For instance, if we made the operation named **advance** return a flag holding the outcome of the advancement, then we'd have

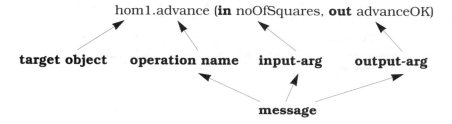

Thus, the structure of a message to a target object is defined by the signature of the target operation to be invoked. This signature comprises three parts: the operation name, the list of input arguments (prefixed by **in**), and the list of output arguments, also called return arguments (prefixed by **out**). Either argument list may be empty.[15] For brevity, I normally omit the keyword **in**, taking it to be the default.

The arguments of a message reflect another fundamental contrast between object-oriented software and traditional software. In a pure object-oriented environment (such as Smalltalk's), message arguments are not data; they're object handles. Message arguments are therefore like objects on the hoof!

For example, Fig. 1.10a shows **hom1.advance (noOfSquares, out advanceOK)**, a message from the hominoid program, in an informal graphic notation.

---

[15] The same argument may appear in both lists or may appear once, prefixed by **inout**. However, this is rare in pure object orientation. (See Exercise 3 at the end of this chapter.)

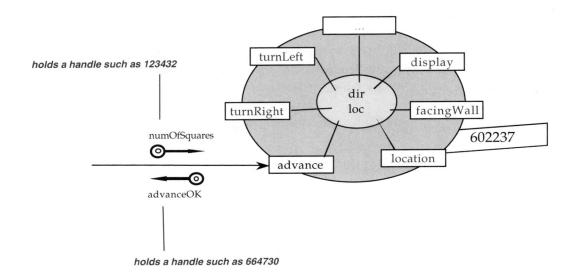

*Fig. 1.10a: The message* **hom1.advance (noOfSquares, out advanceOK)** *shown in informal graphics.*

If we were to snapshot the running hominoid program while it was executing this message and dump out the values of the message's arguments, we would find something unexpected. We might find, for instance

|  |  |
|---|---|
| noOfSquares | set to 123432 |
| advanceOK | set to 664730 |

Why these strange numbers? Because 123432 might be the handle of the object (of class **Integer**) that we normally think of as the integer **2**, and 664730 might be the handle of the object (of class **Boolean**) that we normally think of as the logical value **true**.[16]

Incidentally, if you prefer a more formal notation for the above message, Fig. 1.10b presents it in UML notation, which we'll cover in depth in Chapters 3 through 7.

---

[16] I'm not suggesting that your object-oriented environment would use these exact numbers. I use them for the purpose of illustration only.

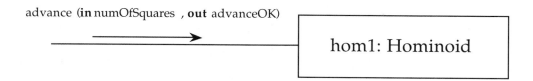

advance (**in** numOfSquares , **out** advanceOK)

hom1: Hominoid

*Fig. 1.10b: The message* **hom1.advance (noOfSquares, out advanceOK)** *shown in UML.*

As another example, if we were executing an object-oriented personnel system and did the same thing, we might find the argument **empOfMonth** set to 441523. 441523 would perhaps be the handle of the object (of class **Employee**) that represents Mr. Jim Spriggs.

### 1.5.3 The roles of objects in messages

In this section, I review the four roles that we've seen objects play in an object-oriented system. An object may be

- the sender of a message
- the target of a message
- pointed to by a variable within another object (as we saw in Section 1.4)
- pointed to by an argument passed back or forth in a message (as we saw in Section 1.5.2)

A given object may play one or more of these roles during its lifetime. In Fig. 1.11, we can see all these roles choreographed together.

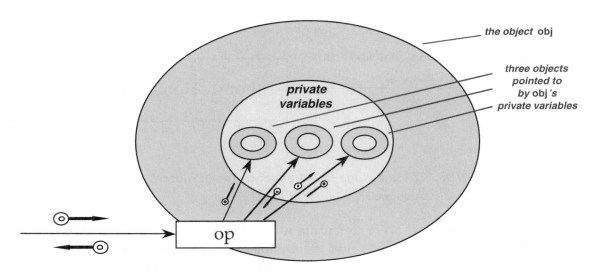

*Fig. 1.11: An operation of an object sending messages to the three objects pointed to by variables.*

In the figure, we see an operation **op** of an object **obj**. It sends messages to the objects pointed to by each of **obj**'s three variables. The first message has only an input argument; the second has only an output argument; the third has both input and output arguments. Each of these arguments is itself a pointer to an object. This structure is very, very typical of how an object's operations interact with an object's variables.

Some authors suggest that each object is a "born sender" or a "born target." This isn't so, as Fig. 1.12 illustrates.

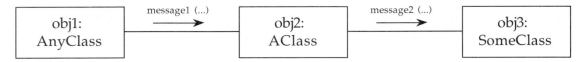

*Fig. 1.12: Two messages between pairs of objects.*

For **message1**, **obj1** is the sender and **obj2** is the target. For **message2**, **obj2** is the sender and **obj3** is the target. So we see that, at different times, the same object can play the part of sender or target. The terms "sender" and "target" are therefore relative to a given message. They aren't fixed properties of the objects themselves.

A pure object-oriented environment contains only objects, each of which plays one or more of the four roles that we saw above. In pure object orientation, there is no need for data, because objects can do all of data's necessary software jobs. And in Smalltalk (a very pure object-oriented language), there really *isn't* any data! At run-time, there are only objects pointing to other objects (via variables) and communicating with each other by passing back and forth handles of yet other objects.

However, in C++ (which is a mixed language in that it's both data/function-oriented and object-oriented), arguments can be pointers to anything. If your C++ code is as pure as Smalltalk, then all your arguments will be pointers to objects. But if you mix objects and data in your program, then some of your arguments may be simple data (or pointers to data).[17] A similar comment applies to Java code, although Java is far less freewheeling a language than C++.

### 1.5.4 Types of message

There are three types of message that an object may receive: informative messages, interrogative messages, and imperative messages. In this section, I briefly define and give an example of each kind of message, using the hominoid once more. We'll return to these message types at the very end of the book, in Chapter 12, when we examine different design options for communicating objects.

> An *informative message* is a message to an object that provides the object with information to update itself. (It is also known as an *update*, *forward*, or *push* message.) It is a "past-oriented" message, in that it usually informs the object of what has already taken place elsewhere.

An example of an informative message is **employee.gotMarried (marriageDate: Date)**. This message tells an object representing an employee that the actual employee got married on a certain date. In general, an informative message tells an object something that's happened in the part of the real world represented by that object.

---

[17] See Exercise 4 at the end of this chapter for more on the distinction between objects and data values.

> An *interrogative message* is a message to an object requesting it to reveal some information about itself. (It is also known as a *read, backward,* or *pull* message.) It is a "present-oriented" message, in that it asks the object for some current information.

An example of an interrogative message is **hom1.location**, which asks the hominoid to tell us its current location on the grid. This kind of message doesn't change anything; instead, it's usually a query about the piece of the world that the target object represents.

> An *imperative* message is a message to an object that requests the object to take some action on itself, another object, or even the environment around the system. (It is also known as a *force* or *action* message.) It is a "future-oriented" message, in that it asks the object to carry out some action in the immediate future.

An example of an imperative message is **hom1.advance**, which causes the hominoid to move forward. This kind of message often results in the target object's execution of some significant algorithm to work out what to do.

Similarly, imagine that we could send the following imperative message to a hominoid:

hom1.goToLocation (square: Square, **out** feasible: Boolean)

This message would request that the hominoid go to a particular square, so long as that were feasible. (The calculation that the hominoid would have to carry out would be immense.)

Real-time object-oriented systems, in which objects control pieces of hardware, often contain many imperative messages. These systems clearly illustrate the future-oriented spirit of an imperative message. Consider this example from the world of robotics:

robotLeftHand.goToLocation (x, y, z: Length, theta1, theta2, theta3: Angle)

This message sets a robot's left hand to a given position and orientation in space. The algorithm may require the robot's hand, the robot's arm, and/or the robot itself to move. The six arguments represent the six degrees of freedom of the hand, a three-dimensional thing in space.

Next, we move from messages to yet another indisputably fundamental property of object orientation, the object class.

## 1.6 Classes

Recall that in the hominoid software we created an object (to represent a hominoid) by executing **Hominoid.New**. **Hominoid**, an example of a *class*, served as a model from which we created hominoid objects (such as the one with the handle 602237). Whenever we execute the statement **Hominoid.New**, we instantiate an object that is structurally identical to every other object created by the statement **Hominoid.New**. By "structurally identical," I mean that each hominoid object has the same operations and variables as the others—specifically, the operations and variables that the programmer coded when he wrote the class **Hominoid**.[18] See Fig. 1.13.

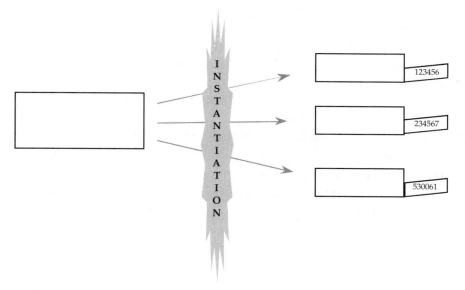

*Fig. 1.13: Three objects instantiated from the same class.*

[18] By the way, throughout this book, I intend an indefinite "he" to mean "he or she." In other words, as they say in British Civil Service paperwork, it is to be understood in the following document that "he" embraces "she."

> A *class* is the stencil from which objects are created (instantiated). Each object has the same structure and behavior as the class from which it is instantiated.
>
> If object **obj** belongs to class **C**, we say "**obj** is an instance of **C**."

There are two differences between objects of the same class: Each object has a different handle and, at any particular time, each object will probably have a different state (which means different "values" stored in its variables).

At first, you may be confused about the distinction between a class and an object. The simple way to remember the distinction is this:

- A class is what you design and program.
- Objects are what you create (from a class) at run-time.[19]

Popular software packages provide a close analogy to classes and objects. Let's say that you buy a spreadsheet package called Visigoth 5.0 from the Wallisoft Corp (founded by Wally Soft himself). The package itself would be the analogue of the class. The actual spreadsheets that you create from it would be similar to objects. Each spreadsheet has all the "spreadsheet machinery" available to it as an instance of the Visigoth class.

At run-time, a class such as **Hominoid** may spawn 3, or 300, or 3,000 objects (that is, instances of **Hominoid**). A class therefore resembles a stencil: Once the shape on a stencil is cut, the same shape can be traced from it thousands of times. All of the tracings will be identical to one another and, of course, to the shape on the original stencil.[20]

---

[19] So *object-oriented programming* should really be termed *class-structured programming*. However, I don't expect this term to catch on!

[20] The standard analogy from the "Objects Are Yummy" School is that a class is like a cookie-cutter and objects are like cookies. Presumably, the garbage collector is much like a cookie monster.

To clarify this further, let's look more closely at the population of objects generated from a single class.  As we've seen, all of the objects of a class have the same structure: the same bunch of operations and attributes.  Thus, each object (instance) of a class has its own copy of the set of methods it needs to implement the operations and the set of variables it needs to implement the attributes.[21] There are at a given time, in principle, as many copies of the methods and variables (0, 3, 300, ...) as there are instantiated objects at that time.  See Fig. 1.14.

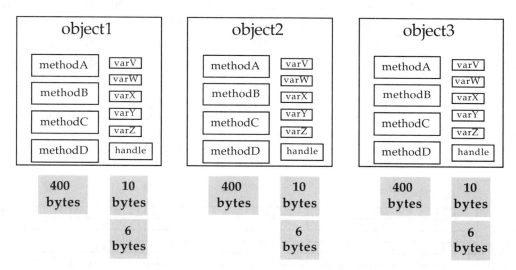

Fig. 1.14: *The methods, variables, and handles for three objects of the same class, together with the objects' memory requirements.*

For a moment, if you don't mind, I'll descend deep into computer implementation in order to explain further the real structure of a bunch of objects of the same class, which I'll call **C**.  Let's assume that each method implementing one of Fig. 1.14's operations occupies 100 bytes, every variable occupies 2 bytes, and every handle occupies 6 bytes. Therefore, **object1** will occupy 416 bytes of memory (that is, 4 * 100 + 5 * 2 + 6).  The three objects together will therefore occupy 1,248 bytes (that is, 3 * 416).  Fifteen such objects would occupy 6,240 bytes (that is, 15 * 416).

But this approach to allocating memory to objects would be very wasteful, because each of the 15 sets of methods of the 15 objects is identical.  And, since

---

[21] A method is the implementation of an operation.  In programming terms, you can think of a method as the code of a procedure's (or function's) body.  Similarly, a variable is the implementation of an attribute, and a handle is the implementation of an object identifier.

each set of methods contains only procedural code, a single set can be shared by all the objects. So, although in principle each object has its own set of operational methods, in practice (to save space) they all share the same physical copy.

On the other hand, although the handles and the variables of each object are identical in structure from object to object, they *cannot* be shared among objects. The reason, of course, is that they must contain different values at run-time.

So, since **C**'s objects all share the same set of operations, the total memory consumed by **C**'s 15 objects will actually be only 640 bytes (400 bytes for the single set of methods, 150 bytes for the 15 sets of variables, and 90 bytes for the 15 handles). This 640 bytes is much better than 6,240 bytes and it's the normal way that an object-oriented environment allocates memory to objects. See Fig. 1.15.

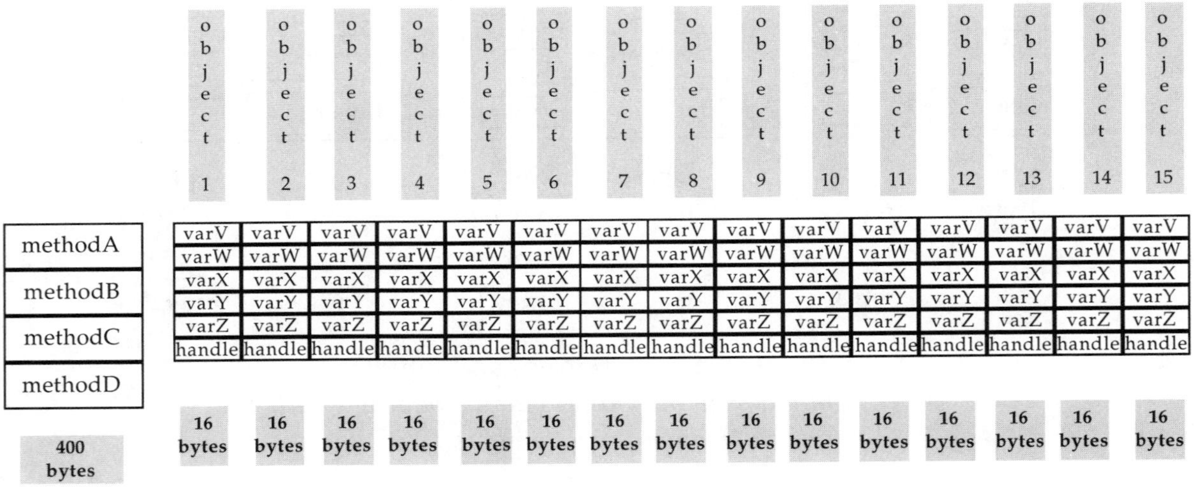

*Fig. 1.15: Schematic depiction of the actual memory (640 bytes) used by 15 objects of the same class.*

Almost all of the operations and attributes that we've looked at in this chapter belong to individual objects. They're called *object instance operations* and *object instance attributes,* or *instance operations* and *instance attributes* for short. However, there are also *class operations* and *class attributes.* By definition, there's exactly one set of class operations and class attributes for a given class at all times—regardless of how many objects of that class may have been instantiated.

Class operations and class attributes are needed to cope with situations that cannot be the responsibility of any individual object. The most famous example of a class operation is **New**, which instantiates a new object of a given class.

The message **New** could never be sent to an individual object. Say, for example, that we had three objects of class **BankCustomer**, representing actual bank customers (let's refer to these objects as **bob**, **carol**, and **ted**) and we wanted to instantiate a new **BankCustomer** object (say, **alice**). To which object would we send the message **New**? There would be no particular reason to send it to **bob**, as opposed to **carol** or **ted**. Worse still, we could never have instantiated the first bank customer, because initially there wouldn't have been any object of class **BankCustomer** to which to send the **New** message.

So, **New** is a message that must be sent to a class, rather than to an individual object. The example from the hominoid game was **Hominoid.New**. This was a class message to the class **Hominoid** to execute its class operation **New** and thus create a fresh object, a fresh instance of the class **Hominoid**.

An example of a class attribute might be **noOfHominoidsCreated: Integer**. This would be incremented by **New** each time **New** executed. However many hominoid objects there were, there would be only one copy of this class attribute. You may design a class operation to provide the outside world with access to this class attribute.

Figure 1.16 shows the structure of memory if the class **C** has two class operations (each of whose methods occupies 100 bytes) and three class attributes (each of whose variables occupies 2 bytes). The number of bytes for "class machinery" (206 in this example) will remain constant regardless of the number of objects that **C** has instantiated. With this class machinery added, **C** and its flock of 15 objects now consume a total of 846 (that is, 206 + 640) bytes of memory.

Note that both in principle and in practice, there's only one set of class methods per class. This is in contrast to instance methods, where, *in principle*, each object has its own set. (Only to save memory do we make objects share the same set of methods for their operations.) The distinction between class variables and instance variables is clearer: Each class has only one set of class variables, whereas there's one set of instance variables for each object of that class, both in principle and in fact.

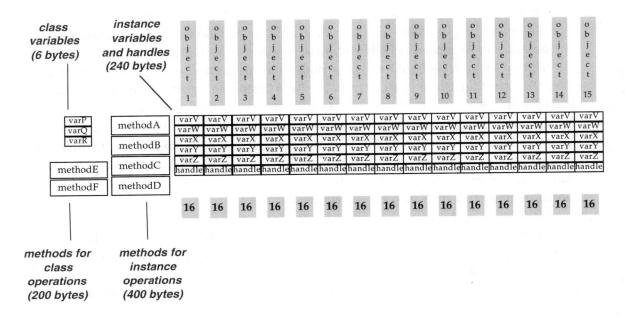

*Fig. 1.16: Schematic depiction of the actual memory (846 bytes) used by 15 objects and the "class machinery."*

If you've studied abstract data-types (ADTs), perhaps at university, you may wonder what the difference is between a class and an ADT. The answer is that an ADT describes an interface. It's a facade that declares what will be provided for users of that ADT, but says nothing about how the ADT will be implemented. A class is a thing of flesh and blood (or at least of internal design and code) that implements an ADT. Indeed, for a given ADT, you could design and build several different classes. For example, one such class could yield objects that run very efficiently, while another class for the same ADT could yield objects that take up little memory.

I say much more about abstract data-types, classes, and the differences between them in Part III of the book. Until then, however, I'll treat "class" and "ADT" as synonyms. With that in mind, let's move on to the important concept of inheritance.

## 1.7 Inheritance

What would you do if you wrote a class **C** and then later discovered a class **D** that was almost identical to **C** except for a few extra attributes or operations? One solution would be simply to duplicate all the attributes and operations of **C** and put them into **D**. But not only would this be extra work for you, the duplication would also make maintenance a nuisance. A better solution would be to have the class **D** somehow "ask to use the operations" of the class **C**. This solution is called inheritance.

---

*Inheritance* (by **D** from **C**) is the facility by which a class **D** has implicitly defined upon it each of the attributes and operations of class **C**, as if those attributes and operations had been defined upon **D** itself.

**C** is termed a *superclass* of **D**. **D** is a *subclass* of **C**.

---

In other words, through inheritance, objects of class **D** can make use of attributes and operations that would otherwise be available only to objects of class **C**.

Inheritance represents another major way in which object orientation departs from traditional systems approaches. It effectively allows you to build software incrementally in this way:

- First, build classes to cope with the most general case.
- Then, in order to deal with special cases, add more specialized classes that inherit from the first class. These new classes will be entitled to use all the operations and attributes (both class and instance operations and attributes) of the original class.

An example may help to illustrate the principle. Let's say that we have a class **Aircraft** in an aviation application. **Aircraft** may have defined on it an instance operation named **turn** and within it an instance attribute named **course**.

The class **Aircraft** deals with activity or information pertinent to any kind of flying craft. However, there are special kinds of aircraft that carry out special activities and thus require special pieces of information. For example, a glider carries out special activities (for example, releasing its towline) and may need to record special information (for example, whether it is attached to a towline).

Thus we may define another class, **Glider**, that inherits from **Aircraft**. **Glider** will have an instance operation named **releaseTowline** and an instance attribute named **whetherTowlineAttached** (of class **Boolean**). This will give us the structure shown in Fig. 1.17, in which the open-headed arrow denotes inheritance.

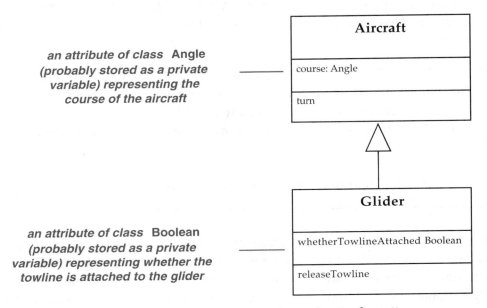

*an attribute of class* **Angle** *(probably stored as a private variable) representing the course of the aircraft*

*an attribute of class* **Boolean** *(probably stored as a private variable) representing whether the towline is attached to the glider*

*Fig. 1.17:* **Glider** *is a subclass that inherits from its super-class,* **Aircraft**.

Now we'll look at the mechanics of inheritance by imagining some object-oriented code that first spawns objects from the classes **Aircraft** and **Glider** and then sends messages to those objects. The code is followed by a discussion of the four statements tagged (1) through (4).

```
var ac: Aircraft := Aircraft.New;
var gl: Glider  := Glider.New;
    ...
ac.turn (newCourse, out turnOK);    (1)
gl.releaseTowline;                  (2)
gl.turn (newCourse, out turnOK);    (3)
ac.releaseTowline;                  (4)

    ...
```

(1) The object pointed to by **ac** receives the message **turn (newCourse, out turnOK)**, which causes it to apply the operation **turn** (with the appropriate arguments). Since **ac** is an instance of **Aircraft**, **ac** will simply use the operation **turn** that has been defined on the class **Aircraft**.

(2) The object pointed to by **gl** receives the message **releaseTowline**, which causes it to apply the operation **releaseTowline** (which needs no arguments). Since **gl** is an instance of **Glider**, **gl** will simply use the operation **releaseTowline** that has been defined on the class **Glider**.

(3) The object pointed to by **gl** receives the message **turn (newCourse, out turnOK)**, which causes it to apply the operation **turn** (with the appropriate arguments). Without inheritance, this message would cause a run-time error (such as **Undefined operation - turn**) because **gl** is an instance of **Glider**, which has no operation named **turn**.

However, since **Aircraft** is a superclass of **Glider**, the object **gl** is also entitled to use any operation of **Aircraft**. (If **Aircraft** had a superclass **FlyingThing**, **gl** would also be entitled to use any operation of **FlyingThing**.) Therefore, the line of code marked (3) will work successfully, and the operation **turn**, as defined on **Aircraft**, will be executed.

(4) This will not work! **ac** refers to an instance of **Aircraft**, which has no operation named **releaseTowline**. Inheritance is no help here, since **Glider** is the only class that has **releaseTowline** defined on it, and **Glider** is a *subclass* of **Aircraft**. Since inheritance doesn't work in this direction, the system will stop with a run-time error. This makes sense, since **ac** may point to a big jet plane, for which **releaseTowline** would have no meaning.

In Section 1.6, we saw the distinction between class and object. Now we see that there's also a subtle distinction between object and instance. Although up to now we've used "object" and "instance" almost synonymously, we see that inheritance in a sense permits a single object to be simultaneously an instance of more than one class.

This corresponds well to the real world. If you own a glider, you own exactly one object with one identification (handle) on its tail. Yet this glider is (obviously!) an example of a glider and, at the same time, an example of an aircraft. Conceptually then, the object representing the thing that you own is an instance of **Glider** *and* an instance of **Aircraft**.

Indeed, the above example demonstrates a telling test for the valid use of inheritance: It's called the *is a* test. If you can say: "a D *is a* C," then **D** almost certainly should be a subclass of **C**. Thus, because "a glider *is an* aircraft," the class **Glider** should be a subclass of **Aircraft**.[22]

Let's explore this topic further by taking a behind-the-scenes look at inheritance. The object referred to by **gl** will be represented at run-time by an amalgamation of two parts. One part will be the instance operations and instance attributes defined for **Glider**; the other part will be the instance operations and instance attributes defined for **Aircraft**, as shown in Fig. 1.18.[23]

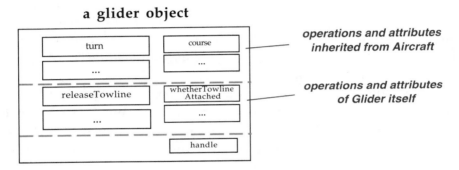

*Fig. 1.18: The instance operations and instance attributes available to an object of class* **Glider**.

In most languages, the inheriting subclass inherits everything that the superclass has on offer; the subclass doesn't get to pick and choose what it inherits. However, there are some tricks by which a subclass can override (that is, cancel out) inherited operations, as I discuss in Section 1.8.

The actual code to implement inheritance in good object-oriented languages is straightforward. You simply state the superclass in the class definition of each subclass that is to inherit from the superclass. For example,

**class** Glider **inherits from** Aircraft;

...

---

[22] I go much further into the *is a* topic and the correct uses of inheritance in Chapters 10, 11, and 12.

[23] In fact, a tool called a *class-flattener*—built into environments such as Eiffel—provides exactly this view.

The example of inheritance in this section is one of *single inheritance,* which means that each class has at most one direct superclass. *Multiple inheritance* is also possible. With multiple inheritance, each class may have an arbitrary number of direct superclasses.

Multiple inheritance converts the inheritance tree of single inheritance into an inheritance lattice. See Fig. 1.19.

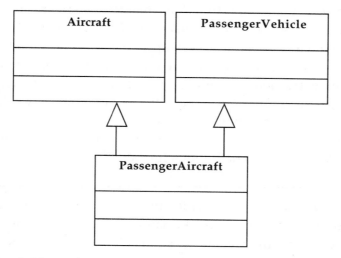

*Fig. 1.19: Multiple inheritance—a subclass with two or more superclasses.*

Multiple inheritance introduces some difficult design issues, including the possibility of a subclass inheriting clashing operations (or attributes) from its multiple ancestors. (Clashing operations have the same name and the inheriting subclass cannot easily tell which one to inherit.)

Difficulties such as the name-clash problem have given multiple inheritance a bad reputation. Over the years, both condemnation and defense of multiple inheritance have reached a fever pitch. I should reveal that I'm in favor of multiple inheritance, because the real world frequently calls for multiply inheriting subclasses. As we saw in Fig. 1.19, the class **PassengerAircraft** could reasonably inherit from both **Aircraft** and **PassengerVehicle**.

Nevertheless, since multiple inheritance may create complex and incomprehensible structures, you should use multiple inheritance judiciously—even more judiciously than single inheritance.[24]  At the time of this writing, two major languages (C++ and Eiffel) support multiple inheritance, while two others (Java and Smalltalk) do not.

## 1.8 Polymorphism

The word "polymorphism" comes from two Greek words that mean, respectively, "many" and "form."  Something that's polymorphic therefore has the property of taking on many forms, as in the episode of *Red Dwarf* (called, appropriately enough, *Polymorph)* in which the spaceship's crew was continually attacked by an alien being that could rapidly switch from one bodily form to another.

Object-oriented textbooks contain two definitions of polymorphism, neither one quite as dramatic as the *Red Dwarf.*  In the definition box below, I've marked them (A) and (B).  Both definitions are valid and both properties of polymorphism work hand in hand to bring a great deal of power to object orientation.  Later in this section, I explain the two definitions further.

---

(A) *Polymorphism* is the facility by which a single operation or attribute name may be defined upon more than one class and may take on different implementations in each of those classes.

(B) *Polymorphism* is the property whereby an attribute or variable may point to (hold the handle of) objects of different classes at different times.

---

Assume that we have a class **Polygon**, which represents the kind of 2-D shape that Fig. 1.20 exemplifies.

---

[24] I return to the issue of multiple inheritance several times in the book, especially in Chapters 11, 12, and 13.  You may also want to look at [Meyer, 1992] for a discussion of multiple inheritance and its less-useful cousin, repeated inheritance (whereby a class inherits features from the same superclass more than once).

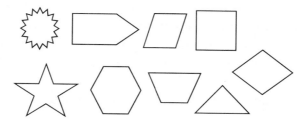

*Fig. 1.20: Some plane—but not plain—polygons.*

We may define an operation named **getArea** on **Polygon** that would return the value of a **Polygon** object's area. (Note that **area** is an attribute defined on **Polygon** and, via inheritance, on **Polygon**'s subclasses.) The operation **getArea** would need a fairly sophisticated algorithm because it would have to take care of any of the oddly shaped polygons of Fig. 1.20.

Now let's add some more classes—say **Triangle**, **Rectangle**, and **Hexagon**—which are subclasses of (and thus inherit from) **Polygon**. This makes sense, because a triangle *is a* polygon; a rectangle *is a* polygon; and so on. See Fig. 1.21.

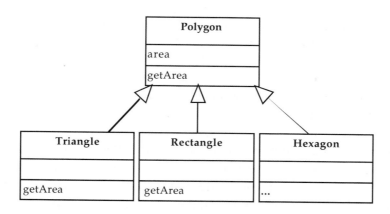

*Fig. 1.21:* **Polygon** *and its three subclasses.*

Notice that in Fig. 1.21 the classes **Triangle** and **Rectangle** also have operations named **getArea**. These operations accomplish the same job as **Polygon**'s version of **getArea**: to compute the total surface area bounded by the shape.

However, the designer/programmer of the code to implement **getArea** for **Rectangle** would write the code very differently from the code of **getArea** for **Polygon**.

Why? Because computing the area of a rectangle is simple (**length * breadth**), the code for the **Rectangle**'s operation **getArea** is consequently simple and efficient. However, since the algorithm to compute the area of an arbitrary complex polygon is complicated and less efficient, we would not want to use it to calculate the area of a rectangle.

So, if we write some code that sends the following message to an object referred to by **twoDShape**:

    twoDShape.getArea;

we may not know which algorithm for computing area will be executed. The reason is that we may not know exactly to which class **twoDShape** belongs. There are five possibilities:

1.  **twoDShape** is an instance of **Triangle**. The operation **getArea**, as defined for **Triangle**, will be executed.

2.  **twoDShape** is an instance of **Rectangle**. The operation **getArea**, as defined for **Rectangle**, will be executed.

3.  **twoDShape** is an instance of **Hexagon**. Since **Hexagon** lacks an operation named **getArea**, through inheritance the operation **getArea**, as defined for **Polygon**, will be executed.

4.  **twoDShape** is an instance of a general, arbitrarily shaped **Polygon**. The operation **getArea**, as defined for **Polygon**, will be executed.

5.  **twoDShape** is an instance of a class **C** (such as **Customer**) that isn't any of the four classes above. Since **C** probably doesn't have an operation named **getArea** defined on it, the sending of the message **getArea** will result in a compile-time or run-time error. That's reasonable, of course, because something called **twoDShape** shouldn't be pointing to a customer.

You may think it odd that an object may not know the exact class of the target object to which it's sending a message. However, that situation is quite common. For example, in the final line of code below, at compile-time we can't tell to what class of object **p** will point at run-time. The actual object pointed to will be determined by a last-minute user choice (tested by the **if** statement).

```
var p: Polygon;
var t: Triangle := Triangle.New;
var h: Hexagon := Hexagon.New;
...
if     user says OK
then p := t
else  p := h
endif;
...
p.getArea;                // here p may refer to a Triangle or a Hexagon object
...
```

Notice that in the above piece of object-oriented code, we don't need a test around **p.getArea** to determine which version of **getArea** to execute. This is an example of very convenient implementation hiding. It allows us to add a new subclass of **Polygon** (say, **Octagon**) without changing the above code in any way. Metaphorically, the target object "knows how to give its area," and so the sender doesn't need to worry.

Notice too the declaration **var p: Polygon**. This is a safety restriction on the polymorphism of the variable, **p**. In the programming syntax that I use here, it means that **p** is permitted to point only to objects of class **Polygon** (or to objects of one of **Polygon**'s subclasses). If **p** were ever assigned the handle of a **Customer** object or a **Horse** object, then the program would stop with a run-time error.

The operation **getArea**, being defined on several classes, provides a good example of polymorphism, as defined under (A). The variable **p**, being capable of pointing to objects of several different classes (for example, **Triangle** and **Hexagon**), is a good example of definition (B). The whole example shows how the two aspects of polymorphism work together to simplify programming.

An object-oriented environment often implements polymorphism through *dynamic binding*. The environment inspects the actual class of the target object of a message at the last possible moment—at run-time, when the message is sent.

> *Dynamic binding* (or *run-time binding* or *late binding)* is the technique by which the exact piece of code to be executed is determined only at run-time (as opposed to compile-time).

The above example, in which the operation **getArea** is defined on **Polygon** and **Triangle**, also demonstrates the concept of *overriding*.

> *Overriding* is the redefinition of a method defined on a class **C** in one of **C**'s subclasses.

The operation **getArea**, which was originally defined on **Polygon**, is overridden in **Triangle**. **Triangle**'s operation has the same name, but a different algorithm.

You may occasionally use the technique of overriding to *cancel* an operation defined on a class **C** in one of **C**'s subclasses. You may cancel an operation by redefining it simply to return an error. If you rely heavily on cancellation, however, it's probably because you've begun with a shaky superclass/subclass hierarchy.

Related to polymorphism is the concept of *overloading*—not to be confused with overriding.

> *Overloading* of a name or symbol occurs when several operations (or operators) defined on the same class have that name or symbol. We say that the name or symbol is *overloaded*.

Both polymorphism and overloading often require that the specific operation to be executed be picked out at run-time. As we saw in the small sample of code above, the reason is that the exact class of a target object—and thus the specific implementation of the operation to be executed—may not be known until run-time.

The normal distinction between polymorphism and overloading is that polymorphism allows the same operation name to be defined differently across different classes, while overloading allows the same operation name to be defined differently several times within the same class.[25]

---

25 Or, to be more general, within the same name-scope.

Which polymorphic operation is selected depends only on the class of the target object to which the message is addressed. But, with an overloaded operation, how is the correct piece of code bound to the operation name at run-time? The answer is, by the signature—the number and/or class of the arguments—of the message. Here are two examples:

> 1a.    product1.markDown
> 1b.    product1.markDown (hugePercentage)
> 2a.    matrix1 * i
> 2b.    matrix1 * matrix2

In the first example, the price of a product is reduced by the operation **markDown**. If **markDown** is invoked with zero arguments (as in 1a), then the operation uses a standard discount percentage; if **markDown** is invoked with one argument (the **hugePercentage** argument of 1b), then the operation applies the supplied value of **hugePercentage**.

In the second example, the multiplication operator * is overloaded. If the second operand is an integer (as in 2a), then the operator * is scalar multiplication. If the second operand is another matrix (as in 2b), then the operator * is matrix multiplication.

## 1.9 Genericity

> *Genericity* is the construction of a class **C** so that one or more of the classes that it uses internally is supplied only at run-time (at the time that an object of class **C** is instantiated).

The best way to illustrate the concept of genericity is by means of a story from the thrilling days of yesteryear. When I was a university student, I took a course called Data Structures 101. One semester, Professor Rossini gave us an assignment to design and program a sorted, balanced, binary tree of integers. (See Fig. 1.22.) The main feature of a balanced tree is that all its leaves "bottom out" at the same level (give or take one level).

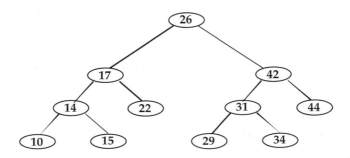

*Fig. 1.22: A balanced binary tree of sorted integers.*

That's all very straightforward—until you have to insert another integer into the tree (say 5, as in Fig. 1.23). Then, the tree may become unbalanced and you have to execute some painful node-twisting until the tree regains its balance.

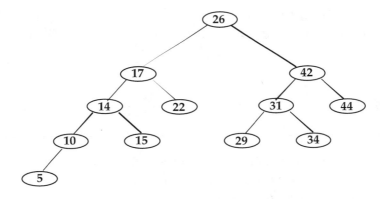

*Fig. 1.23: A tree that's just become unbalanced.*

After various amounts of desktop design and on-line debugging, most of us got our algorithms to work. With self-satisfied smiles, we turned in our programs, went on vacation, and made repeated nightly efforts to forget about sorted, balanced, binary trees.

But, sad to tell, Professor Rossini's balanced-tree exercise was an overture to a much bigger assignment. As part of an application during the next semester (in Business Applications 101), we needed to keep sorted lists of customers and products. Those of us from Data Structures 101 who hadn't managed to completely obliterate our memories of sorted, balanced, binary trees simply dragged out our old code and copied it twice. In one copy, we replaced **Integer** with **CustomerID**; in the other, we replaced **Integer** with **ProductID**.

This cloning of old code greatly increased our productivity. However, this approach is not a silver bullet, because there's significant clone danger. The danger comes from the fact that we now have to maintain three copies of almost identical code.

Thus, if we found a better balanced-tree algorithm, we'd have to revise three pieces of code. Not only would this be extra work, but managing the three versions would also be complicated (unless we could come up with an automated clone changer—and pronto). What we needed was a way to write the basic structure of the balanced-tree algorithm only once and then (without merely cloning) to be able to apply it as many times as we wished to integers, customers, products, or whatever else.

At this point, genericity comes galloping up on a white horse to rescue us. If we define **BalancedTree** to be a parameterized class (formerly known as a generic class), it means that at least one of the classes used within **BalancedTree** needn't be assigned until run-time.[26] That would presumably be the class of the items to be stored in the nodes of the particular balanced-tree object that we instantiate.

I could therefore write the class **BalancedTree** as follows:

```
class BalancedTree <ClassOfNodeItem>;
   ...
   var currentNode: ClassOfNodeItem := ClassOfNodeItem.New;
   ...
   currentNode.print;
   ...
```

Notice the parameterized class argument **ClassOfNodeItem**. This is a formal argument, whose actual "value" will be supplied only at run-time. For example, when we instantiate a new object of class **BalancedTree**, we will supply a real class name as an argument, as follows:

```
   ...
   var custTree: BalancedTree := BalancedTree.New <Customer>;
   var prodTree: BalancedTree := BalancedTree.New <Product>;
   ...
```

---

[26] A parameterized class is known in C++ as a *template class*.

Thus, **custTree** now points to an object (an instance of **BalancedTree**) that keeps instances of class **Customer** in its nodes, as shown in Fig. 1.24. (Similarly for **prodTree**, of course.)

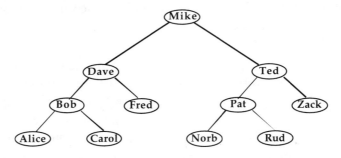

*Fig. 1.24: A balanced binary tree of* **Customer** *objects. (I represent the customers held at the nodes by their first names.) This tree is the object that the variable* **custTree** *points to.*

It's as if we'd cloned the first piece of code twice (once for **Customer**, once for **Product**) to read

    **class** BalancedCustomerTree;
        ...
        **var** currentNode: Customer := Customer.New;
        ...
        currentNode.print;
        ...
    **class** BalancedProductTree;
        ...
        **var** currentNode: Product := Product.New;
        ...
        currentNode.print;
        ...

Finally, notice the statement **currentNode.print**. This is a fine piece of polymorphism, because when we write that statement in the parameterized class **BalancedTree**, we don't know what **currentNode**'s class might be. Thus, anyone who instantiates a **BalancedTree** had better take care that the operation **print** actually is defined upon any class that is used to instantiate a particular tree.

As another example, if you design a parameterized class **HashTable <C>**, you should point out that any class (such as **Symbol**) provided as the actual argument to **C** must have the operation **hash** defined on it. (I cover this possible peril of genericity in detail in Chapter 12.)

You may have realized that there's a way to write **BalancedTree** without genericity and without cloning. We could let the nodes of a balanced tree accept an object of the very topmost class in the superclass/subclass hierarchy. If we name this top class **Object**, then the code would be

```
class BalancedTree;
    ...
    var currentNode: Object := Object.New;
    ...
    currentNode.print;
    ...
```

Now each node of a balanced tree would accept the insertion of absolutely *any* kind of object. In particular, we could mix customers, integers, products, polygons, cowboys, and horses in the very same tree. This would almost certainly be nonsense. Worse still, it would be very unlikely that all these different classes of objects would understand the message **print**.

Both **BalancedTree** and **HashTable** are examples of *container classes*. A container class serves to hold objects in some (often sophisticated) structure. Genericity is often used in object orientation to design such container classes. Although genericity isn't strictly necessary to write reusable code for container classes, it's certainly superior to cloned code or to a fragile design where objects of arbitrary classes are mixed within the same container.

## 1.10 Summary

Since "object orientation" lacks an *a priori* meaning in English, there's been little historical consensus on the set of properties that define it. I consider the following properties to be central to object orientation: encapsulation, information/implementation hiding, state retention, object identity, messages, classes, inheritance, polymorphism, and genericity.

Object-oriented encapsulation yields a software structure (an "object") that comprises a ring of protective operations around attributes representing the state of the object. (In implementational terms, the operations' methods manipulate variables that maintain the state of the object.) Such encapsulation ensures that any change (or access) to an object's internally stored information is via the object's operations.

Information/implementation hiding is the payoff for good encapsulation. Good encapsulation allows information local to an object and design decisions about the internal implementation of the object to be protected from the gaze and meddling of outsiders.

State retention is the property by which an object can retain information indefinitely, including during the intervals between activation of its operations.

Object identity gives every object a unique and permanent identity that's independent of its current state. The object handle is the usual mechanism for assigning an identity to an object.

The handle of an object must be known to any objects that wish to send messages to that object. A message consists of the name of an operation defined for the target object, together with any arguments to be passed to or from the operation. Arguments may be data or pointers to data. However, in a pure object-oriented environment, arguments refer or point only to objects.

Objects derived from the same class share the same structure and behavior. A class is a stencil that is designed and programmed to be the structure from which instances of the class—objects—are "manufactured" at run-time. A class may have a set of class operations and class attributes.

In principle, each object has its own set of methods to implement its instance operations and its own set of variables to implement its instance attributes. In practice, however, objects of the same class normally save memory usage by sharing the same copy of each of their instance methods.

Classes may form inheritance hierarchies (or, more properly, lattices) of superclasses and subclasses. Inheritance allows objects of one class to use the facilities of any of the superclasses of that class. Selectively, operations of a class may be redefined ("overridden") in a subclass.

Polymorphism is the facility by which a single operation name may be defined upon many different classes and may take on different implementations in each of those classes. Alternatively, polymorphism is the property whereby an attribute is permitted to point to (hold the handle of) objects of different classes at different times.

Polymorphism adds a new twist to implementation hiding and gives object orientation much of its power. For example, a sender object may send a message without knowing the exact class of the target object. So long as the designer knows that all the possible classes to which the target may belong have access to an operation with the right name and signature, the selection of the particular operation can be left to the run-time environment.

Overloading is a concept similar to polymorphism in which one of a number of different implementations of an operation is chosen at run-time by inspecting the number and/or classes of the arguments of a message. Both polymorphism and overloading typically call for dynamic (or run-time) binding.

Genericity allows a parameterized class to take a class as an argument whenever an object is instantiated. This allows for the easy creation of "generic" container classes, which serve as skeletal classes on which the specific flesh can be added at run-time. Parameterized classes offer the advantages of cloned code without the overhead of replicated maintenance.

## 1.11 Exercises

1. (a) Rewrite the hominoid-navigation algorithm to make it more robust.

   (b) Can you find any problems with the operation **insertHominoid (hom: Hominoid, location: Square, out insertOK: Boolean)**, which is defined on **Grid**?

2. Does an object know its own handle? If so, how does an object refer to its handle?

3. Why would it be rare for the same argument name to appear both as an input argument and an output argument in the signature of a message? (Assume that the argument points to—that is, holds the handle of—an object.)

4. In Section 1.5.3, I said that "In pure object orientation, there is no need for data." In other words, everything is an object—an encapsulation of operations around variables, which themselves point to objects (via the variables that implement them). But surely there must be data "at the bottom of it all," or wouldn't we spiral down into an infinite recursive descent? So, can everything *really* be an object? And what about integers and reals, of which there are millions of instances? How do they get created?

5. An instance operation may refer to a class variable. However, in a truly object-oriented environment, a class operation cannot directly refer to an instance variable within an object. Why not?

6. When we executed **Glider.New** in Section 1.7, how many objects did we create?

7. How does an object-oriented program get started?

8. What happens to all your objects when you turn the computer off?

9. What happens to all your classes when you turn the computer off?

10. Can you think of a simple way to circumvent object orientation's robust encapsulation mechanism in a language such as C++?

11. Peter Wegner, in a *tour de force* paper, categorized environments as being *object-structured*, *object-based*, *class-based*, or *object-oriented*. The first has only encapsulation and state-retention; the second adds object-identity; the third adds the concept of the class; and the last adds inheritance and the other properties in this chapter.[27] Decide which of these four terms is most appropriate for the language that you're currently using.

12. I mentioned in this chapter that the language Java supports single- but not multiple-inheritance. This is because a class **extends** at most one other class. However, a class potentially **implements** many interfaces. So, was my statement correct? If you're familiar with the language, comment on the distinction in Java between **extends** and **implements** as inheritance mechanisms.

13. Rewrite the hominoid pseudocode on page 8 in the object-oriented programming language of your choice.

14. Consider a piece of software that you (or your company) have purchased, which, its vendor claims, is "object oriented." What characteristics of the software did the vendor identify as being "object oriented"? Do you believe that the vendor's claims were justified? What benefits, if any, did you derive from the touted object-oriented characteristics of the product?

---

[27] I've modified Wegner's definitions somewhat. The original definitions are in [Wegner, 1990].

## 1.12 Answers

1. (a) Two suggestions: Suppose that the START square is completely surrounded by walls and suppose that someone forgot to mark the FINISH square in the grid. Modify the algorithm to cope with those two situations and with any other anomalies that you have considered, such as the fact that there's no safety check on whether **advanceOK** is indeed OK.

   (b) The problem is this: What does the **insertHominoid** operation of the **Grid** object *do* with the information **location: Square** (which is the start location of the **Hominoid** object)? It should use that information to tell the **Hominoid** object what its initial location is, but **Hominoid** does not have an operation **setLocation** defined on it! Because of this, instead of having **insertHominoid** defined on **Grid**, we should have an operation **insertIntoGrid (grid: Grid, location: Square, out insertOK: Boolean)** defined on **Hominoid**. Incidentally, we also need an operation **isAWallLocation: Boolean** defined on **Grid**. (Extra credit: Why?)

2. Yes. An object has a variable (actually, a constant) that you don't need to declare, which holds its own handle. The variable is named by the keyword **self**, **this**, **this**, or **Current** (in Smalltalk, C++, Java, or Eiffel, respectively).

3. It would imply that the target of the message had changed the handle in one of the arguments, which is a nasty design practice. A sender of a message should have the right to assume that its variables hold the same handles after it sends a message as they did before. A few languages specifically forbid this practice; their manuals contain wording such as, "Arguments are object references that are passed by value and cannot be changed by code in the target operation."

4. In a dyed-in-the-wool object-oriented language such as Smalltalk, everything *is* an object; in fact, Smalltalk has unwaveringly adopted the position that "there is no data." For example, in Smalltalk the following act of addition

   $$x <- 5 + 7$$

   is interpreted as "send the message **plus** to the object **5** with the object **7** as the argument." The assignment (<-) is interpreted as "place the handle of the object **12** in the variable **x**."

Not all object-oriented languages, however, are as austere as Smalltalk. In a language such as Eiffel, there are still data-types (such as **integer**, **real**, **char**, **Boolean**, and so on). However, any grander structures are classes that create object instances—not data instances—at run-time. Eiffel compromises the principle that "everything is an object" for a pragmatic reason: Treating integers, characters, and so forth as data-types allows interface compatibility with C code.

In C++, standard C code with standard data-types may be arbitrarily mixed with C++ code. So in C++, all bets are off!

But when I tell people that pure object orientation has no data, they often hurl assorted legumes at me. The most popular examples that people counter me with are **Integer** and **Date**. How can these be classes, rather than old-fashioned data-types? Do we have to say **Integer.New** before we can use the number 5, and **Date.New** before we can use 25th September 1066?

No. Classes such as **Integer** or **Date** are known as *literal classes*. The objects that belong to them are known as *literal objects*. A literal object is simply what its value is. Most literal objects are also *immutable:* They never change value.[28]

Although each object-oriented language has its own treatment of literal classes, most languages make the assumption that all instances of literal classes are predefined (or are created *in situ* by converting text strings like "15th March"). Other languages treat such "classes" as standard data-types, in which the instances are indeed old-fashioned data values rather than objects.

In either case, instantiations from literal classes are unnecessary and illegal:

```
Integer.New;        // illegal code!
Date.New;           // illegal code in most languages!
```

5.  The difficulty is, "attribute of *which* object?" Remember that for a given class, there may be thousands of objects of that class around at run-time. The only way for the class to "get at" the intended object is for the class to have the handle of that object and send a message to it. The object may then graciously return the attribute's information to the class that sent the message.

---

[28] What would life be, without exceptions? In Smalltalk, for example, a string is a literal object that *can* change its value. In Java, **Date** is a regular class, to which **new** is applied.

6. One. (Whenever we execute the class operation **New**, we always create exactly one object with, of course, one handle.) However, this object, which we named **gl**, is an instance of **Glider** and, via inheritance, also an instance of **Aircraft**.

7. The initiation of an object-oriented program depends on both the language and the operating system that you use. However, there are three popular ways in which an operating system may transfer control to your application program:

   • Begin execution at a main function, which, as in a regular procedural language, gains control at program start-up.
   • Automatically instantiate an object of a programmer-defined **Root** class, which, on its initiation, begins the execution of the entire program.
   • Bring up an object-oriented browsing environment, usually with a graphical interface. The user/programmer may then interactively send a message to an appropriate class (or object) to get things going.

8. When you turn the computer off, you lose all your objects in volatile memory, together with the information that they contain. If that's a problem, then you must store that information on disk before your object-oriented program terminates. With an object-oriented database-management system (ODBMS), you can store your objects more or less directly. But if you're using, say, a relational database, you'll have to "unpack" the objects' information into normalized, tabular form before you store them.

9. When you turn the computer off, nothing happens to your classes (in most environments, anyway). Your classes are code that you've compiled and stored on your permanent disk. This illustrates again the difference between classes, which are permanent forms, and objects, which are mercurial, ever-changing, run-time units.

10. In some languages, an unspeakably naughty designer can set up ways for outsiders to "climb over an object's walls" and mess with its variables directly. One way is through C++'s "friend" mechanism. Like most other

design sins, this one is usually perpetrated in the name of the great god Efficiency.

11. Now that you've chosen a term for your current language, consider which of its object-oriented properties (if any) you find most valuable. If your language isn't fully object oriented, which of the properties that I've outlined in this chapter do you most wish that your language had? Why?

12. Java indeed supports only single inheritance in the sense of "inheriting capability," which is how I described inheritance in this chapter. Let's say that a class S has in it the following statement:

   **extends** C **implements** I1, I2

   This means that **S** has access to all of **C**'s operations (Java methods). In other words, through the **extends** construct, **S** inherits not only **C**'s interface but also **C**'s capability—the code that makes its interface work. However, **S** inherits responsibility, *not capability*, through the **implements** construct. In this example, the designer/programmer of **S** is responsible for providing working Java methods for all the operations defined in the interfaces **I1** and in **I2**.

13. Following is what you might come up with for the hominoid rewrite in Java. I assume that the algorithm is contained in the operation **navigate**, which will be an operation of the class **Grid**. (Accordingly, any reference to the grid object itself will be through **this**.) I also assume that the grid object is properly initialized (for example, that any hominoids previously inserted into it have been removed).

```
public boolean navigate ( )

{ // Places a new hominoid on the start square of the grid and navigates
  // the hominoid to the grid's finish square, displaying the hominoid at each
  // step.  Returns false if any problems in the algorithm; true otherwise.

     Hominoid hom = new Hominoid ( );   // creates new instance of Hominoid,
                                        // which will be pointed to by hom
     int oneSquare = 1;                 // constant
     int initialTurnCount;

     Square startSquare = this.start;
     boolean insertOK = this.insertHominoid (hom, startSquare);
                            // insertHominoid returns true if successful

     if (! insertOK)    return false;
                            // abort if hominoid not placed OK in grid

        // set the hominoid in the right direction:
        // turn the hominoid 4 times max or until the hominoid has a
        // clear path ahead of it

   initialTurnCount = 1;
   while (initialTurnCount <= 4 && hom.facingWall)
      {hom.turnLeft(); initialTurnCount ++; }
   //endwhile

   this.display();                    // display the grid ...
   hom.display();                     // ... and the hominoid

   while (hom.location != this.finish)
      { if (hom.facingWall)
           {hom.turnLeft();

              if (hom.facingWall)   {hom.turnRight(); hom.turnRight(); }
              //endif
        } //endif

        hom.advance (oneSquare);
        hom.display;

      } //endwhile
                                      // hominoid is at finish—success !
   return true;

} //end navigate
```

# A Brief History of Object Orientation

Now that we've examined the intrinsic properties of object orientation, let's look at how object orientation fits into the wider landscape of software development.

Upon hearing that Professor Wolfgang Pauli had proposed a new fundamental particle (the μ-meson or muon), Professor Isidor I. Rabi immediately retorted: "Who ordered *that?*" I begin this chapter by listing some of the people who "ordered" object orientation. I next set object orientation in a social context by discussing the attitudes that have arisen toward this software approach. Then, I set object orientation in an engineering context by making a parallel between object orientation and electronics. Finally, I indicate what object orientation might actually be good for, with respect to the programmers, analysts, and managers who make up your shop.

## 2.1 Where Did Object Orientation Come From?

Unlike many developments in human discovery, object orientation did not spring forth at a single moment. Rather than being the "Eureka!" inspiration of a single person in a bathtub, it's the outpouring of work from many people in bathtubs over many years. The concepts of object orientation, which we covered in Chapter

1, are like several tributaries that have flowed together almost by historical accident to form the river of object orientation.

So—with my apologies if I've left out your favorite software researcher—here (approximately in chronological order) are some of the folks who, I believe, have made significant theoretical or practical additions to the object-oriented deluge:

### 2.1.1 Larry Constantine

Since no catalog of software contributors would be complete without him, let's start with the antediluvian Larry Constantine. Although in the 1960s Constantine did nothing under the heading "object orientation," he did research extensively into the fundamental criteria for good software design [Constantine, 1968]. Indeed, he was one of the first people even to suggest that software *could* be designed before it was programmed. Many of Constantine's notions (such as coupling and cohesion) have proven relevant to today's world of object orientation.

### 2.1.2 O.-J. Dahl and K. Nygaard

Dahl and Nygaard introduced several ideas that are now part of object orientation. The best example is the idea of the class, which first appeared in the language Simula [Dahl and Nygaard, 1966].

### 2.1.3 Alan Kay, Adele Goldberg, and others

Kay, Goldberg, and their colleagues introduced the first incarnations of the Smalltalk language at the Xerox Palo Alto Research Center in the years around 1970 [Kay, 1969]. This research gave us many of the concepts that we now consider central to object orientation (such as messages and inheritance). Many people still consider the Smalltalk language and environment (see, for example, [Goldberg and Robson, 1989]) to be the purest implementation of object orientation in existence today.

### 2.1.4 Edsger Dijkstra

Dijkstra, the Conscience of Software Correctness, has been causing us constant guilt for lo! these many decades. In his early work, he proposed the ideas of building software in layers of abstraction with strict semantic separation between successive layers. This represents a strong form of encapsulation, which is central to object orientation.

### 2.1.5 Barbara Liskov

Liskov made significant progress in the 1970s on the theory and implementation of the abstract data-type (ADT), which forms a foundation for object orientation. One of the most salient results of Liskov's work was the CLU language, in which the notion of hidden internal data representations is solidly supported. See [Liskov et al., 1981], for example.

### 2.1.6 David Parnas

In a landmark paper, Parnas wrote about the principles of good modular software construction [Parnas, 1972]. Although the constructs of object orientation transcend traditional procedural modules, many of Parnas' basic tenets of information hiding are still applicable in object-oriented systems.

### 2.1.7 Jean Ichbiah and others

Ichbiah and his group developed the "Green" Programming Language, which the U.S. Department of Defense adopted as the language Ada (now known as Ada-83).[1] Two of Ada-83's constructs (genericity and the package) are at the very heart of object orientation. A later version of the language, Ada-95, supports object orientation more fully.

### 2.1.8 Bjarne Stroustrup

The language C++ has an interesting genealogy. Once upon a time, there was Martin Richards' BCPL language [Richards and Whitby-Strevens, 1980]. This begat a language B, which was an abbreviation (!) for BCPL. B begat C, and C (through the work of Stroustrup) begat the object-oriented language C++.

As Stroustrup describes it [Stroustrup, 1991, p. 4], the "begetting of C++" sounds a tad chancy:

> C++ was primarily designed so that the author and his friends would not have to program in assembler, C, or various modern high-level languages. Its main purpose is to make writing good programs easier and more pleasant for the individual programmer.

---

[1] Ada® is a registered trademark of the United States government.

There never was a C++ paper design; design, documentation and implementation went on simultaneously.

Since the object orientation of C++ was grafted upon an earlier, non-object-oriented and fairly low-level language, its syntax is not always clean. Nevertheless, despite the rise of Java, C++ is still the most widely used object-oriented language. Its C ancestry has given it portability across many machines and operating systems and has therefore vastly increased the popularity of object-oriented programming. In that respect, Stroustrup's contribution to the field has been huge.

### 2.1.9 Bertrand Meyer

Meyer's strength is the melding of the best ideas of computer science with the best ideas of object orientation. The result: a language and environment called Eiffel. Eiffel is a rarity in the software world, for it appeals simultaneously to academics, to software engineers, and to those folks in the trenches who need robust code. Whatever the chosen object-oriented language of your shop, you should definitely learn the concepts behind Eiffel if you want to become a real object-oriented professional.[2]

### 2.1.10 Grady Booch, Ivar Jacobson, and Jim Rumbaugh

These three characters are known collectively by the droll sobriquet of *The Three Amigos*.[3] Although each of them has his own claim to object-oriented fame, as a group their claim comes from their collaboration in the late 1990s to rationalize object-oriented notation (which in the early 1990s was a Tower of Babel). The result of their work was the Unified Modeling Language (UML), a graphical modeling language with both a visual form of expression and a thorough semantic underpinning. I cover UML in Chapters 3 through 7 of this book.

## 2.2 Object Orientation Comes of Age

In this section, I describe how the software industry has reacted to the glorious advent of object orientation.

---

[2] An excellent book for learning Eiffel is [Wiener, 1995].

[3] Their nickname refers to the title of a 1986 John Landis movie—but so far I've failed to see much resemblance between Ivar Jacobson and Steve Martin. Incidentally, in South America this group of methodologists is known as *Los Tres Buddies*.

Aged biologists are fond of uttering this old saw: *Ontogeny recapitulates phylogeny.* This mouthful means that the development of an individual embryo often mimics the evolutionary development of its species as a whole. (An example would be the transient development of gills in the human embryo.) Of course, there's an enormous difference in time scale. Ontogeny takes months, whereas phylogeny takes eons.

Although the old biological saw is much discredited, a new software-engineering saw claims: *The history of object-oriented software engineering recapitulates the history of traditional software engineering.* Of course, there's an enormous difference in time scale. It took us decades to get our act together (sort of!) in procedural and database constructs; we're getting to grips with object-oriented software in a matter of years.

Software development began simply with programming. As system size and human experience both grew, people realized that merely writing code for an application in a torrent of consciousness wasn't good enough. Even if such an application miraculously worked, its code would be so disorganized that any changes to it would be nigh impossible to make.

Enter design. Designing software made it possible to lay out a plan for a rational organization of code before a single line was actually chiseled into the coding pad. This radical idea even allowed people to assess potential maintenance problems at the paper-tiger stage.

So far, so good. Now we were capable of turning out exquisitely crafted software. However, some astute individuals noticed that much of this exquisite software didn't meet the users' needs. To satisfy the users' quirky passion for useful software, orderly and more rigorous analysis was ushered in.

Finally, we were blessed with Computer-Aided Software-Engineering (CASE) tools. At first, these tools were criminally rickety. But later, when they reformed and became only slightly rickety, they were allowed to change their names under a Federal Protection Program. Nowadays, the erstwhile CASE tools are known as automated modeling tools. Modeling tools help us with the disciplines of analyzing requirements, designing software, and building software. They also make software development and maintenance more manageable.

During the entire history of software, people have attempted to achieve reusability. Unfortunately, most procedural units of code aren't self-contained enough to be reused independently. But now, with object orientation, we have another chance to gain the paradise of reuse.

However, object orientation guarantees no miracles. If object classes are not designed carefully, along guidelines such as those that I set out later in this book, then object orientation will fall short of providing reusable and reliable software. Should this unhappy situation come to pass, all we'll get to reuse will be tales of woe from managers who have failed to realize the benefits of object orientation.

As I mentioned above, object-orientation's history has paralleled that of the software mainstream. However, with object orientation, the progression from implementation toward abstraction has occurred at an extraordinary pace. Object-oriented programming first attained popularity in the 1980s. That same decade saw the introduction of both object-oriented design and object-oriented analysis. Object-oriented database-management systems (ODBMSs) and object-oriented modeling tools began to creep in around 1990.

The rapid arrival of these object-oriented fields led to a strange amnesia. Some of the people undergoing object-oriented ontogenesis suddenly forgot their mainstream phylogenesis. Their slogan became: "Anything known before 1990 isn't worth knowing!" They were the hot-blooded, take-no-prisoners, die-hard, object-oriented *revolutionaries*. They denounced the then-current software establishment as bourgeois imperialist paper-tigers of an outmoded COBOL dynasty, deserving only a one-way ticket to Ekaterinburg.

Now their revolutionary fervor has cooled. The object revolution has been won, and its instigators and followers have themselves become part of the establishment. Many of the tools and techniques we find in today's software marketplace routinely and casually rely on object orientation. This is especially true in the world of client-server and other distributed systems.

But the realm of software is in perpetual revolution. The next advance toward a programmer's paradise, distributed component software, is already upon us. With distributed components come yet more of the benefits that the original object revolutionaries promised in their early fiery speeches.

I address the application of object orientation to component software in Chapter 15.

## 2.3 Object Orientation As an Engineering Discipline

In the 1980s, Brad Cox observed that a software object in some ways resembles the hardware integrated circuit (IC) upon which so much of today's life depends [Cox, 1986]. I recalled this appealing analogy recently as archaeologists from the

University of Washington were digging through the strata of paper in my office. They unearthed a book called *Introduction to Radar Systems* by Merrill Skolnik, in which Mr. Skolnik makes the observation that

> Electronic engineering may be categorized according to: (1) components, (2) techniques and (3) systems. Components are the basic building blocks that are combined, using proper techniques, to yield a system.

If we make a small substitution in Mr. Skolnik's prose, replacing "electronic" with "software" and "components" with "classes," we have this:

> Software engineering may be categorized according to: (1) classes, (2) techniques and (3) systems. Classes are the basic building blocks that are combined, using proper techniques, to yield a system.[4]

Although this image is alluring, we shouldn't forget that the choice of worthwhile circuits to encapsulate on a chip depends on engineers' ability to identify useful abstractions. People will rush out to buy ICs for operational amplifiers, audio amplifiers, timers, line-drivers, and so on. But no one would even toddle out to buy an ultra-large-scale IC of random transistors, inductors, and resistors. Before the first useful IC was built, engineers had had decades to discover the useful patterns that crop up in system after electronic system.

In software, by analogy, we must make sure that the classes that we develop are based on sound, robust, handy abstractions. Classes such as **Customer** and the lovable, furry old **Stack** are likely to receive standing ovations; classes such as **Egabragrettu** are more likely to be dumped at the edge of town.

Mr. Skolnik's second point is about techniques. Since ICs that couldn't be combined would be almost useless, it's fortunate that electronic engineers have at their disposal printed-circuit boards (PCBs) that hook ICs together.

Similarly, in developing object-oriented software, we must also attend to the "macro" level of design. This level deals with the ways that classes (and the objects that classes generate at run-time) are interconnected. Clearly, there'll be a strong correlation between what we design at the intra-class level and what we design at this higher, inter-class level. That's to be expected of course, since the

---

[4] In Chapter 15, I explore a software construct that is the analogue of the electronic printed-circuit board. This construct is actually called a *component*.

layout of a PCB certainly depends to some extent on the design of the ICs that sit on it.[5]

There can be good and bad object-oriented designs at both the intra-class level and the inter-class level. Thus, good object-oriented systems, like good electronic systems, depend not only upon high-quality abstractions but also upon high-quality techniques for building with those abstractions. Parts II and III of this book deal with these issues. But first, we must ask a basic question: What is object orientation good for?

## 2.4 What's Object Orientation Good For?

The title of this section is an invitation to cynics and fanatics.

Some reactionaries would say that object orientation is good for nothing; it's merely a religious cult, or a global conspiracy based somewhere on the West Coast. Some revolutionaries will say that object orientation is the first and only miracle solution to all our software woes. Not only will it do windows, but it will also slice and dice vegetables, wax floors, and top off desserts—all under the latest multitiered distributed Web-enabled architecture.

I dwell at neither of these extremes. I believe that object orientation *is* useful, that it's *not* a miracle, that it's not even perfect, and that its specific utility depends upon how you put it to use in your software-development process.

No respectable software-engineering approach should be treated as a "Fad of the Year." A Fad of the Year is an approach that becomes all the rage for a few months or a year.[6] Its adherents espouse it hysterically as the solution to every roaming software problem. Skeptics are dragged aboard its bandwagon by the forces of fanaticism. Later, after the approach has been used and abused indiscriminately to mediocre effect, its adherents abandon it *en masse* and swarm forth to next year's Fad. If your shop "surfs on technology," moving rapidly from fad to fad, you're likely to benefit little from object orientation.

Neither is object orientation a silver bullet, a mindless solution to the problems besieging your shop. Instead, as we'll see in this book, object orientation is a powerful, though challenging, approach to developing software. A mature, pro-

---

[5] If you've studied standard structured design (see [Page-Jones, 1988], for example), you'll remember a similar principle: The coupling among a set of modules largely depends on the cohesion of each module in the set.

[6] See [Page-Jones, 1991] for more details on "Fad of the Year."

fessional shop doesn't play with object orientation with all brains in the OFF position; rather, it works hard at the object-oriented approach and integrates object orientation into its long-term plans for developing professional software.

In the rest of this section, I discuss object orientation's potential effects on six of a shop's typical software activities.

### 2.4.1 Analyzing users' requirements

Advocates of structured techniques never reached détente on where to place the boundary between process and data analysis. The process world of the dataflow diagram has always coexisted uneasily with the data world of the entity-relationship diagram. Process and data analysis became clashing tectonic plates, meeting in some places, subducting each other seismically in other places, and missing altogether in yet others. The clash was especially noticeable in real-time system modeling, where (for example) the correspondence between the control process and the data model was often unclear.

An object-oriented approach to analysis melds process and data investigation early in the lifecycle. Although we can't really say "process and data analysis" when we talk about object orientation (as mentioned in Chapter 1)—"dynamic and static analysis" would be better—the up-front use of object-oriented concepts brings sweeter harmony to these two aspects of analysis. Some people have likened object orientation's blending of process and data to Einstein's fusing of space and time in his theories of relativity, although I must say I find that comparison extravagant.

### 2.4.2 Designing software

In design, object orientation is both a boon and a bane.

Object orientation is a boon because it allows a designer to hide behind the scenic walls of encapsulation such software eyesores as: convoluted data structures, complex combinatorial logic, elaborate relationships between procedure and data, sophisticated algorithms, and ugly device drivers.

Object orientation is a bane because the structures that it employs (such as encapsulation and inheritance) may themselves become complex. In object orientation it's all too easy to create a Gordian hammock of inextricable interconnections that either is unbuildable or will result in a system that runs about as fast as a horse in a sack race. Avoiding such problems is a major challenge for object-oriented designers.

The purpose of this book is to offer some ideas, techniques, and principles with which you can counter object orientation's design challenges. In Part II of the book, I introduce the most useful features of UML, which is the most popular way to depict and explore design decisions.

In Part III, I offer several design principles and criteria by which you can judge a design. Using these design principles and criteria, you can create object-oriented constructs that will cooperate when you construct systems from them, and yet will be independently maintainable. Although object-oriented design will sometimes demand exceptionally diligent work, it's work that, when well done, will reward you with the taming of larger units of complexity than you could tame with other design techniques.

### 2.4.3 Constructing software

The qualities that are most frequently touted for systems built in an object-oriented way are reusability, reliability, robustness, extensibility, distributability, and storability.

*Reusability*

Object orientation enhances reusability because it promotes reuse of code at the class level rather than at the level of the individual subroutine. By developing and tending a library of classes for *your* applications in *your* shop, you are, in effect, creating a new, very-high-level language tailored specifically to your needs.

It appears empirically that the object class is a sophisticated-enough organism to be able to migrate from application to application across your company as a self-contained unit of software. At least, that's true if the class takes with it the framework of ancillary classes that it needs to get its job done. (I explore that topic further in Sections 9.1 and 9.2.)

*Reliability*

Reliable code works repeatedly and consistently. Your code will attain these qualities only if you can verify its correctness in some way. Object-oriented code lends itself to verification through the use of certain assertions called *class invariants*.

A class invariant is a condition that every object of a given class must satisfy. (For example, an invariant of class **Person** may be **dateOfBirth <= todaysDate**.)

Class invariants (and other assertions that I also cover in Chapter 10) make it possible to verify code very thoroughly. In a walkthrough or inspection, you can check that a design or its resulting code meets the intended invariants. Although—even using object orientation—you can never prove code *absolutely* correct, object orientation does make it easier to check that the code will do what you think it should.[7]

## Robustness

Robustness in software is its ability to recover gracefully whenever a failure occurs. (Typical failures are assertion violations, memory violations, external-device errors, and arithmetic overflows.) Software becomes robust when it can trap such an unexpected failure (usually termed an *exception)* and can execute a routine (usually termed an *exception handler* or *rescue clause)* to recover from the failure.

Many modern object-oriented languages and environments support exception detection and handling and thus encourage the development of robust software. An excellent way to achieve robustness of object-oriented code is to combine the idea of assertions and invariants with that of exception handlers. In some object-oriented environments, you can monitor class invariants and other assertions at run-time and also have your software deftly recover if (Heaven forfend!) an assertion should be violated.

The alternative to exception handling is no exception handling: Never detect exceptions and simply let the software crash when an exception occurs. That's not robustness, of course!

## Extensibility

Easy extensibility of software depends technically on what's called a "homomorphism between the domain of specification and the domain of implementation." Ouch! In less formal words, it means that you should make the shape of the solution fit the shape of the problem. By doing this, you ensure that a small user

---

[7] The ultimate reason is that the concept of correctness is not an absolute one that's fixed for all observers, but one that's relative to the frame of reference of a particular observer. In other words, correctness is ultimately subjective.

change will not become a major system nightmare. And when you modify your object-oriented code, you find that you create fewer arcane problems in faraway damp, dark places. Because object orientation builds units of software with higher-level, more true-to-life abstractions, object orientation comes closer to achieving this "homomorphism" than traditional techniques did.

Extensibility and inheritance often go hand in hand. Users often want to extend a system by adding variations to an already stated theme. For example: "Instead of just *customers,* we now want to have *domestic and foreign customers.*"[8] Using object orientation, you can make such extensions incrementally by adding inheriting subclasses under an already implemented superclass.

### Distributability

In 1989, a body known as the Object-Management Group (OMG) took on a Herculean task: getting dozens of major hardware and software vendors to agree on interoperability standards for object orientation. I was amazed that they undertook such an endeavor—I was astounded when they succeeded!

The most visible fruit of their undertaking has been the Common Object Request Broker Architecture (CORBA), an agreed standard architecture for software to support object-oriented systems distributed across multiple platforms.[9] In itself, that's impressive. However, CORBA also allows objects to "talk to one another," not only across similar machines, but also across machines that are different models, running different operating systems, and connected by an assortment of different networks.

Under CORBA, the objects themselves can even be created from classes written in diverse languages and compiled with different compilers. And, on top of all that, an implementation of CORBA includes various standard services (such as replication, proxy, relationship-handling, and transaction-mediating services) that automate away the screeds of code you'd otherwise have to craft by hand to set up your distributed system.

In other words, with CORBA, the distributed and heterogeneous nature of the platforms becomes transparent to you, the application designer and programmer. You can write messages similar to the usual, single-processor way and let CORBA services handle many of the grungy infrastructure details.

---

[8] However, this is a glib example. As we'll see in Chapters 11, 12, and 13, most real-life examples aren't so neat and easy.

[9] For more on CORBA, see [Mowbray and Zahavi, 1995] and [Orfali et al., 1996].

*Storability*

This section wouldn't be complete without a mention of object-oriented database-management systems. An ODBMS is useful if you're building any object-oriented application, and it's especially useful if your application manipulates sound or graphics, neither of which is easily held in a standard relational, tabular form.

An ODBMS will hold objects of arbitrary classes (not only classes such as **String**, **Real**, **Integer**, and **Date**, but also **Customer**, **Aircraft**, **CityMap**, **VideoClip**, and so on), and it provides object-oriented encapsulation, inheritance, polymorphism, and other important object-oriented features. Most ODBMSs come with a query language (such as object-query language, OQL) that replaces the SQL of relational DBMSs.

## 2.4.4 Maintaining software

The qualities of reusability, reliability, robustness, and extensibility are the four pillars of maintainability. (Maintenance, of course, is what many shops spend most of their money on.) Because it enhances these four qualities, object orientation can reduce system maintenance costs in the following ways:

- Reusability reduces the overall body of code that your shop must maintain. It cuts down the amount of new code that has to be written and later maintained for a system, especially after your first one or two object-oriented projects.
- Reliability in software diminishes users' winces of discontent and their pained cries for fixes.
- Robustness ensures that software being maintained won't fall completely to pieces on the operating table.
- Extensibility takes advantage of the users' natural tendency to ask for "base-displacement" kinds of modifications to their systems, whereby they continually ask for many, comparatively minor, modifications to existing software.

## 2.4.5 Using software

Graphical applications have always been a popular choice for object orientation. In particular, people often implement modern graphical user interfaces (GUIs) through object orientation. There are two reasons for this: The first is conceptual; the second, implementational.

Conceptually, the metaphor of object orientation fits well with the typical window/mouse/icon interface. Let's say that you have an icon on a screen. This icon may be a visible representation of an object, say a customer. Click on the icon with a mouse to select that customer. Then bring up a menu. The options on the menu may correspond closely to methods that apply to a customer. For example, there may be an option to **changeAddress**, another to **reassessCreditLimit**, and so on. Also, a domestic customer's menu could be different from an export customer's menu. Each menu would list just the business actions that apply to the particular type of customer.

Even polymorphism—the ability for a method to take on different meanings or implementations with respect to different classes—may appear at the user interface. Let's say you have one icon on the screen representing a spreadsheet object and another representing a document object. When you double-click on the **Open** menu item, you will attach either the spreadsheet program or the text-processing program to the object, depending on which of the two icons was highlighted. In other words, the particular version of the **open** method that's executed depends on whether the class of the highlighted object was **Spreadsheet** or **Document**.

Implementationally, many commercially available software libraries that let you build window/mouse/icon interfaces are written in an object-oriented language. Since a window naturally has many properties of an object, most development tools for windowing interfaces also have a seam of object orientation running through them.

So, while it's not quite true to say that object orientation per se makes software more usable, it is true that a good graphical user interface makes software more usable and that object orientation may be the best approach to building software libraries that support GUIs.

### 2.4.6 Managing software projects

So far, I've directed almost everything that I've introduced in this book toward technical people. But what of the poor manager? Is object orientation another technical innovation that must be borne in silent suffering until its advocates wither away or join another shop? Or worse, is object orientation merely another silver bullet with which a manager can shoot himself in the foot?

No. Object orientation isn't just for nerds anymore. Object orientation's technical advantages are advantages for managers too. For example, a technique that reduces maintenance clearly frees up a manager's resources to attack the pressing application backlogs. But, for managers, object orientation goes further than the mere technical. Object orientation brings change both to a shop's organization and to managers' jobs.

When a shop adopts object orientation, its organization will change for several reasons. Reuse of classes will require a class library and a class librarian. Each programmer will migrate into one of two groups: the group designing and coding new classes or the group using classes to create new applications. With less emphasis on programming (reusability implies less new code), requirements analysis will become relatively more important.

A new notation, such as UML, will also have an impact. Although requirements analysis and software design are two different beasts, UML is widely used to model both of them. This gives modern O.O. a notational continuity that the structured techniques of yore sorely lacked. I thought that this seamlessness would be a blessing to all concerned, until I met a manager at a newly object-oriented shop who told me the following:

> In the old days, I knew that when they were drawing round things [processes on a data flow diagram] they were doing analysis and when they switched to square things [modules on a structure chart] they'd moved on to design. Now I never know what they're doing, and I'm worried that they don't either!

As a manager whose shop is moving into object orientation, you should be aware of such organizational changes. You will need to train your staff for their new roles. You will need to manage people in these roles. You will need to encourage reuse, rather than recoding. You will need to give people time to think through their class designs so that the classes they construct are fit for reuse. In short, you will need to run project teams that are suddenly using different terminology, different tools, and a different lifecycle, and—at the same time—aiming at goals that are new, or at least have found a new significance.

Object orientation works well only if managers treat it as a means, rather than an end. Object orientation is the means to—pick one that interests you—maintainability, extensibility, robustness, distributability, GUI support, reduced delivery time, and so on. As a manager, you should focus on your goal at all times and use object orientation as a technology to achieve that goal. As one manager said: "When I buy soap, I always remember that I'm really after clean hands."

If you don't keep your goal in mind, then object orientation with all its transitional costs (financial, organizational, social, and emotional) will seem like an expensive boondoggle. However, if you know not only what you're doing, but also *why* you're doing it, you'll derive the stamina to score the object-oriented goal you're seeking.

## 2.5 Summary

Part of the appeal of object orientation is the analogy between object-oriented software components and electronic integrated circuits. At last, we in software have the opportunity to build systems in a way similar to that of modern electronic engineers: We can connect prefabricated components that implement powerful abstractions. But, to take advantage of this, we must first identify sound software abstractions and have ways to link them constructively.

Techniques for achieving these "software integrated circuits" fall broadly under the rubric of object orientation. "Object orientation" is a term that gathers together the ideas of many software researchers from the 1960s to the present day. However, not everyone would agree with this point of view. Some people (object-oriented revolutionaries) would say that object orientation represents a complete break with the past. Others (reactionaries) take the opposite position: Object orientation is, at most, a veneer of jargon over the "same old stuff."

My experience is that object orientation is neither the same old stuff nor a complete break from everything we ever learned about software. Instead, it's a welcome evolutionary step that goes far toward meeting the challenge of developing ever-more-complex software.

Object orientation also addresses two problems of structured techniques. The first is the rift between process and data and the mismatch between the requirements-analysis model and the software-design model. The second is the gap between so-called information and real-time systems-development approaches. In my opinion, a good object-oriented approach should span both categories of system.

Object orientation makes itself felt in all phases of software development. In analysis, it demands a deep investigation of the abstractions within the users' dominions—at least if true reusability is to be achieved. In design, it calls for the sound organization of software constructs, many of which are more sophisticated than those found in traditional structured design.

Constructing reliable and robust object-oriented software requires establishing various assertions, such as class invariants, that can be monitored for exceptions at run-time. Software maintenance is improved not only because reusability yields "less code to maintain" but also because the software is built on sounder abstractions.

Although object orientation isn't just for graphics anymore, it's still valuable for building graphical user interfaces. For this reason, the object-oriented abstractions fit well with the friendly, natural interfaces that many users have come to expect.

Finally, object-oriented software development will be successful only if it is managed intelligently. Managers should introduce object orientation smoothly and then manage its demands (such as software-engineering discipline) and results (such as reusability) carefully.

## 2.6 Exercises

1. Most analogies break down somewhere. As you read through the chapters of this book, consider the flaws in the analogy between a software object class and an electronic integrated circuit.

2. From what you know of object orientation, where would you place yourself in the spectrum *reactionary . . . evolutionist . . . revolutionary?* Justify your position by comparing developments in object orientation with those in the traditional mainstream of software development.

3. In your opinion, is it necessary for a shop to choose a language (or operating environment) that has *all* of the object-oriented properties that I described in Chapter 1? In other words, do you concur with some object-oriented revolutionaries, who tend to sneer at shops that choose something less than full object orientation?

4. Consider the Object-Oriented Hall of Fame of Section 2.1. Whom, in your opinion, have I left out? What contribution did he or she make to the theme of object orientation?

## 2.7 Answers

1.  One flaw in the analogy stems from the way that software ICs are wired together in most current object-oriented languages. Electronic ICs remain symmetrically anonymous to one another. Wiring goes from one IC socket to another IC socket and at no time does an IC "know" to which other ICs it's connected; it "knows" only its own pins and not the pins of other ICs.

    Not so with classes and objects. Classes are connected to other classes by explicit name. For example, if **ClassA** inherits from **ClassB**, then **ClassA** will contain a line of code such as **inherits from ClassB**. An object sends a message by naming an operation of another object. This is like connecting an IC to another by soldering a lead from the inside of one to a pin of the other.

    Peter Wegner discusses this concept further in Section 6.1.3 of his paper [Wegner, 1990]. (In the remainder of this book I also cover the connections among classes in more detail.)

2.  If you're an object-oriented reactionary, then look back at the key abstractions of object orientation that I covered in Chapter 1. Check each one carefully to see whether you can find reference to a similar abstraction in some pre-object-oriented publication. If you're an object-oriented revolutionary, read for example Yourdon and Constantine's book on structured design [Yourdon and Constantine, 1979]. Can you make a case that the major concepts of this work (such as coupling and cohesion) are irrelevant to our brave, new, object-oriented world?

3.  In my opinion, the debate over whether I Am More Object Oriented Than Thou is a religious, moot point having little to do with engineering. The engineering issue is, Which benefits of object orientation are most important to us in achieving our shop's goals? A partially object-oriented environment has *some* of the software-engineering advantages of object orientation and lacks others. Therefore, a shop exercising good judgment understands its needs and chooses an environment that satisfies those needs.

4.  In determining other people to add to my Object-Oriented Hall of Fame, you may want to consider the authors of methodologies, languages, or tools that you're using in your shop. One possibility: Research the early history of the Java language at Sun Microsystems.

"Behold, how good and joyful a thing it is:
brethren, to dwell together in unity!"

—*The 1662 Book of Common Prayer,* 133:1

# Part II: The Unified Modeling Language

Part I explored object orientation through its key abstractions and its context in software engineering. Part II (Chapters 3 through 7) presents a graphic notation for representing object-oriented design constructs.

In the late 1990s, as I mentioned in Chapter 2, Grady Booch, Ivar Jacobson, and Jim Rumbaugh came up with the definitive version of Unified Modeling Language (UML), which is now a standard adopted by the Object-Management Group (OMG), among other organizations. UML notation bears a resemblance to that of the Object Modeling Technique (OMT), which Rumbaugh and others developed in the early 1990s. Predictably enough, UML also exhibits the influence of the Booch and Jacobson branches of this ancestral triumvirate.

I congratulate Booch, Jacobson, and Rumbaugh (and their numerous collaborators worldwide) on their splendid effort to remove the notational, terminological, and semantic chaos that bedeviled the early, frenzied years of object orientation. As I well know, it's very difficult to come up with a notation for object orientation that's simple enough to use but powerful enough to merit using.

In 1990, Larry Constantine, Steve Weiss, and I developed a prototype object-oriented design notation. It was called Uniform Object Notation (or UON), meaning that it could be used "uniformly" to depict systems built using structured techniques, object-oriented techniques, or a mixture of both. However, UON addressed only some of the constructs found in object-oriented systems.[1]

Later, Brian Henderson-Sellers and Julian Edwards extended UON beyond its primitive beginnings into a notation (EUON) that became part of their MOSES methodology.[2] Working partly with Henderson-Sellers and Edwards and partly on my own, I developed UON further, into a notation called Object-Oriented Design Notation (or OODN). As it turned out, however, neither UON nor OODN ever acquired mass appeal.

However, elaborating on the still-primitive EUON, Don Firesmith, Ian Graham, and Henderson-Sellers created a splendid alternative to UML. Their notation is called the OPEN Modeling Language (OML), and it is part of a comprehensive OPEN approach to expressing and developing object-oriented systems. But, despite its rigor and underlying meta-model, OML does not seem destined for widespread application.

Now back to UML. It is a language with a semi-formal semantic specification that includes abstract syntax, well-formedness rules, and dynamic semantics. UML can capture the structure of object-oriented systems at a level above that of individual lines of code, and it can be expressed in diagrams that span the gamut of constructs that appear in typical object-oriented systems. These diagrams include, for instance, the class diagram (which features the constructs of inheritance, semantic association, composition, and aggregation), the sequence diagram, the collaboration diagram, and the state diagram.

A good design notation should show overall system structure in a graphic form and leave detailed semantic definitions (of algorithms, class invariants, preconditions, and postconditions, for example) to text. For that reason, UML doesn't try to replace textual definitions of classes and their methods. Instead, the language provides a graphic framework for organizing design constructs and then defining each construct via appropriate text.

Before I launch into UML itself, let me relate the goals that Messrs. Booch, Jacobson, and Rumbaugh set for themselves in developing UML. You may want to mentally gauge the degree to which they've achieved these goals as we review UML in the following chapters.[3]

---

[1] See [Page-Jones et al., 1990] for an account of UON.

[2] See [Henderson-Sellers and Edwards, 1994] for the MOSES notation.

[3] My take: With only a few exceptions, they've done a very good job, because it's hard to meet all of these (sometimes opposing) goals. For the latest statement of the goals, check **www.rational.com**.

The following seven goal statements are excerpted from UML's principal authors themselves.

1. **Provide users a ready-to-use, expressive visual modeling language so they can develop and exchange meaningful models.**

   It is important that the OOAD standard support a modeling language that can be used "out of the box" to do normal general-purpose modeling tasks. If the standard merely provides a meta-meta-description that requires tailoring to a particular set of modeling concepts, then it will not achieve the purpose of allowing users to exchange models without losing information or without imposing excessive work to map their models to a very abstract form.

   The UML consolidates a set of core modeling concepts that are generally accepted across many current methods and modeling tools. These concepts are needed in many or most large applications, although not every concept is needed in every part of every application. . . .

2. **Provide extensibility and specialization mechanisms to extend the core concepts.**

   We expect that the UML will be tailored as new needs are discovered and for specific domains. At the same time, we do not want to force the common core concepts to be redefined or re-implemented for each tailored area. Therefore we believe that the extension mechanisms should support deviations from the common case, rather than being required to implement the core OOA&D concepts themselves. The core concepts should not be changed more than necessary.

   Users need to be able to

   1. build models using core concepts without using extension mechanisms for most normal applications;

   2. add new concepts and notations for issues not covered by the core;

3. choose among variant interpretations of existing concepts, when there is no clear consensus; and

4. specialize the concepts, notations, and constraints for particular application domains.

### 3. Be independent of particular programming languages and development processes.

The UML must and can support all reasonable programming languages. It also must and can support various methods and processes of building models. The UML can support multiple programming languages and development methods without excessive difficulty.

### 4. Provide a formal basis for understanding the modeling language.

Because users will use formality to help understand the language, it must be both precise and approachable; a lack of either dimension damages its usefulness. The formalisms must not require excessive levels of indirection or layering, use of low-level mathematical notations distant from the modeling domain, such as set-theoretic notation, or operational definitions that are equivalent to programming an implementation.

The UML provides a formal definition of the static format of the model using a metamodel expressed in UML class diagrams. This is a popular and widely accepted formal approach for specifying the format of a model and directly leads to the implementation of interchange formats. . . .

### 5. Encourage the growth of the OO tools market.

By enabling vendors to support a standard modeling language used by most users and tools, the industry benefits. While vendors still can add value in their tool implementations, enabling interoperability is essential. Interoperability requires that models can be exchanged among users and tools without loss of information. This can only occur if the tools agree on the format and meaning of all of the relevant concepts. Using a higher meta-level is no solution unless the mapping to the user-level concepts is included in the standard.

6. **Support higher-level development concepts such as collaborations, frameworks, patterns, and components.**

   Clearly defined semantics of these concepts is essential to reap the full benefit of OO and reuse. Defining these within the holistic context of a modeling language is a unique contribution of the UML.

7. **Integrate best practices.**

   A key motivation behind the development of the UML has been to integrate the best practices in the industry, encompassing widely varying views based on levels of abstraction, domains, architectures, life cycle stages, implementation technologies, etc. The UML is indeed such an integration of best practices.

---

Although the authors didn't initially identify the following four goals for UML, I've found that, by later intention or by pure good fortune, they achieved them anyway. So, I would append the following items as self-fulfilled goals:

1. **Inclusion of a simpler UML within a general, comprehensive UML**

   The average designer has no desire to confront a mob of marauding symbols in order to express his everyday designs. This impels UML to be *small*. On the other hand, a comprehensive notation like UML must depict constructs from several major object-oriented languages and must also anticipate the needs of designers working on the esoteric extremes of O.O. This impels UML to be *large*.

UML turns out to be both large and small. It contains quite a variety of modeling constructs and the ability for users to build even more. On the other hand, I've found that I use perhaps only half of UML to express the majority of my design work.

So, don't feel obliged to use the entire set of UML, just because it's there. It's OK to choose only those symbols that are relevant to your language, your environment, and your project. Chances are that you, like me, will find your own small workaday subset of useful UML symbols for the projects in your shop.

## 2. Usefulness in several modeling perspectives

A modeling perspective (or viewpoint) states the parts, the level of detail, and the abstractions of the subject matter that the model with that perspective intends to emphasize. In *Designing Object Systems*, for example, authors Steve Cook and John Daniels point out three important modeling perspectives in an object-oriented project.[4] To paraphrase,

- The first is the *essential perspective*, which models concepts from the business, without reference to implementation technology.
- The second is the *specification perspective*, which models the characteristics of software that will meet the requirements of a business solution.
- The third is the *implementation perspective*, which models the construction of the software.

Although I was skeptical at first, I find UML to be useful in all three of these modeling perspectives, using the same UML symbology and terminology for each modeling perspective (although some symbols and terms may be more prevalent in one perspective than in another). A popular phrase for this kind of versatility is "seamlessness across models."

## 3. Correspondence to code, close enough to permit reengineering

UML depicts the structure of object-oriented code at the level just above that of the code itself. Therefore, it should be possible for tools to take existing code and, automatically or manually, represent its salient structure in UML.

---

[4] [Fowler and Scott, 1997] echo the notion of modeling perspectives.

### 4. Computer-aided, as well as manual, usage

Since automated modeling tools (or CASE tools) are widespread, a modern object-oriented notation needs to cater for the screen, the mouse, and the printer. But, despite the availability of modeling tools, plenty of system modeling still takes place on whiteboards and on the backs of envelopes. Happily, the majority of UML's most useful symbols are sketchable with humble pencil and paper, prior to their subsequent glorious reincarnation in an electronic medium.

Now let's turn to the layout of Part II. Each of the five chapters introduces diagrams and symbols that cover a particular group of object-oriented design constructs.

Chapter 3 introduces the class (or pin-out) symbol, which shows a class and its attributes and operations, together with their formal signatures.

Chapter 4 presents the class diagram, which shows classes' single or multiple inheritance hierarchies and classes' other interconnections via the association, composition, and aggregation constructs. The composition and aggregation constructs are typically used to depict the objects that as a group comprise an object of a given class. Association is used to capture the semantic (or business-oriented) relationships among objects of various classes.

Chapter 5 covers sequence and collaboration diagrams, both of which show (in different ways) run-time interactions among objects. The former diagram, which has a firm format, strongly emphasizes timing and message sequence by showing objects' operations scaled roughly to their execution times. This diagram is particularly useful for designing systems with concurrent execution and asynchronous messaging. The latter diagram, which has a freer format, emphasizes the messages (and actual arguments) passed between objects at run-time.

Chapter 6 addresses the state diagram, which shows how objects make transitions from state to state within the state-space defined for their class. Many of the issues in Chapter 6 relate to the adaptation of traditional state-transition diagrams for object-oriented design.

Chapter 7 wraps up Part II with three more specialized diagrams. The first is the package diagram, which shows the grouping of software elements into encapsulation structures at a level higher than that of the single class. The second is the deployment diagram, which represents the overall system architecture by showing units of technology and their physical communication links. It also portrays how a software system is partitioned across the various pieces of underlying hardware and software technology. The third kind of diagram in Chapter 7 isn't part of traditional UML. It's the window-navigation diagram, which shows the application-meaningful paths between windows in a graphical user interface.

I don't intend for this book to be a reference manual on every symbol and nuance of UML.[5] Therefore, since about 40 percent of UML will probably express about 98 percent of your design deliverables, I concentrate on the portion of UML that yields the biggest design bang per symbol. However, I certainly present enough UML for you to understand the diagrams in Part III of the book.

In selecting the portion of UML to present here, I've omitted use cases and action diagrams. Use cases are tremendously valuable during requirements analysis and are important enough to warrant an entire book in their own right.[6] However, they are not central to the object-oriented design principles that I address in this book. As for action diagrams, I find them too graphically verbose to express the design ideas that I want to get across here.

Occasionally, I point out a minor variation on UML that you may prefer when drawing a particular design construct on a whiteboard. Which notation style you choose will depend on your taste and your drawing technique. However, since I bet you'll use an automated modeling tool to create most of your formal deliverables, you'll probably have to work within the notational dialect of that tool in order to print your design diagrams out. Incidentally, from what I've seen so far, UML modeling tools stray far less from the straight and narrow in their iconography than tools for other notations have, so in practice, you won't be overwhelmed by confusing notational mutations.

---

[5] For a complete UML reference manual, that duty falls to [Rumbaugh et al., 1999] and any subsequent updates they publish. Several other books have been devoted to UML, too. Two excellent ones for your further pursuit are [Fowler and Scott, 1997] and [Muller, 1997].

[6] See [Rosenberg and Scott, 1999], for example.

# Basic Expression of Classes, Attributes, and Operations

In this chapter, I describe UML notation for classes and then explore UML notation for the features (attributes and operations) that you may allocate to a class. I conclude the chapter with UML for two variations on the basic class: the utility package and the parameterized class.

We begin at the beginning, with the fundamental class notation.

## 3.1 The Class

The class symbol on the left of Fig. 3.1 is central to any application of UML. The topmost of the symbol's three compartments shows the class name, by convention starting with an uppercase letter. This one's imaginatively named **SomeClass**. Into this compartment, you may also add some further information about the class, as discussed in Section 3.7. The convention for modeling tools is to show the class name in boldfaced font, but I've never managed to write in boldface on a whiteboard.

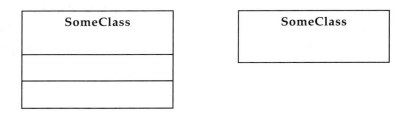

*Fig. 3.1:* *Symbol for a class in its full and abbreviated forms.*

The middle compartment shows the attributes of the class, and the bottom compartment shows its operations. We'll come back to these two compartments in the next section. Additional compartments may be added to the standard three, and they may be given user-defined names (such as *invariants* or *exceptions)* that express their purposes.

An alternative symbol for a class appears on the right side of Fig. 3.1. This abbreviated symbol (which omits the attribute and operation compartments) is handy when you want to show only a class and its name.

Figure 3.2 shows the equivalent symbols for depicting an object. As we saw in Chapter 1, when an object is spawned from a class, it obtains a structure that is almost identical to that of its class.[1] Naturally enough, then, UML uses the same symbol for an object as for a class.

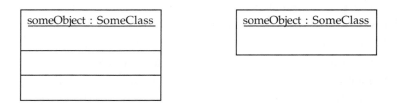

*Fig. 3.2:* *Symbol for an object (an instance of a class) in its full and abbreviated forms.*

---

[1] The main difference is that an *object*—an instance of a class—has *no* class attributes or operations. However, typical classes have *very few* class attributes and operations. Most attributes of a typical class are instance attributes (that is, attributes of *objects* of the class) and most operations are instance operations (that is, operations of *objects* of the class).

The most noticeable differences in notation between an object and its class are evident in the name compartment. For example, in contrast to the style used for a class name, an object's name is underlined and not in boldface. These typographical differences allow your eye to differentiate quickly between classes and objects. Moreover, the syntax of an object's name takes the form of <u>instanceName:</u> <u>ClassName</u>. As I pointed out in Chapter 1, an object doesn't actually have a name of its own—just a handle. Nevertheless, in most design contexts, such as when one object is sending another object a message, the objects are known by some name (for example, **thisCustAccount** or **leftFlap**). If you don't have a good name for it—which is possible in your early design work—you can leave it anonymous. In that case, **: ClassName** is acceptable notation.

## 3.2 Attributes

Here's a quick review of attributes, before we explore their representation in UML. (For clarity, I'll limit my discussion to publicly visible instance attributes.)

- An attribute represents information about an object.
- The term *attribute* is not quite synonymous with *variable*. An attribute represents an abstractly defined property, independent of how that property is internally implemented. A variable, on the other hand, is an internal implementation mechanism.

  Nevertheless, eight times out of ten, an attribute turns out to be implemented as a simple variable, identical in nature to the attribute itself. For example, the **length** attribute may be implemented with a **length** variable.

  On the ninth occasion, however, some manipulation may be involved. For example, a **date** attribute may be passed into and out of an object in the form **YYYY/MM/DD**, whereas it may be stored in a **date** variable as an integer (say, the number of days since the birth of King Grog the Magnanimous).

  On the tenth occasion, the derivation of an attribute value may involve several variables. For example, the **capacity** attribute of a cuboid is presumably computed by multiplying the values of **Cuboid**'s **length**, **breadth**, and **height**. See right for a helpful illustration of a cuboid.

- In general, an attribute is both gettable and settable from outside the object.
- On the other hand, some attributes are read-only—that is, only *gettable* from outside the object.[2] Typically—but not necessarily—these attributes are derived from others; for example, **capacity** of a **Cuboid** object, or **age** of a **Person** (derived from **dateOfBirth**).

    Note that although **capacity** is a read-only attribute, it is *not* a constant; it may be changed by executing operations on the object, such as **scale** (which enlarges or shrinks a cuboid).

Now let's see how UML represents attributes. The **Person** class in Fig. 3.3 has three attributes listed in its middle compartment: **name**, **dateOfBirth**, and **age**. Each attribute name is followed by its respective class (or data-type), after a colon. I preface read-only attributes with a forward slash (**/**); for example, **/ age**.[3] The **Cuboid** class in Fig. 3.3 has four attributes: **length**, **breadth**, **height**, and **capacity**, the last of which is not directly settable (in other words, it's read-only).

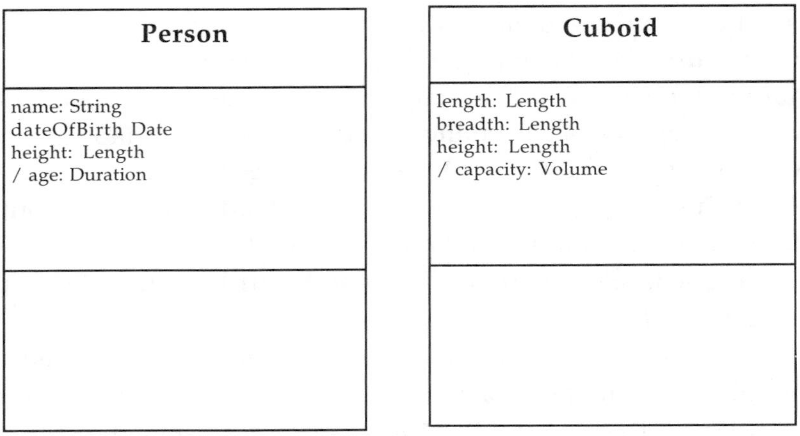

| Person |
| --- |
| name: String<br>dateOfBirth Date<br>height: Length<br>/ age: Duration |
|  |

| Cuboid |
| --- |
| length: Length<br>breadth: Length<br>height: Length<br>/ capacity: Volume |
|  |

*Fig. 3.3: Attributes.*

---

[2] This corresponds to the notion in the CORBA interface-definition language (IDL) of the term *readonly*. I suppose that an attribute *could* be settable, but not gettable, from outside the object. However, I haven't seen many such attributes and I don't think that UML has any notation for that situation.

[3] In UML, the forward slash (**/**) formally signifies a derived attribute. However, I think that whether an attribute is derived or not is an implementation decision. Externally, we should only see whether an attribute is directly settable or not, for which purpose I find the forward slash concise and informative. Although the forward slash means "not directly settable" in this book, you and your team should decide how to use it on your projects.

## 3.3 Operations

In this section, we review operations and explore their representation in UML at the same time. As shown in Fig. 3.4, operations appear in the lowest compartment with their full formal signatures. Each formal signature comprises the operation name, together with the list of the operation's formal input and output arguments.[4]

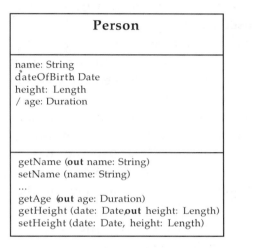

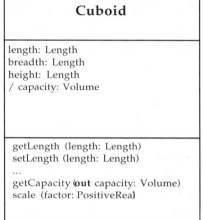

*Fig. 3.4: Operations.*

The UML standard calls for the keywords **in** and **out** before each argument to show its direction—into or out from the operation (and **inout** signifies an argument that is both **in** and **out**). In this book, I designate input arguments as the default, so I omit the keyword **in**. Where there are output arguments, I use the keyword **out** followed by one or more arguments. (I don't use any **inout** arguments.)

- A typical attribute requires two standard operations: a *get operation* and a *set operation*.[5] As shown in Fig. 3.4, **Person** has a **getDateOf-**

---

[4] *Formal argument* is a traditional term in computer science for an argument that appears in the definition of a function (usually in the function header, which defines the function's interface). By contrast, an *actual argument* is supplied by a caller of the function. In object orientation, the same distinction between formal and actual applies to the arguments of operations.

[5] A get operation is an example of a query (or accessor) operation, whose execution leaves the state of the system unchanged. A set operation is an example of a non-query (or modifier) operation, whose execution may change the state of the system.

**Birth** operation, which returns the value of the person's date of birth to whoever needs it, and a **setDateOfBirth** operation, which establishes a date of birth for a person. Similarly, **Cuboid** has **getLength** and **setLength** operations, among others.

- Obviously, an attribute that's read-only doesn't need a set operation. So, for example, the class **Person** has defined on it only one operation corresponding to the **age** attribute, named **getAge**, and **Cuboid** has **getCapacity** but not **setCapacity**.

- A few attributes call for operations that need input arguments. Such attributes often hold data on the previous history of that attribute. For example, the attribute **height** defined on a **Person** varies over time. If the application keeps the history of this attribute, then the operation **getHeight** will take **date** as an input argument and return the person's height on that date. This operation's formal signature would be **getHeight (date: Date, out height: Length)**. The method implementing this operation may use a table lookup to obtain the height or it may compute it somehow, but that detail is hidden from us here.

- Some operations require communication with other objects, through message passing. For example, to change the job of a **Person**, you would need an operation such as **changeJob (newJob: Job, effectiveDate: Date)**. This would result in considerable communication with personnel-related objects (of class **Organization** and so on). We'll look at the UML for such communication in Chapter 5.

The operation names **getDateOfBirth** and **setDateOfBirth**, mentioned earlier, follow a popular naming convention for the get and set operations of a typical attribute, **dateOfBirth**. However, there are alternative conventions for naming and depicting operations in UML. For example, some shops would prefer to name the first operation simply **dateOfBirth**, especially if they intend to program it as a function, rather than as a procedure. So, instead of a message **person1.getDateOfBirth (out dateOfBirth)**, they would have the nicer-looking message, **person1.dateOfBirth**. I show this convention in Fig. 3.5.

| Person |
|---|
| name: String<br>dateOfBirth Date<br>height: Length<br>/ age: Duration |
| name: String<br>setName (name: String)<br>...<br>age: Duration<br>height (date: Date): Length<br>setHeight (date: Date, height: Length) |

| Cuboid |
|---|
| length: Length<br>breadth: Length<br>height: Length<br>/ capacity: Volume |
| length: Length<br>setLength (length: Length)<br>...<br>capacity: Volume<br>scale (factor: PositiveReal) |

*Fig. 3.5:   Attributes with a functional naming convention<br>for get operations.*

Notice that under this naming convention, most get operations are identical in form to their corresponding attributes (although the **height** operation of the **Person** class still needs the input argument **date**). This leads many shops to omit all basic, uninteresting get and set operations from their UML class symbols. See Fig. 3.6, for example.

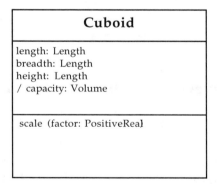

| Person |
|---|
| name: String<br>dateOfBirth Date<br>height: Length<br>/ age: Duration |
| height (date: Date): Length<br>setHeight (date: Date, height: Length) |

| Cuboid |
|---|
| length: Length<br>breadth: Length<br>height: Length<br>/ capacity: Volume |
| scale (factor: PositiveReal) |

*Fig. 3.6:   Class symbols with basic get and set operations<br>omitted.*

Of course, the get and set operations are still there implicitly and will have to be programmed. But, by not showing them, modelers can significantly reduce the clutter on—and the size of—their UML class symbols.  This is the convention that I adopt for the rest of this book, except where I want to highlight a get or set operation by listing it explicitly in the bottom compartment of a class symbol.  When I do show a get operation, I tend to name it by the functional naming convention: That is, I favor the name **price** over **getPrice**.

Some academics refer to the class symbol, with its operations, as an *ADT-definition diagram*, where "ADT" stands for "abstract data-type."  But other people nickname it as the *pin-out symbol*, because it resembles the diagram of IC pins in an integrated-circuit catalog.

To reinforce the analogy between a class and an integrated circuit, I show (in Fig. 3.7) an example of a pin-out diagram for an electronic IC, a fictitious timer. The diagram shows what each of the eight pins requires as input or provides as output.  The behavior of some of the pins is also implied by their names.  The pins of the IC are analogous, of course, to class operations.

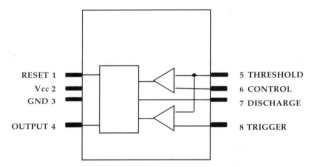

*Fig. 3.7: A pin-out diagram for a fictitious IC, a timer.*

## 3.4 Overloaded Operations

Operations that are overloaded will appear many times on the class diagram, each time with a different signature (that is, with a different number of arguments or with different classes of arguments).[6]  In Fig. 3.8, for example, the operation **markDown** of the class **SellableProductLine**, which reduces the price of an item, may have two versions.  The first **markDown** takes an input argument, which is a percentage discount.  The second **markDown** brooks no input argument; it always reduces the price by the same (default) amount.

---

[6] You may recall from Chapter 1 that an operation is overloaded if it is defined more than once on the same class.

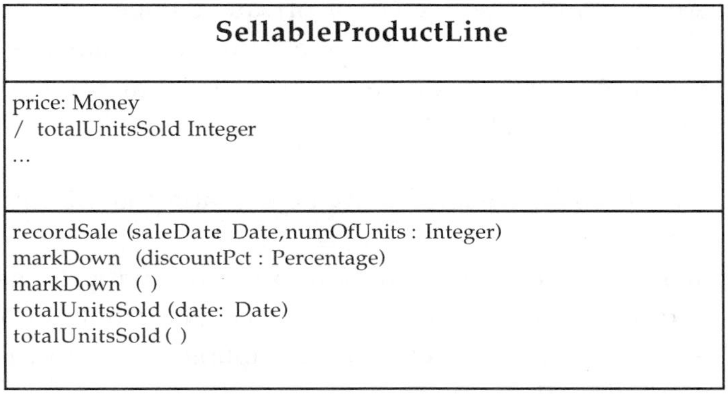

```
┌─────────────────────────────────────────────┐
│              SellableProductLine              │
├─────────────────────────────────────────────┤
│ price: Money                                  │
│ /  totalUnitsSold Integer                     │
│ ...                                           │
│                                               │
├─────────────────────────────────────────────┤
│ recordSale (saleDate Date,numOfUnits : Integer)│
│ markDown  (discountPct : Percentage)          │
│ markDown  ( )                                 │
│ totalUnitsSold (date: Date)                   │
│ totalUnitsSold ( )                            │
│                                               │
└─────────────────────────────────────────────┘
```

*Fig. 3.8: Two pairs of overloaded operations.*

There's a second overloaded operation, the get operation **totalUnitsSold**. The first version takes the input argument **date** and returns the total number of product line units sold on that date. The second version (with no input argument) returns the total number of product line units sold since the Big Bang. (Incidentally, the operation **recordSale** probably updates an internal variable that remembers how many units were sold on a given date.)

## 3.5 Visibility of Attributes and Operations

UML attaches a prefix to an attribute or operation name to indicate the feature's visibility. As Fig. 3.9 shows, public attributes or operations are prefixed with a plus sign (**+**). Protected attributes or operations are prefixed with a number sign (**#**), and private attributes or operations with a minus sign (**–**). However, since you usually want a class diagram to show only public attributes and operations, most designers (and most modeling tools) omit the plus sign, except to provide special emphasis.

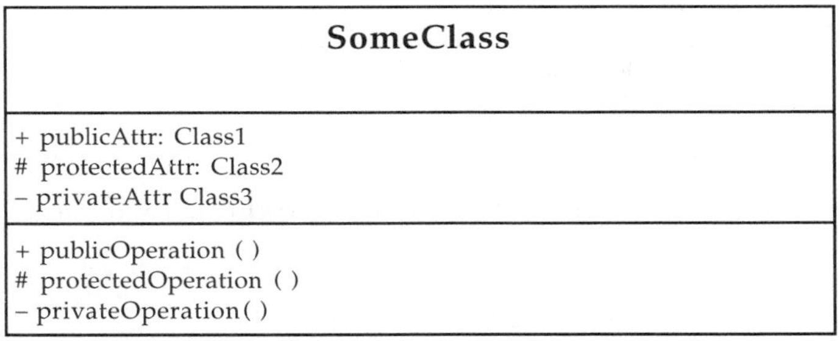

```
┌─────────────────────────────────────────────┐
│                  SomeClass                    │
│                                               │
├─────────────────────────────────────────────┤
│ + publicAttr: Class1                          │
│ # protectedAttr: Class2                       │
│ – privateAttr Class3                          │
├─────────────────────────────────────────────┤
│ + publicOperation ( )                         │
│ # protectedOperation ( )                      │
│ – privateOperation( )                         │
└─────────────────────────────────────────────┘
```

*Fig. 3.9:  Public, protected, and private attributes and operations.*

Although what we call public, protected, or private is dependent on what language is used, it's possible to come up with some definitions that are valid in several languages.[7] For example, let's describe a feature **f**, an attribute or operation that is defined on an object **obj** of class **C**.

- If **f** is *public,* then **f** is visible to any object, and **f** is inherited by the subclasses of **C**.
- If **f** is *private,* then **f** is visible only to **obj**. Alternatively, as defined in C++ and Java: If **f** is private, then **f** is visible only to objects of class **C**—in other words, to **obj** and its siblings; also, in this case, **f** is not inherited by the subclasses of **C**.
- If **f** is *protected,* then **f** is visible only to objects of class **C** and to objects of **C**'s subclasses; also, in this case, **f** is inherited by the subclasses of **C**.

Ultimately, however, designers will use the UML **+**, **–**, or **#** prefixes that best express the definition of visibility supported by their programming language.

## 3.6 Class Attributes and Operations

In Fig. 3.10, the underlined names indicate class attributes and operations. Given this, you may ask: "Hey, why does UML use underlining to depict *class* features? Didn't you say earlier that underlining signifies *instances?*"

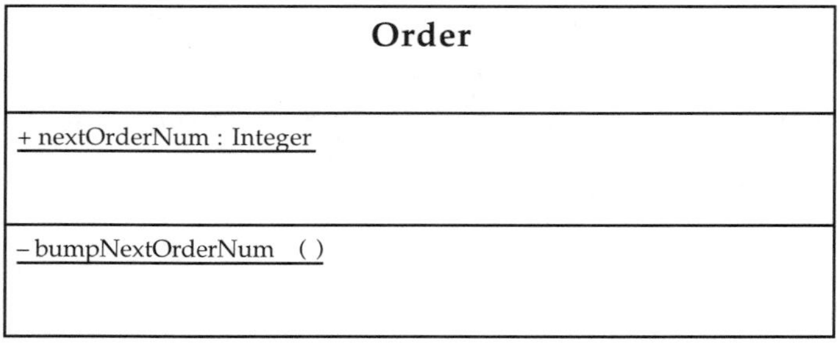

| Order |
|---|
| + nextOrderNum : Integer |
| – bumpNextOrderNum   ( ) |

*Fig. 3.10: A public class attribute and a private class operation.*

---

[7] For a merry discussion of just how diverse the definition of "protected" can be, see [Fowler and Scott, 1997, pp. 100–101].

I'm not glad you asked me that. I could pull out the excuse that I don't make the news, I just report it. However, there is a reason for underlining class attributes and operations—albeit an odd sort of reason. If you're a trusting soul, you can accept the notation at face value, skip to the next section, and have a happy, carefree day. If not, hang on tight for the official rationalization of this notation.

The object-oriented operating environment sees a single class (say, **C**) as an instance of the class called **Class**, of which every class is an instance. Therefore, from the environment-level perspective, each class feature of **C** exists at the instance level and must be underlined.

I know it's a stretch. Perhaps you should do what the trusting souls do (myself included): Forget the explanation and just remember the notation. Or, when modeling on a whiteboard, prefix names of class attributes and operations with a dollar sign (**$**). This is the old UML convention, and I still find it handy.

## 3.7 Abstract Operations and Classes

An operation is *abstract* if it has no implementation (this is equivalent to a base-class pure-virtual function in C++ or a deferred feature in Eiffel). In other words, it has an interface and a defined functionality, but no implementation method with actual code!

An *abstract class* (or deferred class, in Eiffel) doesn't instantiate objects, usually because it has at least one abstract operation defined on it. If it did create an object, a message invoking the object's abstract operation would cause a run-time error. Given this, the following message is illegal on an abstract class:

SomeAbstractClass.New;   // illegal code![8]

On the face of it, an abstract operation and the class on which it's defined may seem useless. So, why have them in an object-oriented language?

The answer relates to inheritance. An abstract operation in a class **C** serves as a common placeholder, indicating to the reader that classes below **C** in the inheritance hierarchy will provide a *concrete* implementation of the operation (also known as an *effective* or *non-abstract* implementation). Ultimately, each of the

---

[8] In Exercise 4 of Chapter 1, we saw that instantiation from literal classes (such as **Integer.New**) is illegal in most languages. An abstract class is similar in this respect to a class of literals. Otherwise, however, it's a distinct concept. An abstract class doesn't have objects, but a literal class can have many, predefined objects.

lowest subclasses will probably apply its own method for implementing the operation, perhaps optimized to meet the specific needs of that subclass.

For example, using the **Polygon** class of Chapter 1, we could change **getArea** into an abstract operation of **Polygon**, which would then become an abstract class. This change would have two implications:

1.  We'd be *obliged* to provide a concrete operation **getArea** for **Hexagon**. (We already have concrete operations for **Triangle** and **Rectangle**.)

2.  We would never instantiate an object of class **Polygon**. That is, we would never write **Polygon.New**, because a message to its operation **getArea** would cause an error. We should instantiate an object only of one of the classes **Triangle**, **Rectangle,** or **Hexagon**. (Indeed, this guideline is enforced as a rule in Eiffel, Java, and C++.) However, we could still have written **var p: Polygon**. This declaration (in the O.O. pseudocode language I use in this book) means that **p** may (polymorphically) hold the handle of an object of any of the classes, **Triangle**, **Rectangle**, or **Hexagon**.

Figure 3.11 shows **Polygon** as an example of an abstract class, with the name of the abstract class in italics and the property **{abstract}** in braces under the name. Some modeling tools drop the property name and let the italic font do all the work. That's sufficient in most cases, but I find italics a bit tough to manage on a whiteboard. The abstract get operation *getArea* also appears in italics, with the property **{abstract}** in braces after its name.

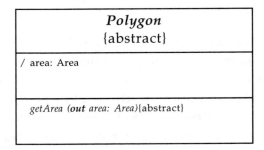

*Fig. 3.11: An abstract class, with an abstract operation,*
**getArea**.

## 3.8 The Utility

The *utility* (or *utility package)* is a group of procedures and functions encapsulated into a single unit with a set of private data. It differs from the class in that individual objects are never instantiated from it; the utility is more like a group of traditional functions and procedures (like a dynamically linked library) or an Ada-83 package.[9]

The utility is like a class with no objects: Its operations are, in effect, class operations. (Alternatively, you could regard a utility as a class with only one, predefined object.)

Figure 3.12 shows the UML notation for a utility. The class name is prefaced by the stereotype **«utility»**, enclosed in what my publishing friends tell me are guillemets (not to be confused with guillemots, which are birds). Notice that none of the operation names in Fig. 3.12 is underlined. Although a utility's operations are in effect class operations, by convention UML doesn't underline their names.

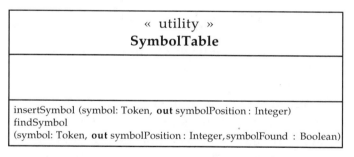

*Fig. 3.12: A utility to handle a symbol table.*

The utility is valuable for implementing a software construct with only one instance, such as a mathematics package or a daemon. (A daemon is a piece of software that acts as a monitor for changing conditions. For example, a daemon may watch system inputs for the occurrence of events in the environment and another daemon may watch a database for some condition to become true.)

---

[9] I don't use the term *package* here, because UML uses package for a different (but related) concept. In Ada, you can create new packages from a generic one, using the keyword **new**. However, this is not fully analogous to object instantiation. The usual COBOL implementation for a utility is a subprogram with multiple, discrete entry-points. A system designed around utilities rather than classes is usually termed *object-based*. In structured design, the term for a utility is *information cluster* or *information-strength module*.

The utility is also useful in that it can provide a veneer of object orientation to programs written in traditional languages, such as C or COBOL. A well-defined utility built around some venerable old COBOL or other legacy code is commonly called a *wrapper*.

## 3.9 Parameterized Classes

UML shows a *parameterized class* (also known as a *generic class* or, in C++, as a *template class*) with a dotted box over the top right of the standard class symbol. Into this box goes the list of formal class arguments (of which there's usually just one). See Fig. 3.13.

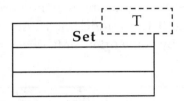

*Fig. 3.13: A parameterized class, with one formal class argument.*

Figure 3.13 shows **Set**, a typical container class, which takes a class formally named **T** as an argument. When an actual class, such as **Car**, is supplied for **T** (or, put more formally, "bound to **T**"), each of the objects of that class will represent a set of cars. The name of the bound, parameterized class is then given as **Set <Car>**, which is shown on the left side of Fig. 3.14.

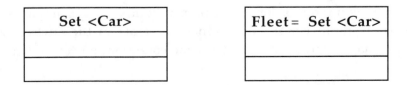

*Fig. 3.14: A bound class, formed from a parameterized class.*

On the right side of Fig. 3.14, I show the class **Fleet**, which is simply a more memorable synonym for **Set <Car>**. (The equal sign is my shorthand for their synonymity.)

Figure 3.15 shows the class **Fleet** again, this time in a more sophisticated UML diagram. Here, we see the specific binding of the actual class argument, **Car**, to **Set**'s formal class argument, **T**. The dotted arrow, pointing upward, explicitly and graphically depicts binding (indicated by the **«bind»** stereotype).

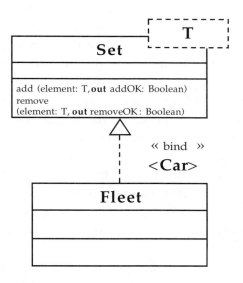

*Fig. 3.15: A bound class, formed from a parameterized class—another depiction.*

## 3.10 Summary

The class symbol is central to UML. It is typically shown with three compartments; from top to bottom, they contain the class name and any supplementary information, the attributes, and the operations, respectively. Objects appear in a similar form to classes, except that the object's name, in the top compartment, is underlined and usually expressed as **<u>obj: Class</u>**.

An attribute represents a piece of information about an object and appears in the middle compartment of the class symbol: Each attribute is listed by name, followed by its class (or data-type). By implication, when an attribute is listed, the operation compartment contains a get operation and a set operation. If the set operation is not necessary or is not allowed—for example, if the value of the attribute is derived by an algorithm—I precede the attribute name with a forward slash (/).

In the third compartment of the class symbol, each operation is listed with its full formal signature (its name, followed by the formal input and/or output arguments a message must supply to invoke the operation). Conventionally, get and set operations are omitted for brevity, unless a designer needs to emphasize an operation—such as a get operation that requires an input argument.

Many operations carry out more complex activities than simply setting or getting attribute values—activities that possibly require communication with other objects or external devices. The implementation of such operations is termed the operation's *method.*

The names of public, protected, and private attributes and operations are prefixed by a plus sign (**+**), a number sign (**#**), and a minus sign (**–**), respectively. However, the plus sign is normally dropped because visibility is public by default. Class attributes and operations, which are not instantiated for individual objects, are given underlined names. An operation is overloaded if it appears several times on a class diagram, each time with a different signature (with a different number of arguments or with different classes of arguments).

The name of an abstract class appears in italics and is followed by the property **{abstract}**. An abstract operation's name also appears in italics and has the property **{abstract}**. The name of a utility class is preceded by the **«utility»** stereotype. Although a utility's operations are in effect class operations, by convention their names are not underlined.

A parameterized class (or, generic or template class) appears with a dotted box over its top right corner. The dotted box contains the list of formal argument names, each of which represents a specific class to be supplied (or "bound") to the parameterized class. A bound class, which is a parameterized class that has already been bound with specific classes, is named according to the following syntax:

ParameterizedClass <SuppliedClass1, SuppliedClass2, SuppliedClass3>

Alternatively, the bound class can be given a meaningful name:

MeaningfulName = ParameterizedClass <SuppliedClass1, SuppliedClass2, SuppliedClass3>

Notationally, the binding of the specific classes is shown by an arrow from the bound class to the parameterized class. The arrow is labeled with the **«bind»** stereotype and the list of supplied classes.

## 3.11 Exercises

1. Summarize the differentiating characteristics of classes (such as abstract versus concrete) that we covered in this chapter and Chapter 1.

2. Summarize the differentiating characteristics of operations (such as instance versus class) that we covered in this chapter and Chapter 1.

3. Summarize the UML symbols used to prefix the name of a feature (an attribute or operation). Assume for this exercise that class attributes and operations have a dollar sign (**$**) prefix.

4. The class **Person** has an operation **height** that—although just a get operation for its attribute **height**—had to be shown as an explicit operation because it needs an input argument. (See Fig. 3.6.) Why not "parameterize" the attribute **height** instead, as **height (date: Date): Length**, and so remove the need to show its get and set operations explicitly?

5. Research the UML notation to express a class whose objects are immutable (a concept I covered in the exercises of Chapter 1).

6. On page 98, I gave the name **Fleet** to the bound parameterized class **Set<Car>**. Is this the best name for such a class? (Hint: Speculate about some applications that would use **Set<Car>**, together with the applications' current and future scopes of applicability.)

7. From what you've seen so far, how would you characterize the difference between a UML property and a UML stereotype?

8. Show in UML notation a class of your choice (such as the **Hominoid** class of Chapter 1). Include attributes and operations.

## 3.12 Answers

1.   Here are some differentiating characteristics of classes that we've considered in this chapter and in Chapter 1.  For each pair, I mention the "normal" class first—the kind of class you'll come across most often:

   (i)   <u>Nonutility versus utility class</u>.  The former gives rise to distinct objects. The latter doesn't (or should be considered the sole object of its "class").

   (ii)   <u>Non-literal versus literal</u>.  The former supports run-time instantiation of objects.  The latter has all its objects "instantiated" implicitly by the compiler, and the objects' "handles" are their literal values.

   (iii)   <u>Mutable versus immutable</u>.  The objects instantiated from the former may change state after instantiation (for this, the class should really be called *a class with mutable objects*.)  The latter has objects whose states do not change after instantiation.  Most immutable classes are literal classes and most literal classes are immutable classes.

   (iv)   <u>Concrete versus abstract</u>.  (Non-deferred versus deferred.)  The former is a class with no abstract operations.  No objects can be instantiated from the latter kind of class, usually because it has one or more abstract operations.  (However, objects can be instantiated from a concrete subclass of an abstract class.)

   (v)   <u>Non-parameterized versus parameterized</u>.  (Nongeneric versus generic; non-template versus template.)  The former is a simple class that needs no class names bound to it.  The latter is a class that binds class names as arguments upon instantiation of objects.

2.   Here are some differentiating characteristics of operations that we've considered in this chapter and in Chapter 1:

   (i)   <u>Instance versus class</u>.  The former operation is defined on an individual instance (an object).  The latter is defined on a class and does not directly access variables of individual objects.

(ii) <u>Query versus non-query</u>. (Accessor versus modifier.) Execution of a query operation does not change the state of the system. Execution of a non-query operation usually does. Most query operations are get operations, which access attribute values. Most other operations are non-query operations, including set operations, which change attribute values.

(iii) <u>Public versus protected versus private</u>. A public operation is visible outside the class or object on which it's defined. A protected operation is visible only to objects of the same class (or to its subclasses). A private operation is visible only to the object on which it is defined.

(iv) <u>Concrete versus abstract</u>. (Non-deferred versus deferred.) The former is the normal kind of operation, with an implementation that can be executed (a method composed of a body of code). The latter operation lacks an actual implementation and must be overridden in an inheriting subclass by a concrete, executable implementation.

(v) <u>Procedural versus functional naming</u>. (I admit that this distinction is more at the programming-language level than at the design level.) The former returns its values via arguments, rather than via the operation name. The latter kind of operation returns a value via the operation name and is convenient for get operations.

3. The following table summarizes the use of UML prefixes on feature names:

| Group | Symbol | Meaning |
|-------|--------|---------|
| A |   | readable and writeable attribute (both "gettable" and "settable") |
|   | / | read-only attribute (only "gettable") |
| B |   | instance attribute or operation |
|   | $ | class attribute or operation |
| C |   | public (or yet-to-be-decided) attribute or operation |
|   | + | public attribute or operation |
|   | − | private attribute or operation |
|   | # | protected attribute or operation |

For an attribute, choose one from Group A, one from Group B, and one from Group C. For an operation, choose one from Group B and one from Group C. In orthodox UML, Group B is actually represented by *no underlining* or *underlining*, respectively.

4. I don't show parameterized attributes in this book, because they're not supported in UML. However, I confess that I use parameterized attributes informally, on whiteboards, especially when I'm nailing down attributes but I'm not quite ready to address operations.

5. Reasonably enough, UML indicates immutability with the property, **{immutable}**. If you place this property in the top (name) compartment of a class, then the class's objects are completely immutable (that is, *all* their attributes are immutable after instantiation). If you place this property alongside a single attribute in the middle compartment of a class, then only that attribute is immutable. (As you can see, "immutable" is just a fancy O.O. word for "constant.")

   Remember, immutability is different from the idea of being "not directly settable." For example, the **location** attribute of a hominoid is not directly settable—and so is marked with a forward slash (/)—yet it isn't immutable: Its value changes whenever the hominoid advances.

6. A fleet can be a bunch of cars, but it can also be a bunch of boats or a bunch of airplanes. Today, a corporation may own only a fleet of cars, but in the future, its pampered executives may be whisked across the country by corporate jets and paddled across large lakes by corporate canoes. In that case, we would need, for example, **AirplaneFleet** and **BoatFleet**. However, the name **Fleet** would then be less effective, especially if we needed **Fleet** to be a superclass of **AirplaneFleet**, **BoatFleet**, and **CarFleet**. So, in order to avoid extensive name changes later, we should name **Set<Car>** as **CarFleet**—not just **Fleet**—from the beginning.

   This epitomizes a couple of vexing questions that arise when you develop object-oriented systems with reuse in mind: Where will this class need to be reused? What will the scope of the business be in the future?

7.  A UML property represents a particular characteristic of a standard UML element. For example, the property **{abstract}** is added to the top component of an abstract class symbol to represent a particular kind of class. A UML stereotype, on the other hand, represents a new modeling construct. For example, the stereotype **«utility»** is added to the top compartment of the class icon to represent UML's utility construct, which is distinct from the class. (Most other notations assign a unique symbol to each construct, which leads to a confusing plethora of made-up symbols.)

    UML properties and stereotypes are very useful. Unfortunately, however, some shops seem to find the distinction between "property" and "stereotype" to be so subtle that they apply them interchangeably.

8.  Figure 3.16 shows some attributes and operations that may be defined on **Hominoid**.

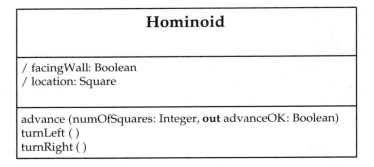

*Fig. 3.16: UML for the class* **Hominoid**.

There are a couple of points to note in this example:

(i)   The attributes **facingWall** and **location** should not have corresponding set operations; hence, they require the forward slash (**/**) notation.

(ii)  Although most operations have input or output arguments, the operations **turnLeft** and **turnRight** have none. This is legal, but it's often a hint to a designer that an operation could be generalized. For example, we could replace the two operations with a single, more general operation such as **turn (turnAngle)**. I return to this issue in Section 14.2.

# Class Diagrams

This chapter introduces UML for class diagrams, which offer modelers three important object-oriented constructs: the inheritance structure, the association structure, and the whole/part association.

Section 4.1 presents the inheritance (or superclass/subclass) structure. As we saw in Chapter 1, inheritance is a vital structure for building classes upon other classes. It's also the major framework upon which you build a class library.

Section 4.2 presents the association structure. An association between classes occurs when there is some conceptual relationship (usually involving the business being modeled) that links their instances.[1] UML depicts associations with—no surprise here—the association construct.

Section 4.3 presents whole/part associations, by which, for example, a chair comprises a back, a seat, and four legs. This structure is as common and as useful in object orientation as it is in everyday life. There are two forms of whole/part associations in UML: composition (expressed by the composition adornment on the association symbol) and aggregation (expressed by the aggregation adornment).

---

[1] Indeed, the UML term *association* is termed *relationship* in many other notations.

## 4.1 The Generalization Construct

In UML, the generalization construct (shown as an arrow with an "open" head) allows a design to indicate either single or multiple inheritance.

### 4.1.1 *Single inheritance*

Figure 4.1 shows an inheritance hierarchy with single inheritance (each subclass has one superclass). Notice that the direction of the arrow is from the subclass (the more special, inheriting class) to the superclass (the more general, inherited-from class). This may seem odd: In everyday life, doesn't inheritance "travel" *downward?* That is, doesn't one inherit Trans-Siberian Railway Shares and a large Etruscan pot *from* one's great-uncle?

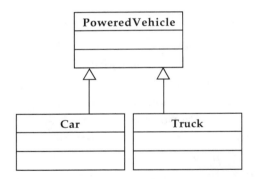

*Fig. 4.1: A single-inheritance hierarchy.*

The inheritance arrow points upward in the hierarchy, however, because the direction of class reference is upward. In other words, a subclass **Car** may refer to its superclass **PoweredVehicle**, but **PoweredVehicle** normally has no reference to **Car**. The arrow turned out to have another valuable intuitive connotation: It also depicts the path along which an object of a given class will search for the operation it needs to inherit and execute. (First, it searches its own class, then its parent class, then its grandparent class, and so on.)

Figure 4.2 shows an alternative style for depicting inheritance.[2] Instead of separate arrows to the superclass, there is just one, branching at the subclasses. Although Fig. 4.2 is semantically equivalent to Fig. 4.1, I prefer this style because, as we'll see below, it allows us to specify properties of the subclasses (such as partitioning constraints) on the diagram.

---

[2] UML refers to this tree-like diagramming as the "shared target" style.

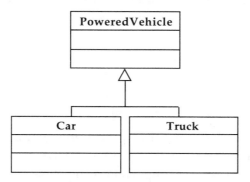

*Fig. 4.2.: A single-inheritance hierarchy—shared-target notation.*

Figure 4.3 shows another style for superclasses and subclasses, this time without compartments for attributes and operations. I normally use this abbreviated style when I don't need to show any details beyond the class names themselves.

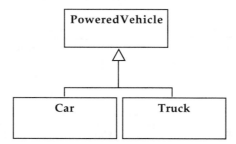

*Fig. 4.3.: A single-inheritance hierarchy—normal abbreviated notation.*

Incidentally, if you want to document a single-inheritance class hierarchy without feature names,[3] a diagram isn't necessary: You can document your hierarchy with simple indented text. This is exactly how many vendor-supplied library-browsers depict inheritance.[4]

---

[3] As a reminder, a *feature* is a term for an attribute or operation.

[4] Multiple inheritance can also be expressed textually in the form of a direct-inheritance matrix, a Boolean matrix that shows which class is a direct superclass of which. The total-inheritance matrix is derived from this first matrix by computing its so-called transitive closure. But don't try this at home; it's definitely a job for an automated modeling tool.

For example, if **Car** and **Truck** are subclasses of **PoweredVehicle**, you could write

**PoweredVehicle**

   **Car**

   **Truck**

However, the indented-list portrayal of inheritance cannot simultaneously show attributes and operations very easily, whereas UML's generalization notation can happily show these features superimposed on the class symbols.

### 4.1.2 Multiple inheritance

Figure 4.4 shows UML for multiple inheritance, whereby a class inherits directly from more than one superclass. In UML, there's nothing significant in the left-to-right ordering of a class's direct superclasses. (Moreover, there's nothing significant in the left-to-right ordering of a class's subclasses, either.)

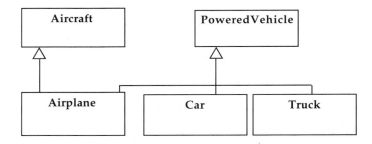

*Fig. 4.4: A multiple-inheritance hierarchy.*

### 4.1.3 Subclass partitioning

Figure 4.5 shows **PoweredVehicle** and its three subclasses again. Note that I've annotated the generalization arrow in this diagram with the properties **disjoint** and **incomplete**. Let me explain what these terms mean.

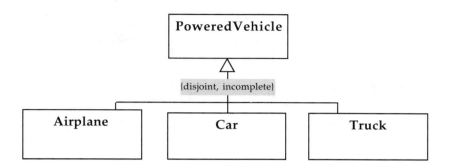

*Fig. 4.5: A disjoint, incomplete hierarchy.*

The term disjoint partitioning (as opposed to overlapping partitioning) applies to two or more groups of things that are cleanly partitioned. In other words, no single thing can belong to more than one group at the same time. For example, dogs, pigs, and horses are—at the time of writing!—disjoint groups. For an illustration of the terms disjoint and overlapping, see Fig. 4.6.

*Fig. 4.6: An illustration of disjoint and overlapping groups.*

The term *incomplete partitioning* (as opposed to *complete partitioning*) applies to subgroups of a group. It means that not all of the group's possible subgroups are included in the model. In other words, the group may have some members that don't belong to any of the modeled subgroups. This doesn't imply that the modeler intends to add more subgroups to the model; the currently modeled subgroups may be all that are necessary to the application at hand.

For an illustration of complete partitioning and incomplete partitioning, see Fig. 4.7, where the group as a whole is represented by the dotted outline and the subgroups by the solid outlines.

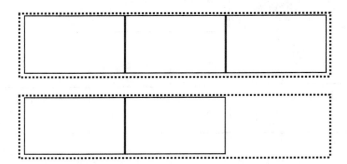

*Fig. 4.7:    An illustration of complete and incomplete sub-groups for a group.*

To illustrate incomplete partitioning in words, let's say that the group is people and the subgroups are: trapeze artists, sky divers, confidence tricksters, snake-unction peddlers, and methodologists.  Clearly, the subgroups are incomplete (with respect to a group of all people), because they don't include, for instance, help-desk personnel or ferret-tamers.  (I'm not sure whether or not they're over-lapping.)

If you're using a modeling tool, note that incomplete partitioning is not deter-mined by the portion of the diagram that's visible on your display.  Many model-ing tools use ellipses (...) to indicate that some subclasses are not shown in the open window.  The subclasses that are shown may be incomplete, but the model as a whole may still have complete partitioning.

The term *dynamic partitioning* (as opposed to *static partitioning)* applies to a thing's membership in more than one subgroup over time.  With dynamic parti-tioning, a thing may begin life as a member of one subgroup but later become a member of a different subgroup.  For example, as Fig. 4.8 illustrates, an employee may be a non-manager this year, but a manager next year—or vice versa!

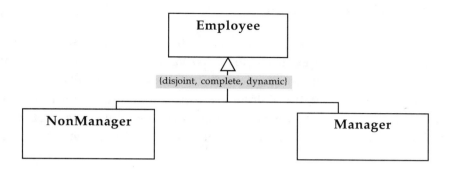

*Fig. 4.8: A dynamic inheritance hierarchy.*

Although the concepts of disjoint/overlapping partitioning, complete/incomplete partitioning, and dynamic/static partitioning are valuable early in a project (when the team is analyzing business requirements), they remain valuable in design, too.

If you know that two classes are mutually overlapping, then you know that there could be a useful subclass that inherits from both of them. For example, in Fig. 4.9, **Animal**'s overlapping subclasses, **Herbivore** and **Carnivore**, could have a common (multiply inheriting) subclass, **Omnivore**. Furthermore, if a class is partitioned completely into subclasses, you may decide to design it as an abstract class, as shown in the next section.

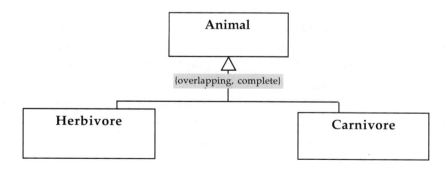

*Fig. 4.9: An overlapping, complete inheritance hierarchy.*

I return to the design implications of dynamic partitioning later in the book, especially in the final exercise of Chapter 14.

### *4.1.4 Partitioning discriminators*

Figure 4.10 shows an inheritance hierarchy with two levels. At the upper level, **Vehicle** has two subclasses: **ExternallyPropelledVehicle** and **InternallyPropelledVehicle**. (I've marked this partitioning as disjoint because I'm not considering my old Rolls Canardly, which, though nominally self-propelled, has spent much of its life being pushed.) The partitioning is complete because I assume that a vehicle's propulsion source must be either external or internal—there's no other option.

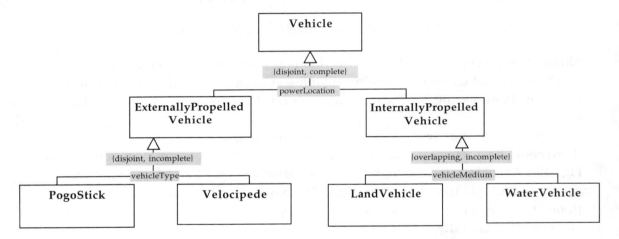

*Fig. 4.10: An inheritance hierarchy with discriminators.*

Notice the new annotation in Fig. 4.10, the discriminator **powerLocation**. Informally, this says: "What differentiates vehicles that belong to **ExternallyPropelledVehicle** from vehicles that belong to **InternallyPropelledVehicle** is the location of their propulsive power." In object-oriented design terms, objects of class **Vehicle** will probably have an attribute named **powerLocation**. Objects of class **ExternallyPropelledVehicle** will have that attribute set immutably to the constant value **external**, while objects of class **InternallyPropelledVehicle** will have that attribute set immutably to the constant value **internal**.

As I mentioned above, a superclass that's completely partitioned into subclasses may become an abstract class (one with no objects instantiated from it). This is because, in a complete partitioning, there are no "stray" objects: Every object that *could* be instantiated from the superclass has a more precise home in one of the subclasses. For example, in Fig. 4.10, **Vehicle** would become an abstract class since every actual vehicle object we create will be an instance of either **ExternallyPropelledVehicle** or **InternallyPropelledVehicle**.

At the lower level of the inheritance hierarchy, I've marked the subclass partitioning of **ExternallyPropelledVehicle** (under the discriminator **vehicleType**) as disjoint and incomplete. The disjointness is obvious; the partitioning is certainly incomplete because the subclass **OstrichCart** (among many others) is missing. So, I bet that **ExternallyPropelledVehicle** won't become an abstract class—we'll probably need instantiations such as,

> **var** myOstrichCart := ExternallyPropelledVehicle.New

I've marked the subclass partitioning of **InternallyPropelledVehicle** (under the discriminator **vehicleMedium**) as overlapping and incomplete. It is overlapping in that an amphibious vehicle can navigate both land and water. Indeed, when I pushed my Rolls Canardly into the river as an insurance scam, it floated away like a true canard and was returned to me two days later. (Claim denied!) These overlapping subclasses will probably have a common subclass.

The partitioning of **InternallyPropelledVehicle** is incomplete because air and space vehicles (among others) are missing. **InternallyPropelledVehicle** will presumably be designed as a concrete class to allow air and space objects to be instantiated.

## 4.2 The Association Construct

An association in UML represents a varying population of relationship links between instances of classes. What this mouthful means is best revealed by example: Let's say that we have two classes, **LibraryPatron** and **LibraryBook**. An association between them might be **Borrowing**, a set of relationship links stating which patron is currently borrowing which book. Today, the **Borrowing** association may contain these seven links:

| | | |
|---|---|---|
| Fred | is borrowing | *Igloo Construction for Beginners* |
| Sally | is borrowing | *The Thrill of Cost Accounting* |
| Mary | is borrowing | *Quantum Mechanics for Surrealists* |
| Stan | is borrowing | *Three Generations of Wellingtons in the Field* |
| Stan | is borrowing | *Woolly Thinking* |

| | | |
|---|---|---|
| Genghis | is borrowing | *Across the Andes by Frog* |
| Brunhilde | is borrowing | *Downsizing in Action: Snow White and the Three Dwarfs* |

Tomorrow, **Borrowing** may contain these eight links:

| | | |
|---|---|---|
| Fred | is borrowing | *Cold Comfort: The Road Back from Hypothermia* |
| Mary | is borrowing | *Quantum Mechanics for Surrealists* |
| Mary | is borrowing | *Four-Dimensional Relativistic Tensor Calculus for Dummies* |
| Stan | is borrowing | *Bring Me My Anorak of Desire* |
| Genghis | is borrowing | *Biggles Flies Down* |
| Genghis | is borrowing | *Biggles Pulls It Off* |
| Wally | is borrowing | *Biggles Holds His Own* |
| Brunhilde | is borrowing | *Confessions of a Teenage Software Architect* |

Next month—the library is closed for remodeling—there may be no instances of **Borrowing**.

As this example shows, each link in a (binary) association hitches together one instance of the first class with one instance of the second class, reflecting a particular business relationship between those instances. The business relationship in this example is book borrowing.

Notice that **Borrowing** represents a bunch of links, the actual number of which changes over time: first seven, then eight, then zero. In this respect, an association is really like a class whose links are its instances.

### 4.2.1 The basic UML notation for associations

Figure 4.11 contains three associations, each shown as a line between two classes.[5] The name of the association appears on that line. For instance, since companies employ persons, there is an association named **Employment** between the two classes **Company** and **Person**.

---

[5] In certain cases, the same class appears at both ends of the association.

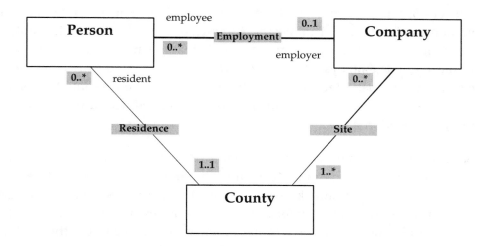

*Fig. 4.11: Three associations between pairs of classes.*

The role of each class in the association may appear beside it at the end of the line. In Fig. 4.11, **Person** has the role of **employee** in the **Employment** association, while **Company** has the role of **employer** in the **Employment** association. The multiplicity of the association also appears at the ends of each line.[6] For example, a given person is an employee at 0 or 1 companies; a given company is an employer of 0 to many persons—that is, any number of persons.

Modeling associations is the backbone of a powerful analysis technique called information modeling, and I shan't try to do justice to it here. However, I will highlight a few points, in the interest of clarity:

1.  You may use association diagrams to capture information from several different modeling perspectives.[7] For example, from an essential perspective, you may simply show class names. From a specification perspective, you may add the operations and attributes that support the associations. From an implementation perspective, you will need to consider how your object-oriented code will support efficient navigation across associations. (See Section 4.2.4 for more on navigation.)

2.  As association, or *relationship*, is usually named with a verb form in traditional information modeling (if such a thing exists—since there are 94

---

[6] Some people use the term *cardinality* for *multiplicity*.

[7] I discussed modeling perspectives in Chapter 2.

dialects of IM, each guarded by a ferocious tribe). For example, many information modelers would name the **Employment** association as **is employed at** (reading from **Person** to **Company**) and reading from the other direction, would name it **employs**. Modelers in the object-oriented world, however, prefer to name an association with a singular noun. The reason: An association is effectively a class, which is most naturally named with a noun. (We return to this in Section 4.2.2.)

3. Some of the multiplicity shown in Fig. 4.11 may be debatable. For example, how can a person be employed at *no* companies? Why are we interested in such a person? Without knowing the goal of the project that produced this model fragment, I can't say for sure. If we're interested in a business domain that includes only employed people, then we should change the multiplicity to **1..1**. If not—that is, if we have a mix of employed and unemployed people in our domain of interest—then we should leave the multiplicity as it is. Similarly, how can a company have no persons employed? It probably can't, but the issue is whether our software should *enforce* a lower limit on personnel count.

4. The association on the left in Fig. 4.11 shows that we're interested in which person has a residence in which county. We can guess that the multiplicity refers to one's primary residence, because a person seems to have residence in exactly one county. But guessing isn't good enough, especially if the multiplicity could be incorrect. Analysts must carefully define business terms such as *residence*. If they fail to, then we as designers have a moral imperative to scream, yell, and rend our shirts in protest.

5. The association on the right shows that we're interested in which company has a site in which county. The multiplicity of the **Site** association implies that we're interested in *all* of the counties in which a company has a site, not just the primary site or headquarters. Perhaps we need this association for tax purposes—but that isn't good enough: A righteous and upstanding analyst must carefully define and document the meaning and purpose of this association.

And now some points specifically about UML notation for associations:

1. UML doesn't insist on a name for an association. However, you should try to name *all* your associations (unless they are the composition and aggregation associations that I cover in the next section). It's good discipline, and you'll feel better afterwards (endorphins, I expect).

2. UML doesn't require role names either. Legally, you may have one UML association with no role names, another with one, and another with two. That's fine by me. Try to find meaningful role names where possible, but don't strain user-credulity to come up with artificial ones, especially when the class at the end of the line itself indicates the role.[8]

3. UML modeling tools often abbreviate multiplicity like this: **0..\*** (any number) becomes simply an asterisk (**\***). Similarly, **1..1** (exactly one) is shown as **1**.

### 4.2.2 Associations depicted as classes

Figure 4.12 shows an ownership association between persons and dogs, reflecting the fact that a person may own any number of dogs and a dog must be owned by exactly one person (no stray dogs and no joint custody, in this model). As usual, I've named the association; it's **DogOwnership**.

*Fig. 4.12: A basic association between two classes.*

Figure 4.13 shows an association that's semantically identical to the one in Fig. 4.12. However, the name of the association (**DogOwnership**) has moved up to become the name of a class, which is attached to the association line by a dotted line.

---

[8] Some skilled, experienced modelers take an opposite point of view and model associations using *only* role names and without an association name. Unfortunately, in less skilled hands, this practice often leads to vague or ambiguous associations.

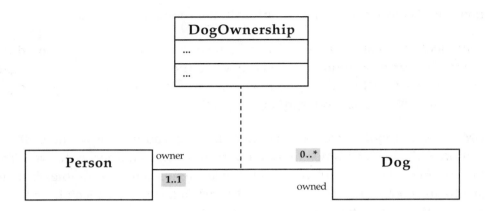

*Fig. 4.13:* **DogOwnership** *promoted to a class.*

Promoting the association to a class allows us to attach attributes and operations to it, those that properly belong to dog ownership rather than to a dog or person.[9] For example, we could have **/ acquisitionDate: Date** and **/ terminationDate: Date** as attributes. We could also have **cedeOwnership (terminationDate: Date)** as an operation. We could even model another association (such as **Licensing** between **DogOwnership** and **County**), reflecting our interest in knowing which county licensed which instance of dog ownership.

### 4.2.3 Higher-order associations

So far, we've looked at the binary association of two classes, which UML depicts as a line. But how does one show a ternary or three-way association? As Fig. 4.14 reveals, the answer is a diamond, which beautifies the junction of the three association lines. (UML borrowed the diamond symbol from the Chen dialect of information modeling.)

Figure 4.14's association is part of a purchasing model for buying items from vendors. In this business, the unit price depends on three factors: the item type (the product); the company that's selling it (the vendor); and the quantity of items you purchase (the price-break level). We therefore need a ternary association

---

[9] Remember that, formally speaking, the association has been a class all along (whose instances are links). So, like many in my own career, this promotion is only symbolic.

among **ItemType**, **Company**, and **PurchasedQuantity** in order to have a suitable home for the **unitPrice** attribute, which is determined by the instances of those three classes.

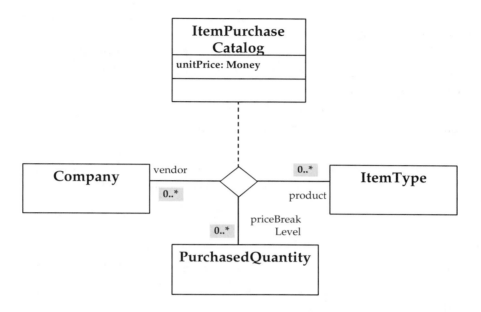

*Fig. 4.14: A ternary association.*

Let me make a couple of pragmatic points about ternary relationships:

1.  You can bet that the multiplicity on all three classes will be **0..\***. (If not, then the ternary association can usually be resolved into two or three binary associations.)

2.  You will probably need to promote the association to a class of its own—here, it's **ItemPurchaseCatalog**—because the association will have at least one attribute or operation. (If not, then the ternary association may again be resolved into two or three binary associations.)

Useful ternary associations are much rarer than binary ones. Quaternary (or four-way) associations are rarer still. If one crops up on your next project, you can show it in UML just like a ternary one (but with four solid lines touching the diamond).

### 4.2.4 Navigability of associations

Navigability is a UML concept that I reserve entirely for O.O. implementation models. In other words, I tend to add the navigability symbols to my diagrams toward the end of design (if I add them at all). That said, let's look at what navigability is and how UML shows it.

In Fig. 4.15, the first navigability (the arrow from **Person** to **Dog**) indicates that the implementation will support a quick and easy traversal from a **Person** object to the owned **Dog** objects. That is, if you know a person, you'll be able to find his dogs quickly. However, there's no guarantee of the reverse. That is, if you know a dog, it may take a long time to produce the owner.

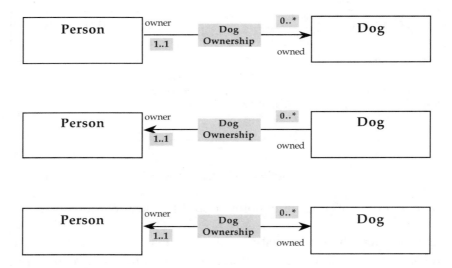

*Fig. 4.15: Three possible navigabilities for an association between two classes.*

You can build this navigability into each **Person** object by referring to a set of dogs with the following variable declaration within the class **Person**:[10]

    ownedDogs: Set <Dog>;

The second navigability in Fig. 4.15 (the arrow from **Dog** to **Person**) indicates that the implementation will support a quick and easy traversal from a **Dog** object to

---

[10] I return to the implementation options at the end of Section 4.3.1 and discuss them further in Exercise 4 of Chapter 14.

the **Person** object that owns it. That is, you'll be able to find the owner of any given dog quickly. Again, there's no guarantee of the reverse. That is, if you know an owner, this mechanism will offer no easy way to find his dogs.

You can build this navigability into **Dog** with the following simple declaration, taking advantage of the multiplicity of 1 from **Dog** to **Person**:

    owner: Person;

The third navigability in Fig. 4.5 simply combines the first two. With it, you'll be able to traverse the association quickly in both directions. **Person** and **Dog** will have references to each other in their variable declarations.

## 4.3 Whole/Part Associations

UML has special notation for two whole/part associations: *composition* and *aggregation*. Over the past few years, debate on the meanings of this infamous pair has left many people unable to see the forest for the trees. The problem is that there are actually seven or eight varieties of whole/part construct in the real world, and an attempt to shoehorn them all into composition and aggregation can result in confusion and aggravation.[11]

Nevertheless, with a little cerebral toe-wiggling, you can manage the shoehorning in most situations. But, if your project team finds it all too painful, then my recommendation is this: Resolve to use only one construct (say, aggregation). As we'll see in this section, you can use standard UML multiplicity notation to express any further whole/part subtleties.

### 4.3.1 Composition

Composition is a common structure in software systems, object-oriented or not, because many composite objects appear in everyday life. For example, a dog is a composite of a head, a body, a tail, and four legs (one at each corner). Other compositions are more conceptual or software-specific: For example, an e-mail missive is a composite containing a header and a few text paragraphs. In turn, the header is a composite of the sender's name, the receiver's name, the message title, and some other e-stuff.

---

[11] You can find an illuminating summary of the various whole/part constructs in [Martin and Odell, 1995]. I also mention some of them in the exercises at the end of this chapter.

Now, before we continue, some terminology. This whole/part association is called *composition;* the "whole" is called the *composite [object];* the "part" is called the *component [object].*[12]

The three most important characteristics of composition are as follows:

1. The composite object does not exist without its components. For example, remove the bristles, the handle, and the little rubber thingee from a toothbrush and you no longer have a toothbrush. Indeed, just remove the bristles from a toothbrush and it hardly qualifies as a toothbrush. In this sense, a composite object's lifetime cannot transcend its components' lifetimes.

2. At any time, each given component object may be part of only one composite.

3. Composition is typically heteromeric. The components are likely to be of mixed types: some wheels, some axles, some bits of wood . . . and there's your wagon.

Now it's time to look at the UML for a modeling composition. The composite object in Fig. 4.16 represents a simplified glider. It has four components: a fuselage, a tail, a left wing, and a right wing.

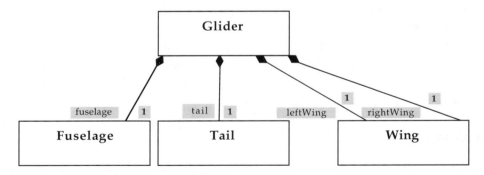

*Fig. 4.16: A composite object and its components.*

Let's dissect this figure to see how the UML works:

1. An association between the composite object and each of the component objects appears on the diagram as an association line with a little black diamond adorning the end beside the composite object.[13]

---

[12] Here, I use the term *component* in its traditional sense of "part"; I don't ascribe to it the meaning of prefabricated software construct that is the "component" of Chapter 15.

[13] Unlike the class-inheritance diagrams we saw in Section 4.1, composition diagrams usually show hierarchies in the "separate target" or "non-tree" style.

2.  The class of the composite, **Glider**, appears at one end of the association line. The class of each component—**Fuselage**, **Tail**, **Wing**, and **Wing**—appears at the other end.  Note that a component like **Wing** only needs to appear once, even though it's the class of two components.

3.  The role of the component object in the composition appears at the component end of the association line.  The roles **leftWing** and **rightWing** are good examples:  Each is an object of class **Wing**, but each plays a different role in a glider.  (OK, I know that left wings and right wings aren't exactly interchangeable, but I said that this was a simplified glider.)[14]

4.  You may (and should) show multiplicity at the component end of each association line.  If the multiplicity at the composite end isn't shown, then it's assumed to be exactly 1.  In Fig. 4.16, every multiplicity is exactly 1.

5.  The association line has no name, which is the norm for both composition and aggregation.  The reason:  Rarely does a name for a composition association add any significance beyond the whole/part meaning already indicated by the symbology.  Trivial verbs, such as **has**, **comprises**, **consists of**, and so on, add nothing to the model.

Since composition is a form of association, you may implement navigability in the same ways that we discussed in Section 4.2.4.  For example, the class **Glider** may have the following variables declared within it:

>   fuselage: Fuselage;

>   tail: Tail;

>   leftWing: Wing;

>   rightWing: Wing;

When an object—let's refer to it as **glider1**—of class **Glider** is instantiated (and initialized), the variable **tail** will point to an object representing the tail of **glider1**. Similarly, the variables **fuselage**, **leftWing**, and **rightWing** hold the handles of the other components of a **Glider** object.

---

[14] Gray boxes, such as those around **leftWing** and **rightWing** in Fig. 4.16, are for graphic clarity only and have no semantic significance.

This implementation supports navigability from a composite object to its component objects. To show this in Fig. 4.16, you may add navigability arrows from **Glider** to **Fuselage**, **Tail**, **Wing**, and **Wing**, respectively. You may also let the component objects hold the handle of the composite in order to implement navigability from component to composite. Your choice of navigability design will depend on the following factors:

- how often and how fast the composition needs to be traversed in each direction
- whether the components need to be reused in another situation, without the composite (if so, they should not contain any references to the composite)

Composition often goes hand-in-hand with message propagation. For example, to move a rectangle symbol on a screen, you could tell the rectangle object to move itself. In turn, the rectangle could send a message to each of its component lines, to tell them to move. Similarly, to find the weight of a chair, you could send a message to each component of the chair, requesting the component's weight.

Where you need message propagation like this, you usually support it by designing navigability into your composition associations. In the latter example above, you would make sure that for any **Chair** object, you could quickly get the handle of the **ChairSeat** object, the **ChairBack** object, and each of the **ChairLeg** objects that compose it. In Chapter 5 (on the object-interaction diagram), I show the UML notation for messages to the components of a composite object.

### 4.3.2 Aggregation

Like composition, aggregation is a familiar construct whereby software systems represent structures from real life. For example, a city is an aggregate of houses, a forest is an aggregate of trees, and a flock is an aggregate of sheep.[15] In other words, aggregation is a group/member association.

---

[15] In fact, the flock of sheep was the original aggregate, as revealed by the etymology of the word (where *grex* means *flock*).

Again, some terminology. The association is called *aggregation;* the "whole" is called the *aggregate [object]*; the "part" is called the *constituent [object]*.[16] The three most important characteristics of aggregation are as follows:

1. The aggregate object may potentially exist without its constituent objects. For example, even if you fire all the employees from a department, you still have a department. However, this property isn't always useful. I can imagine an empty, razed city, but what about an empty flock? Inquiring Zen masters want to know: Can you watch a null flock?[17]

2. At any time, each object may be a constituent of more than one aggregate. Again, a real-world aggregate may or may not avail itself of this property. A person may belong to more than one frequent-eating club, but can a sheep belong to more than one flock? The aforementioned Zen masters are again mute on this moot point.

3. Aggregation tends to be homeomeric. This means that the constituents of a typical aggregate will belong to the same class. For example, the constituents of a paragraph are all sentences and the constituents of a forest are all trees.

Let's look now at the UML notation for aggregation. Figure 4.17 shows a management report that is composed of paragraphs of text (for simplicity). You can make the following observations about Fig. 4.17:

1. An association between the aggregate and its constituents is denoted by a little open diamond on the aggregate end of the association line.

2. The classes of the aggregate (**MgmtReport**) and of the constituent (**Paragraph**) appear at the respective ends of the association line. The role of the constituent object **textPart** also appears at the constituent end of the association line.

---

[16] Although I tend to use the simple term *member* rather than the grandiose *constituent,* which is the standard UML term, I avoid using "member" here because it's gotten me into trouble in C++ shops where it's short for *member function.* If you want to be really baffling, try *aggregand.* But, if you want a simple life, stick to *whole* and *part* for both composition and aggregation.

[17] Hmmm. Perhaps that's why it took shepherds so long to invent the concept of zero.

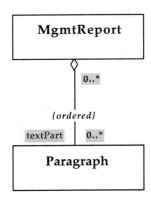

*Fig. 4.17: An aggregate object and its constituents.*

3. With aggregation, you should show multiplicity at both ends of the association line because you cannot *assume* the multiplicity anywhere, as you can with a composition association. The multiplicity at the aggregate end of Fig. 4.17 is **0..\***; this means that a paragraph may belong to many management reports at the same time or it may belong to one or none. The multiplicity at the constituent end is also **0..\***; this means that a management report may comprise many paragraphs or one or none (an empty report).

4. The **{ordered}** property on the association reveals that the paragraphs are in a defined sequence. Although you may also find this property on multiple components in a composition or on other associations, I've encountered it most often on constituents of an aggregate. Occasionally, you may add other properties to an association with **0..\*** or **1..\*** multiplicity. For example, **{Bag}** would allow (in this example) the same paragraph to appear several times in the same report. The default is **{Set}**, which forbids duplicates. To emphasize implementation details in your design, you may even specify **{List}** or **{Tree}**, though you should avoid burdening your associations with properties that are irrelevant to your readers.

As with composition, you may implement aggregation through the use of variables. For navigability from the aggregate to the constituents, a variable in the aggregate will point to the constituents. For example, the class **MgmtReport** may contain the following declaration:

textPart: Set <Paragraph>;

Other examples of aggregation appear in Figs. 4.18 and 4.19.

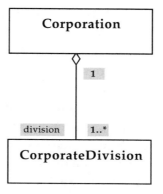

*Fig. 4.18: A corporation is an aggregation of several divisions.*

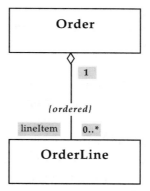

*Fig. 4.19: An order is an aggregation of several order lines.*

Each of these has a different multiplicity from that in Fig. 4.17. A corporate division can belong to only one corporation, and a corporation must contain at least one corporate division (according to *this* model, anyway). An order line can belong to only one order, but an order may contain no lines (perhaps as it's being built over several minutes or hours). Notice that in both of these examples, we're using multiplicity to revoke a constituent's theoretical ability to belong simultaneously to more than one aggregate.

## 4.4 Summary

UML depicts inheritance with a generalization arrow that extends from the inheriting subclass to the "inherited from" superclass. This notation handles both single inheritance and multiple inheritance (in which a class inherits from several superclasses). However, you may choose to represent single inheritance as an indented list of classes. For large hierarchies, such a textual representation may be more concise, though less graphically immediate, than UML.

UML indicates subclass partitioning properties with one term from each of these pairs: disjoint/overlapping and complete/incomplete. The criterion for partitioning may be indicated by a partitioning discriminator.

UML models a binary association with a line drawn between the two associated classes. The name of the association (typically a noun) appears on the line. Each multiplicity of the association appears at its respective end of the line in the form **min..max**, where **min** and **max** are usually shown by numerals for zero or one, or by an asterisk for many. The role of each class in the association may also appear at the end of the association line, if it adds meaning to the model. You may further characterize an association with the implementation detail of navigability. This appears as an arrowhead at one or both ends of the association line, indicating the direction in which navigation will be facilitated.

When you want to accentuate the fact that an association is a class in its own right—perhaps to show its attributes or operations—you may convert the association into an ordinary class. You then attach the class's symbol via a dotted line to the line between the two associated classes. For ternary and higher-order associations, you join lines from the associated classes at a diamond. Such an association is normally treated as a class in its own right, and its class symbol is attached via a dotted line to the diamond.

Each of the whole/part constructs of composition and aggregation is a special case of an association. For composition, UML adorns the association line with a small black diamond at the composite end. For aggregation, UML adorns the association line with a small open diamond at the aggregate end. For both composition and aggregation, you typically show cardinalities and roles and, if appropriate, navigability. However, the name of the association is usually omitted unless it adds further information beyond the whole/part nature of the relationship.

## 4.5 Exercises

1. Could the designers of UML have unified the subclass-partitioning concepts of disjoint/overlapping and complete/incomplete into a single set of possible combinations? If so, how? (Hint: Under each of the four partitioning combinations, think about the number of subgroups to which a member of a group could simultaneously belong. Figures 4.6 and 4.7 may help you to visualize the answer.)

2. In Fig. 4.10, the discriminator under which I partitioned **ExternallyPropelledVehicle** was **vehicleType**. However, the discriminator under which I partitioned **InternallyPropelledVehicle** was **vehicleMedium**. Does this lack of symmetry disturb you?

3. In Fig. 4.10, I marked the subclass partitioning of **InternallyPropelledVehicle** as overlapping. What implication does this have for the design and programming of the discriminator **vehicleMedium**? What implication does an incomplete partitioning have for the value(s) of a discriminator?

4. Section 4.1.4 contained the following words:

   The partitioning of **InternallyPropelledVehicle** is incomplete because air and space vehicles (among others) are missing. **InternallyPropelledVehicle** will presumably be designed as a concrete class to allow air and space objects to be instantiated.

   In what ways is this naïve?

5. Draw a class-inheritance diagram that captures the two categories of a company's customers: external customers, which are other companies, and internal customers, which are all the divisions within the company.

6. When is it appropriate to model with composition? For example, why not use the UML composition notation to show that a dog is composed of height, weight, color, and date of birth?

7. One so-called characteristic of composition—which I read about all the time but don't find convincing—is the *cascading delete:* When a composite object is deleted, the component objects get deleted, too. Can you think of a situation in which you'd want to delete a composite object but retain the component objects?

8. A sliced loaf is made of bread slices. Is the association between the loaf and its slices composition or aggregation?

9. Draw an object-aggregation diagram for a book chapter with the following structure: A chapter comprises several sections, each of which comprises several paragraphs and figures. A paragraph comprises several sentences, each of which comprises several words. (You may ignore punctuation and you needn't pursue the structure of a figure any further.)

## 4.6 Answers

1.  To postulate a unified set of subclass partitionings, consider the following: Let **G** be a group of things and **t** be an arbitrary thing. Assume that **G** is partitioned into subgroups. Then,

    A complete partitioning means that **t** must belong to at least one subgroup of **G**.

    An incomplete partitioning means that **t** must belong to at least zero subgroups of **G**.

    A disjoint partitioning means that **t** can belong to at most one subgroup of **G**.

    An overlapping partitioning means that **t** can belong to many subgroups of **G**.

    These four UML partitioning combinations can be summarized with the following:

    | | |
    |---|---|
    | Incomplete, disjoint: | **t** can belong to **0..1** subgroups of **G**. |
    | Complete, disjoint: | **t** can belong to **1..1** subgroups of **G**. |
    | Incomplete, overlapping: | **t** can belong to **0..\*** subgroups of **G**.[18] |
    | Complete, overlapping: | **t** can belong to **1..\*** subgroups of **G**. |

    These verbose combinations of properties could be written as **0..1**, **1..1**, **0..\***, and **1..\***, respectively. However, some people don't find the terse notation intuitive.

2.  The lack of symmetry bothers me. Why didn't the analysts partition externally propelled vehicles by their medium? Conversely, why *did* the analysts partition internally propelled vehicles by their medium?

    Perhaps land-based externally propelled vehicles have something in common that can be factored into the same class, whereas the same is not true for land-based internally propelled vehicles. That sort of nuance should be checked with the subject-matter experts.

---

[18] As usual, an asterisk (\*) stands for "many."

3.  As we saw in Answer 1, above, an overlapping partitioning implies that the partitioning discriminator can have multiple values (for example, both **land** and **water** at the same time). An incomplete partitioning implies that the discriminator may have a null value. For this reason, some UML purists insist that discriminators are only merited by complete, disjoint partitionings. I have no such qualms; I show a partitioning discriminator whenever I think it will explain the reason for the partitioning more clearly.

4.  The statement from Section 4.1.4 implies that air and space vehicle objects would be instantiated by a simple appeal to **InternallyPropelledVehicle.New.** However, air and space vehicles are highly specialized, with lots and lots of attributes and operations. Such objects will require their own subclasses or even hierarchies of subclasses. Air and space vehicle objects would then be instantiated from their respective subclasses.

    A further level of naïveté is that any class hierarchy for a realistic assortment of vehicles is incredibly difficult to derive—even more so than for the notorious subclass hierarchy of **Customer**.

5.  Figure 4.20 shows one class-inheritance diagram for the internal and external customers. The most interesting portion of this structure is the class **InternalCustomer**, which inherits multiply from **CorporateDivision** and **Customer**.

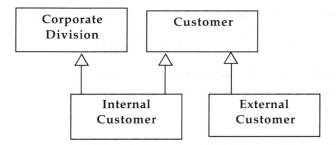

*Fig. 4.20: An inheritance hierarchy for* **Customer**.

You could refine this class-inheritance diagram by introducing another class, **ExternalCompany**, and then having **ExternalCustomer** inherit multiply from **Customer** and **ExternalCompany**. This approach would separate customer properties completely from corporate-entity properties and would also improve the symmetry of the class structure.

6.  You should use UML to model only significant compositions, such as those that are based on the physical composition of real things like gliders or chairs. Other significant compositions are characterized by several layers, where component objects themselves are composites of yet other components. An e-mail missive is a small example of this structure, as mentioned in Section 4.3.1.

    Conversely, although it's possible, you wouldn't use composition to show that a dog is composed of height, weight, color, and date of birth. These are attributes of a dog, not components. If you use composition to depict attributes, your diagrams won't have much lasting value and your models will seem contrived.

7.  First we must ask, What does it mean to delete a chair? Even if you dismantle a chair, you may still want to reuse (and so *not* "delete") its legs, seat, or back for use in another chair. In general, you may still be interested in the component objects of a deleted object, perhaps to compose something else from them.

    I encountered a particularly telling problem with the cascading delete when I was working on an application that had a whole/part construct very similar to that of a chair. In fact, for this example, I'll pretend that it actually *was* a chair. In one piece of the application, a chair was "deleted," together with its parts (when the chair was sold). In another piece, however, a chair was "deleted"—*but its parts were retained* (when it was disassembled).

    So, if we followed the cascading delete principle in this application, we'd be on the tusks of a dilemma: Should a chair be modeled as a composite or as an aggregate object? (As we saw in Section 4.3.1, it should be a composite object.)

    Some authors of UML books assert that, "An object is a composite object if and only if, when it's deleted, its component objects are also deleted. Otherwise, it is an aggregate object." However, I don't find this "principle" useful—or even valid!

8.  At first, the association seems like composition, because each slice belongs to at most one loaf at a time. But wait! The association seems like aggregation in that all the slices are alike and they can be arbitrarily removed from the loaf. Arghh! After some thought (and a few sandwiches), I decided to call it composition. My reason: When I eat the last slice, I no longer have a loaf. (By the way, Jim Odell has coined a special term for this sliced-loaf phenomenon: *object-portion composition*.)

9. Figure 4.21 shows one possible aggregate structure for the book chapter.

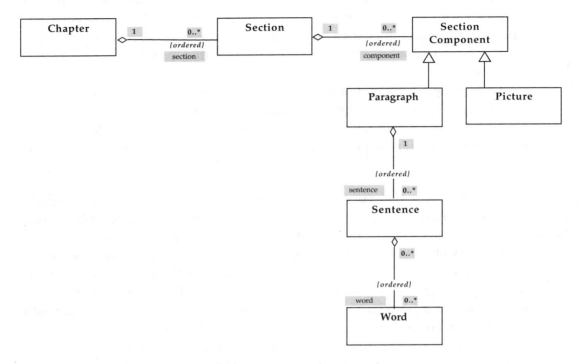

*Fig. 4.21: The structure of a book chapter.*

The object-aggregation diagram shows that a chapter is an ordered collection of sections. The structures for a paragraph and a sentence are similar to the structure of a chapter.

The structure of a section is a little tricky, because a section comprises a mixture of paragraphs and diagrams. A good way to design this is to create a class called **SectionComponent**, from which both **Paragraph** and **Picture** inherit. This allows each component of a section to be either a paragraph or a picture.

Note that Fig. 4.21 contains the assumption that a section appears in exactly one chapter. If a section could appear in multiple chapters, then there would be a **1..\*** multiplicity at the composite end of the association. Review the other parts of Fig. 4.21 to identify similar assumptions.

Also note that I allow a chapter with zero sections. While this is arguably correct—you might want to save a null version at the start of your author-ship—you may consider changing this multiplicity to **1..\***.

# 5

# Object-Interaction Diagrams

So far in this discussion of UML, we've looked mainly at the static structure of the object-oriented source code that lies lexically in leisure upon your listing. Now we turn to the execution, run-time, or dynamic structure of an object-oriented system. (Obviously, the static and dynamic structures are highly related, since it's the compiled lexical code that actually runs.)

Central to the execution of an object-oriented program is the sending of messages. As we saw in Chapter 1, a message is a request by a sender object to execute an operation of a target object. The *object-interaction diagram* of UML depicts the messages and message arguments that objects send to one another. This diagram performs a job similar to the structure chart in prehistoric structured techniques: It shows the run-time communication structure of the system.

The object-interaction diagram (often referred to as the *interaction diagram)* is ideal for modeling the procedure of a single *use case,* which is defined in [Jacobson, 1992] as a "behaviorally related sequence of transactions in a dialogue with a system." In other words, an object-interaction diagram often depicts the dialogue between a user and a system as they perform a useful unit of work, such as entering a purchase order or scheduling a machine run.

The object-interaction diagram comes in two styles: the *collaboration diagram* (covered in Section 5.1) and the *sequence diagram* (covered in Section 5.2). The two styles of diagram capture the same content—indeed, one style of diagram can be automatically converted into the other.

The collaboration diagram tends to be more free-form and flexible in how it's drawn. It also gives similar weight to static object relationships and dynamic object messaging. The sequence diagram, on the other hand, is more tightly organized and emphasizes temporal sequence.

Messages also come in two basic flavors: *synchronous* (during which a sender object must wait for the target to finish execution) and *asynchronous* (during which a sender object needn't wait). Sections 5.1 and 5.2 deal with the UML notation for synchronous messages, the usual form of messages in most object-oriented systems. Section 5.3 looks at the UML for asynchronous messages, which are important in many real-time systems.

## 5.1 The Collaboration Diagram

In the UML collaboration diagram, objects that interact by messages appear as standard UML "boxes," each bearing an object's name. See Fig. 5.1, for example.

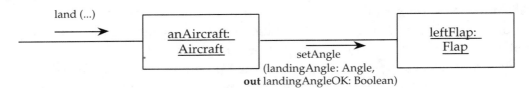

*Fig. 5.1: A collaboration diagram for the message* **leftFlap.setAngle**.

Notice that each object's name has the form <u>objName: ClassName</u>, where the underlining emphasizes that we're dealing with instances, not classes. On a collaboration diagram, each object is identified with the name that other objects use to send it a message, since objects don't really have names of their own. In other words, a target object assumes the name of the variable in the sending object that holds the handle of the target.

### 5.1.1 Depicting a message

On a collaboration diagram, a synchronous message is depicted with a small arrow that points from a sender object (**sendobj**) to a target object (**targobj**).[1] The message arrow is labeled with the name of a target-object operation, followed by the operation's actual input and output arguments.

The message arrow sits alongside a line from the sender to the target that represents a communication path between the two objects. A communication path usually exists because there's a link between **sendobj** and **targobj**.[2] However, there are other ways that such a path could come about. For example, **sendobj** could have received the handle of **targobj** in a previous message from a third object.

The simplified avionics example in Fig. 5.1 shows the operation **land** (in a sender object of class **Aircraft**) sending a message to a target object **leftFlap** (of class **Flap**). The message requests that **leftFlap** set itself to an appropriate landing angle. The return argument **landingAngleOK** is set to **true** whenever the value of **landingAngle** is valid. The message that you'd read in the code of the sender's operation **land** would be

>     leftFlap.setAngle (landingAngle, **out** landingAngleOK)

Remember that on a collaboration diagram—or on a sequence diagram, which we'll discuss in Section 5.2—an argument's name is the *actual* argument name. That is, it's the argument name used in the sender's argument list, as opposed to the formal name used by the target in its operation header.[3] An example of an actual argument name is **landingAngle**, in Fig. 5.1. (The formal argument name inside the operation **setAngle** is probably named **requiredFlapAngle**.[4])

---

[1] The sender and target objects are usually, but not necessarily, different objects. Also, they usually, belong to different classes.

[2] As you may recall from Chapter 4, a link is an instance of an association. In other words, an association exists between classes, while a link exists between objects.

[3] A reminder: The arguments following the keyword **out** in the argument list (if any) are output arguments (arguments from the target back to the sender). The other arguments are input arguments (arguments from the sender to the target).

[4] Most people omit class names alongside message arguments on an object-interaction diagram. In other words, I normally write (**landingAngle, out landingAngleOK**), rather than (**landingAngle: Angle, out landingAngleOK: Boolean**). However, for clarity, I've included class names in the examples of the first part of this chapter.

Figure 5.2 is semantically identical to Fig. 5.1. However, the box on the left of this collaboration diagram represents a single operation (**land**), rather than a whole object (**aircraft**). I find this approach useful for two reasons: The first is that it provides a tidy start to the diagram at the operation whose execution begins the whole collaboration. The second is that you can pinpoint the fact that particular messages emanate just from a particular operation, rather than vaguely from the object as a whole.

To show which class the operation **land** belongs to, I qualify the name **land** using the syntax **objectName: ClassName.operationName**, that is, **anAircraft: Aircraft.land**.[5]

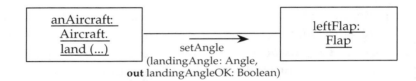

*Fig. 5.2:*  *A collaboration diagram for the same message (**setAngle**), with the invoking operation (**land**) shown explicitly.*

Figure 5.3 shows an example from a simplified banking application. The idea is to transfer some funds from one account (**fromAccount**) to another (**toAccount**).[6] Notice the little numbers before the messages, which signify the sequence in which the messages get sent.

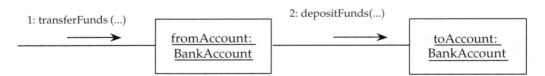

*Fig. 5.3:*  *A collaboration diagram for the message **fromAccount.transferFunds**.*

---

[5] To distinguish name qualification syntax from message syntax, I prefer to use the C++ convention of the double-colon, thus: **anAircraft: Aircraft::land**. However, UML favors the dot and reserves the double-colon for package components, which I discuss in Chapter 7.

[6] You could argue that instead of being on **BankAccount**, **transferFunds** should be an operation on the class used in Fig. 5.3, a more application-specific class, such as **Transfer**. Later in this chapter, I'll introduce **Transfer**.

I have to confess that I'm not a big fan of sequence numbers. My reasons? The first is that they don't help me much: Either the sequence is very straightforward (and then who needs the numbers?) or it isn't (and then how do you assign a meaningful temporal sequence to a complicated algorithm?). Instead of adding sequence numbers to a complicated algorithm, you can specify the message sequence by writing pseudocode for a method—the implementation of an operation—a topic I cover in Section 5.2, The Sequence Diagrams.

The second reason I'm not a fan of sequence numbers is that they're a pain to keep up-to-date, although some tools can help with this. Even with a tool, though, you'll *have to* add sequence numbers to your messages if you want your tool to automatically convert collaboration diagrams into sequence diagrams.[7]

Figure 5.4 shows another simplified banking example, this time a withdrawal from an account at the First Draconian Bank of Greed, where customers may make only one withdrawal per day from any of their respective accounts. Therefore, as Fig. 5.4 indicates, the object **custAccount** (of class **Account**) updates the **cust** object (representing the customer who owns the account) with the date and time of the withdrawal. This is done by invoking the set operation **setLastWithdrawalTime (lwTime: DateTime)**.[8]

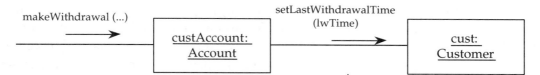

*Fig. 5.4:  A collaboration diagram for the message*
**cust.setLastWithdrawalTime**.

Figure 5.5 shows another message between the same pair of objects. This is actually the prior message from **custAccount** to **cust**, to find the date and time of the customer's most recent withdrawal. **custAccount** obtains this information by invoking the get operation **lastWithdrawalTime: DateTime**.

---

[7] Some tools use hierarchical, nested sequence numbers for that purpose. See [Fowler and Scott, 1997], for example.

[8] This is not the only—or even the best—object-oriented design to fulfill the application's requirement, by the way. For a discussion of alternatives, see Exercise 3 of Chapter 14.

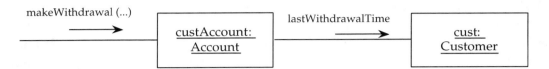

*Fig. 5.5: A collaboration diagram for the message* **cust.lastWithdrawalTime**.

There's something counterintuitive about the message arrow of Fig. 5.5: The information flows from **cust** to **custAccount**, but the message arrow points from **custAccount** to **cust**. In other words, the information for this get operation flows in the direction opposite to the arrow. The reason for this is that a UML message arrow shows who invokes whom, not "who has something interesting to pass to whom." If this seems unnatural, then perhaps you could name this get operation **getLastWithdrawalTime**, in order to provide more clarity.

### 5.1.2 Polymorphism in the collaboration diagram

Polymorphism brings great power to object orientation. And now the bad news. Polymorphism and dynamic binding, which is polymorphism's run-time implementation mechanism, also bring headaches to notation developers. In the structured-design world, we always knew where we were: **call A** always meant **call A**. But if object-oriented polymorphism applies, the sender object may not be aware of the exact class of the target object. So, then, what name should we give to the class of the target?

The answer is this: Make the target's class the lowest class in the inheritance hierarchy that is a superclass of all the classes to which the target object could possibly belong. For example, if the message is **icon.scale** and the target object (pointed to by **icon**) may be of class **Triangle**, **Rectangle**, or **Hexagon**, then the class name on the target object would be **Polygon** (assuming that **Polygon** is the direct superclass of those three classes).

Some shops emphasize the polymorphism of a target object by means of parentheses, as in Fig. 5.6. When the determination of the target object's exact class can be made with certainty at design time (which is equivalent to static binding), these shops show the target class name without parentheses. When the exact class will be determined only at run-time (dynamic binding), they show the target class name in parentheses.

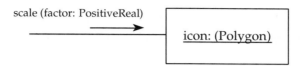

scale (factor: PositiveReal)

icon: (Polygon)

*Fig. 5.6:*   *The method to implement* **scale** *will be from* **Polygon** *or one of its subclasses and will be dynamically bound to the target object,* **icon**.

Another example of polymorphism:  If we had **x.print**, where **x** could point to a target object of class **Spreadsheet**, **Textdoc**, **Customer**, or several others, then we'd probably be obliged to choose as the target class name the highest class of all, which may be the class **Object**.  There probably isn't another class that is a superclass of all those classes.

### 5.1.3 Iterated messages

An *iterated* message is one that's sent repeatedly, typically to each constituent of an aggregate object.  For an example of an iterated message, let's first assume that a number of icons are displayed on a computer's metaphoric desktop (its screen), as modeled in Fig. 5.7.

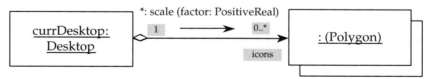

*Fig. 5.7:*   *The message* **scale** *is sent iteratively, that is, in turn to each of several* **icons** *contained in* **currDesktop** *(the sender object).*

Now, suppose that at some point, the desktop needs to enlarge or reduce all its icons by some factor.  To do so, the desktop merely sends the same message— **scale (factor: PositiveReal)**—to each icon in turn.

The iterated message appears in UML as a normal message with three peculiarities:

1.  The message is prefixed by an asterisk (**\***), signifying multiplicity, as usual.

2.  The name of the collection (in Fig. 5.7, **icons**) appears in its usual position, but each individual target object remains unnamed.

3.  The target-object symbol is doubled, again to signify multiplicity.[9]

An iterated message usually requires some kind of message to initialize the iteration within the program. For example, if your icons are in a **List**, you'll need a **first** message to get the head of the list (and then the iteration will repeatedly call for the **next**). Typically, I don't show those traversal messages in my designs, although you certainly may.

Incidentally, the example of Fig. 5.7 is a beautiful set-piece illustration of object orientation at work. An object sends the same message to each object within a group. However, since each member of that group may have a different class (**Hexagon**, **Circle**, **Drawing**, and so on), each may execute the message in its own special way. Through the miracle of polymorphism, the sender object remains blissfully unaware of this complication.

### 5.1.4 Use of self in messages

The term **self** often appears in messages on UML diagrams.[10] **self** is an instance constant (that is, not a variable) that holds an object's own handle. This allows an object sending a message either to

1.  Pass **self** as an argument, thereby telling the target object which object sent the message, or to

2.  Send a message to itself.

In UML, you would show the first usage (passing **self** as an argument) simply by naming one of the message arguments **self**. See Fig. 5.8.

---

[9] However, when I draw such an iterated message on a whiteboard, I don't bother with the doubled symbol. Your tool may or may not insist on showing it.

[10] **self** is not an official UML term; it's a term from Smalltalk. You may prefer the C++ and Java term, **this**, or the Eiffel term, **Current**.

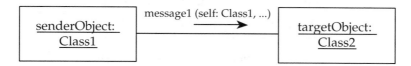

*Fig. 5.8:* **self** *passed as an argument.*

Passing **self** as an argument occurs most often when the target needs to look up the sender's handle in a table that, perhaps, relates the sender to some other object(s). Some beginners to object orientation splatter their diagrams with **self** arguments, thinking that a target object needs the handle of the sender to "somehow get the output arguments back to the right object." Not so! The synchronous message arrow implies automatic return of execution control from the target object to the sender object. In fact, all major object-oriented programming languages take care of return of control to the sender object in this way.[11]

So, use **self** judiciously as an argument. Beware, too, of "yo-yo messaging," wherein sender and target objects continually swap roles and engage each other in a seemingly endless dialogue of messages! The indicator of this on an object-interaction diagram is **self** arguments flying back and forth like shuttlecocks.

In UML, you could show the second usage of **self** (if an object sends a message to itself) by naming the target object **self**, as shown in Fig. 5.9.[12]

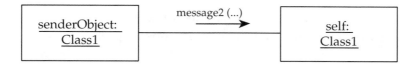

*Fig. 5.9:    A sender object sending a message to itself,*
*where **self** is the target object.*

---

[11] However, in a so-called callback mechanism, the target *does* need the handle of the sender. I cover this in Section 5.3.2.

[12] As you can see from Fig. 5.9, it's quite acceptable to repeat object symbols on a collaboration diagram. Such repetition may help out if lines begin to cross or curve very tightly (as in Fig. 5.10). For the rest of this chapter, by the way, I'm no longer going to include class names alongside arguments in messages. Most tools also omit class names in actual arguments, showing them only in formal arguments.

Figure 5.10 shows an alternative, more evocative, style, whereby the reference line turns back on itself and has the stereotype **«self»**.

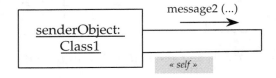

*Fig. 5.10: The reference line turns back to the sender.*

In strictly programming terms, a message from an object to itself might not be necessary. If the sender method and the target method belong to the same object, the sender method *could* directly manipulate the same variables as the target method since it has access to all of the object's variables.

However, that approach has two drawbacks. First, it may duplicate some code in the two methods. Second, it spreads knowledge of the representation of the variables to too many methods. Having an object send a message to itself is therefore useful when a designer wants to use the key idea of implementation hiding to hide the implementation of one operation from another operation in the same class. Some classes are therefore designed with "rings of operations," a topic that we'll return to in Chapter 13.

## 5.2 The Sequence Diagram

The sequence diagram is a type of object-interaction diagram that emphasizes temporal sequence over static-object relationships. I prefer the sequence diagram to the collaboration diagram when there are half-a-dozen or so messages scuttle-butting among objects in a group; with the sequence diagram, I can clearly see "who says what to whom and when." Also, I certainly prefer it whenever procedural or timing issues become tricky, because no other diagram illuminates timing so well.

As the sequence diagram in Fig. 5.11 shows, time increases downward along the vertical axis, and a list of objects that will receive messages extends along the horizontal axis, at the top. (These objects may be listed by their class names, if that's precise enough.) The body of the diagram shows the activated operations, sized to reflect their approximate duration: The symbol for an activated operation is roughly proportional vertically to the length of time during which the operation is active. The arrows between operations depict messages, just as they do in the collaboration diagram.[13] The optional sequence numbers on the messages convey temporal sequence, just as they do on a collaboration diagram.

Now let's look at what's going on in Fig. 5.11, which contains another example of a bank transfer.[14] Let me quickly walk you through the messages' execution sequence.

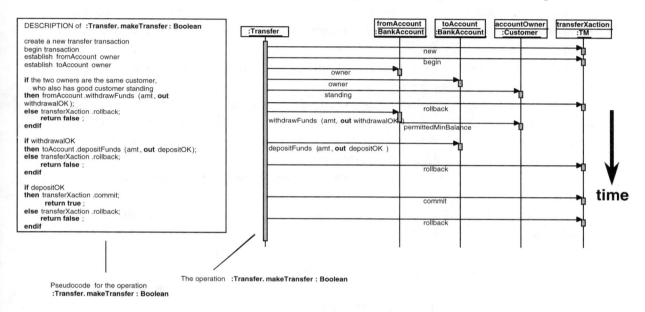

Fig. 5.11: A sequence diagram for transferring funds.

The sequence begins with the unnamed **Transfer** object at the left. An operation of that object, **makeTransfer** (shown as the long vertical bar on the left), carries out the transfer of funds from one account (**fromAccount**) to another one owned by that same customer (**toAccount**). I assume that another operation of the **Transfer** object, something like **setUpTransfer**, has initialized the object with information such as the accounts involved, the amount of money, and so on.

The operation **makeTransfer** sends a message **new** to create an object for transaction monitoring named **transferXaction** of class **TM**.[15] **makeTransfer** then

---

[13] As in the collaboration diagram, the arrows point unidirectionally toward the operation the message invokes. In a synchronous message, control returns to the message sender after the invoked operation has executed, but the notation treats the return as implicit.

[14] This funds-transfer example is more realistic than the one in Fig. 5.3. Thanks to Ken Boyer for arranging the diagram.

[15] Some tools show object instantiation by having the message arrow touch the object box itself.

sends a **begin** message to initialize **transferXaction**. We need the transaction monitor so that in case there's a failure, the system will roll back any partially completed changes as indicated by the **rollback** message. We don't want to withdraw money from one account and fail to deposit it into the other, even though the bank manager thought that was a nifty idea!

The next two messages go to **fromAccount: BankAccount** and **toAccount: BankAccount**, respectively, eliciting the **owner** of the account. The **Transfer** object needs to know the account owners for two reasons: to verify that the two accounts have the same owner and to find the **standing** of the owner (with values like good, bad, abject, deadbeat, or despicable).

The next message, **withdrawFunds (amt, out withdrawalOK)** goes to **fromAccount: BankAccount**, which sends the message **accountOwner.permittedMinBalance** to check that the withdrawal would not reduce the account's balance to an amount below the customer's permitted minimum. As the pseudocode in the side box states, the output argument of **withdrawFunds (amt, out withdrawalOK)** is set to **true** if everything's okay.

Finally, if all is well, the message **depositFunds (amt, out depositOK)** increments the money held in **toAccount** and the message **commit** informs **transferXaction** that it's fine to irrevocably commit the entire set of updates. If all is not well, the message **rollback** informs **transferXaction** that it should discard any changes that occurred since **begin**. (By the way, I'm not sure how **depositOK** ever would become false—maybe only when **amt** is negative.)

Most of the sequence diagram is intuitively understandable, but it does have some limitations. In the sequence diagram of Fig. 5.11, it's not clear that the **rollback** and **commit** messages are mutually exclusive; one gets sent, but not both.

So where do the algorithmic nuances go? Formally, they belong as pseudocode for one or more methods. Informally, you can tack these descriptive boxes onto sequence diagrams like sticky notes, and some tools include a facility for this. If you're using a sequence diagram to model a use case, you can put the textual use-case specification in the box on the left. (See [Rosenberg and Scott, 1999] for more details.)

In this example of a sequence diagram, the names along the top of the diagram refer to objects. Alternatively, you can use class names, as I mentioned earlier, or you can place tasks or entire processors along the top of the diagram to model the execution behavior of a system's architectural artifacts.[16]

---

[16] In this book, I tend to use the word "artifact" to mean a piece of technology (such as a processor task or database) that is capable of executing software instructions or holding data.

## 5.3 Asynchronous Messages and Concurrent Execution

In Sections 5.1 and 5.2, I assumed that all messages are synchronous—that is, that they are processed by the target object one at a time, while the sender waits. I also assumed that all execution in an object-oriented system is single-threaded, meaning that only one object is active at a time.  To put it more explicitly, I assumed the following:

- Only one object in a system can send a message at a given time.
- The sender object must wait for the target object to process the message.
- The target object will process only one message at a time.

Although this is how many mainstream O.O. environments currently work, synchronous messaging is only a special case of object execution in general.  In this section, I explore the more general case, the *asynchronous* message, which allows the sender of the message to continue executing while the target object is processing the message.  Asynchronous messages demand multiple threads of control in the system, in order for several objects to execute at the same time.  Without multiple threads of control (that is, without *concurrency*), all messages would have to be synchronous.[17]

### 5.3.1 Depicting an asynchronous message

You can show asynchronous messages on either form of object-interaction diagram (collaboration or sequence) by using a half arrowhead on the asynchronous message arrow, as in Fig. 5.12.  When an asynchronous message is sent, at least two loci of execution are active in the system, because the target begins to execute while the sender remains in execution.

---

[17] Since this section is about modeling concurrency and asynchronous messages in UML, I won't dwell on the specific mechanisms by which concurrency may be implemented (such as non-blocking message-sends), but I will mention a few terms here.  If the system as a whole has concurrency but each target object handles only one message at a time, there is *system-level concurrency*.  If a target object can handle multiple messages at a time, there is *object-level concurrency*.  If a single operation can handle multiple messages at a time, there is operation-level concurrency.  (An operation could simultaneously process several messages by having several execution threads through reentrant code, or alternatively the system could simply run several copies of the operation.)  A processor may also simulate concurrency (termed *pseudo-concurrency)* by means of, say, time-slicing.  See [Booch, 1994] or [Atkinson, 1991], for example, to find out more about the various forms of concurrency.

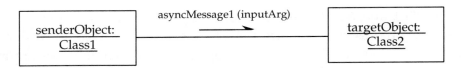

*Fig. 5.12: A collaboration diagram showing a basic asyn-
chronous message.*

Figure 5.13 shows a specific example with asynchronous and synchronous messages. It's from a real-time system that authorizes personnel to pass through
electronically controlled doors. (The employee inserts an ID card into a reader,
and if the employee is authorized to enter, the system plays jingly music, displays
a greeting such as "In comes Mr. Mellor," and slides the door open.)

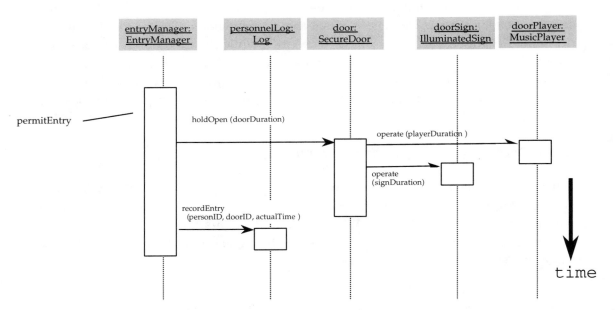

*Fig. 5.13: A sequence diagram for concurrently executing
objects.*

The operation that manages this piece of the application is **permitEntry** (defined
on the class **EntryManager**), which appears on the left of Fig. 5.13. After determining that the employee is allowed through the door (by means of a piece of code

within **permitEntry** that isn't shown in Fig. 5.13), **permitEntry** sends the synchronous message **holdOpen** to the object **door** (an instance of **SecureDoor**).

The operation **holdOpen** then handles the sound, lights, and action associated with opening the door. For the action of opening the door, **holdOpen** sends messages to a hardware driver (for brevity, these messages aren't shown in Fig. 5.13). For the sound-and-light show, **holdOpen** sends two asynchronous messages, both named **operate**: one to **doorPlayer** and one to **doorSign**. (It's useful to have an operation of **SecureDoor** take care of the player and sign operation, because each **SecureDoor** object presumably knows best about its player and sign configuration.) The two operations named **operate** execute concurrently; **door**, trusting that the hardware and firmware behave correctly, pays no further heed to them.

Since the message to **holdOpen** was synchronous, **permitEntry** waits for **holdOpen** to finish its execution and then sends the synchronous message **recordEntry** to **personnelLog**, which notes the employee's passage through the doorway.

### 5.3.2 The callback mechanism

In the great existentialist novel *A Legion of Disasters*, by Eric Lurch, the character Philippe leans over and speaks to his fellow legionnaire, Ferdinand, in the bunk below:

> I can take the heat but I can't stand this damn waiting. I must sleep for a while. Wake me up when the camels get to town.[18]

This bit of dialogue illustrates the *callback mechanism*, a popular use for asynchronous messages in which the following events occur:

1. The subscriber object **subscrobj** registers an interest in some event type via an asynchronous message to the target object **listenobj**. (In the example above, Philippe registers an interest in the event type "the camels get to town" with his pal Ferdinand.)

2. **subscrobj** continues with other activities while **listenobj** monitors for the occurrence of an event of the registered type. (Philippe takes a nap while Ferdinand watches out for camels.)

---

[18] See [Lurch, 1972].

3. When an event of that type occurs, **listenobj** sends a message (usually asynchronous) back to **subscrobj** to notify **subscrobj** of the occurrence. This is the *callback*. **listenobj** may then continue with other activities. ("Ferdinand shouted: 'Wake up, Philippe, wake up! The camels are here and we don't want to be late like last time.' Then, without waiting to see whether Philippe had heard, he began to put on his boots.")

In case you've forgotten your Foreign Legion days, Fig. 5.14 expresses the callback mechanism in a more object-oriented way. Here's the blow-by-blow account:

1. **subscrobj** sends an asynchronous message **registerForEventType1** to **listenobj** with the argument **furtherDetails**. (This argument isn't always needed, but it may be used, for example, as a further filter on interesting events.) The subscriber also supplies its handle (via **self**), which will provide the return address for later callback.

2. The operation of **subscrobj** that sent the asynchronous message **registerForEventType1** continues executing for a while and then terminates. **listenobj** notes (in a table perhaps) that **subscrobj** is interested in an occurrence of event type 1.

3. When an event of type 1 occurs, **listenobj** sends the asynchronous message **eventType1Occurred** to **subscrobj**, with the argument **eventDetails**. (This argument isn't always needed: It may contain information about the specific event that occurred.) **listenobj** then continues with its activities, which often include calling back dozens of other subscriber objects that have registered an interest in an occurrence of that event type.[19]

---

[19] Note that although **listenobj** doesn't know anything about the subscriber objects (apart from their handles), it must have faith that each of them has the operation **eventType1Occurred**, which is required to receive and understand the callback message. Even so, these subscriber objects may be of many different classes, and they may contain definitions/implementations of the **eventType1Occurred** operation that are polymorphically different in each.

*Fig. 5.14: The callback mechanism via asynchronous mes-
sages in a concurrent environment.*

The sequence diagram in Fig. 5.15 shows an example of the callback mechanism,
where the event of interest is the arrival of e-mail with an urgency above a certain
threshold.[20]

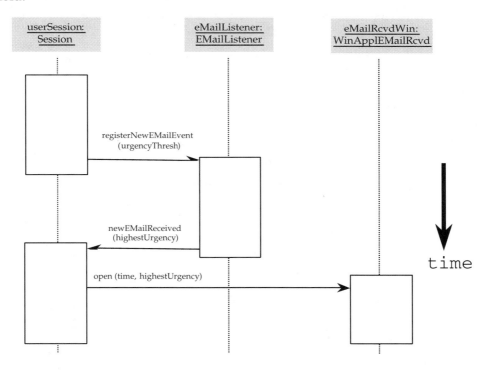

*Fig. 5.15: Callback mechanism used to detect e-mail.*

The **userSession** object registers its interest in new e-mail with the **eMailListener**
object by sending the message **registerNewEMailEvent (urgencyThresh)**. I'm assuming here that one **eMailListener** "works for" only one **userSession** and that **userSes-**

---

[20] I show only the chief messages for the callback mechanism here, omitting any instantiation and
initialization messages that may be needed.

**sion** has already passed **self**, **eMailUserID**, and so on when it instantiated and initialized **eMailListener**. When e-mail that's urgent enough arrives, **eMailListener** calls back **userSession** with **newEMailReceived (highestUrgency)**, whose argument indicates the highest urgency among the messages that actually arrived. **userSession** then opens a window (**eMailRcvdWin**) that displays the following message:

> Hi there! You received new mail with emergency urgency from the President of Ruritania at 12:12 on 2001/02/02.

The sequence diagram of Fig. 5.16 shows a "listener" object that doesn't just wait for an event to happen—it sets it up to happen. (I placed "listener" in quotes because in this case it doesn't need to listen; it's in charge of the event occurrence.)

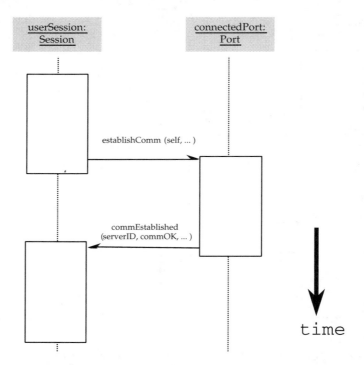

*Fig. 5.16: Callback mechanism to connect a session to a remote computer.*

The job of the system fragment shown in Fig. 5.16 is to get a user logged on to a remote computer system. First, the object **userSession** (of class **Session**) sends an asynchronous message **establishComm** to a target object **connectedPort** (of class **Port**) asking to establish communication with the remote computer. Since establishing this communication may take a while, **userSession** can get on with any other initialization required for the session.

When the operation **establishComm** has completed its job—once the remote computer starts communication—it sends an asynchronous callback message **commEstablished (serverID, commOK)** to **userSession**. (Here, **commOK** is set to **true** only if a connection to a server on the remote machine was successfully achieved.) Then, **userSession** can log on to the remote machine, perhaps obtain remote database authorization, and so on.

There are two differences between this pattern of callback and the one in Fig. 5.15. The first is that the "listener" object does not sit idly, passively waiting for some event to take place. The second is that the event of interest occurs just once. Therefore, there's no formal registration of interest in an event type. Indeed, the only reason for a callback mechanism (with its two asynchronous messages), rather than a single synchronous message from **userSession** to **Port**, is this: **userSession** can use the concurrency to proceed with other activities that would otherwise have to execute serially.

### 5.3.3 Asynchronous messages with priority

Once we allow concurrency, we also allow a target object to be bombarded by messages from lots of concurrently executing sender objects. Since these messages may arrive faster than the target can process them, they'll have to go somewhere to wait their turn. They go into a "waiting room," more often known as a *message queue.*

The target object ushers arriving messages into the message queue. The object then repeatedly removes a message from the front of the queue, invokes the operation that will process the message, and takes the next message from the queue. Messages that overflow the queue will be rejected. An object with no queuing facility will reject all messages that cannot be immediately processed. (Rejected messages may be returned to sender with an exception indicator.)

Messages in a queue may be ordered by priority. You can picture this as a set of parallel queues at the target, each queue with its own priority level, as Fig. 5.17 shows.

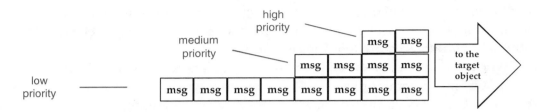

*Fig. 5.17: Three parallel queues, each with its own priority.*

Figure 5.18 shows how I annotate an asynchronous message with its priority level. Here, in part of an electronic-mail system, an asynchronous message is being sent to the **eMailPort** object, asking it to transmit some outgoing e-mail. Sometimes, e-mail messages arrive at **eMailPort** faster than they can leave, so they have to go into a multiple-priority queue. The property **{priority = 3}** alongside the message arrow indicates that the message in Fig. 5.18 has a priority of 3.[21]

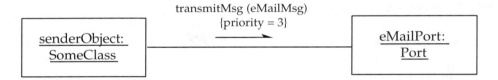

*Fig. 5.18: An asynchronous message (with priority 3) going to an object with a multiple-priority message queue.*

---

[21] Although I show *message*s with priorities here, I haven't discussed exactly how the implementation of message priorities might work. The simplest approach is to have an object process its messages in descending order of priority. Sender objects may also have priority levels. If so, a rule such as "A message may not have a higher priority than that of the sending object" will allow parts of a system to obtain guaranteed execution priority. For example, if a nuclear reactor is about to melt down, it may be a good idea to ensure that the reactor-cooling software executes before the monthly personnel report software. Since in many environments priorities are defined as properties of tasks, an operation might farm out its messages to one of a group of similar tasks, each of them running with a different priority. But these simple approaches don't cope with particularly pesky priority problems, such as *starvation* and *priority inversion*. See [Sha et al., 1990], [Lampson and Redell, 1980], or [Grehan et al., 1998] for more details.

### 5.3.4 Depicting a broadcast (nontargeted) message

An object sending a message normally holds the handle of the object that's the target of the message. However, in systems with concurrency and asynchronous messaging, this isn't always true. In the extreme case, a sender may *broadcast* a message—that is, treat every object in the system as a potential target. A copy of the message goes into the queue of every object in the system.

An object may broadcast a "to whom it may concern" message in response to some external event that it detects. For example, an object might detect a security compromise and broadcast to all objects the need for a priority system shutdown. An object may ignore a broadcast message because it has no operation with which to process it. Another object may choose to ignore the message temporarily until it reaches a suitable state.[22] But most objects that understand the message will take some action immediately upon its receipt.

Figure 5.19 shows the UML for a broadcast message, where I use the stereotype **«broadcast»** to indicate the broadcast nature of this message. In this example, a start-up sequencer is getting every object in the system that exists at start-up time to load itself. (Perhaps this means "Load your variables from stored information," a process sometimes called *object rehydration*.)

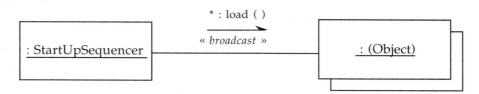

*Fig. 5.19: A broadcast message.*

A broadcast message is similar to an iterated message in that it goes to many objects—hence the double symbol on the target (if you choose to use it) and the asterisk (*) prefix to the message. (Incidentally, [Muller, 1997] likes to use the symbol *‖ to emphasize the parallel nature of a true broadcast.) Since the target class name **Object** implies that the targets are objects of class **Object** or its subclasses, the message goes out to everyone. Some people prefer to use the class name **Any** to indicate that the target is all classes and objects.

---

[22] I cover object states in Chapters 6 and 10.

In the real-time application shown in Fig. 5.20, an operation of the unnamed object **: DashboardMonitor** (perhaps an operation called **signalTimeToRefreshDisplays**) "watches a clock" to determine when it's time to refresh the instrument displays on a vehicle dashboard. The class name of the target indicates that only objects of class **Instrument** (and its subclasses) will get the message. I term such selective broadcasting as *narrowcasting.* As we saw earlier, through polymorphism, each object of a subclass of **Instrument** (such as **Speedometer** or **Tachometer**) may carry out its own version of the operation **displayCurrentReading**.

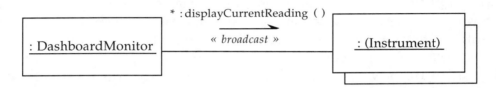

*Fig. 5.20: A narrowcast message.*

For comparison with Fig. 5.20, I show in Fig. 5.21 the UML for a standard (non-broadcast) iterated message, where the object **: DashboardMonitor** holds the handles of all the relevant instruments (in a **List** or **Set** named **instruments**). This time, of course, there's no stereotype **«broadcast»** on the message.

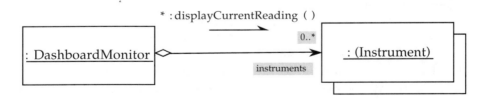

*Fig. 5.21: An iterated message.*

## 5.4 Summary

This chapter looked at the two styles of UML object-interaction diagram: the collaboration diagram and the sequence diagram. Although both styles depict the messaging interaction of objects during system execution, each style has its own special features.

The collaboration diagram is more free-form and shows temporal message sequences only numerically. It depicts static object relationships and dynamic object messaging together. The sequence diagram shows temporal message sequences graphically, so it's useful for clarifying the sequence of interactions among several communicating objects. However, the sequence diagram does not show static object relationships.

Objects are shown on collaboration diagrams as boxes, with each object's name expressed as <u>objName: ClassName</u>, where the underlining emphasizes the instance nature of the symbol. If an object is the singleton of its class, you may leave it anonymous, in the form <u>: ClassName</u>. A target object's name is usually chosen to be the name by which the sender refers to the target.

Polymorphism complicates the naming of the target object's class, because the sender—or indeed even you, the designer—may not know the target's class precisely. With polymorphic targets, choose the name of the lowest class in the inheritance hierarchy that's a superclass of all the classes to which the target object could belong. If you wish, you can highlight the polymorphism by enclosing this name in parentheses.

A message on a collaboration diagram is an arrow alongside the line depicting the link (association instance) between the sender and target objects. The arrow is labeled with the name of the operation to be invoked on the target object, together with the actual input and output arguments for the operation. An iterated message is prefixed with an asterisk (*) followed by the sequence of iteration in square brackets, if that's important. To emphasize iteration, you may also duplicate the target object's box.

The sequence diagram depicts object interactions with time running from north to south on the diagram. Each object appears as a vertical dotted line with the object name at the head. Each execution of an operation of the object appears as a thin box on the dotted line, with a length roughly proportional to the execution time of the operation. Messages between objects appear as horizontal lines connecting one execution box to another. You may highlight algorithms for methods by attaching pseudocode to the sequence diagram. Sequence diagrams have the same naming conventions as collaboration diagrams.

Both the collaboration diagram and the sequence diagram can show synchronous messages, in which the sender object waits for the target to complete execution, and asynchronous messages, in which the sender object continues execution after sending the message. UML shows synchronous messages with a full arrowhead and asynchronous messages with a half arrowhead.

Asynchronous messages are often used to implement the callback mechanism, in which a subscriber object sends an asynchronous message to a listener object to register its interest in an event type. The listener object then sends an asynchronous message to the subscriber when an event of the prescribed type occurs.

Asynchronous messaging requires some concurrency of execution in the system. As a result, messages may sometimes need to queue up at an object and be prioritized for execution. You may show the priority of a message as a UML property.

In a broadcast message, the sender object may not have the handles of the target objects, but sends the message to all (or, in a narrowcast, to some) of the objects who can understand it. The broadcast message is prefixed with an asterisk (*) and stereotyped with **«broadcast»**. The class of the target is **(Object)** or **(Any)**.[23] A narrowcast message has a target of a more specific class.

---

[23] As a reminder, the parentheses indicate polymorphism in UML. For example, **(Object)** means "class **Object** or a subclass of **Object**."

## 5.5 Exercises

1.  Draw a sequence (or collaboration) diagram for an operation of your choice. (In my answer, I chose Chapter 1's algorithm for navigating a hominoid through a grid, which I placed in an operation of a new class named **Navigator**.)

2.  For the class you chose in Exercise 1, is any object-level concurrency possible? What operations could execute simultaneously on the same object? Are there any pairs of operations that you *wouldn't* want to execute simultaneously on the same object?

3.  In this chapter, I've subtly implied that when a sender object holds the handles of its target objects, it sends out several messages in series (iteratively). Conversely, when a sender doesn't hold the handles of its target objects and emits a broadcast message, it sends out several messages in parallel. Are these two implications entirely correct?

## 5.6 Answers

1.  Figure 5.22 shows the sequence diagram for navigating the hominoid through the grid to the finish square. (I assume that this is a sequence diagram for the method implementing an operation defined on class **Navigator**.) I show part of the algorithm in the box at the left; in practice, you would probably show the entire algorithm, especially if your tool supported that capability.

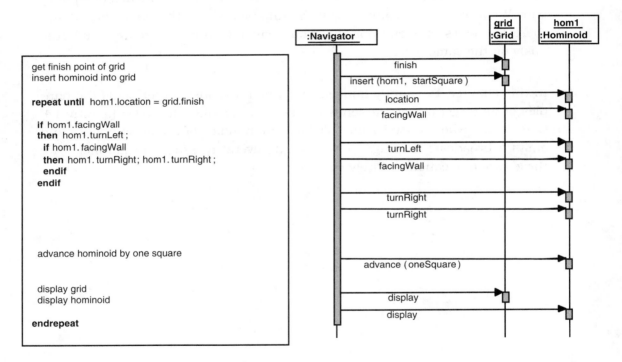

*Fig. 5.22: A sequence diagram for navigating the hominoid.*

2. In **Hominoid**, the get operations **facingWall** and **location** (for example) could execute together, because neither of these accessor operations changes the state of a hominoid, or anything else. However, there would have to be *some* restrictions on concurrency. I doubt, for example, that the operation pairs **turnLeft/turnRight** or **step/turnLeft** could execute simultaneously. If the software were actually installed in a real hominoid, imagine what that would do to the poor hominoid's hardware!

3. No. Strictly speaking, *holding target handles* and *iterating messages* are distinct ideas: A broadcast message could be sent iteratively to all objects. Indeed, at some level of implementation (even in a concurrent system), that's probably what happens—the iteration sequence being defined by the operating system. Also, in an asynchronous/concurrent environment, an object could send messages in parallel to all the objects whose handles it holds, if that made sense in the application under design.

# 6

# $S$tate Diagrams

A state diagram for a class shows the states that objects of that class may assume and the transitions the objects may make from state to state.[1] Following the work of David Harel and others (see [Harel, 1987] or [Henderson-Sellers and Edwards, 1994], for example), the authors of UML extended the basic state-transition notation with, for instance, nested states. In this chapter, I briefly describe the basic state diagram and then explore some useful elaborations on it: the use of nested states; the incorporation of message arguments; the representation of concurrent, interacting states; and finally, the accommodation of continuously variable attributes on the state diagram.[2]

---

[1] In extremely rare cases, a class itself (as opposed to its objects) has states worth modeling with a state diagram. This is analogous to the idea of a class attribute versus an instance attribute, which we discussed in Chapter 3.

[2] The official UML term is *statechart diagram*, which is shortened here as *state diagram*. It's a bit easier to say, and it removes the redundancy built into the official wording. Note also that traditional state *tables* remain valuable—see [Ward and Mellor, 1985], for example, for more details.

## 6.1 Basic State Diagrams

A state diagram is ideal for modeling an attribute with these two characteristics:

- The attribute possesses few values, and
- The attribute has restrictions on permitted transitions among those values.

For example, consider the class **SellableItem**, which contains the instance attributes **salePrice: Money** and **currInspectionStatus: InspectionStatus**. There are two qualitative differences between these attributes:

1. **salePrice**, being an instance of **Money**, has a large number of possible values, such as $1.98, $4.95, $5.95, and so on. **currInspectionStatus**, on the other hand, has only a small set of possible values, such as **received** (just arrived from the vendor), **inInspection** (being scrutinized, even as we speak), **accepted** (passed the inspector's deepest scrute), and **rejected** (cast out as unworthy).

2. There's probably little business restriction on permitted changes to **salePrice**. In other words, an object's **salePrice** may change from $4.95 to $5.25, or from $6.50 to $5.99, or whatever. However, an object's **currInspectionStatus** cannot change directly from **received** to **accepted** without first passing through the value **inInspection**.

**salePrice** is not a suitable candidate to be modeled by means of a state diagram, because it has lots of possible values and almost no restrictions on its transitions among those values. The attribute **currInspectionStatus**, on the other hand, has the two properties that make it ideal for a state diagram. As we saw above, this attribute has only a few possible values and there are significant restrictions on its transitions from one value to another. An instance attribute, such as **currInspectionStatus**, with the two ideal characteristics listed above and values that reflect the natural states of its owner object, is termed a *state attribute*. A state attribute is a mechanism to represent the states of an object.

Figure 6.1 shows a state diagram for **SellableItem.currInspectionStatus**. In the figure, each of the boxes contains a value of **currInspectionStatus** and represents a state of a **SellableItem** object.[3] The arrows represent transitions between states.

---

[3] As we'll see in Chapter 10, a box on a state-transition diagram denotes a region in the state-space of the class. The region may comprise a single point or a group of points.

Each transition is annotated with a two-part label. The text above the line describes an *event*, which is usually caused by an inbound message to the object. An event triggers a transition from one state to the other. The presence of multiple events above the line indicates that *any one* of those events may cause the transition.[4]

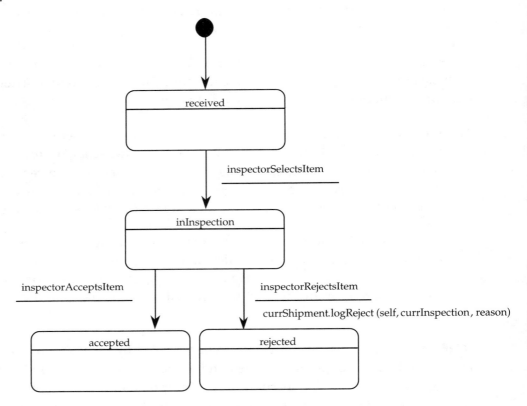

*Fig. 6.1: State diagram for* **SellableItem.currInspectionStatus**.

The text below the line describes the action that's triggered by a transition between states. This action is usually an outbound message from the object. The presence of multiple actions below the line indicates that *all* of the actions are carried out during the transition. For some transitions, there may be no associated actions.

---

[4] Stylistically, standard UML prefers to use a forward slash (/) to separate events from actions, rather than a horizontal line. So, in this section, you may want to substitute the words "before the slash" for "above the line" and "after the slash" for "below the line."

In Fig. 6.1, I show just one example of an action: an outgoing message to log the fact that there was a rejected item (namely **self**) within the current shipment.

The initial state of a state diagram, marked by a black dot as at the top of Fig. 6.1, is a state in which the object spends no time. Instead, the object immediately transitions to the state that it first acquires on its instantiation or initialization. This transition from the initial state is normally not labeled, although you may label it with the event that creates the object, if you wish.

The final state of a state diagram, marked by a bull's-eye, represents an object's completion of activity. There's an example of a final state in Fig. 6.6 on page 172. (More precisely, as we'll see when we look at nested states in the next section, the final state represents the completion of activity within the enclosing state.)

The UML state diagram that I've described so far associates actions with transitions, which is often called the Mealy convention. However, UML also supports actions associated with states, called the Moore convention. I show an example of actions on states later in this chapter. So, in UML, there's something for everyone—whether you're a Mealy shop, a Moore shop, a Mearly shop, a Moorly shop, or just merely a shop.

## 6.2 Nested States

Not all state diagrams are as simple as the one in Fig. 6.1. Some state diagrams require inner states, nested within outer ones. As an example, let's consider the state diagrams for the class **Machine**, which represents a shop-floor machine in a factory-control application.

**Machine** has two statuses: a current operating status represented by the attribute **opStat** and a current service status represented by the attribute **serviceStat**. As Fig. 6.2 shows, **opStat**, the machine's operating status, has four states: **standingBy**, **accelerating**, **running**, and **decelerating**.

In the state diagram, the event

> **when** (**self**.actualSpeed >= runningSpeed)

is a UML *change event* (known in other approaches as a *Boolean transition* or *predicate transition*). It's deemed to occur at the moment when the Boolean expression in parentheses (after the keyword **when**) switches from **false** to **true**.

Also in Fig. 6.2, the expression

> [**self**.serviceStat = inService]

in Fig. 6.2 is known as a *guard*. A guard on a transition means that the transition takes place only if the Boolean expression in brackets evaluates to **true** when the triggering event occurs. In this example, the machine will only start under the operator's command if it is in service.

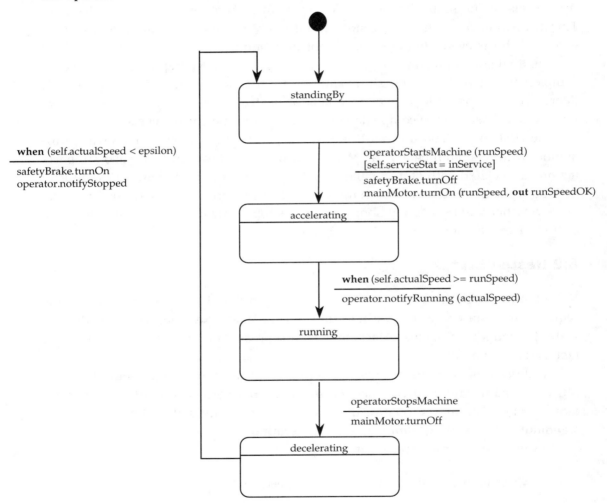

*Fig. 6.2: The state diagram for* **Machine.opStat**.

This brings us neatly to Fig. 6.3, which shows the three states of **serviceStat**, the machine's service status: **inService**, **waitingForRepair**, and **inRepair**.

At first glance, **Machine** may appear to have twelve possible states—three for **serviceStat** times four for **opStat**. But that's not true if we make the reasonable

assumption that within this application only an in-service machine can meaningfully accelerate, decelerate, and so on.  Thus, there are really just *six* legitimate
states, because the two attributes, **serviceStat** and **opStat**, aren't mutually independent:  **opStat** has meaning only when **serviceStat = inService**.

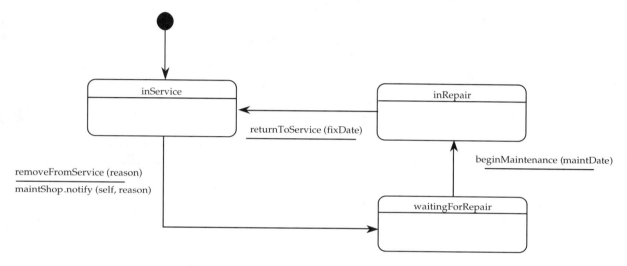

*Fig. 6.3: The state diagram for* **Machine.serviceStat**.

Figure 6.4 shows the combination of the two state diagrams from Figs. 6.2 and
6.3, where the second diagram is nested into the **inService** state of the first.[5]  This
nesting of the four **opStat** states within the **inService** state illustrates the constraint that **opStat** has meaning only when **serviceStat = inService**.  Indeed, this
nesting is useful only when there are constraints such as these across state diagrams for a class.

Note that the nested **running** state now indicates that the machine has both
the operating status of **running** and the service status of **inService**.  Conversely,
since the **inRepair** state has no nested states, the machine's operating status is
undefined when it has the service status of **inRepair**.  With this constraint added
to our model, we may remove the guard **[self.serviceStat = inService]** from the
**standingBy/accelerating** transition shown in Fig. 6.2, because the transition is
meaningful only for an in-service machine.

In Fig. 6.4, there are two initial-state symbols—the little black dots.  The outer
dot indicates that when an object of class **Machine** is created, the value of **service-**

---

[5] I omitted the annotations on the transitions only for purposes of clarity in this example.

**Stat** should be initialized to **inService**. The inner dot means that whenever an object of class **Machine** enters the state **inService**—that is, whenever **serviceStat**'s value becomes **inService**—the value of **opStat** should be initialized to **standingBy**.

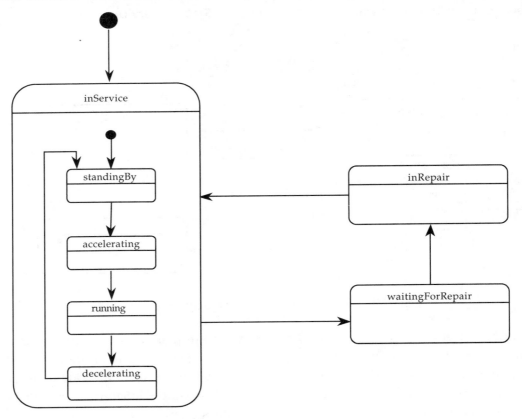

*Fig. 6.4:*  *The combined, or nested, state diagram for*
**Machine.serviceStat** *and* **Machine.opStat**.

Figure 6.5 shows part of the state diagram for a washing machine. Rather like the factory machine in Fig. 6.4, the washing machine goes through its cycle only when it's in service, which for the washing machine means that its door is closed. However, there's a crucial difference between the washing machine and the factory machine: If the washer's door gets opened and then closed, it must return not to its initial state—**stopped**—but to its state just before the door was opened. In other words, the washer must be able to restore the previous substate of **runnable** when the state **runnable** is reentered.

To depict this, UML follows David Harel in employing the *history symbol,* an H in a small circle (see [Harel, 1987]). This symbol means: Enter whatever substate was active last, upon subsequent entry to the enclosing state. If the history symbol has a transition to a substate (as it does to **stopped** in Fig. 6.5), then it means, Enter this substate, upon first entry to the enclosing state. The history symbol may then replace the initial-state symbol for a substate, as it does in Fig. 6.5.

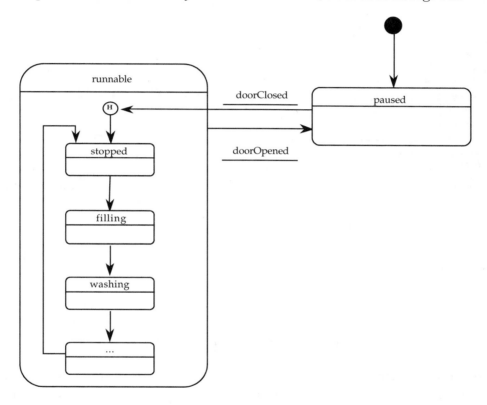

*Fig. 6.5: A state of* **WashingMachine** *with history.*

## 6.3 Concurrent States and Synchronization

This section covers the concurrent states that an object may have and goes deeper into the topic of nested states. I use a running example of a fairly realistic commercial order from a company named Smibley and Futz, Inc. Although the life of a Smibley and Futz order is quite complex, it's still a simplification of what an order at your own company may undergo. As you read, bear in mind that a real order may have multiple items in a variety of states, or partial items, when only a part-quantity can be shipped.

Let's look first at Fig. 6.6, which shows the states of an order's **custAuthorizationStatus** (the state attribute whose values are driven mainly by customer whim, rather than by Smibley and Futz decisions).

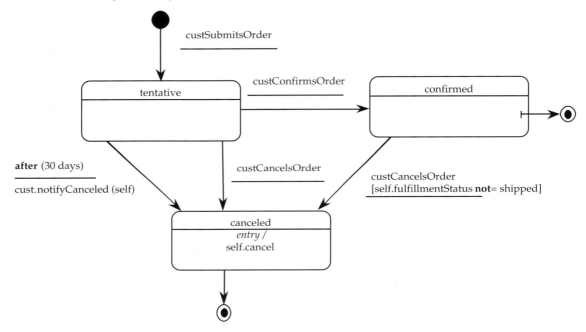

*Fig. 6.6: State diagram for* **Order.custAuthorizationStatus**.

When a customer calls with an order, the company treats the order by default as **tentative**, a state in which it's submitted perhaps for a price quotation but not to be immediately fulfilled. When the customer confirms the order, which may occur during the initial phone call, the order assumes the **confirmed** state. According to S&F's policy, this is the only state in which real processing can occur; we'll return to it shortly.

The customer may cancel an order unless the goods have already been shipped—hence the guard, **[self.fulfillmentStatus not= shipped]**. If the customer cancels, the order becomes—you guessed it!—**canceled**. As Fig. 6.6 shows, the entry action to the **canceled** state is the message **self.cancel**, which causes the **Order** object to undo any stock allocation that may have been made for it.[6] Notice

---

[6] In order to concentrate on state diagrams, this chapter doesn't elaborate on the actions that are mentioned on the diagrams.

that tentative orders are automatically canceled after thirty days, giving us an example of a UML **after** clause:  **after (timePeriod)** represents a temporal event that occurs when the interval **timePeriod** has elapsed after entry to the given state.

Now it's time to look again at the **confirmed** state.  The small line within the state in Fig. 6.6 is a UML *stub*, which indicates an expanded diagram in which the stub and other subsumed details of the state blossom in full.  Figure 6.7 is an expansion of the **confirmed** state.

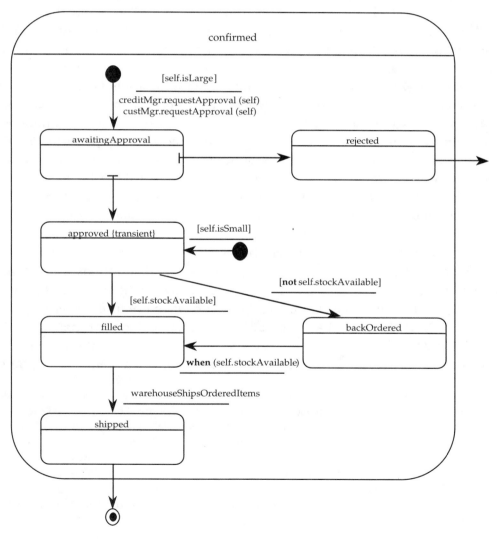

Fig. 6.7:   *State diagram for* **Order.fulfillmentStatus**, *an expansion of the* **confirmed** *state.*

The policy at S&F is that large orders must be approved by both a credit manager and a customer manager. (I don't define "large" here, but **self.isLarge** returns **true** for a large order.) This gives a large confirmed order the initial substate **awaiting-Approval**, which I discuss below. A small confirmed order, which gets automatic approval, begins in the substate **approved**.

Once an order is approved, it is ready to be filled, a state in which specific items of the product types are allocated for delivery to the customer. But first, inventory must be checked: Either the stock is available and the transition to **filled** is activated, or the stock is depleted and the transition to **backOrdered** is activated. I show this on the diagram as two transitions with guards—**[self.stock-Available]**, for instance—and no events.

When I show this approach to my clients and students, they often stop me and ask, "Why didn't you use a **when** clause, such as **when (self.stockAvailable)**?" My answer is that **approved** is actually a *transient state* (or *flow-through state*), meaning that it does not persist. (Note its **{transient}** property in Fig. 6.7.) In other words, rather than hanging around in a transient state, an object makes an instantaneous transition to another state, without waiting for an event. (Some people term such an eventless transition a *triggerless transition*.) So, a transient state is like a fork in the road, where the object makes a transition based on whichever guard evaluates to **true**.

The **approved** state is transient because, in this computerized application, we needn't wait for Smibley's nephew to go out back and count boxes of Whizzo™ No-Cholesterol Dream Whip. Therefore, since the system knows whether or not the stock is there and acts accordingly, there's no **when** event to model.[7]

Note that the state **backOrdered** is a regular old non-transient, with **when (self.stockAvailable)** causing the transition to **filled**.[8] When the warehouse sends out the ordered items, the state becomes **shipped**. I was tempted to pull **shipped**

---

[7] In fact, a **when (self.stockAvailable)** leading from **approved** would be problematic: If the stock were already available on entry to **approved**, the event would never occur. I once proposed the clause **whenever (self.stockAvailable)**, which combines **when (self.stockAvailable)** and the guard **[self.stockAvailable]** and allows the states **approved** and **backOrdered** to be combined. However, this clause hasn't caught on. Instead, some modelers, including authors of other UML works, are finessing the issue by using **when** to mean **whenever**. Other modelers are more absolute in their rejection of transient states, but because of the above problem, I find transients very convenient. In the next section, I show another way to represent them, which may get me into further trouble with the Ministers of the New World Modeling Order.

[8] For convenience in this model, I assume that the **Order** object itself has an attribute **stockAvailable** that returns a Boolean value after checking inventory for availability.

out of the superstate **confirmed**, because S&F won't cancel a shipped order. However, since that would have left the state **shipped** out in the cold or would have required another nesting, I decided to model that requirement with the guard **[self.fulfillmentStatus not= shipped]**, as shown in Fig. 6.6.

The stub in Fig. 6.7's **awaitingApproval** indicates an expansion, which is shown in Fig. 6.8. This state diagram models a large order's purgatorial wait for the blessings of the credit managers and the customer managers. Since these managers are independent beings, we divide **awaitingApproval**'s expansion into two *concurrent* diagrams, using a vertical dotted line.

But we're not done yet! Approval at S&F means waiting for *both* managers to give the thumbs-up; a rejection from either casts an order to its doom. To handle this situation, I exploit the *synchronization bar* of UML, shown at the bottom of **awaitingApproval** in Fig. 6.8. This big black bar indicates that *both* **creditMgr-Approved** and **custMgrApproved** must be reached before we can proceed. When both states are entered, we immediately move to **approved**.

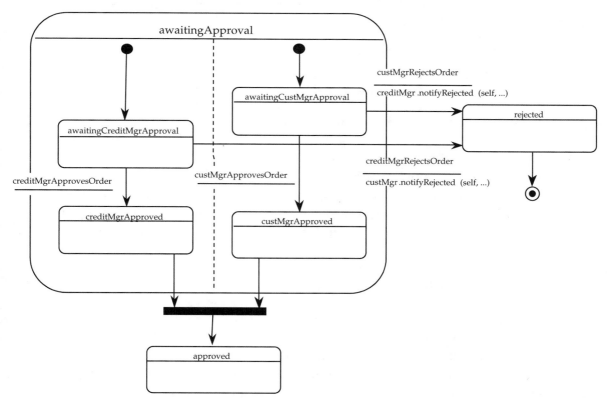

*Fig. 6.8:* State diagram for **Order.approvalStatus**, an expansion of the **awaitingApproval** state.

Since the transition to **rejected** can occur from either **awaitingCreditMgrApproval** or **awaitingCustMgrApproval**, we don't need any synchronization—just a couple of straight transitions out to **rejected**. Incidentally, the message **custMgr.notify-Rejected (self, ...)** is just a courtesy message telling the other manager not to bother reviewing an already rejected order.

## 6.4 Transient States from Message-Result Arguments

As we discussed in Section 6.2 on nested states, the Boolean guard and **when** expressions are built from a combination of these elements:

- attributes of an object (or sometimes private variables)
- arguments of input messages to the object
- arguments returned from outbound messages to other objects

We saw examples of the first two of the above elements in Fig. 6.2. For instance, the guard

> [**self**.serviceStat = inService]

contains an attribute, **serviceStat**. The **when** expression

> **when** (**self**.actualSpeed >= runSpeed)

has another attribute, **actualSpeed**, and an input message argument, **runSpeed**, which came from **operatorStartsMachine (runSpeed)**.

So far, however, we haven't seen the impact of the third kind of argument, a return argument of an outbound message. An example from the shop-floor machine model in Fig. 6.2 was **runSpeedOK**, in the outbound message to **mainMotor**:

> mainMotor.turnOn (runSpeed, **out** runSpeedOK)

The message **turnOn** tells the object **mainMotor** to spin up the actual shop-floor machine's motor to **runSpeed**. However, if the value of **runSpeed** exceeds what's possible for the installed brand of motor, then **mainMotor** will grumble and do nothing except return **runSpeedOK** as **false**. But now we have a modeling problem. If **runSpeedOK** comes back as **false**, we can't just make a blithe transition to **accelerating**, because the machine's *not* accelerating—it's still stopped!

Ideally, we would put a pair of guards here—one for each value of **runSpeedOK** (**true** or **false**)—as we would if **mainMotor.turnOn** were an inbound rather than outbound message. But it's too late for a guard under the action **mainMotor.turnOn** because the guard is testing a return argument (**runSpeedOK**) of the message **mainMotor.turnOn** itself. To handle this kind of situation, I use a transient state, **turningOnMotor**, as shown in Fig. 6.9, a revised extract from Fig. 6.2.

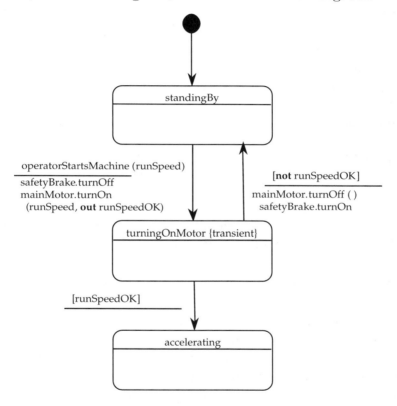

*Fig. 6.9: Part of state diagram for* **Machine.opStat**.

This transient state in the middle of Fig. 6.9 is a vehicle for the two guards **[run-SpeedOK]** and **[not runSpeedOK]**. In other words, it makes the transition from **standingBy** to **accelerating** a transition that's conditional on the value of **run-SpeedOK**.

Finally, the transition back to the **standingBy** state causes two further outbound messages to be issued (to turn off the main motor and to apply the safety brake again).

## 6.5 Continuously Variable Attributes

Conceptually at least, some attributes of real-world things vary continuously, rather than discretely. In other words, if we measured them with ultimate precision, we would find an infinite number of values rather than a few, discrete ones. I term these *continuously variable attributes*.[9]

For example, a reaction in a chemical factory's reaction vessel has a current temperature, which is continuously variable. As Fig. 6.10 shows, the attribute **Reaction.currTemp** represents the reaction's temperature (where **Reaction** is the class of chemical reactions in a vessel). Although **currTemp** is a continuous rather than a discrete attribute, it too may play a role in a state diagram.

Notice that each of the state diagram's three "Goldilocks" states—**tooCool**, **tooHot**, and **justRight**—corresponds to a range of values of **currTemp**:[10]

| | |
|---|---|
| > maxTemp | // too hot |
| ≤ maxTemp and ≥ minTemp | // just right |
| < minTemp | // too cool |

Notice, too, that most of the transitions on the diagram are triggered by a **when** statement (apart from the initial one). This is typical of transitions between states that are simply conditions of an attribute. If you find this modeling approach too littered with **when** statements, consider the alternative in Exercise 6 at the end of this chapter.

The state diagram in Fig. 6.10 illustrates the Moore convention of placing outbound messages on states, rather than on transitions (which is the Mealy convention).[11] For example, whenever the state **tooCool** is reached, the message **heater.turnOn** is sent. The keyword **entry** in the state **tooCool** indicates that the message is sent on entry to the state. (Other possible UML keywords are: **exit**, for the action taken on leaving a state; and **do**, for the activity carried out while in a state. Note that **entry** and **exit** denote atomic actions, whereas **do** denotes an ongoing activity.)

---

[9] I base the term *continuously variable attribute* on the term *continuous data-flow* used in [Ward and Mellor, 1985]. The idea is that such an attribute—in principle, anyway—varies continuously rather than only after discrete events. The pressure of the air in your room is an example of a continuously variable attribute.

[10] As we'll see in Chapter 10, any such assertion is actually equivalent to the definition of a region of the class's state-space.

[11] Note that Fig. 6.10 uses *both* the Mealy and Moore conventions in the same state diagram, which is perfectly acceptable in UML.

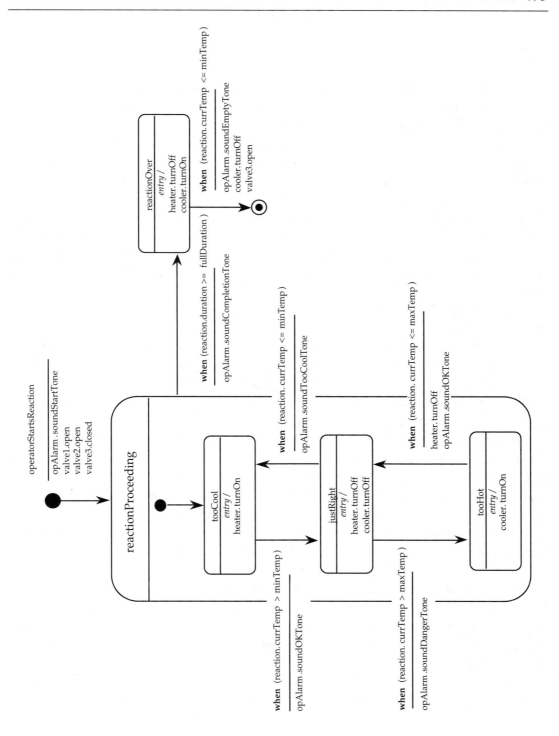

*Fig. 6.10: State diagram for* **Reaction**.

## 6.6 Summary

A state diagram shows the permitted states that objects of a given class may assume and the permitted transitions between pairs of states. The diagram is useful for modeling classes whose objects have a state attribute with these two properties: The attribute can take on a small number of allowed values, and the permitted transitions among those values are restricted. An attribute that exhibits these properties, with values that reflect the natural states of its owner object, is termed a state attribute.

Each simple, non-nested state on the state diagram corresponds to one possible value of a state attribute or, sometimes, to a range of values of the attribute. The initial transition of a state diagram, which takes an object to its first state, is indicated by a black dot at the tail of the arrow. The final transition has a bull's eye on its arrowhead.

Each transition between a pair of states appears as an arrow on the state diagram. The trigger for a transition between states is an event, annotated above a horizontal line or before a forward slash, in some tools. The presence of more than one event above the line indicates that *any* of the listed events may trigger the transition. A guard in the form of a **[booleanExpression]** may appear after an event, signifying that if the **booleanExpression** evaluates to **true**, the transition may take place as soon as the triggering event occurs.

There are three kinds of UML event: a *call event*, a *change event*, or an *elapsed-time event*. A call event occurs upon receipt of an inbound message from another object. (A variation on the call event is the *signal event*, which occurs upon receipt of an explicit signal from another object.) A change event, indicated by a **when (booleanExpression)** clause, occurs on the transition of a **booleanExpression** from **false** to **true**. An elapsed-time event, indicated by an **after (timePeriod)** clause, occurs at the expiration of a **timePeriod**, which is normally measured from the time of entry to a given state.

An action is normally defined as an outbound message to another object or to **self**. Actions that accompany a transition between states (known as the Mealy convention) appear below a horizontal line or after a forward slash, in some tools. The presence of more than one action below the line indicates that *all* of the listed actions occur.

Actions that take place at states (known as the Moore convention) are listed within the state symbol itself, following one of these keywords: **entry** (for actions taken upon entry to the state), **exit** (for actions taken upon exit from the state), and **do** (for actions taken during residence within the state).

A class may have two or more state attributes that can be profitably modeled with state diagrams. Using state diagrams this way often leads to having more than one state diagram for the class, or to having nested state diagrams, if the attributes are not completely independent of each other. A nested state diagram shows inner states within outer states. To avoid graphic clutter, UML allows a modeler to show nested states as stubs, which are expanded in full detail on a separate state diagram. UML directs the return to a previously departed nested state—the enclosing state's last active substate—with a stylized H inside a small circle (for "history"). A black dot on an inner state designates it as the first inner state to become active when the outer, enclosing state is entered, unless an H symbol is present.

Even when state attributes appear on separate state diagrams (that is, when they aren't nested within each other), they may still have some interdependence. For example, the transition of one attribute may only occur if another attribute is at a given value. (This constraint can be modeled with a guard statement.) Similarly, the transition of an object to a state may be permitted only after both attributes have arrived at appropriate values, regardless of which arrived first. Although a guard can again be pressed into modeling service here, UML offers the synchronization bar to mark graphically the rendezvous point between the two concurrent state attributes.

Object orientation complicates the traditional state-transition diagram, because an outbound message sent during guarded transitions from a state may have return arguments that appear in the Boolean expressions of the transitions' guards. This situation requires the addition of a transient state to the state diagram, as a branch point for the transition that causes the outbound message to be sent. The original guarded transitions would then become transitions from the additional transient state.

Some classes—especially those in process-control systems—have attributes that are conceptually continuous, rather than discrete, in the values that they may assume. Some of these continuously variable attributes may yield worthwhile state diagrams. States that are based on a continuously variable attribute are typically based on ranges of the attribute's values. A hallmark of such a state diagram is the many change events that trigger the transitions.

## 6.7 Exercises

1. Suppose a designer has created a state diagram with 57 states and 93 transitions, many of them guarded. The consensus of reviewers is that the diagram is hopelessly tangled and incomprehensible. How would you advise this designer? ("Emigrate to Baffin Island" is not an acceptable answer.)

2. What if another designer had spent a day staring at a class and was about to leap from the 38th floor because he couldn't come up with a worthwhile state diagram for it? What would be your advice to *this* designer?

3. The state diagram in Fig. 6.4 has two initial-state symbols, the big black dots: One leads to the state **inService** and one leads to the substate **standingBy**. Could one of these be dropped without changing the meaning of the diagram? If so, which one? Is it good practice to eliminate initial-state symbols like this?

4. There are some problems with the state diagram in Fig. 6.10. For example, valve 1 and valve 2, which presumably release reactive chemicals into the reaction vessel, never get closed. (Valve 3, the output valve that drains the vessel, opens and closes.) The final **when** clause, **when (reaction.currTemp <= finalTemp)**, also has a problem: If **reaction.currTemp** is already less than **finalTemp** upon entry to the **reactionOver** state, the **when** will never get executed. How would you fix these problems and any others you've found in Fig. 6.10?

5. The example in Section 6.4 implied that continuously variable attributes are to be found only in the real-time, process-control world. Is this accurate? In what sense might **Share.price** be a continuously variable attribute? Could it have a meaningful state diagram?

6. How might you use a table rather than a state diagram to model the transitions among value ranges of a continuously variable attribute like **currTemp** in Fig. 6.10?

7. Consider an application at Larnham Goode, Inc., a small seminar company. For simplicity, assume that the company offers only one seminar and has only one (worn-out and frazzled) instructor. Each week of the teaching calen-

dar is an instance of the class **SeminarWeek**. The reservation status of a given week is held in **SeminarWeek.reservationStat**, which can contain the values **available**, **tentativelyReserved**, and **firmlyReserved**. When a new **SeminarWeek** is created (when it's placed on the calendar), it is given the initial **reservationStat** of **available**.

A customer can make a reservation for a given week, with or without a deposit. A deposit entitles the customer to a firm reservation; without it, the customer gets only a tentative reservation. Show the state diagram for the three states of **reservationStat** that I just described.

8. One day, Mr. Larnham Goode, the esteemed president of the seminar company, realizes that some weeks are more in demand than others. So, the company establishes the concept of peak (highly popular) weeks, as opposed to normal weeks. The constant **isPopular** captures the popularity of a **SeminarWeek**. (In other words, for a popular week, **isPopular** is set to the fixed value **true** when the popular-week object is instantiated.) Only firm reservations are allowed in peak weeks; to secure a firm reservation, a customer must plunk down a large deposit. "Large" is defined as "at least the amount represented by **peakDeposit**," and we can assume that **peakDeposit > 0**. How would you modify your state diagram from Exercise 7 to reflect this new policy?

## 6.8 Answers

1.  Make sure that your state diagrams are *abstractions* of class behavior. A
    state diagram doesn't—and shouldn't—capture *every* possible facet and algo-
    rithm of the class. If you find that your state diagram is becoming a hodge-
    podge of states and conditions, then you probably want to rethink your
    notion of the class—or at least further abstract your diagram. You'll also
    benefit from breaking your tangled single diagram into multiple state dia-
    grams, each based on a particular state attribute.

    If your state model of a class is still horribly complicated, then you should
    consider factoring out subclasses, each subclass taking on the behavior of
    one major state of the original class. For example, you could introduce two
    or three subclasses of **Machine**, such as **InServiceMachine**, **WaitingForRepair-
    Machine**, and **InRepairMachine**. (This idea of subclassing based on states is
    very strongly emphasized in [Shlaer and Mellor, 1992].)

2.  Don't worry if the class on which you're working reveals nothing profound via
    a state diagram. Many classes have no worthwhile state diagram, because
    their attributes can take on hundreds of values or because their transitions
    are unrestricted. Capture such classes' behavior through class invariants and
    the definitions of the classes' operations and attributes, and don't bother with
    state diagrams for these classes. (I cover these definitions in Chapter 10.)

3.  Yes, if you drop the initial-state symbol leading to **inService**, the surviving ini-
    tial-state symbol would imply that a new **Machine** object would begin in the
    state/substate **inService/standingBy**. However, I don't like to do this. My
    reason: What if we later had another set of substates within another state,
    with its own initial-state symbol? Then our deletion of the outer black dot
    would render the diagram ambiguous.

4.  For the perpetually open valves, you presumably need to add a state such as
    **vesselFilling** to address the first problem. If your shop uses **when** to mean
    **whenever**, then you don't have the second problem. If **when** just means **when**
    (as in, "at the *exact* moment that **false** flips to **true**"), then you could introduce
    a transient state before **reactionOver** to check whether **reaction.currTemp <=
    finalTemp**.

5. Although continuously variable attributes crop up most obviously in real-time, process-control systems, you may also encounter them in some business systems. Just as the attribute **Reaction.currTemp** of Section 6.4 would theoretically prove to be continuous if we could measure it with enough frequency and precision, the attribute **Share.price** could be considered continuously variable. Although we may not measure it quite so often as **Reaction.currTemp**, our application could be fed a stream of share prices (rather like temperatures from a reactor), with no clue about any "upstream events" that ultimately drive changes in price.

Share.price could therefore have a state diagram very similar to that of **Reaction.currTemp**, with the state names changed to **fairlyPriced**, **overPriced**, and **underPriced** to preserve the application. A transition to **overPriced**, for example, could cause an outbound message to sell the position in that share. The message may be one such as,

    equityAccount.sellPosition (**self**)

6. The simplest approach would be to place the value ranges of the continuously variable attribute in both the rows and the columns of the table. Then the actions for each transition would appear as outbound messages in the appropriate square of the table. The chemical reaction example of Fig. 6.10 might appear as shown in the table below:

| FROM: | TO: | tooCool | justRight | tooHot |
|---|---|---|---|---|
| **tooCool** | *entry/* heater.turnOn | — | opAlarm. soundOKTone | // impossible |
| **justRight** | *entry/* heater.turnOff cooler.turnOff | opAlarm. soundTooCoolTone | — | opAlarm. soundTooHotTone |
| **tooHot** | *entry/* cooler.turnOn | // impossible | opAlarm. soundOKTone | — |

The first column indicates the original state before the transition. The second column indicates the Moore actions—the actions associated with a specific state rather than with a particular transition. The third, fourth, and fifth columns show the Mealy actions—the actions that occur during a particular transition.

7.    The three values of **reservationStat** are shown as states in Fig. 6.11.

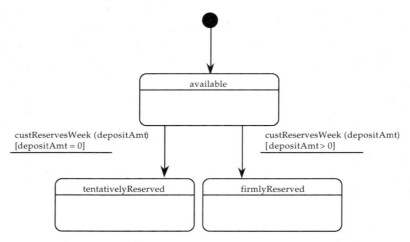

*Fig. 6.11: Part of the state diagram for* **SeminarWeek.reservationStat**.

The inbound message **custReservesWeek** causes a transition to either the state **tentativelyReserved** or the state **firmlyReserved**. The mutually exclusive guards, **[depositAmt = 0]** and **[depositAmt > 0]**, differentiate between the two possible transitions. Incidentally, a negative **depositAmt**, if it were technically feasible, would prevent any transition from the state **available**.

8.    Figure 6.12 shows this new twist to reservations. To reflect the new complexity in company policy, the guard on each of the transitions has now become more complex. I had some trouble writing the two guards in a meaningful way, so I experimented with several forms of these long Boolean expressions. I tried **not self.isPopular**, for instance, but found **self.isPopular = false** more readable. You may want to experiment further to derive better forms for the Boolean expressions, perhaps using this logic table as grist, evaluating the **and** of the row and column values:

| AND: | isPopular = false | isPopular = true |
|---|---|---|
| depositAmt = 0 | tentativelyReserved | tentativelyReserved |
| 0 < depositAmt < peakDepositAmt2 | firmlyReserved | tentativelyReserved |
| depositAmt >= peakDepositAmt | firmlyReserved | firmlyReserved |

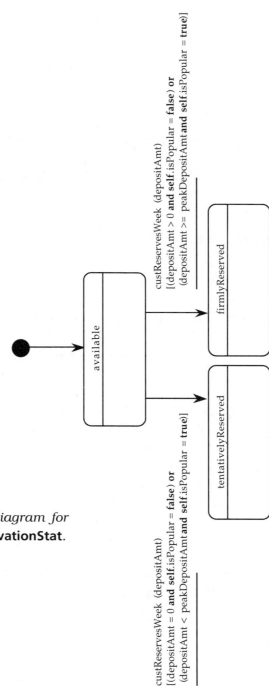

*Fig. 6.12:* *Part of the state diagram for* **SeminarWeek.reservationStat**.

# Architecture and Interface Diagrams

C hapters 3 through 6 covered the concepts you'll use daily for object-oriented design, the heart and soul of UML. In this chapter, the first section introduces UML for modeling system architecture, which encompasses the following:

- software architecture, such as packages (covered in Section 7.1.1)
- hardware architecture, such as multiple processors (covered in Section 7.1.2)
- the interaction of software architecture with hardware architecture, such as the assignment of software constructs to hardware artifacts (covered in Section 7.1.3)

The second section of this chapter shows the notation for modeling the windows in the human interface and the navigation paths among the windows. Since there is little in current UML that directly assists with modeling the human interface, I have created some UML stereotypes for this purpose.

## 7.1 Depicting System Architecture

*Architecture modeling* starts with an essential model (one that is uncommitted to any particular technology) and maps it to a chosen technology. You can use UML to show both the interconnections among technology artifacts and the distribution of your software system across these artifacts. In this section, we look at UML packages that only show software partitioning, UML deployment diagrams that only show hardware partitioning, and UML deployment diagrams that show both hardware and software partitioning.

### 7.1.1 Packages

Since no two shops have exactly the same notion of a *package*, I can best describe it generally as a grouping of software elements. Within an object-oriented system, a package is often a collection of classes. It might be a collection of classes in a purchased library, a collection of classes for a particular application, or a collection of classes that capture aspects of a real-world thing (such as **CustomerFinancials**, **CustomerShipping**, and **CustomerProfile**, each of which addresses one set of customer characteristics).

UML depicts a package as a stylized folder, similar to the folder icon used in many desktop applications, as Fig. 7.1 exemplifies.

*Fig. 7.1: A simple UML package diagram showing two interdependent packages.*

The two packages in Fig. 7.1 presumably dwell in the library of a hospital Information Systems (IS) shop. **PatientPackage** is a collection of classes relating to a patient, such as **Patient** and **PatientMedicalHistory**. **HospitalWardPackage** is a collection of classes relating to a ward, such as **Ward**, **Bed**, and **Nurse**.[1] The fully

---

[1] In some methodologies, packages such as **PatientPackage** and **HospitalWardPackage** are termed *subdomains* of the business domain. I return to the subject of domains in Chapter 9.

qualified name for this **Bed** class is **HospitalWardPackage::Bed**. Using the fully qualified name distinguishes *this* class from a **Bed** class in any other package, such as in **HospitalInventory**.

A dotted arrow between two packages signifies dependency. In this example, the arrowhead at each end of the arrow shaft reveals a dependency in each direction. The rightward arrow indicates that **PatientPackage** depends on **Hospital-WardPackage** (perhaps **Patient** refers to the occupied **Bed**) and the leftward arrow indicates that **HospitalWardPackage** depends on **PatientPackage** (perhaps **Nurse** contains a reference to **Patient**).

The UML package diagram in Fig. 7.2 illustrates how packages can be contained within packages, much as folders can be contained within folders in file-management utilities.

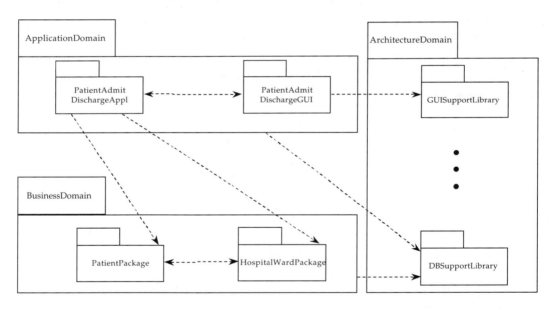

*Fig. 7.2: A UML package diagram for an application.*

The **BusinessDomain** package is simply a grouping of the two packages we saw earlier. The **ArchitectureDomain** package is a grouping of purchased library packages for the hardware/software platform on which the application is to be run: **GUISupportLibrary** (which contains classes to implement graphical user interface features) and **DBSupportLibrary** (which contains third-party add-on classes for database support). The vertical ellipses indicate that there are other libraries in the **ArchitectureDomain** package.

The **ApplicationDomain** package contains two packages that are specific to a single application for patient admission and discharge.

The **PatientAdmitDischargeAppl** package contains the software that implements the policies and procedures for admitting and discharging a patient. Since the classes in this package make many references to classes in both **PatientPackage** and **HospitalWardPackage**, I placed dependency arrows from **PatientAdmitDischargeAppl** to **PatientPackage** and **HospitalWardPackage**. Alternatively, I could have shown this with a single arrow to the entire **BusinessDomain** package.

The **PatientAdmitDischargeGUI** package contains the software for the interface to the application. The classes within the **PatientAdmitDischargeGUI** package are built using artifacts from the **GUISupportLibrary**—hence the dependency arrow from the former to the latter.

### 7.1.2 Deployment diagrams for hardware artifacts

Figure 7.3 illustrates the hardware technology of a three-tier client-server system.[2] On the users' desks, workstations are connected to a departmental file-server via a local-area network (LAN). The departmental file-server may hold individual objects (specifically, their instance variables) and/or the executable code for object classes. The departmental file-servers are, in turn, connected to the corporate server via a wide-area network (WAN). The corporate server may contain information that is central to the corporation or that needs to be kept securely. Each department has an operator workstation that is directly connected to the file-server via LAN and to the corporate server via WAN.

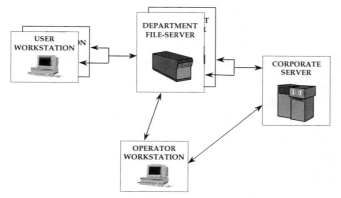

Fig. 7.3: *A schematic of the technology in a three-tier client-server business system.*

---

[2] I use the term *tier* to mean hardware tier.

Figure 7.4 shows an abstraction of Fig. 7.3 called a UML *deployment diagram*, which depicts the location of the technology units and the communication links between them.[3]

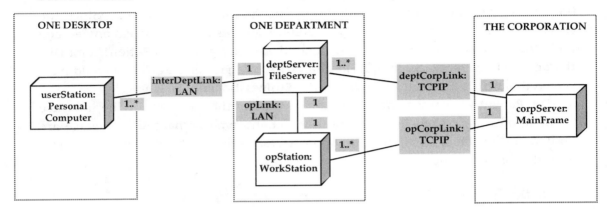

*Fig. 7.4:   A deployment diagram for the three-tier client-server business system.*

The example in Fig. 7.4 shows that several user workstations are connected to a single departmental file-server via a local communication link (named **inter-DeptLink**, of class **LAN**). Each departmental file-server is attached to an operator workstation via a link (named **opLink**, also of class **LAN**). The departmental file-servers and the operator workstations are connected to the corporate server via links (named **deptCorpLink** and **opCorpLink**, respectively, both of class **TCPIP**).

A deployment diagram, such as the one in Fig. 7.4, is a framework to which you can attach all kinds of statistics and model numbers to specify the technology units and their links. For example, you might specify a certain workstation to be of class **Blatz-888-100** (a fabulous workstation from Ignatius Blatz Enterprises), with so many gigabytes of RAM and so many terabytes of fixed-disk. Or, you might define **interDeptLink** to be of class **MellactoLAN** (the best-selling LAN from Sid Melly Networks), with a certain protocol and bandwidth.

You may also indicate the multiplicity of the connected nodes, as I have in Fig. 7.4. For example, we see from the diagram that each **userStation** is connected to exactly one **deptServer** and that a given **deptServer** has at least one **userStation** connected to it.

---

[3] This is roughly equivalent to the architecture-interconnect diagram of [Hatley and Pirbhai, 1988] and [Hatley et al., 2000].

### 7.1.3 Deployment diagrams for software constructs

In Fig. 7.5, there are three processors: a guidance machine (a Blatz Super5000), a main control-surface controller (a WiggleZap 2B), and a backup control-surface controller (also a WiggleZap 2B). The guidance machine talks to each control-surface controller via a guidance bus.

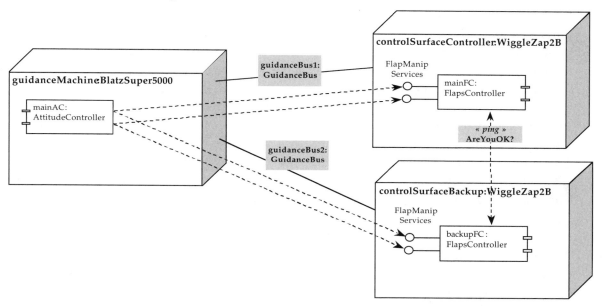

*Fig. 7.5:   A deployment diagram for part of a (simplified) aircraft-control system.*

Well, that's all hardware stuff—like the deployment diagram in Fig. 7.4. But Fig. 7.5 also has software allocations.[4] Each control-surface controller has a flaps controller running on it (each an instance of **FlapsController**). Also, the guidance machine has an attitude controller running on it.[5] These three pieces of software are UML *software components*, each depicted by a rectangle with little open bars on one side.[6]

---

[4] This deployment diagram is roughly equivalent to the architecture-flow diagram of [Hatley and Pirbhai, 1988] or the processor model of [Ward and Mellor, 1985].

[5] An attitude controller controls the various flight angles of the airplane and not, as one of my students thought, the mood of the passengers.

[6] Oddly, the "little open bars on one side" have no connectional purpose in UML diagrams (although the "little open lollipops" certainly do, as we shall see). My colleague Stan Kelly-Bootle points out that little open bars should *always* have a connectional purpose. Nevertheless, when I draw a software component on a whiteboard, I replace the bars with little lines—or nothing at all.

The criteria for designating UML software components seem to vary from shop to shop. Formally speaking, a UML software component is any element of software that has both an abstract specification (as an interface) and a concrete realization (as a body).[7] I've seen some shops define a software component to be any separately compilable software unit, including: a class; a dynamically linked library (DLL); a C++ pair, comprising a header file (**.h**) and a code file (**.cpp**); or a CORBA IDL interface wrapped around a body of legacy code. Other shops choose packages to be the software components of deployment diagrams, using the component symbol to depict the package, rather than the UML symbol that I introduced in Section 7.1.1.[8]

But now, back to Fig. 7.5. A component interface—a "little lollipop," such as those on the left side of **flapsController**—shows a service that a software component makes available to the outside world, via an interface. In this example, I've shown **FlapManipServices**, an interface that provides operations (such as, say, **setAngle**) for manipulating flaps. (Another interface might be **FlapTestServices**.)

A dashed arrow pointing to a component interface represents communication. The initiator of the communication is at the tail end. However, information may pass in both directions, as with the in- and out-arguments of a message. For example, in Fig. 7.5, I added a "ping" between the main and backup flap-controller components to illustrate the application of a UML stereotype to a deployment diagram's communication arrow. The ping allows each component to check the other's operational status periodically. The **«ping»** stereotype can then be defined for protocol, frequency, and so on.

Sometimes, you need to model explicitly certain architectural relationships, such as which software components run on which hardware nodes. Figure 7.6 uses two stereotypes to accomplish this.

---

[7] I elaborate on this definition in Chapter 15.

[8] When I recently proposed to Professor Sid Dijkstra—an internationally feted expert on the UML package symbol—that UML's package and component symbols be merged into a single symbol, he was aghast. "Meilir, you idiot!" he exclaimed with vehemence. "Don't you realize that packages depict static, lexical properties of systems, whereas components depict dynamic, run-time structure?" Oh well—can't win 'em all, I suppose!

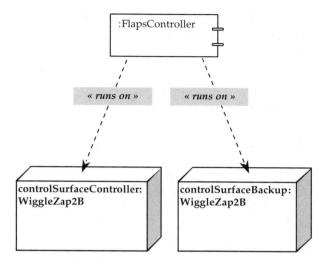

*Fig. 7.6: A form of deployment diagram that shows which software components may run on which hardware nodes.*

Figure 7.7 models a less specific relationship, answering the general question, "Which hardware platforms are compatible with a given software component?"

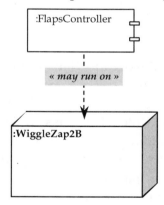

*Fig. 7.7: A less specific form of deployment diagram.*

Deployment diagrams are also found in business shops, as often as in real-time shops—although "as rarely" may be a better description of my experience. For example, in Fig. 7.8, we see a deployment diagram for part of a bank's automated teller application. The **atmProcessor** (a **ScroogeTeller86** machine) communicates via the **atmLink** (a **WAN**) with the **regionalAccountServer** (a **DataBlast12A** machine). On the **atmProcessor**, there's a software component (**CashDispenser**) that controls the doshing out of moolah to the customer. This component communicates with another software component (**AccountDataServer**), which deals with account data via the interface **AccountServices**.

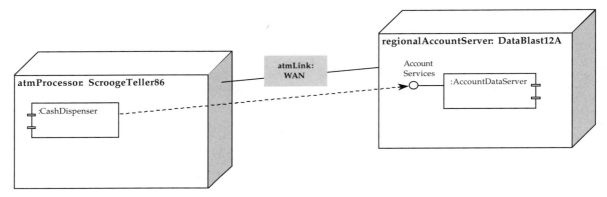

*Fig. 7.8: A deployment diagram for part of a bank's automated teller system.*

## 7.2 Depicting the Human Interface

This section covers two additional diagrams, for window layout and window navigation. Although these two diagram types are not part of traditional UML, they're indispensable for building a typical modern system with a GUIful of windows.

The window-layout diagram, which I discuss in Section 7.2.1, captures the properties of each individual window. The window-navigation diagram, which I explore in Section 7.2.2, captures the transitions among the windows that form the application-specific navigation paths. Section 7.2.3 is a short digression on the "object orientedness" of graphical user interfaces.

### 7.2.1 The window-layout diagram

As Fig. 7.9 shows, a window-layout diagram corresponds in many ways to the actual window that will be delivered for this part of the application. In this case, the application is a sales system.

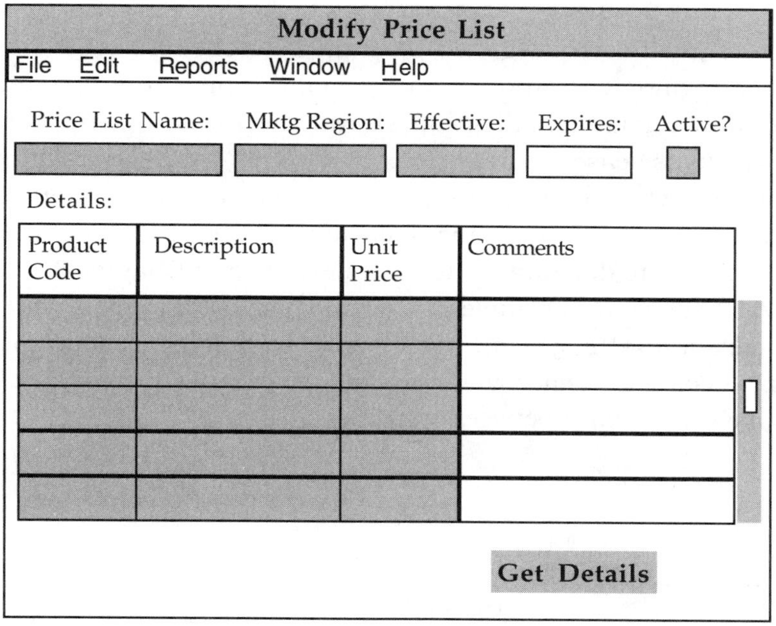

*Fig. 7.9: Example of a window-layout diagram.*

Early in the project—perhaps during a prototyping effort—the diagram will show the fields, buttons, and menus of the windows, but it will not be cosmetically correct. For example, the fields may be unaligned and the colors and fonts may be arbitrary. Later, the development team can enhance the diagram's appearance so that it's more in line with the shop's GUI standards. For example, if the final product will have mandatory fields in cyan and optional fields in white, the team can adjust the window-layout diagram to distinguish the two kinds of field.

Especially during prototyping, the window-layout diagram may be a rough-and-ready tool. Indeed, some shops develop theirs on large yellow sticky notes and slap them up on whiteboards. (This approach is termed *lo-tech* or *lo-fi UI prototyping.*) Other shops maintain their diagrams in machine-readable form, but not necessarily using a purpose-built windowing tool.

The main purpose for the window-layout diagram is to provide a framework for further design specification, which includes required field cross-validations, field synchronizations, database lookups, and so on. A nontrivial window-layout diagram may be the source of several pages of window specifications.

## 7.2.2 The window-navigation diagram

The purpose of a window-navigation diagram is to show how the users may traverse from one window to another along major, application-meaningful paths. Often, a window-navigation diagram shows the human-computer interaction paths for a single use case.

The window-navigation diagram is a straightforward adaptation of the screen-transition diagram (see, for example, [Yourdon, 1989, p. 392]), which is itself an adaptation of the state diagram structure I described in Chapter 6.

Figure 7.10 shows an example of a window-navigation diagram for the product-pricing part of a sales system. I've inserted stereotypes for the specific roles of the diagram's symbols: **«window»** for a window; **«cb»** for a command button; and **«nav»** for a navigation path between windows.

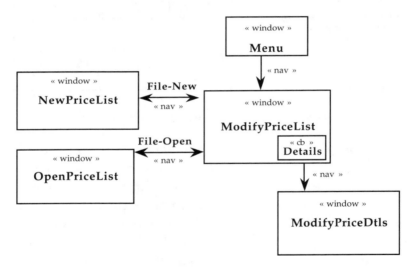

*Fig. 7.10: Example of a window-navigation diagram.*

From a menu, the user arrives at the main window (**ModifyPriceList**) for modifying the price list for a product. At that point, he may select **New** from the pull-down menu under **File**, which will take him to the **NewPriceList** window for starting a new price list. Alternatively, he may select **Open** from the pull-down menu under **File**, which will take him to the **OpenPriceList** window to retrieve an existing price list. In any case, he must return to the **ModifyPriceList** window, where he may then inspect the details of the price list by clicking the **Details** button. He need not return from the **ModifyPriceDtls** window (because, presumably, he may exit from the entire price list modification while he still has that window open).

A window-navigation diagram shows only an abstraction of each window. (The window-layout diagram has the job of showing a window's details.) It shows just the buttons, double-clicks, and so on, that cause transitions from one window to another. Similarly, it shows only the menu items and sub-items that cause transitions. Figure 7.11 provides a key to the symbols of the window-navigation diagram.

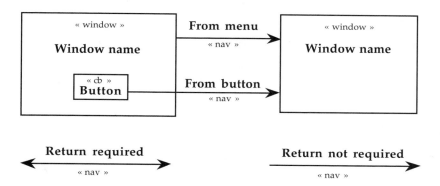

*Fig. 7.11: Key to symbols on a window-navigation diagram.*

Figure 7.12 shows a navigation diamond, which is used to indicate a branch point between two alternative navigation paths. From the main menu (of an order-entry application, in this case), the user arrives at a window for selecting customers. Presumably, this window lists customers (objects of class **Customer**) in a table, with enough information in the columns (such as name and address) for the user to recognize each customer. The user may then select a customer with a mouse—to "bring focus to a customer row." We'll term this selected customer **focusCust**.

Once the user has selected the **focusCust**, the **New Order** button becomes enabled. Clicking this button takes the user to the window for adding the **focusCust**'s new order. However, there are two groups of customers for this company: domestic and overseas. The latter group requires a special window for order entry, with all kinds of special fields for customs, letters of credit, export authorization, and whatnot.

The application must take the user to the order-entry window that's appropriate for that **focusCust**. I show this navigational fork in the road as a black diamond with two paths leading from it, one to each kind of order-entry window. Alongside each navigation path, a Boolean guard expression in brackets indicates which path is enabled for a given customer.

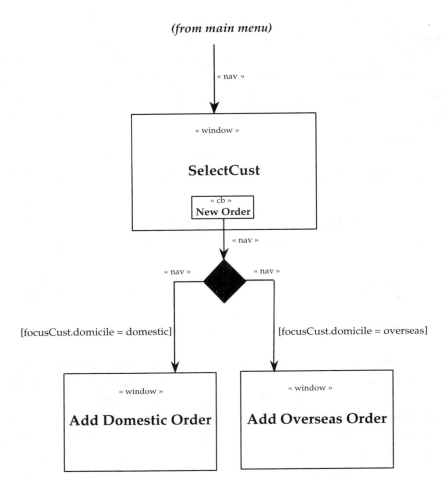

*Fig. 7.12: Alternative navigation paths.*

As a matter of human-interface design, navigation diamonds should be used sparingly, because their overuse may confuse the user. However, when you do need to model them, the diamonds and their guards are very expressive.

### 7.2.3 A brief digression: What's object oriented about a GUI?

Like object orientation itself, graphical user interfaces have attracted diverse responses. Some effervescent folk see GUIs as the pièce de résistance of object orientation, exclaiming, "Wow! GUIs! That means having objects on the screen.

Hey, we're object oriented. Yippee!" But other folks, glum souls, complain that graphical user interfaces shouldn't even be mentioned in a book on object orientation. My view is that since the modern GUI has object-oriented aspects, both philosophically and practically, it does belong in a book on O.O. So, first the philosophy, then the practice.

A system that presents itself to its users as a cooperating set of windows normally follows the *object-action paradigm*. This means that a user selects an object with a single mouse-click (where the object is perhaps shown as an icon or as a row in a table) and then applies an action to the object (perhaps via a menu selection or a double mouse-click).

The object-action paradigm brings object orientation out to the human interface. I say this because the idea of first identifying an object and then requesting it to do something corresponds exactly to sending a message, where we first identify an object by its handle and then invoke one of its operations.

Another object-oriented concept, polymorphism, may also be important in the human interface. As I mentioned in Chapter 2, you may highlight an object on a window and then "tell it to print itself." *How* it prints itself will depend on whether the selected object is a spreadsheet, a text document, or a diagram.

On the practical side, object-oriented design is an approach that's very appropriate for building a system's human interface. You can design the user interface just like any other object-oriented application. For example, when a window of class **UpdatableWindow** closes, it sends a message to a **SaveIgnoreOrCancel** window to warn the user that changes may be lost. (The class **UpdatableWindow** may inherit from the class **Window**.)

Window objects may also exchange messages with business objects. As a simple example, a window of class **ProductItemWin** may send a message to an object of class **ProductItem** in order to display the **sellByDate** of a particular product item that's on the window.

Thus, in both the philosophical (object-action) sense and in the practical (object-oriented design) sense, graphical user interfaces will have a prominent place on the object-oriented stage for many years to come.

## 7.3 Summary

This chapter presented additional modeling notation necessary for developing systems, especially ones with a sophisticated system architecture or a graphical user interface.

UML offers two complementary diagrams for capturing the software and hardware aspects of system architecture. The first is the *package diagram*, which depicts groupings of purely software elements. This diagram is valuable for modeling the high-level structure of the software to be implemented.

The second diagram is the *deployment diagram*, which depicts the technology units (especially hardware such as processors and mass storage, together with their physical communication links) on which the system will be implemented. The deployment diagram can also model how software will be distributed across the chosen technology units, by superimposing software components and their interconnections onto a deployment diagram that represents pure physical technology (such as processors).

A software component is a body of run-time code with a well-defined interface that provides services to other components. In practice, a software component on a deployment diagram may be a dynamically linked library, a package, or even (rarely) a single object. Some shops, rightly or wrongly, choose packages to be the software components that they show on their deployment diagrams.

The *window-layout diagram* defines the content of a window to be delivered as part of a system's human interface. It approximates the layout of the windows, but doesn't contain every eventual cosmetic refinement. The window-layout diagram serves both as a prototype of the ultimate window and as a framework on which to specify field validations, window/field behavior, messages between business objects, and so on.

The *window-navigation diagram*, which depicts application-meaningful paths between windows, allows interface designers and users to explore interface navigation before the system is built. It abstracts each window as a skeletal rectangle that bears the window's navigational buttons. The paths between windows appear as arrows, annotated where necessary with menu-selection choices. I use UML stereotypes to indicate windows, buttons, and navigation paths. I also use a navigation diamond where the navigation paths divide, and I place guard expressions along the exit paths of the diamond.

## 7.4 Exercises

1.  The partitioning of software across units of technology can occur at several "levels of granularity." For example, an entire subsystem could live on one processor and another subsystem on another processor. Can you think of other levels of partitioning, especially ones that are finer than the subsystem level, that would be possible with an object-oriented system? (Hint: In what ways could you partition objects and the classes to which they belong?)

2.  The fragment of a window-navigation diagram in Fig. 7.13 shows three windows from the interface to a customer-information system. Start with the window **SelectCust** and, judging from the navigation paths and the names of the windows and buttons, guess what happens at each window shown. To which diagrams would you turn to confirm or refute your speculation?

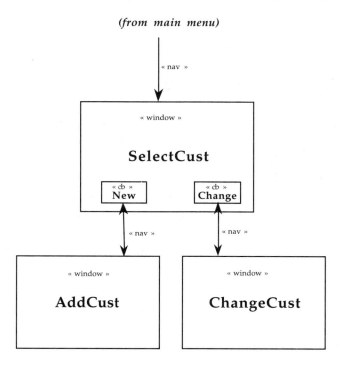

Fig. 7.13: Three windows in part of a window-navigation
diagram.

## 7.5 Answers

1.  One possibility is that the objects of a particular class are distributed across processors. For example, we may have a machine in Paris, a machine in Tokyo, a machine in Rio de Janeiro, and a machine in Terre Haute. The objects of class **Customer** could then be distributed across these machines, for the obvious reason of efficiency: We want to access our Japanese customers quickly on the Tokyo machine, for example. The code for the class **Customer** would presumably be fully replicated on the four machines, because the code must execute on all four machines. Partitioning a population of objects like this is termed *horizontal partitioning*.

    The objects could also be fully replicated, perhaps to allow the Paris office quickly to access information about *les Hoosiers*. However, such redundancy would make it complicated to maintain mutual consistency across copies of the same object.

    You could even split an individual business object into parts that abide on different machines. This is a very fine partitioning, but it might prove useful in some circumstances. For example, say you've designed a class Customer for an application handling both shipping and finances. Customer's objects will thus contain aspects of financial information, shipping information, credit information, and so on.

    Even when designing non-distributed applications, you should try to split a large class (one like **Customer**, which probably contains a multitude of attributes) into several "aspect" classes, using the composition construct to link their objects. For example, you could create three customer aspects: **CustomerFinancials**, **CustomerShipping**, and **CustomerProfile**. An object of class **Customer** would contain references to the objects of all three. As we saw in Section 7.1.1, these customer aspect classes could then be grouped for convenience into a package named **CustomerPackage**.

    If the Rio office is purely a shipping office, then perhaps the objects at that location will rarely be asked to provide customers' financial information. Therefore, the **CustomerFinancials** class and all its instances could be dropped from the Rio machine in order to save space (and possibly to enhance security). A message from a **Customer** object on the Rio machine to a **CustomerFinancials** object would therefore require network communication. (Of course, network security may be weaker than the Rio machine's security!)

Splitting objects apart in this manner is termed *vertical partitioning.* Vertical partitioning introduces problems of consistency again (for example, ensuring that the physically separated pieces are kept consistent) and is usually implemented so that at least one machine holds whole, unpartitioned objects.

A third possibility is that a class lives on one machine and its objects live on another. In this case, the second machine may specialize in holding and manipulating large volumes of information (as a so-called database engine), while the first machine may specialize in processing or number-crunching. To execute a message, the appropriate object is transferred from the second machine to the first. For this approach to be worthwhile in efficiency, the two machines should normally be close to each other.

Although there are several other ways to partition object-oriented software, the above three are the most typical. Incidentally, notice again how important it was in the above paragraphs to maintain the distinction between the term "class" and the term "object."

2.    From the main menu in Fig. 7.13, the user arrives at a window for selecting customers, which operates similarly to the **SelectCust** window of Fig. 7.12. But once the user has selected a customer (say, **focusCust**), the **Change** button becomes enabled. Clicking this button takes the user to the **ChangeCust** window for modifying customer information.

When the **ChangeCust** window is displayed, the user can review all of the externally visible information about the customer represented by the **focusCust** object, and he can modify any of the updatable fields on the window. He must return from this window to the selection window (as indicated by the two-way arrow). In other words, he can only close the **ChangeCust** window and return focus to the **SelectCust** window; he cannot open some other window, such as one for adding a customer.

The **AddCust** window for adding a new customer operates similarly to the window for modifying an existing one. However, the **New** button on the **SelectCust** window is presumably always enabled, whether the user has a customer selected or not. (There's no need to select an existing customer in order to add a new one.)

Some of the above explanation is speculative. To confirm my speculations in practice, we should also look at the window-layout diagrams for the three windows, which list the fields that each window contains. More importantly, the definitions behind the diagrams tell us what each window does when it opens and closes, when each of its buttons becomes enabled and disabled, what happens when a button is clicked, what the validation rules are for fields, and so on. Together with the window-navigation diagram, window-layout diagrams would complete our understanding of this piece of the graphical user interface.

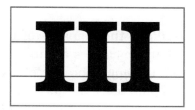

"The logic of our understanding contains the laws of correct thinking upon a particular class of objects."

—Immanuel Kant, *Critique of Pure Reason*

# Part III: The Principles of Object-Oriented Design

The chapters of Part III cover the principles behind good object-oriented design and the criteria by which you can evaluate the quality of your designs. In other words, Part III addresses the question, What makes a good object-oriented design and what makes a bad one?

The question is certainly meaningful, for I've seen object-oriented code in one application that was extensible and modifiable and object-oriented code in another application that was hideous, gnarled, and infuriating to maintain. Since the programming of the two applications was similar and the requirements that the applications were trying to implement were similar, the variation must have been due to the applications' design structure. (Then again, maybe the designer of the second application was also hideous, gnarled, and infuriating.)

I begin Chapter 8 by contrasting the encapsulation structure of object-oriented software with that of traditional software. I then build the idea of connascence upon the principle of encapsulation. Connascence, which is a generalization of structured design's coupling and cohesion to more complex encapsulation structures, is a yardstick of how well a designer has exploited the potential encapsulation that object orientation offers.

Classes at distinct levels of design abstraction have distinct design characteristics and properties. They also have different degrees of reusability. Chapter 9

207

outlines the domains of classes that you're likely to find in an application, and what the classes are in each domain. The chapter introduces a quantitative metric, the encumbrance of a class, and shows how it relates to class domains. The chapter uses the idea of domains and encumbrance to evaluate three kinds of class cohesion. (Class cohesion indicates how closely knit the attributes and operations of a given class are and whether they "belong together" in that class.)

Chapters 10 and 11, which explore the design fundamentals of object orientation, are at the heart of Part III. Chapter 10 introduces the ideas of state-space and the behavior of classes, along with the concepts of class invariants and operation preconditions/postconditions, which form the foundations of design by contract. Chapter 11 looks at the properties of subclasses in terms of state-spaces, together with the design principles of type conformance and closed behavior, which guide the development of robust class hierarchies.

In Chapter 12, I use concepts from the earlier chapters of Part III to identify and remove the dangers that lurk in some object-oriented constructs, including the prized mechanisms of inheritance and polymorphism. Chapter 13 dissects two actual designs to illustrate techniques for operation organization that can improve the resilience of class design. Chapter 14 further addresses the question of what constitutes good object-oriented design by inspecting the quality of a class's interface and by showing the criteria for a class to properly implement an abstract data-type.

# Encapsulation and Connascence

This chapter covers the two fundamental properties of object-oriented system structure: encapsulation and connascence. Although both of these properties of software structure were present in traditional systems, object orientation, with its new complexities, elevates their significance considerably. The understandability and maintainability of object-oriented software—even the value of object orientation itself—rest fundamentally on encapsulation and connascence.

In the first section of this chapter, I discuss encapsulation; in the second, I discuss connascence and then explore how good object-oriented software depends on a combination of good encapsulation and good connascence.

## 8.1 Encapsulation Structure

As I mentioned in Chapter 1, software emerged in the 1940s from the primeval swamp as a collection of unicellular creatures known as machine instructions. Later, these evolved into other unicellular creatures known as lines of assembler code. But a grander structure soon appeared, in which many lines of code were gathered into a procedural unit with a single name. This was the subroutine (or procedure), with examples such as **computeLoanRepayment** and the all-time star of The Subroutine Hall of Fame, **computeSquareRoot**.

The subroutine introduced encapsulation to software. It was the encapsulation of lines of code into a structure one level higher than that of the code itself. The subroutine was a marvel of its time. As I mentioned in Chapter 1, it saved precious machine memory by hiving off dozens of instructions, and it saved human memory, too, by giving programmers a single term (such as **computeLoan-Repayment**) to refer to dozens of lines of code. No wonder the subroutine's advent induced boundless rapture among ecstatic programmers and gave rise to all-night coding parties.

### 8.1.1 Levels of encapsulation

I term the subroutine's level of encapsulation *level-1* encapsulation. (Raw code, with no encapsulation, has *level-0* encapsulation.) Object orientation introduces a further level of encapsulation. The class (or object) is a gathering together of subroutines (known as operations) into a yet higher-level structure. Since operations, being procedural units, are already at level-1 encapsulation, the class is at *level-2* encapsulation. See Fig. 8.1.

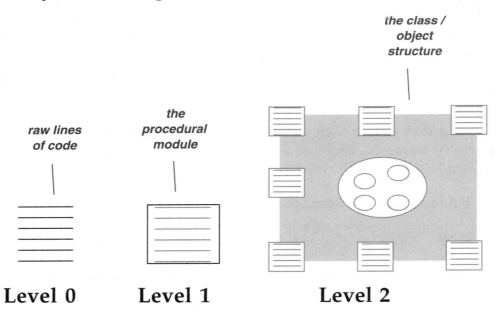

Fig. 8.1: *Three levels of encapsulation exhibited by software constructs.*

My analogy between organisms and software structures, though far from profound, isn't entirely gratuitous. Procedural modules, such as those found in structured design, didn't realize the reusability people expected.[1] Classes stand alone far better than procedures do. Classes come closer to biological organs in their ability to be transplanted from application to application. And components, which I discuss in Chapter 15, do even better than classes!

"But why stop at level-2 encapsulation?" you ask. A good question! We are already seeing level-3 and level-4 encapsulation, in which classes are grouped into even higher-level structures, such as the packages and components I discuss in Chapters 7 and 15. Outside level-3 and higher structures, only *some* classes (or parts of their interfaces) are made visible.

Business classes in a large object-oriented organization are often grouped "horizontally" into level-3 structures by respective subject area, much as we did in Chapter 7. For example, an airline might have a subject area related to the passenger, another for the airport, another for the personnel, and another for the aircraft. Since a class related to a passenger's frequent-flyer program wouldn't have much to do with a class for aircraft inventory, the two classes could be encapsulated in two different level-3 packages.

Level-3 structures can also be grouped "vertically."[2] For example, classes that would work together to implement the policy for **UpgradeFrequentFlyer** might include: **Passenger** (especially its **Preferences** and **FrequentFlyer** aspects), **Reservation**, **Leg** (of a **Flight**), **AirplaneSeatingConfiguration**, **Seat**, and lowlier classes such as **PrioritizedQueue**, **Date**, **Time**, and so on.

(By the way, a typical policy to move frequent fliers who've requested upgrades from economy to first class is triggered, say, 72 hours before departure. The system assigns each passenger wishing to upgrade a priority according to a combination of **FrequentFlyer.status**, **Reservation.dateMade**, **Reservation.fareBasis**, and so on. The highest-priority passengers are given upgrades, followed in descending order by the next-highest-priority passengers until the available seats are filled.)

---

[1] The Module of the Month Club offered an illustration of this. After joining this club, one could order the latest in tremendously reusable procedural modules. Unfortunately, the club soon went out of business.

[2] A *horizontal group* of classes comprises classes from the same domain that do not necessarily interact. (Packages typically exhibit this structure.) A *vertical group* of classes interact to implement a piece of business activity; they typically come from several domains. (Components normally exhibit this structure.) For more on which classes belong to which domains, see Section 9.1.

## 8.1.2 Design criteria governing interacting levels of encapsulation

Table 8.1 summarizes some traditional structured-design criteria in terms of the encapsulation levels of Section 8.1.1. It shows which criterion applies to each pair of encapsulation levels. For example, cohesion is a classic measurement of the quality of the relationship between a procedure (a level-1 construct) and the lines of code (level-0 constructs) within the procedure. I briefly describe each of the table's boxes in the paragraph and definitions that follow it.

*Table 8.1.*

*The Structured-Design (or Level-1) Criteria Governing Interrelationships Among Elements at Each Pair of Encapsulation Levels.*

| FROM: / TO: | level-0 construct (line of code) | level-1 construct (procedure) |
|---|---|---|
| level-0 construct (line of code) | Structured programming | Fan-out |
| level-1 construct (procedure) | Cohesion | Coupling |

The principles of structured programming govern the relationship between a line of code and other lines of code within the same procedure. Fan-out, cohesion, and coupling are terms from structured design.[3]

- *Fan-out* is a measure of the number of references to other procedures by lines of code within a given procedure.
- *Cohesion* is a measure of the "single-mindedness" of the lines of code within a given procedure in meeting the purpose of that procedure.
- *Coupling* is a measure of the number and strength of connections between procedures.

---

[3] See, for example, [Page-Jones, 1988] and [Yourdon and Constantine, 1979] for detailed discussions of fan-out, cohesion, and coupling.

Table 8.2 is an extension of Table 8.1 to include level-2 encapsulation. Notice that although the original (level-0 and level-1) section remains basically the same, level-2 encapsulation gives us five more boxes to name.

Class cohesion is an obvious analogue to the cohesion of a procedure, but it's at one level of encapsulation higher. It refers to the single-mindedness of a set of operations (and attributes) in meeting the purpose of the class. Class coupling is a measure of the number and strength of connections between classes.

Although the other three boxes don't have names, we could give them names (or we could dig out names from the mystic depths of the object-oriented literature). Then we'd have nine names. And, if we included level-3 encapsulation, we'd have sixteen names.

But enough names already! When the number of fundamental particles of physics exploded, physicists began to wonder whether their particles were quite so fundamental after all. When the number of fundamental design criteria explodes like this, perhaps we should look for a deeper criterion behind them all. If we can find such a criterion, then it should apply to software elements at all levels of encapsulation—even level-5, if we're ever blessed with such a level.

In the next section, I propose such a criterion: *connascence*.

*Table 8.2.*
*An Extension of Table 8.1 to Include Level-2 Encapsulation (Classes).*

| TO: / FROM: | level-0 construct (line of code) | level-1 construct (operation) | level-2 construct (class) |
|---|---|---|---|
| level-0 construct (line of code) | Structured programming | Message fan-out | — |
| level-1 construct (operation) | Cohesion | Coupling | — |
| level-2 construct (class) | — | Class cohesion | Class coupling |

## 8.2 Connascence

*Connascence*, which is derived from Latin, means "having been born together." An undertone to this meaning is "having intertwined destinies in life." Two software elements that are *connascent* (or that *connate)* are born from some related need—perhaps during requirements analysis, design, or programming—and share the same fate for at least one reason. Following is the definition of *connascence* as it applies to software:

> *Connascence* between two software elements **A** and **B** means either
>
> 1. that you can postulate some change to **A** that would require **B** to be changed (or at least carefully checked) in order to preserve overall correctness, or
>
> 2. that you can postulate some change that would require both **A** and **B** to be changed together in order to preserve overall correctness.

In this section, I explore the varieties of connascence. My chief purpose is to present the concept as a general way to evaluate design decisions in an object-oriented design, even if that design includes level-3 or level-4 encapsulation structures.

### 8.2.1 Varieties of connascence

I'll begin with a simple, non-O.O. example of connascence. Let's take software element **A** to be the single line of traditional code declaring

     **int** i;        *// line A*

and element **B** to be the assignment:

     i := 7;        *// line B*

There are at least two examples of connascence between **A** and **B**. For instance, in the (unlikely) situation that **A** were changed to **char i;** then **B** would certainly have to be changed, too. This is *connascence of type.* Also, if **A** were changed to **int j;** then **B** should be changed to **j := 7;.** This is *connascence of name.*

Now, some variations on the theme of connascence: The above example of **i** on lines **A** and **B** showed *explicit connascence,* which is in effect connascence that's detectable by a good text editor. In other words, it's connascence that leaps off the page and says, "This element is connascent with that one."

Some connascence, however, is *implicit.* For example, in an assembler routine I once saw

```
X: JUMP Y+38
...
Y: CLEAR R1
...                 // 38 bytes of code here
    CLEAR R2        // This is the instruction being jumped to from X—call it Z
...
```

There are 38 bytes between **CLEAR R1** and **CLEAR R2**. Exactly 38 bytes! This *connascence of position* between these two innocent instructions at **Y** and **Z** is forced upon them by the nasty jump at line **X**. Although the need for this offset of precisely 38 bytes isn't apparent in the code after line **Y**, woe betide anyone who inserts another instruction somewhere in those 38 bytes.[4]

Clearly, explicitness and implicitness are neither binary nor absolute. Instead, connascence has a spectrum of explicitness. The more implicit connascence is, the more time-consuming and costly it is to detect (unless it's well documented in an obvious place). Connascence that spans huge textual distances in a class-library specification or other documentation is also likely to be time-consuming and difficult to discover.

Note that

1. Two software elements needn't communicate with each other in order to be connascent. (We saw an example of this in the connascence of position between lines **Y** and **Z** in the above assembler routine.)

---

[4] That, by the way, is exactly what a maintenance programmer did. The next time the system ran, it crashed shortly after line **X** was executed.

2.  Some forms of connascence are *directional*. If element **A** refers to an element **B** explicitly, then **A** and **B** would be *unidirectionally connascent* (the direction being *from* **A** *to* **B**). Many examples of connascence of name are directional—for example, the connascence of name introduced when one class inherits from another. If element **B** also referred to element **A** explicitly, then **A** and **B** would be *bidirectionally connascent*.

3.  Some forms of connascence are *nondirectional*. Elements **A** and **B** would be nondirectionally connascent if neither one referred explicitly to the other. For example, **A** and **B** are connascent if they use the same algorithm, although neither one refers to the other at all.

Most of the connascence I've described above is *static connascence*. That's connascence that applies to the code of the classes that you write, compile, and link. It's connascence that you can assess from the lexical structure of the code listing.

The following list (which isn't exhaustive) gives some further varieties of static connascence.

**Connascence of name**

> We saw this in the first example (lines **A** and **B**) above, in which two programming variables needed to have the same name in order to refer to the same thing. Another example: A subclass that uses an inherited variable of its superclass must obviously use the same name for the variable that the superclass uses. If the name is changed in the implementation of the superclass, then it must also be changed in the subclass if correctness is to be preserved.

**Connascence of type or class**

> We also saw connascence of type in the example with the data-type **int**. If **i** is assigned the value **7** on line **B**, then **i** should be declared to be of type **int** on line **A**.

## Connascence of convention

Let's say that the class **AccountNumber** has instances in which positive account numbers, such as 12345, belong to people; negative ones, like –23456, belong to corporations; and 00000 belongs to all internal departments. The code will be sprinkled with statements like

> **if** order.accountNumber > 0
> **then** ...

There's a connascence of convention among all the software elements touching an account number. Unless this convention of **AccountNumber** meaning is encapsulated away, these elements may be widespread across the system.[5]

The hominoid of Chapter 1 furnishes us with another example. Let's say that **Hominoid** had the attribute **direction**. **direction** could be represented in many ways, for instance

> 0 = north; 1 = east; 2 = south; 3 = west
> N = north; E = east; S = south; W = west
> 0 = north; 90 = east; 180 = south; 270 = west

Every client of **Hominoid** who uses the attribute will be exposed to the chosen convention for representing **direction**; this will create great connascence of convention. Thus, it is important to choose a decent convention (say, the third one) to represent **direction**.

## Connascence of algorithm

Connascence of algorithm is similar to connascence of convention. Example: A software element inserts symbols into a hash-table. Another element searches for symbols in the table. Clearly, for this to work, they must both use the same hashing algorithm. Another example: the encoding and checking algorithms for check-digits in a customer's account number.

A bizarre example of connascence of algorithm that I saw recently was caused by a bug in the implementation of one of a class's operations. This operation was supposed to return an array of values, sorted into ascending

---

[5] This is actually a connascence of "value/meaning convention." It's similar to hybrid coupling in structured design and has caused many a maintenance problem in systems.

order. But, because of the bug, the last two array values were always switched. Owing to the absence of the source code, no one was able to correct the bug.

So the "fix" was this: Every class that invoked this operation had code added to it that switched back the two offending array values. This yielded horrid connascence of algorithm, which hurt everyone badly when the original defect was finally corrected. Then, all the code patches (in more than forty places) had to be found and removed.

### Connascence of position

Most code in a procedural unit has connascence of position: For two lines of code to be carried out in the right execution sequence, they must appear in the right lexical sequence in the listing. There are several kinds of connascence of position, including *sequential* ("must appear in the correct order") and *adjacent* ("must appear next to each other"). Another example of connascence of position is the connascence in a message between the formal arguments in the sender and the actual arguments in the target. In most languages, you must set out actual arguments in the same sequence as the formal ones.

*Dynamic connascence* is connascence that's based on the execution pattern of the running code—the objects, rather than the classes, if you like. It, too, has several varieties:

### Connascence of execution

Connascence of execution is the dynamic equivalent of connascence of position. It comes in several kinds, including *sequential* ("must be carried out in a given order") and *adjacent* ("must be carried out with no intervening execution"). There are many examples of connascence of execution, including initializing a variable before using it, changing and reading the values of global variables in the correct sequence, and setting and testing semaphore values.

## Connascence of timing

Temporal connascence crops up most often in real-time systems. For example, an instruction to turn off an X-ray machine must be executed within $n$ milliseconds of the instruction to turn it on. This timing constraint remains true no matter how much the operating system needs to preempt the **xRay-Controller** task in order to carry out the workload of its other tasks.

## Connascence of value

Connascence of value usually involves some arithmetic constraint. For example, during the execution of a system, the **lowPointer** to a circular buffer can never be higher than the **highPointer** (under the rules of modulo arithmetic). Also, the four corners of a rectangle must preserve a certain geometric relationship in their values: You can't move just one corner and retain a correct rectangle.

Connascence of value is notorious for occurring when two databases hold the same information redundantly, often in different formats. In that situation, procedural software has to maintain a bridge of consistency between the databases to ensure that any duplicated data have identical values in each database. The maintenance of this software, which is probably performing awkward format translations, may be cumbersome.

## Connascence of identity

An example of connascence of identity is provided by a typical constraint in an object-oriented system: Two objects, **obj1** and **obj2**, each of which has a variable pointing to another object, must always point to the same object. That is, if **obj1** points to **obj3**, then **obj2** must point to **obj3**. (For example, if the sales report points to the March spreadsheet, then the operations report must also point to the March spreadsheet.) In this situation, **obj1** and **obj2** have connascence of identity; they must both point to the same (that is, identical) object.

## 8.2.2 Contranascence

So far, I've tacitly equated connascence with "sameness" or "relatedness." For example, two lines of code have connascence of name when the variable in each of them must bear the same name. However, connascence also exists in cases where *difference* is important.

First, I'll offer a trivial example. Let's say that we have two declarations:

**int** i;
**int** j;

For correctness—indeed, merely for the code to compile!—the variable names, **i** and **j**, must differ from each other. There's a connascence at work here: If, for some reason, we wanted to change the first variable name to **j**, then we'd also have to change the second name *from* **j** to something else. Thus, the two declarations are not independent.

I've heard this kind of connascence called "connascence of difference" or "negative connascence." I use the shorter term *contranascence*. Although it sounds like the opposite of connascence, contranascence is actually a form of connascence in which difference, rather than equality, must be preserved.[6]

A familiar case of contranascence crops up in object-oriented environments with multiple inheritance (the ability of a subclass to inherit from multiple superclasses). If class **C** inherits from both classes **A** and **B**, then the features of **A** and **B** should not have the same names: There's a contranascence of name between **A**'s features and **B**'s features.

As a more concrete example of contranascence, consider an application in a video-rental store.

The class **ProgramRentalItem** may inherit from both **PhysicalInventoryItem** and **RecordingMedium**. These two classes (or their superclasses) may each have an attribute named **length**. But **PhysicalInventoryItem**'s **length** may mean the physical length of an item in inches, and **RecordingMedium**'s **length** may mean the playing time of the program (the movie or whatever is on the video tape).

Although you could argue that **duration** would be a more appropriate name for the second attribute, you may have to take what you get from your class library. In our case, the class **ProgramRentalItem** needs to inherit both of the attributes named **length**, and this clash in names brings a serious problem.

---

[6] The highfalutin term for absence of connascence is *disnascence:* Two software elements are disnascent if one has absolutely nothing to do with the other. Of course, *independence* works pretty well, too!

Across an entire library of classes, of which any pair may share a subclass, there's a contranascence of name across *all* classes because of this risk of name clashes under multiple inheritance. No wonder multiple inheritance has acquired a bad reputation, and no wonder good object-oriented languages contain mechanisms that remove this rampant contranascence.[7]

### 8.2.3 Connascence and encapsulation boundaries

I'll go so far as to say that connascence and contranascence are at the heart of modern software-engineering constructs.

To explain this, I'd like to return to Section 8.1's topic, encapsulation. Although I defined encapsulation and the levels to which it may aspire, I didn't say much about why encapsulation is important.

Encapsulation is a check on connascence, especially contranascence. Imagine a system comprising 100,000 lines of code. Imagine further that the entire system resides in a single module, say a main procedure. Imagine next that you have to develop and maintain this system. The contranascence among the hundreds of variable names would of itself be a nightmare: Simply to pick a name for a new variable, you'd first have to check dozens of other names to be sure of avoiding a clash.

Another problem would be the deceptive nature of the code. Consider two lines of code that are adjacent on a source listing. You might wonder *why* the two lines are adjacent: Is it because they *must be* adjacent (owing to connascence of position) and that inserting a line would wreck the system? Or did they just *happen to* wind up adjacent when the code was all shoveled into the same module?

So, a system that's not broken into encapsulated units has two problems: rampant connascence (chiefly through contranascence), and the confusion over what is *true* connascence and what is accidental similarity or adjacency. (An example of accidental similarity would be two variables named **i**, in two entirely separate and unconnected classes. There would be no connascence of name here; either variable could be renamed **j** with no sad consequences.)

Connascence is also why object orientation "works." Object orientation eliminates—or at least tames—some of the connascence that runs wild in traditional modular systems with only level-1 encapsulation. Again, I'll explain with an example: the hash-table example of Section 8.2.1.

---

[7] One of the best language mechanisms is Eiffel's **rename** keyword. See [Meyer, 1992], for example. See also Exercise 5 in Chapter 12 for another look at this example.

I'll assume a system that maintains a single hash-table and is designed with only level-1 encapsulation (which is the level of encapsulation of, say, structured design). The system must access the hash-table from several (at least two) places in the code: location(s) that update the table and location(s) that look up symbols in the table. The code in these locations will have connascence of algorithm; if you think up a better hashing algorithm, then you'll have to find all the code locations that use the current algorithm and make the necessary changes.

Level-1 encapsulation will neither guide you to where these places are nor tell you how many places there are. Even if there are only two places with the hashing algorithm, they may be close together or far apart in the system listing. You'll be on your own (unless you can find some friendly and accurate documentation).

An object-oriented system, with at least level-2 encapsulation, has a natural home for the hashing algorithm in the single class **SymbolTable**. Although there will still be a connascence of algorithm between the operation **insertSymbol** and the operation **lookupSymbol**, the connascence will be under control. It will be encapsulated within the boundary of a single element (the class **SymbolTable**). If good object-oriented design has been used, then there will be no connascence due to the hashing algorithm anywhere else in the system (that is, anywhere outside **SymbolTable**).

### 8.2.4 Connascence and maintainability

Connascence offers three guidelines for improving system maintainability:

1. Minimize overall connascence—this includes contranascence, of course—by breaking the system into encapsulated elements.

2. Minimize any remaining connascence that crosses encapsulation boundaries. (Guideline 3, below, will help here.)

3. Maximize the connascence within encapsulation boundaries.

The above guidelines transcend object orientation. They apply to any software-construction approach with level-2 encapsulation or level-3 encapsulation, or an even higher level. Also, as you may have noticed, the guidelines express a very old principle in design: Keep like things together and unlike things apart. However, this old principle never told us what "like things" were; in fact, they're software elements with mutual connascence.

Figure 8.2 shows two classes with connascence between them. (The connascence is directional, with the direction indicated by arrowheads.) Some of this connascence (shown by the broad lines) violates object-oriented principles by connecting the internal design of one class to the internal design of another: "Like things" have been placed in different software structures.

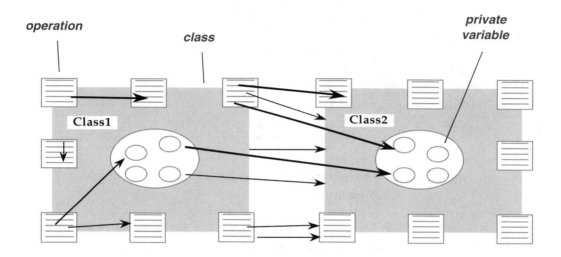

*Fig. 8.2:*  *Lines showing connascence (for example, con-*
*nascence of name), with broad lines violating*
*encapsulation boundaries.*

For example, a line from a method of **Class1** that refers to a variable within **Class2** violates object-oriented encapsulation. (Note that directional connascence violates encapsulation only when it crosses *into* an encapsulated unit.)

Figure 8.3 shows two other classes that have no offending encapsulation-busting connascence.

Connascence represents a set of interdependencies in software. Explicit connascence is apparent in the source code and can often be discovered with little more than a text editor's search or a cross-reference listing. Implicit connascence (connascence not readily apparent from the code itself) may be detectable only by human ingenuity, aided by whatever documentation exists for the system under examination.

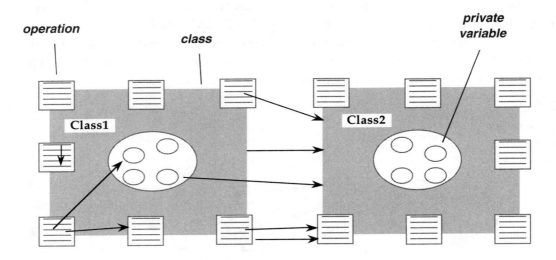

*Fig. 8.3: Lines showing connascence, with none violating encapsulation boundaries.*

The human mind is a very expensive (and fallible) tool for keeping track of widespread connascence. Implicit connascence, especially when it straddles encapsulation boundaries, presents an extra challenge to system maintainers. Implicit connascence becomes particularly difficult to track several months after the code has been designed and written. Perhaps future CASE tools will assist people in monitoring connascence and in revealing implicit connascence. This would be especially helpful in large systems that exhibit level-2 (or higher) encapsulation.

### 8.2.5 Connascence abuses in object-oriented systems

As we saw in Section 8.2.3, the level-2 encapsulation capabilities of object orientation are a tremendous boon for a designer trying to tame connascence. However, in this final section on connascence, I give three examples of how object-oriented designers sometimes violate the principle of "keeping connascence at home"—that is, within class boundaries. The first concerns the friend function of C++, the second concerns a misuse of inheritance, and the third concerns a gratuitous introduction of connascence in breach of object-oriented principles.

## 1. The friend function of C++

The friend function of C++ was created expressly to violate encapsulation boundaries. It's an element outside the boundaries of a class that has access to the private elements of objects of that class. So, if a friend function **ff** gets the handle of an object of class **C1**, it can mess about in the internals of that object willy-nilly. The connascence between **ff** and **C1** is therefore high; it includes connascence of name, type, convention, and so on. Every change that a designer makes to the internal design of **C1** will require **ff** to be thoroughly checked and possibly changed.

If **ff** is the friend of only one class, then you could argue that **ff** is really part of that class and to all intents lies within its boundary. Fair enough. However, if **ff** is also the friend of **C2**, **C3**, and **C4**, then that argument fails. Unfortunately, many C++ designs have exactly that structure . . . and with friends like those, who needs enemies!

One legitimate use of the friend construct, however, is as a scaffold to inspect the internal states of objects under test. Since object-oriented encapsulation limits white-box scrutiny of objects, it ironically hinders the testing of object-oriented systems. The friend function lifts the veil of secrecy from the implementation of the class under test.

## 2. Unconstrained inheritance

The construct of inheritance—although wildly popular in most object-oriented shops—may sometimes introduce raging connascence. If you allow a class to make use of both externally visible and internally visible elements of a superclass, then you will introduce a great deal of connascence across major (class) encapsulation boundaries. This will include connascence of name, connascence of class, and other varieties of connascence.

In a shop where I once consulted, an analysis/design team had begun to build its class library with some very well-thought-out hierarchies of Smalltalk classes. For example, **DomesticShipment** and **ExportShipment** were both (reasonably enough) subclasses of **Shipment**. However, the team's language and design strategy allowed subclasses unbridled access to programming variables within superclasses. This meant that the maintainers of subclasses **C1**, **C2**, and so forth, had to stay aware—almost on a minute-to-minute basis—of any changes to the internal design of the superclass **C**, because **C**'s maintainer could create disastrous results in descendant classes just by making an innocuous change to an (ostensibly private) variable name.

The team worked around this problem by having Jim be responsible for, say, **DomesticShipment**, **ExportShipment**, **Shipment**, and other related classes. Jim would make sure that any changes he made to **Shipment** were propagated to classes connascent with **Shipment**—and there were actually many such classes. Unfortunately, however, the rampant connascence among the classes couldn't be parceled out to individual team members like the classes themselves could. The result was that every class maintainer had the tedious chore of keeping abreast of internal design changes to all that class's superclasses. Thus every change to the class library caused high anxiety all round, since time pressures denied the team any chance to keep the library documentation up to date.

If Jim and his colleagues had taken into account the guideline that connascence should not cross encapsulation boundaries, it would have told them that inheritance by a subclass should be restricted to only those features of the superclass that are already externally visible. (Another way to say this is: The notion of inheriting abstract behavior should be divorced from the notion of inheriting the internal implementation of such behavior.[8]) Had their library been designed according to this principle, their lives would have been less fraught with trouble, and maybe they wouldn't have called their shop The Land of the Midnight Fix.

### 3.   Relying on accidents of implementation

In another shop of yore, a programmer named The Weasel—don't ask me why!—had created a class **Set** that furnished the behavior of a mathematical set. (Its operations included **add**, **remove**, **size**, and so on.) The class appeared to be well designed and written and it always performed fine.

The Weasel used **Set** in several places in his own applications. For example, he used the **retrieve** operation, which retrieved elements of the set one by one in random order until every element had been provided. However, The Weasel knew that **retrieve** happened to retrieve elements in exactly the *same* order in which they'd been added to the set, even though that wasn't documented or supposed to be a property of the operation. He made use of this accidental, undocumented fact several times in his application. He had thus

---

[8] See [Porter, 1992] for a further discussion of this point.

created a connascence of algorithm across the encapsulation boundary between his application and the internals of the **retrieve** operation.

When **Set** was later replaced by a different implementation—one that happened not to preserve order in the same way—many of The Weasel's applications blew up. Many of the users also blew up, but The Weasel was nowhere to be found. It was rumored that he had taken up another identity and had gone underground in the Middle East. So, let's all hope that The Day of The Weasel has passed forever.

### 8.2.6 *The term* connascence

Although I didn't make up the word "connascence"—it's in *Chambers' Twentieth Century Dictionary,* for example, and in *Webster's Third New International Dictionary* (as "connate")—I have taken a lot of flak over the past few years for using it. I carried out some market research on *coupling* as an alternative term, but at one shop, the developers huddled together upon hearing the word and a muttering arose in their midst. Then, turning to me, they spake as with one voice, saying: "Hey, don't waste our time with that ancient structured crap!"

I tried *interdependence* at another shop, but apparently that term was too bland to register a single blip on the team's cognitive radar. That's why I like *connascence:* It's a term that gets people's attention and doesn't need to skirt around any prior usage.

Once, however, I got burned. A developer at one shop said, "Hey, I've used connascence for years with a different meaning. I say that two objects are connascent when they get instantiated together at run-time." Since I could hardly argue with his use of the term as meaning "born together," I told him he could substitute the humbler term *interdependence* for my more general notion.[9] You can do that, too, if you like—I'm by no means wedded to *connascence.*

---

[9] If two objects *had to* be instantiated together, then I'd say that the two objects had *connascence of instantiation.* If two objects *had to* have the same lifetime, I'd say they had *connascence of lifetime*—or if I wanted to impress people, *connascence of duration.*

## 8.3 Summary

Encapsulation is a venerable concept in software. The subroutine, invented in the 1940s, introduced encapsulation of code into procedural modules; this is level-1 encapsulation. However, object-oriented structures are more sophisticated than traditional procedural structures like the subroutine. Object orientation involves at least level-2 encapsulation. In level-2 encapsulation, operations (implemented by methods) are themselves encapsulated, together with attributes (implemented by variables), into classes.

The complexities of level-2 encapsulation introduce many novel interdependencies among design elements. Rather than give each kind of interdependency its own term, I introduce the general term *connascence*. Connascence exists when two software elements must be changed together in some circumstance in order to preserve software correctness. Contranascence is a form of connascence in which difference, rather than similarity, must be preserved. Disnascence is the absence of connascence.

Connascence comes in several forms. Static connascence derives from the lexical structure of a code listing. Examples include connascence of class and connascence of convention. Dynamic connascence depends on the execution pattern of code at run-time. Examples include connascence of timing and connascence of value. Explicit connascence is immediately apparent from reading a code listing. An example is connascence of name. Implicit connascence is apparent only from a study of the code or its attendant documentation. Connascence of execution or algorithm is usually implicit. Copious implicit connascence raises software-maintenance costs.

The level-2 encapsulation of object orientation addresses the problem of potentially rampant connascence in large, modern systems. This encapsulation provides solid class structures within whose boundaries unbridled connascence can be corralled.

However, there are several ways that connascence may escape encapsulation boundaries—even in an object-oriented design. In this chapter, we saw three examples of poor design: The first was the use of C++'s friend function deliberately to nullify the benefits of object-oriented encapsulation. The second was the misguided use of inheritance to allow a subclass to inherit the implementation of a superclass. The third was allowing the internal (and probably volatile) details of a class's algorithm to be relied on by code in other classes.

The three examples above violate the central principle of object-oriented design: Minimize overall connascence—this includes contranascence, of course—by breaking the system into encapsulated elements. Then minimize any remaining connascence that crosses encapsulation boundaries by maximizing the connascence within encapsulation boundaries.

## 8.4 Exercises

1. A man I met in a pub told me that every idea in modern music can be found somewhere in Haydn's works. One could say something similar about Yourdon and Constantine's book on structured design [Yourdon and Constantine, 1979]: Its pages form a magnum opus of oft-overlooked design ideas, which are "rediscovered" time after time. Check this book to see whether Yourdon and Constantine have anything to say on the subject of connascence.

2. Use of the **goto** statement has become notorious over the past few decades as a cause of incomprehensible software. From the standpoint of connascence, can you justify the **goto**'s bad reputation?

3. Assume that you've become tired of object orientation. You want to create a new software paradigm that employs levels of encapsulation and has various forms of connascence. Explain (in a general way) how you would set forth the design criteria and guidelines for connascence and encapsulation in your paradigm.

4. This chapter discussed connascence mainly in terms of programming code. Are there any other examples of connascence that crop up in the wider context of the overall software-development project?

5. In Section 8.2.4, I suggested that implicit connascence that crosses encapsulation boundaries usually proves particularly troublesome to maintainers of an object-oriented system. Can you give examples of such connascence and suggest how to make it more explicit, and thus easier to track?

6. Further research is needed into the forms of connascence that apply to modern software-design paradigms, especially as object-oriented design becomes popular. Set up an experiment to elicit the degrees of ill caused by the different varieties of connascence (for example, connascence of name and position). The experiment could measure the effects of connascence (both within and across encapsulation boundaries) on presumed dependent factors, such as human comprehension time/cost, debugging time/cost, and modification time/cost. Perhaps you can recruit volunteers to review source code and measure their time to detect bugs deliberately seeded into the code.

## 8.5 Answers

1.  Yes, Yourdon and Constantine begin an exploration of what is essentially connascence in Chapter 3 of their book. However, after introducing connascence (under the vague term *structure)* and touching on it briefly, the chapter goes off at an angle from the general concept. Later, especially in Chapter 6, the book flirts tantalizingly with the topic again.

2.  For a long time, we've known that the undisciplined use of the **goto** statement causes the static and dynamic structures of code to diverge. In terms of connascence, it implies that static connascence of position (in the code listing) gives little clue to dynamic connascence of execution (at run-time). Since maintainers make modifications to the static code, **goto**s increase the risk that a static change will violate some connascence of execution. Furthermore, any **goto** induces an additional connascence of name between the **goto** itself and the label that's the target of the **goto**, together with contranascence among the label names themselves.

3.  Here's one possible framework on which to base a definition of a future software paradigm:

    a.  State the intended purpose and scope of applicability of your paradigm.

    b.  State the paradigm's encapsulation structure. State what the paradigm's components are and which components are contained within which.

    c.  In terms of the above encapsulation structure, state the default visibility rules of the paradigm. This will prescribe the allowed connections among components and will state the "boundaries of privacy" established by the encapsulation structure.

    d.  List the possible forms of connascence inherent in the paradigm. There will be explicit connascence, which appears in the source code, and implicit connascence, which will be more difficult to perceive because it is "invisible." As we saw, implicit connascence becomes especially subtle when it transcends the official encapsulation structure of the paradigm.

e. Classify as much as possible the pernicious effects of each form of connascence in various contexts.

f. Suggest heuristics for deriving or modifying software designed under this paradigm in order to minimize the pernicious effects mentioned above.

4. Yes, there are many examples of connascence that spans project deliverables. For instance, you can find connascence between the model of user requirements and the design model of a software implementation of those requirements. Recently, I encountered a distressingly vast connascence of name when a business decided to change the word **Customer** to **Client**. The havoc this caused was immense! A good "full project life-cycle" modeling tool could keep track of these hundreds of lines of connascence across deliverables and thereby reduce the onus on the human mind to keep track of them.

5. I recently saw two examples of implicit connascence in two separate object-oriented systems.

In the first example, a pair of classes in a business system each contained the number **5** (representing the number of office buildings the company owned). This created implicit connascence of value between the two classes, because to change one **5** (but not the other) to **6** would cause an error. If the literal constant **5** were instead denoted by **numOfOffices**, then the connascence would become explicit and less of a problem: Change the value once, and it would be changed everywhere. To do this, you would presumably store the value of **numOfOffices** in a database.

In the second example, a real-time communications application contained two objects that would issue voluminous communications across a network at exactly the same time. This caused the network to clog unnecessarily, because there was no reason that the objects *had to* start communicating simultaneously. The problem was solved when the two objects were made to stagger their transmissions. In other words, this system had an implicit contranascence of timing, which was made explicit by setting up a scheduling table for the objects' communication. (Notice that in this example, preserving the contranascence of timing is necessary for performance, rather than for strict correctness of the software.)

# Domains, Encumbrance, and Cohesion

Classes in a system are not all alike. For example, in a brokerage application you might find the classes **Equity**, **AccountPosition**, **Date**, **Time**, **List**, and **Set**. In an avionics system, you might find the classes **Flap**, **FuelTank**, **Date**, **Time**, **Set**, and **Tree**.

Notice that there's something about the classes **Equity** and **FuelTank** that sets them apart from the classes **Date** and **Set**. For example, **Equity** seems more complex, intricate, and specialized than the simple **Date** class. That's because **Equity** and **FuelTank** are from the business domain, whereas **Date** and **Set** are from the foundation domain.[1] Moreover, the classes **Equity** and **FuelTank** seem different from each other, as well, because they're from two different industries (brokerage and aviation).

I begin this chapter by defining domains of classes. In the chapter's second section, I introduce encumbrance as a quantitative measure of a class's "sophistication" and show how classes from higher domains normally have higher values

---

[1] Please note that here I mean *business* in the widest possible sense. I include businesses involving avionics, instrumentation, and microwave-oven control, along with the more traditional businesses of banking, insurance, and fishmongery.

of encumbrance. In the chapter's third section, I define a qualitative measure of a class, class cohesion, one of whose recommendations for "class goodness" is that a class should be based in one and only one domain.

## 9.1 Domains of Object Classes

A normal object-oriented system will contain classes from four major domains: the application domain, the business domain, the architecture domain, and the foundation domain. Each of these domains has several groups of classes within it:

- The *application domain*—comprising classes valuable for one application

  Event manager classes
  Event recognizer classes

- The *business domain*—comprising classes valuable for one industry or company

  Relationship classes
  Role classes
  Attribute classes

- The *architecture domain*—comprising classes valuable for one implementation architecture

  Human-interface classes
  Database-manipulation classes
  Machine-communication classes

- The *foundation domain*—comprising classes valuable across all businesses and architectures

  Semantic classes
  Structural classes
  Fundamental classes

In the next sections, I explain the significance of each domain by means of examples, beginning with the most straightforward classes at the bottom of the list above.

### 9.1.1 The foundation domain

The classes in the foundation domain are usable in many applications from many different industries running on a broad range of computer architectures. In other words, the foundation domain comprises classes with the widest possible reusability.

The foundation domain has three groups of classes: *fundamental*, *structural*, and *semantic*. Here are some examples of classes from each group:

- *Fundamental classes* include **Integer**, **Boolean**, and **Char**. These classes are so basic that many object-oriented languages include them as built-in, simple, traditional data-types.

- *Structural classes* implement structures. They read like the curriculum of a Data Structures 101 university course, including **Stack**, **Queue**, **List**, **BinaryTree**, **Set**, and so on. Also known as *container classes*, they're very often designed by means of genericity.

- *Semantic classes* include **Date**, **Time**, **Angle**, **Money**, and **Mass**. (Some people also include in this group of classes basic geometric shapes, such as **Point**, **Line**, **Polygon**, and **Circle**.) Semantic classes have a richer meaning than plain **Integer** or **Char**. Additionally, their attribute values may be expressed in units, such as hours, dollars, meters, or firkins per fortnight.

Classes in the foundation domain, by definition, may prove useful in any application in any business anywhere. A **List** or a **Date** class is as likely to show up in a medical system as in a video-library system.

A foundation class may be built upon other foundation classes. For example, **Angle** may use **Real** in its implementation, and **Polygon** may use **Set**. The way I've ordered the class domains is no accident; the classes lower down in the list tend to be used by the classes higher up, as we'll see again when we look at class cohesion in Section 9.3.

### 9.1.2 The architecture domain

The classes in the architecture domain are usable in many applications from many different industries. However, the reusability of architectural classes is limited to a single computer architecture.

The architecture domain has three groups of classes: *machine-communication*, *database-manipulation*, and *human-interface*. Here are some examples of classes from each group:

- *Machine-communication classes* include **Port** and **RemoteMachine**.
- *Database-manipulation classes* include **Transaction** and **Backup**.
- *Human-interface classes* include **Window** and **CommandButton**.

Architectural classes are useful in any application in any business, so long as the application is implemented on a physical architecture supported by those classes. In other words, there can't be a single architecture-domain class library for the whole world, because classes such as **Port** or **Backup** will have to exist in several versions for the various computer architectures that exist. So, your choice of architecture-domain library will depend on the hardware and software architecture(s) that you use in your shop.

### 9.1.3 The business domain

The classes in the business domain are useful in many applications, but only those *within a single industry*, such as banking, medicine, or avionics.

The business domain has three groups of classes: *attribute*, *role*, and *relationship*. Here are some examples of classes from each group:

- *Attribute classes* capture the properties of things in the business world. Examples are **Balance** (of a bank account) or **BodyTemperature** (of a patient). Although these classes are obviously similar to **Money** and **Temperature** (which are semantic foundation classes), they are not identical. A bank account's balance and a patient's body temperature will be subject to certain business rules that don't apply to general foundation classes. For example, the value of an account balance may be constrained to lie within certain limits. Transgression of those limits may signal an error or trigger some other business activity.

- *Role classes* derive from "roles that things play" in the business.[2] Examples are **Customer** and **Patient**. When you analyze the busi-

---

[2] A role in object-oriented analysis is analogous to the entity-type in information modeling.

ness domain, these classes are likely to be the first and most obvious classes that you identify.

- *Relationship classes* derive from associations among things in the business world. They include **AccountOwnership** (by a bank customer) and **PatientSupervision** (by a nurse).

Some business classes' applicability may be even more narrow than a whole industry: They may be useful only to a single corporation. Indeed, since some large corporations involve themselves in several businesses, the usability of a given business class may not span more than one division. For example, I know of a corporation that is developing seven different classes named **PurchaseOrder**—and the company has only nine divisions! I suspect that they could reengineer the corporation to reduce the number of incompatible **PurchaseOrder** classes. But I doubt that they could ever reduce the number to one, because no two divisions carry out purchasing in exactly the same way.

Again, we see the pattern in which classes in higher domains are built on classes in lower ones. For example, **AccountOwnership** will refer to the classes **Customer** and **Account**, and at least one attribute of **Account** will be of class **Balance**.

### 9.1.4 The application domain

A class in the application domain is used only within a single application (or a small number of related applications).

The application domain contains two groups of classes: *event-recognition* (detection that a particular event has occurred) and *event-management* (execution of the correct business policy for that particular event). Here are some examples of classes from each group:

- *Event-recognizer classes* are event daemons, software constructs that monitor input to check for the occurrence of specific events in the environment. An example is an object of class **PatientTemperatureMonitor**, which looks for the events **patient develops fever** ("he gets too hot") and **patient becomes hypothermic** ("he gets too cold"), among others.

- *Event-manager classes* carry out the appropriate business policy when an event of a given type occurs. An example of an event manager is an object of class **WarmHypothermicPatient**, which immediately sends messages to other objects to increase the patient's warmth and to summon medical attention by sounding an alarm at a nurse's station. (Of course, the **WarmHypothermicPatient** object would only become active in the event that a patient became hypothermic.) Another example, from a different hospital application, is **SchedulePatientForSurgery**. An avionics example of an event-manager class is **SetFlapLandingConfiguration**.

A class in the application domain has very narrow reusability. Indeed, most classes in this domain are relevant to only one application and so have no reusability at all. For example, **SchedulePatientForSurgery** would probably be useful only in the Surgery-Management System.

### 9.1.5 The source of classes in each domain

For most people, the ability to stock libraries with reusable software is the *sine qua non* of object orientation, and many shops rightly devote much of their design effort toward the exquisite reusability of the classes that they build. But, as we saw in the preceding sections, classes in different domains have different degrees of reusability. Classes in the lowest domain have the greatest reusability, while classes in the highest domain have the least, as Fig. 9.1 illustrates.

I realize that this is a circular argument. After all, I defined the foundation domain to be the domain of classes with universal reusability and the application domain to be that of software structures useful only with one application. Nevertheless, the issue of reusability is important when it comes to the famous old question, Where do classes come from? The answer depends greatly on the domain of class concerned.

For the foundation classes, the answer is simple: You buy them from a class vendor. Developing a foundation library is a difficult and expensive undertaking. Don't try it at home. Of course, if you do so and you manage to finish the job, you'll have all the classes you want—but you'll also spend a thousandfold more than the library would have cost.

You'll certainly have to augment your purchased foundation library with some classes of your own. That's okay. But buy, borrow, and beg any foundation classes you need before you fall back on the option of building them.

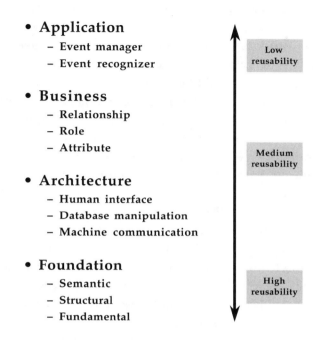

- **Application**
  - Event manager
  - Event recognizer

- **Business**
  - Relationship
  - Role
  - Attribute

- **Architecture**
  - Human interface
  - Database manipulation
  - Machine communication

- **Foundation**
  - Semantic
  - Structural
  - Fundamental

*Fig. 9.1: Domains of classes and their reusability.*

The source of classes in the architecture domain is similar to that of the foundation domain, but there are four differences:

- You may have to buy architectural classes from the vendor(s) of your hardware and software infrastructure (although third-party vendors will supply libraries for popular architectures).

- You may have to suffer annoying incompatibilities across portions of the architectural library that come from different vendors.

- Your architectural-library vendor(s) may have built on a different foundation library from yours.

- Your purchased architectural library will probably need more tailoring, custom-building, and modification than your purchased foundation library, because of the two previous points.

The classes in the business domain are especially interesting—and challenging. These are classes that aren't often possible to buy right now for at least two reasons. First, general vendors don't have the industry expertise to develop classes for hospitals or banks or aviation or telecommunications. Second, the marketplace for such a class library would be a nightmare. Every purchaser would want customization: "Our company prides itself on being special and different. The class **Product** that you sold us doesn't meet our business needs." However, even as I write, the situation is changing. We're now beginning to see business-domain classes and components (see Chapter 15) for some industries (such as, in fact, banking and telecommunications) being offered for sale.

Still, since it will be a while before such business-domain software becomes widely purchasable, today you'll almost certainly have to develop the classes in the business domain yourself. And you'll have to take great care in analyzing their requirements—using techniques such as role-relationship modeling or entity-relationship modeling—because they will become a treasure store of your company's business acumen. Also, you'll have to take great care in their design, because these classes will have significant reusability if they're well analyzed and designed—but virtually none if they're not.

The competitiveness of your company may depend on the time-to-deployment of new software systems, which will depend significantly on the quality of the business classes in your shop library. So, although you'll get a lot of mileage from your foundation and architectural libraries, the strategic success of object orientation in your corporation will eventually rest on how well you build your home-grown business-domain library.[3]

The topmost domain is the application domain. Don't worry too much about design for reusability here; however well you design, you won't get much reusability. The main source for the classes in this domain are the business events that you discover during analysis.

Perhaps "construct" would be a better term than "class" in the previous paragraphs, since event recognizers and event managers may be implemented as traditional procedures or single-instance utility packages, rather than as full-blooded classes. For example, the event manager **WarmHypothermicPatient** could become a stand-alone procedure. Alternatively, it could become the single operation of a new class, or it could become an operation of the existing class **Patient**.

---

[3] I return to the issue of business classes in purchased libraries in Exercise 1 at the end of this chapter.

## 9.2 Encumbrance

Section 9.1 treated class domains in a qualitative way. In this section, I offer a quantitative way to tell how far a class sits above the fundamental domain. The measure is called *encumbrance*.

### 9.2.1 What is encumbrance?

I thought you'd never ask! Encumbrance measures the total ancillary machinery of a class. "Total ancillary machinery" comprises all the other classes that the given class must rely on in order to work. In other words, if you count all the classes referred to by a class **C**, and then count the classes that *they* refer to, and so on, the total number will be the encumbrance of **C**.

In order to define "encumbrance" formally, I first define the terms "direct class-reference set" and "indirect class-reference set." (Note: The next few paragraphs look more difficult than they really are. Please stay tuned, because I need to define "encumbrance" formally just once, and then it will be over. If you wish to avail yourself of anesthetic, go ahead!)

> The *direct class-reference set* of a class **C** is the set of classes to which **C** refers directly.

In most object-oriented languages, a class **C** may refer directly to another class **D** in any of the following ways:

- **C** inherits from **D**.
- **C** has an attribute of class **D**.
- **C** has an operation with an input argument of class **D**.
- **C** has a variable of class **D**.
- **C** has a method that sends a message with a returned argument of class **D**.
- **C** has a method containing a local variable of class **D**.
- **C** supplies **D** as an actual class parameter to a parameterized class.
- **C** has a friend class **D** (in C++).

> Let the direct class-reference set of **C** comprise the classes $C_1$, $C_2$, ..., $C_n$.
>
> Then, the *indirect class-reference set* of **C** is the union of the direct class-reference set of **C** and the indirect class-reference sets of $C_1$, $C_2$, ..., $C_n$.[4]

This definition is obviously recursive. I can stop the recursion by saying that the class-reference set—both direct and indirect—of each class (including **Integer**, **Real**, **Boolean**) in the fundamental domain is empty. (What you choose as your fundamental domain is arbitrary; it doesn't matter what classes you pick so long as you stick to them and you define their class-reference sets to be empty.)

And now—at last—here's the definition of encumbrance:

> The *direct encumbrance* of a class is the size of its direct class-reference set. The *indirect encumbrance* of a class is the size of its indirect class-reference set.[5]

At this point, you're probably tearing your hair out. Fortunately, however, there's a much clearer and more intuitive way to look at encumbrance. Let's use an arrow to show a direct class reference. In the example shown in Fig. 9.2, the direct class-reference set of **C** is $C_1$, $C_2$, $C_3$. Thus, **C**'s direct encumbrance is simply 3.

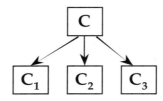

*Fig. 9.2:* **C** *and its direct class-reference set.*

---

[4] If you prefer an even more mathematical definition: The indirect class-reference set of **C** is equivalent to the transitive closure on the direct class-reference set of **C**.

[5] Some authors use the term *total class coupling* for the size of a class's direct-reference set.

Figure 9.3 shows **C**'s indirect reference set. You find the indirect encumbrance of **C** by counting all the classes in this diagram, that is, all the classes in the tree whose root is **C** and whose leaves are the fundamental classes at the bottom (denoted by $F_1$ and so forth). The indirect encumbrance of **C** is therefore 12. (Notice that I include the direct class-reference classes in my count of the indirect class-reference set.)

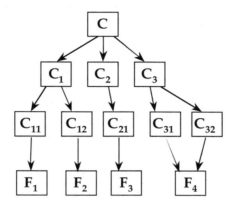

*Fig. 9.3:* **C** *and its indirect class-reference set.*

Figure 9.4 shows a concrete example of encumbrance, in which the indirect encumbrance of **Rectangle** is 4, since it has the four classes **Point**, **Length**, **Real**, and **Boolean** in its indirect reference set.[6]

*Fig. 9.4:* **Rectangle** *and its indirect class-reference set, with each class's indirect encumbrance marked.*

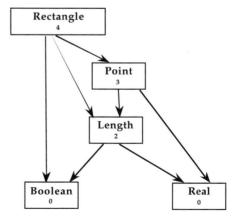

---

[6] A different design for **Rectangle** would give it a slightly different encumbrance.

Although **Real** may refer to **Boolean** (in a comparison operation) and **Integer** (in a rounding operation), I've adopted the usual "zero" convention to set the encumbrance of **Real** (and its fundamental companions) to zero.

### 9.2.2 The use of encumbrance

Encumbrance gives us a measure of class sophistication—that is, how high the class is above the fundamental domain. Thus, classes in higher domains have high indirect encumbrance and those in lower domains have low indirect encumbrance.

An unexpected indirect encumbrance may indicate a fault in class design. For example, if you find a class with high indirect encumbrance to be in a low domain, then there may be a problem with the class's cohesion. (I cover class cohesion in Section 9.3.) Alternatively, if a class in a high domain has low indirect encumbrance, then it has probably been designed from scratch; that is, the designer has built it directly from **Integer**, **Char**, and other fundamental classes, rather than by reusing intermediate classes from the library.

### 9.2.3 The Law of Demeter

Lieberherr and Holland offer the Law of Demeter as a guiding principle for limiting the direct encumbrance of a class by limiting the size of its direct reference set.[7] (However, the authors didn't actually employ the terms "encumbrance" and "direct class-reference set.") A general phrasing of the Law of Demeter is as follows:

---

[7] In Greek mythology, Demeter was the goddess of the harvest. However, this Law of Demeter derives its name from an object-oriented project named Demeter. See [Lieberherr and Holland, 1989] for further details.

> For an object **obj** of class **C** and for any operation **op** defined for **obj**, each target of a message within the implementation of **op** must be one of the following objects:
>
> 1. The object **obj** itself—specifically, **self** and **super** (in Smalltalk), **this** (in C++ and Java), or **Current** (in Eiffel).
>
> 2. An object referred to by an argument within **op**'s signature.
>
> 3. An object referred to by a variable of **obj** (including any object within collections referred to by **obj**).
>
> 4. An object created by **op**.
>
> 5. An object referred to by a global variable.

There are two versions of the law, differing only in their interpretation of Point 3. The Strong Law of Demeter defines a variable as being only a variable defined in the class **C** itself. The Weak Law of Demeter defines a variable as being either a variable of **C** or a variable that **C** inherits from its superclasses.

The Law of Demeter is eminently reasonable, for it restricts arbitrary references to other classes within a given class. Under the law, the code within **C** will refer to only the minimally feasible number of other classes. I prefer the Strong Law of Demeter to the Weak Law because it further limits the connascence across encapsulation boundaries that I decried in Chapter 8—in this case, the class boundaries of **C**'s superclasses.

As we saw in Section 8.2.4, limiting connascence in this way eases system maintenance and evolvability for two reasons:

- It frees the designer of **C**'s superclasses to redesign their internal implementation; and
- It enhances the understandability of **C**, because someone trying to understand the design of **C** isn't continually dragged into the implementation details of **C**'s superclasses or, worse, those of a completely unrelated class.

## 9.3 Class Cohesion: A Class and Its Features

*Class cohesion* is the measure of interrelatedness of the features (the attributes and operations) located in the external interface of a class.

In Table 8.2, I placed the term *class cohesion* in the quadrant formed by level 2 and level 1 to indicate that class cohesion is one encapsulation level higher than procedural-module cohesion.[8] Perhaps, however, *type cohesion* would be an even better term than *class cohesion*, since with this concept we're trying to assess how well a class "hangs together as an implementation of some abstract data-type."

A class with low (bad) cohesion has a set of features that don't belong together. A class with high (good) cohesion has a set of features that all contribute to the type abstraction implemented by the class.

People have tried to define class cohesion by considering how the methods implementing a class's operations use the class's internal variables. The idea: The more overlap in the methods' use of the variables, the higher the cohesion of the class. Although I've tried this approach, I don't find it very attractive—for the following two reasons.

The first reason is that cohesion is a property that should be apparent from the "outside" of an encapsulated software unit. Therefore, it seems wrong to have to look at a class's internals in order to assess its cohesion. The second reason is that such a measurement is unstable and too dependent on the particular internal design of methods, which may change over a class's lifetime. Therefore, an immature class (one that you're just beginning to design) may appear to have lower cohesion than a mature one (one that has grown its final, adult set of features and their implementations). That isn't good.

During my recent meanderings through object-oriented shops, I've observed three tell-tale cohesion problems in the allocation of features to classes: three problems that are observable from a class's external design. I call these three problems *mixed-instance, mixed-domain,* and *mixed-role cohesion.* Of the three, mixed-instance cohesion is typically the greatest sin and mixed-role cohesion the least.

A class can have all, some, or none of these cohesion problems. A class with none of these three mixed cohesions is entirely cohesive and is said to have *ideal cohesion.* In the following sections, I define each of the three mixed cohesions and assess their design symptoms.

---

[8] *Procedural [module] cohesion,* a term from structured design, is a measure of how well lines of code belong together within a single procedural module, such as a function or a procedure.

### 9.3.1 Mixed-instance cohesion

> A class with *mixed-instance cohesion* has some features that are undefined for some objects of the class.

For example, let's say that a sales department has both commissioned and non-commissioned salespeople. Fred is commissioned and Mary is noncommissioned. In the object-oriented application that supports the department, there is a class **Salesperson**, of which the objects pointed to by the variables **fred** and **mary** are instances.

Given the above, the first of these two messages makes sense, but the second does not:

```
fred.issueCommissionPmt;
mary.issueCommissionPmt;
```

We *could* keep both messages and set the commission of the object **mary** to zero. However, that would be a lie. Mary doesn't have zero commission; she has an undefined commission. Even so, **Salesperson** would also need a variable **whether-Commissioned:Boolean** (possibly also available as an attribute). And we should include in the operation **Salesperson.issueCommissionPmt** an **if** statement that prevents the printing of commission checks of $0.00 for "noncommissioned objects."

That would all work, but it would be an ugly design.

The real problem is that the class **Salesperson** has mixed-instance cohesion, because it is too coarse for the application: It lumps both commissioned and noncommissioned salespeople together as one class. We need to add the finer-grained subclasses **CommSalesperson** and **NonCommSalesperson** to our design. These two new subclasses will inherit from their superclass, **Salesperson**. A commissioned salesperson would be represented by an instance of **CommSalesperson**, while a noncommissioned salesperson would be represented by an instance of **NonCommSalesperson**.

The operation **issueCommissionPmt** would then be allocated to **CommSalesperson**, as shown in Fig. 9.5.

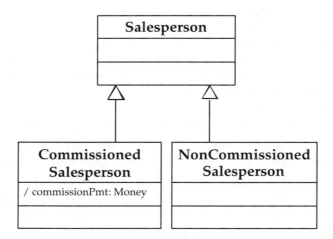

*Fig. 9.5:* *Removing the cohesion problem of* **Salesperson** *by adding subclasses.*

Mixed-instance cohesion usually indicates a class hierarchy that isn't well refined or that simply isn't correct. As we saw, it also leads to some gnarled code (in the form of extra **if** statements) within the offending class itself.

### 9.3.2 Mixed-domain cohesion

> A class with *mixed-domain cohesion* contains an element that directly encumbers the class with an extrinsic class of a different domain.

In the above definition, I use "domain" in the same sense that I did in Section 9.1. But now I need to define "extrinsic."

> The class **B** is *extrinsic* to **A** if **A** can be fully defined with no notion of **B**.
>
> **B** is *intrinsic* to **A** if **B** captures some characteristic inherent to **A**.

For example, **Elephant** is extrinsic to **Person**, because in no sense does "elephant" capture some characteristic of a person. However, **Date** (as in, date of birth) is intrinsic to **Person**.

There are many examples of mixed-domain cohesion, some of which are obvious, some subtle. The first example that I saw was subtle: It was the **Real** (real number) class in a vendor's class library, which had an attribute **arctan**.[9] I stared for a long time at this attribute, for I perceived something gravely wrong with its allocation to the class **Real**. However, although I realized the gravity of the problem, I couldn't figure out exactly *why* I thought that **arctan** didn't belong in **Real**.

One day, as I was sitting beneath an apple tree in my garden, an insight suddenly hit me. (Lacking a sense of historical precedent, I shouted "Eureka!") **Real** has no business messing around with objects of class **Angle**. Where would this designer stop with this encumbrance?

How about adding an operation called **convertTemp** to the class **Real** so we could convert Fahrenheit to Celsius and Kelvin to Réaumur? That would encumber **Real** with **Temperature**. Or, if we wanted to get euros for our dollars, we could encumber **Real** with **Money**. Or **Real** could even return the set of customers whose bank balances were (to the nearest cent) equal to some real number. The list of absurd possibilities is endless, as Fig. 9.6 shows.

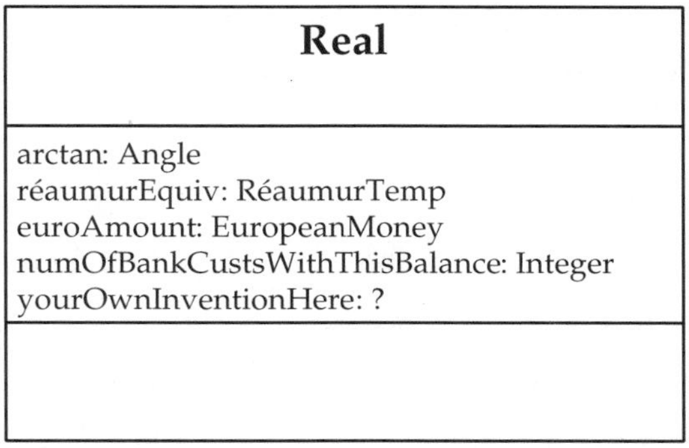

| **Real** |
| --- |
| arctan: Angle<br>réaumurEquiv: RéaumurTemp<br>euroAmount: EuropeanMoney<br>numOfBankCustsWithThisBalance: Integer<br>yourOwnInventionHere: ? |
| |

*Fig. 9.6:* **Real** *with rampant mixed-domain cohesion.*

When you design a class of a given domain, you'll have to include classes from lower domains in your design—that's what reusability's about. But make sure that you need those classes because of intrinsic properties of your class. For

---

[9] In case your school trigonometry is a little rusty, I should explain that **arctan** is the inverse-tangent function. It takes a real number **r** and tells you the angle whose tangent is **r**. The arctan of 1.0 is 45 degrees, for example. (**arccos** is the inverse cosine.)

example, it would be fine for the class **Account** to have an operation that returned an object of class **Money** or even an attribute of class **Date**. However, I'd be very suspicious if the class returned an object of the architecture-domain class **WireXferLink**.

The architecture domain often gets mixed into a business-domain class. This is wrong—unless your business actually *is* building architectural infrastructures. The old object-oriented motto of "a thing should know how to something itself," as in "a document should know how to print itself," can be a little *too* appealing. A **Document** class with specific knowledge of a printer has mixed-domain cohesion.

When you design a class of a given domain, you should be particularly wary of introducing classes of higher domains into the class you're designing. That's why the class **Real** (above) was a problem. **Real** is a fundamental class, and it shouldn't be encumbered with classes of higher domains. Yet, in the poor design that I saw, **Real**'s attribute **arctan** (of class **Angle**) forced **Real** to deal with **Angle**, a class from a higher group of classes (namely, the semantic group).

Another way to get a sense of the relative domains of two classes is to ask the question, Can I imagine this class being built without this other class? I can imagine **Real** being built without the class **Angle** ever existing. However, I cannot envision building the class **Angle** without the class **Real**. This implies that **Angle** is in a higher domain than **Real**.

(Incidentally, the class **Real** that I encountered had another attribute, **arccos**, which isn't even defined for most real numbers. This saddled the poor class with mixed-instance cohesion as well.)

### 9.3.3 Mixed-role cohesion

A class **C** with *mixed-role cohesion* contains an element that directly encumbers the class with an extrinsic class that lies in the same domain as **C**.

Unlike a class with mixed-domain cohesion, a class with mixed-role cohesion doesn't straddle domains. However, it does include more than one role from a single domain (where "role" means an abstraction of a group of like things in the real world).

A famous example involves persons and dogs. Let's say that we have a class **Person** with an attribute **numOfDogsOwned** (the number of dogs that a given person owns). If the get operation for the attribute is a simple function (also named **numOfDogsOwned**), we would use **fred.numOfDogsOwned** to find out how many dogs are owned by an object **fred** (of class **Person**).

The **Person** class doesn't have mixed-instance cohesion, because non-dog-owning objects could simply return a value of zero. It doesn't have mixed-domain cohesion, because **Person** and **Dog** are both in the business domain. But it does have mixed-role cohesion, because **Person** and **Dog** are distinct concepts, extrinsic to each other.

In pure design terms, mixed-role cohesion is the least serious transgression of class cohesion. However, if you're designing your classes for reusability, then you should pay careful attention to mixed-role cohesion. What if you wanted to reuse **Person** in an application that had no dogs? You could do so, but you'd have extra, useless baggage in the class, and you might get some pesky warnings about missing dogs from your compiler (or linker).

And where should we stop with this design philosophy? Why not include these attributes in **Person**: **numOfCarsOwned**, **numOfBoatsOwned**, **numOfCatsOwned**, **numOfFrogsOwned**, . . . ? Not only would these attributes severely encumber **Person** with other classes, but each of them also implies yet another set operation to update the number of things owned.[10]

Mixed-role cohesion, as exemplified by "person owns dog," is all-too appealing because

- It's very easy to write the message code to find out how many dogs someone owns: It's simply **fred.numOfDogsOwned**.
- Many information-modeling approaches do indeed treat **numOfDogsOwned** as an attribute of **Person**.
- In real life, if you want to find out how many dogs Fred owns, you would probably ask Fred himself: "Hey, how many dogs do you own?"[11]

However appealing the above arguments are, you shouldn't be distracted into automatically creating a class **Person** with mixed-role cohesion. There are many

---

[10] Yes, you could generalize all these operations to **numOfThingsOwned**, with **typeOfThing** passed as an argument. But the basic cohesion problem would remain.

[11] I find this anthropomorphic view of object orientation to be specious and irrelevant. I include it because I've often heard it used as an object-oriented "design principle."

other design options that don't compromise the cohesion of **Person**; I explore four of these in detail in the final exercise of Chapter 14.

As an object-oriented designer, you should aim to create classes with ideal cohesion, that is, classes with no mixed-instance, mixed-domain, or mixed-role cohesion. Classes with ideal cohesion have the utmost reusability, and that is many shops' primary objective for object orientation (especially for classes in the business domain).

## 9.4 Summary

A class may belong to one of four domains. These domains are: the foundation domain, which comprises classes valuable across all businesses and architectures; the architecture domain, which comprises classes valuable for one implementation architecture; the business domain, which comprises classes valuable for one industry or company; and the application domain, which comprises classes (as well as some simpler procedural constructs) that are valuable within one application.

Classes of the foundation domain have the greatest reusability, while those from the application domain have the least. (This follows directly from the definitions of the domains, of course.) Each of the four domains has several groups of classes within it.

Direct encumbrance is the size of a class's direct class-reference set, which is the set of other classes to which the class directly refers. Indirect encumbrance is the size of a class's indirect class-reference set, which is the set formed by the transitive closure of the class's direct class-reference set. Informally speaking, the indirect encumbrance of a class is the number of other classes that it needs in order to work.

Classes from higher domains normally have higher indirect encumbrance than classes from lower domains. The Law of Demeter (named after the Demeter Project, in which it was first postulated) offers guidelines for bounding a class's direct encumbrance by limiting its references to other classes.

The cohesion of a class is the measure of how well the features of the class (its operations and attributes) belong together in a single class. A class departs from ideal cohesion if it has mixed-instance, mixed-domain, or mixed-role cohesion. (It may have more than one. See Exercise 4 below.)

A class with mixed-instance cohesion has elements that are undefined for some objects instantiated from the class. A class with mixed-domain cohesion has an element that refers to an extrinsic class belonging to a different domain. A class with mixed-role cohesion has an element that refers to an extrinsic class belonging to the same domain.

Of the three types of cohesion above, mixed-instance cohesion results in the greatest design and maintenance problems, whereas mixed-role cohesion tends to result in the least.

## 9.5 Exercises

1.  A class library that you purchase from a general class vendor will probably contain only foundation classes. Why do you think this is?

2.  How should we handle inheritance when we compute encumbrance? For example, some class hierarchies emanate from a single root class (named, for example, **Object** or **Any**). Since every class in such a hierarchy inherits ultimately from **Object**, doesn't this imply that the indirect encumbrance of every class will be approximately equal?

3.  Did the **Hominoid** class of Chapter 1, as it was designed, have any cohesion problems? If so, suggest an alternative design for **Hominoid**.

4.  If a class may have mixed-instance, mixed-domain, or mixed-role cohesion, how many combinations of cohesion are possible for a class?

5.  I once saw a class **BankCustomer** with an attribute **gender**, which returned the gender of a customer as one of four possible values: **0** (customer's gender was unknown), **1** (male), **2** (female), and—this one took me by surprise—**3** (other!). It turned out that this last value was used for corporate bank customers, whose gender is undefined.

    What is the cohesion of **BankCustomer**? What design change would you introduce to improve its cohesion?

6.  If you have a collection of trigonometric attributes, such as **tan**, **cos**, **sin**, and so on, you could make them instance attributes of the class **Angle**. Attributes such as **arctan**, **arccos**, **arcsin**, and so on, would be class operations of the class **Angle**, because they don't apply to individual instances of **Angle**. In what other way (other than as class and instance features) could you gather all these features into a single construct? (Hint: The construct appeared in Section 3.8.)

7.  Investigate some of the commercially available software with which you're familiar. Is it constructed with any form of domain separation? In particular, is it constructed so that classes in lower domains avoid referring to those in higher domains?

## 9.6 Answers

1. There are several reasons: First, most vendors aim for the maximum commercial marketplace. By definition, foundation classes are useful to the widest possible group of industries and applications. Second, most foundation classes demand a knowledge of general computer science, rather than of any specific business. Thus, a typical class vendor can claim (with credibility) an understanding of foundation classes that's as good as anyone else's.

   Third—and this is the reason that most vendors' libraries *don't* contain business classes—business classes are difficult to analyze and often embody business policy and information that companies consider proprietary. Most companies aren't currently in the business of selling their business expertise as software classes to be reused.

   Nevertheless, I believe that this will change and that we'll soon see industry-specific business-domain libraries for sale on the street, including banking class libraries, telecommunication class libraries, and medical class libraries. Already, many of the task forces of the Object-Management Group are working on industry-specific object components.

2. No. A class is unlikely to derive much of its indirect encumbrance from a class high in the class-inheritance hierarchy, for two reasons: First, inheritance is only one way in which a class refers to other classes; a class's encumbrance is due to many other kinds of reference as well. Second, the highest classes in a class-inheritance hierarchy tend to have low-to-medium encumbrance, because they refer to few other classes. Thus, the contribution of a class high in the hierarchy to the encumbrance of its subclasses isn't likely to be dramatic.

   Nevertheless, one variation of indirect encumbrance (which I saw a shop working on recently) excludes from an indirect class-reference set of a class **C** any classes whose features aren't actually used by methods of **C**. This variety of indirect encumbrance may yield a finer measure of **C**'s encumbrance, but it's also more complicated to compute than the variety I described in this chapter.

3. The **Hominoid** class had mixed-domain cohesion, because it had an operation **display** that presented a hominoid on a screen. So, since **Hominoid** is pre-

sumably mixed up with devices and their formats, we may even need a different version of **Hominoid** for every architecture (printer, plotter, monitor) around the shop. We may even—perish the thought!—require a different version for every possible monitor resolution.

If that doesn't bother you (perhaps because portability and reusability are not issues), then OK. But if it does, you should have **Hominoid** return a reference to an object that holds the display shape of the hominoid (which would be of class **BitPattern** or **LinePattern**). Then, you could send that object in a message to an output-device object, which would then display it.

However, you may dislike the above design approach, because you may consider that exporting the bit-pattern representation of a hominoid shouldn't be part of the abstraction of **Hominoid**. If you want to allow a **display** operation to access information on the appearance of a hominoid but you don't want to export that information from **Hominoid**, you could create another class, **DisplayableHominoid**, to inherit from **Hominoid**, as shown in Fig. 9.7. The operation **display**, defined on **DisplayableHominoid**, would operate on variables defined within **Hominoid**.

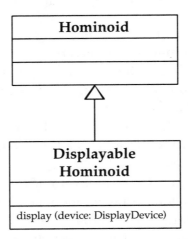

*Fig. 9.7: The design of* **DisplayableHominoid**.

The disadvantage of this design is that access to the hominoid information within **Hominoid** has tightly bound the **DisplayableHominoid** class to the **Hominoid** class. This creates the risk that changes to the internal design of **Hominoid** will ripple into **DisplayableHominoid**.

Yet another design approach is to separate the appearance of a hominoid from its other information and to keep "hominoid appearance" in another class. I cover such a design approach in Section 12.1.4, when I discuss the design of the class **Room**.

4. Table 9.1 shows the six possible combinations of mixed-instance, mixed-domain, and mixed-role cohesion that a class may possess. The reason that there are six (rather than eight) combinations is that a class with mixed-domain cohesion must also have mixed-role cohesion, as combinations 3 and 6 of Table 9.1 indicate. The first combination represents ideal class cohesion. (In the table, the abbreviations MI, MD, and MR stand for mixed-instance, mixed-domain, and mixed-role cohesion.)

*Table 9.1.*
*The Six Possible Combinations of Mixed-Instance,*
*Mixed-Domain, and Mixed-Role Cohesion.*

| Combination | MI | MD | MR |
|:-----------:|:--:|:--:|:--:|
| 1 | N | N | N |
| 2 | N | N | Y |
| 3 | N | Y | Y |
| 4 | Y | N | N |
| 5 | Y | N | Y |
| 6 | Y | Y | Y |

5.  **BankCustomer** has mixed-instance cohesion, because one of its attributes (**gender**) applies to only some of its instances (that is, only to objects representing *human* customers). The designer of this class should factor it into two subclasses, **HumanBankCustomer** and **CorporateBankCustomer**. The first subclass would have attributes such as **gender** and **mothersMaidenName**. The second subclass would have attributes such as **corporationType** and **numOfShareholders**. The superclass, **BankCustomer**, would have attributes such as **customerID** and **customerName** (assuming that corporate customers have the same name format as human customers).

    Once these two subclasses have been factored out from **BankCustomer**, all three classes will have ideal cohesion (so long as they don't have other cohesion problems, such as mixed-domain cohesion, of course).

6.  You could group these features together as a utility package of trigonometry functions, with signatures such as

    tan (angle: Angle): Real;
    arctan (real: Real): Angle;

    This design approach would also avoid the problem of mixed-domain cohesion that I pointed out in Section 9.3.2.

7.  Some of the component-based "application construction kits" that are emerging have exactly the kind of domain separation I discuss in this chapter, whereby there's a strict pecking order of references, from software constructs in the application domain at the top level, down to those in the foundation domain at the bottom.

# 10

# State-Space and Behavior

In the first section of this chapter, I introduce two fundamental properties of classes: state-space and behavior. In the second section, I explore the state-spaces of subclasses. In the third section, I analyze the behavior of subclasses.

The fourth section introduces the class invariant as a restriction on state-space. The fifth and final section explores operation preconditions and postconditions, which together form the contract between an operation and a client of that operation.

Class invariants, preconditions, and postconditions form the backbone of an object-oriented design approach termed *design by contract*. The next chapter, building on these concepts, explores ways to achieve sound class-hierarchy design.

## 10.1 State-Space and Behavior of a Class

> A class should represent a uniform abstraction of the properties of the individual objects that belong to that class.

Although that's a grand-sounding sentence, what do the words in it really mean?

259

By "abstraction" I mean that we don't necessarily have to consider *every* possible property of the real-world things that are represented by software objects. For example, although we may have a class **HumanBankCustomer**, we don't have to include the property **headSize** in that class (although of course we could if we wished to).

By "uniform" I mean that the abstraction we choose for a class applies in the same way to each of the objects belonging to the class. For example, if we're interested in the date of birth for **HumanBankCustomer**, then we're interested in the date of birth of *all* human bank customers.

By "properties" I mean simply this:

> The two *properties* of a class are its *state-space* and its allowed *behavior*.

Most of this chapter is an exploration of the concepts of state-space and behavior and their practical implications for object-oriented design. But, before I formally define "state-space" and "behavior," let me illustrate these terms with a concrete example: a knight on a chessboard—that is, an object of class **ChessKnight**—as shown in Fig. 10.1.

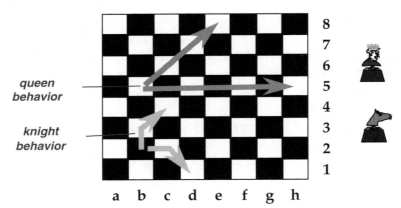

*Fig. 10.1: A chessboard with a queen and a knight.*

The total *state-space* of **ChessKnight** amounts to every square on the board. Next consider the queen. The total state-space of **ChessQueen** is also every square on the board. Nevertheless, we know that the class **ChessQueen** is different from **ChessKnight**. So, what's different? The answer is her behavior.

The queen is permitted to move along any row, column, or diagonal to get to another square. Therefore, she can reach any other square on an empty board—in other words, any other state in her state-space—in only two moves. The knight, on the other hand, with his peculiar behavior, may need up to six moves to reach another square.

Therefore, the classes **ChessKnight** and **ChessQueen** have identical state-spaces but unlike behaviors. Now let's imagine another kind of knight, one that moves like the traditional knight but is not allowed on the central four squares of the chessboard. (See Fig. 10.2.)

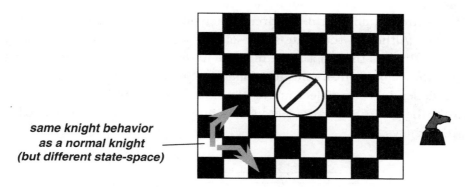

same knight behavior
as a normal knight
(but different state-space)

*Fig. 10.2: A knight that's not permitted in the center of the board.*

So, why is this knight different? The answer is that, although he shares identical behavior with the traditional knight, his state-space differs.

From the above, we see that two classes may differ either in their state-space or in their behavior (or both). Now I'll define "state-space" more exactly. (I define "behavior" in Section 10.3.)

> The *state-space* of a class **C** is the ensemble of all the permitted states of any object of class **C**.
>
> The *dimensions* of a state-space are the coordinates needed to specify the state of a given object.

Informally, the state of an object is the "value" that it has at a given time. More properly, an object's state is the ordered set of objects to which the object refers at a given time. For example, the state of a **SwimmingPool** object right now might be 30, 2, 25 (meters long, meters deep, and temperature in Celsius, respectively). In other words, this **SwimmingPool** object currently points to an object of class **Length** (30 meters), another one of class **Length** (2 meters), and one of class **Temperature** (25 degrees Celsius).

I picture a class's state-space as a grid of points, each point being a state. Each object that's an instance of the class is like a little dot, which spends its lifetime hopping around from place to place (from state to state) within the state-space of its class. A "hop from place to place" is known technically as a transition (in the same sense that I used "transition" in Chapter 6).

Figure 10.3 shows such a grid in three dimensions, the state-space for the class **ProductLine**. (Although the state-space of the actual class may have many more dimensions, three is the most I can manage to draw!) The three dimensions that I've shown are **weight**, **price**, and **qtyAvailable**. Since these three dimensions are mutually independent, an object (a given product line) may be found almost anywhere within the grid. Several objects sit as little dots within the **ProductLine** grid, as Fig. 10.3 shows.

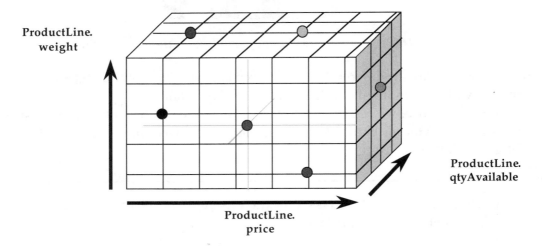

*Fig. 10.3: The state-space of the class **ProductLine** as a grid, with each product line as a "little dot."*

As another example, the **Patient** class may have such dimensions as **age**, **height**, **weight**, **currentTemperature**, and so on. A given **Patient** object may be at (almost!) any point in this multidimensional grid.

The dimensions of a class's state-space are roughly equivalent to the attributes defined on the class.[1] The values marking off the dimensions are the values that the attributes may take on. Since each dimension is itself of some class, the values along that dimension are objects of the dimension's class. For example, the **price** dimension of **ProductLine** would be marked off with objects of class **Money**, and the **height** of a patient would be marked in inches or centimeters, objects of class **Length**.

The classes that mark dimensions aren't always from such a lowly domain as **Money** and **Length**. For example, **Hammer**'s state-space has two dimensions, **Handle** and **Head**, because you make a hammer (a composite object) by selecting one handle and one head (the two component objects).[2] Each of these two classes is itself from the business domain and itself has several dimensions (such as **length**, **weight**, and so on).

## 10.2 The State-Space of a Subclass

This section begins our exploration into subclasses with a look at the state-spaces of two illustrious classes, **A** and **B**.

> If **B** is a subclass of **A**, then the state-space of **B** must be entirely contained within the state-space of **A**.[3] We say that **B**'s state-space is *confined by* **A**'s state space.

---

[1] I say "roughly" because most attributes that could be derived from others aren't normally considered dimensions. For example, the dimensions of **Cube** may be **length**, **breadth**, and **height**, but not **volume** or **area**.

[2] To be consistent, I should term these dimensions **hammer** (of class **Hammer**) and **head** (of class **Head**). I discuss dimensions further in Exercise 1 at the end of this chapter.

[3] Technically, it's the *projection* of **B**'s state-space onto **A**'s that must lie within **A**'s state-space.

The best way to clarify this is with an example. Let's say that the class **A** is **Road-Vehicle**. For simplicity, we'll assume that its state-space has only one dimension: **currWeight**. We'll set lower and upper limits of, respectively, 0.5 tons and 10.0 tons on **RoadVehicle.currWeight**.

Suppose that subclass **B** is **Automobile**. If we set lower and upper limits of, respectively, 1.0 tons and 3.0 tons on **Automobile.currWeight**, then we're in good shape. The state-space of **Automobile** is confined within that of **RoadVehicle** and so **Automobile** is legal as a subclass of **RoadVehicle**.

Figure 10.4 shows the ranges of **RoadVehicle.currWeight** and **Automobile.currWeight** graphically.

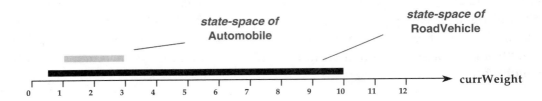

*Fig. 10.4: The 1-D state-spaces of* **Automobile** *and* **Road-Vehicle.**

Note that had we set lower and upper limits of, respectively, 0.2 tons and 13.0 tons on **Automobile.currWeight**, we'd be in trouble. For instance, a 13-ton automobile would be illegal by the above definition of **RoadVehicle**, which limits a road vehicle to 10 tons. Therefore, the state-space of **Automobile** wouldn't be confined within that of **RoadVehicle**, and so **Automobile** couldn't be a subclass of **RoadVehicle**.

This state-space violation would allow an object to be a legal instance of its own class but to be illegal as an instance of the superclass. In other words, my car could be an automobile but not a road vehicle—an absurdity.

Ironically—and this surprises many people—the state-space of a subclass may have *more* dimensions than that of the superclass.

> If **B** is a subclass of **A**, then **B**'s state-space must comprise at least the dimensions of **A**'s—but it may comprise more. If it comprises more dimensions, we say that **B**'s state-space *extends from* **A**'s.

The state-space of **Automobile**, for example, might have the dimension **Automobile.currPassengerCount**, which would not be a dimension of a general non-passenger road vehicle. If so, **Automobile**'s state-space would be an extension from **RoadVehicle**'s.

Perhaps this has left you a little bewildered. How can a subclass's state-space both be *confined by* and *extend from* the state-space of its superclass? The answer is this: Within the dimensions defined on the superclass, the state-space of a subclass may be smaller than that of the superclass—but at the same time, the subclass's state-space may extend into other dimensions that are undefined for the superclass. For example, Fig. 10.5 shows **Automobile**'s state-space simultaneously confined by and extending from **RoadVehicle**'s state-space.

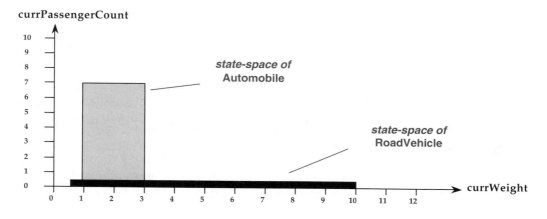

*Fig. 10.5: The 2-D state-space of* **Automobile** *and the 1-D state-space of* **RoadVehicle**.

In the **currWeight** dimension, **Automobile**'s state-space is still confined within **RoadVehicle**'s, because **Automobile.currWeight**'s range still falls within **RoadVehicle.currWeight**'s range. Now, however, **Automobile** has an extra dimension (**currPassengerCount**) in its state-space. Thus, its state-space (shown as a gray area in Fig. 10.5) extends into that second dimension; specifically, as we see, an automobile may have zero to seven passengers aboard. For the more general class **RoadVehicle**, **currPassengerCount** remains undefined.

## 10.3 The Behavior of a Subclass

Most objects (unless they're immutable) make transitions within their class's state-space as one or more of their attributes change value. These transitions constitute a class's allowed behavior, which is defined in the following way:

> The allowed *behavior* of a class **C** is the set of transitions that an object of class **C** is permitted to make between states in **C**'s state-space.

This definition implies that not all possible transitions are legal for an object. An object hops around within the state-space of its class only in the manner prescribed for it by the behavior of the class. As we saw in Section 10.1, although a knight may be found on any of the 64 chessboard squares, its permitted transitions are quite limited (at most, eight transitions from its current square).

What about behavior in subclasses? Do superclass and subclass behaviors have a relationship like state-spaces do? Specifically, does behavior get extended and/or confined in a subclass?

The answer to both these questions is yes. First, let's consider extension, the behavior that **B** (the subclass) possesses, but that **A** (the superclass) lacks. It's obvious that such extra behavior in **B** must exist, for without it, how would an instance of **B** manage to leap about in the part of **B**'s state-space that extends out from **A**'s?

Let's return to **RoadVehicle** and its subclass **Automobile** as our example. **Automobile** will have behavior, facilitated by operations such as **pickUpPassenger** and **dropOffPassenger**, that allow it to increase and decrease its number of passengers. This behavior is clearly beyond any behavior that **RoadVehicle** may have; after all, **RoadVehicle** doesn't even have a notion of passengers!

(To put it more technically: **RoadVehicle** lacks the dimension of **currPassengerCount** in its state-space. Therefore, any behavior that lets an object mosey around in the **currPassengerCount** dimension couldn't possibly be defined on **RoadVehicle**.)

This example shows that **Automobile** may *extend* the behavior of its super-class, **RoadVehicle**, just as **Automobile** extended the state-space of **RoadVehicle**.

**Automobile**'s behavior may also be *confined by* the behavior of **RoadVehicle**, just as **Automobile**'s state-space was confined by the state-space of **RoadVehicle**. A simple example: We can possibly add five tons to the weight of a general road vehicle, as long as it doesn't exceed the ten ton limit. However, we can never add five tons to an automobile's weight because its maximum weight is three tons and doing so would take is out of the state-space of **Automobile**.

In Section 11.3, I return to behavior confinement, whose implications lead to an important principle in the design of bulletproof subclasses: closed behavior.

## 10.4 The Class Invariant as a Restriction on a State-Space

Most of the state-spaces that we've looked at in this chapter have been complete in the sense that an object may occupy any of the places in the state-space grid. However, many classes don't allow their objects such free rein. We saw one such restriction in Fig. 10.2's example of the knight that had to keep out of the middle. In this section, we look at how to define legal state-spaces more precisely.

The legal state-space of a class is defined by its class invariant.

> A *class invariant* is a condition that every object of that class must satisfy at all times (when the object is in equilibrium).

The expression "when the object is in equilibrium" means that an object must obey its class invariant at all times when it's not in the middle of changing states. In particular, an object must toe the invariant line when the object is initialized at instantiation, and before and after any (public) operation is executed.

Let's take as an example the class **Triangle**.[4] If the sides of a triangle are **Triangle.a**, **Triangle.b**, and **Triangle.c**, then part of **Triangle**'s class invariant would be

$$a + b \geq c \text{ \textbf{and} } b + c \geq a \text{ \textbf{and} } c + a \geq b$$

This says that, no matter what object of class **Triangle** we have, the sum of the lengths of any two of its sides must be greater than or equal to the length of its

---

[4] To keep this example simple, I'll ignore the position and orientation of triangles and concentrate on their size. The invariant (with its $\geq$ rather than $>$) allows degenerate triangles that are just straight lines.

third side. (No doubt you can come up with several other, similar constraints on **Triangle**.)

The three-dimensional grid of Fig. 10.6 (with axes labeled **a**, **b**, and **c**) represents the state-space of **Triangle**. But that's not strictly true; it's an overstatement. Only some of the points in the grid—the ones that satisfy the above invariant for **Triangle**—belong to **Triangle**'s true state-space. For example, we couldn't have a triangle with sides of 1, 2, and 5.

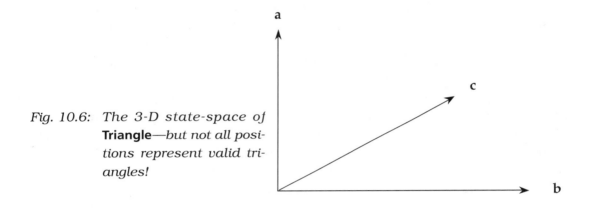

*Fig. 10.6:* *The 3-D state-space of* **Triangle**—*but not all positions represent valid triangles!*

Figure 10.7 shows a hierarchy of triangle varieties.

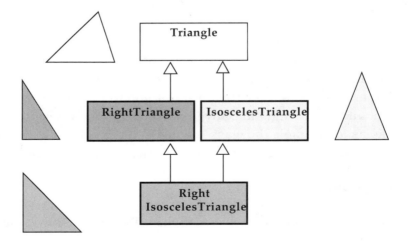

*Fig. 10.7: Four varieties of triangle.*

The class **IsoscelesTriangle** has (within the limits of equality for computer reals) the invariant:

> a = b **or** b = c **or** c = a

and the class **RightTriangle** has the invariant (due to the late Mr. Pythagoras):

> a * a + b * b = c * c     // I assume for simplicity that **c** is the hypotenuse.[5]

Because invariants are inherited, a given class must obey the invariant(s) of its superclass(es). So, since both **IsoscelesTriangle** and **RightTriangle** are subclasses of **Triangle**, they also inherit the invariant

> a + b ≥ c **and** b + c ≥ a **and** c + a ≥ b

Therefore, **IsoscelesTriangle** objects will always obey this entire invariant:

> (a + b ≥ c **and** b + c ≥ a **and** c + a ≥ b) **and** (a = b **or** b = c **or** c = a)

To pursue this further, the class **RightIsoscelesTriangle** (which inherits both from **RightTriangle** and **IsoscelesTriangle**) has a state-space made up of points that are legal for *both* **RightTriangle** and **IsoscelesTriangle**. Its class invariant is therefore the logical **and** of the invariants of **RightTriangle** and **IsoscelesTriangle**,[6] namely

> (a + b ≥ c **and** b + c ≥ a **and** c + a ≥ b) **and**
> a * a + b * b = c * c **and**
> (a = b **or** b = c **or** c = a)

## 10.5 Preconditions and Postconditions

So far, we've looked chiefly at the rules—the invariants—governing classes as a whole. Now, let's turn to the conditions that govern *individual operations*.

Every operation has a *precondition* and a *postcondition*. The precondition is a condition that must be true when the operation begins to execute. If it is not true, then the operation may legitimately refuse to execute and possibly raise

---

[5] See Exercise 4 for more details.

[6] Note that in languages such as C++ and Java, the class invariant is a theoretical construct, not directly implemented in the language. In these languages, class invariants are therefore not really inherited in the same sense that attributes are inherited.

some exception condition. The postcondition is a condition that must be true when the operation ends its execution. If it is not true, then the operation's implementation is defective and must be fixed.

Take, for example, the operation **Stack.pop**, which pops the top element off a normal last-in, first-out stack. The precondition for this operation is

> **not** empty

If the precondition of an operation is met, the operation must ensure that the operation's postcondition will be met when the operation ends its execution. For example, the postcondition for **pop** might be

> (numElements = **old** numElements − 1) **and not** full

wherein the keyword **old** means "whatever value this had before the operation executed."

Bertrand Meyer and others describe the pre- and postconditions of an operation as a contract between an operation and a client who sends a message to that operation.[7] The metaphor of the contract implies that

1. If the sender of the message can guarantee that the precondition is true, then the target operation will guarantee that the postcondition will be true after execution.

2. If, on the other hand, the sender of the message cannot guarantee that the precondition is true, then the whole deal is off: The operation is neither obliged to execute nor to guarantee the postcondition.

Remember that the class invariant is true both when an operation begins to execute and when it ends. So the full story of pre- and postconditions is that an operation is sandwiched between two compound conditions, like this:

> Class invariant **and** operation precondition
>     Operation executes
> Class invariant **and** operation postcondition

---

[7] See, for example, [Meyer, 1988], [Meyer, 1992], or [Wiener, 1995].

As an example, let's take the operation **scaleHoriz**, defined on the class **Rectangle**. The operation, which appears in Fig. 10.8, stretches or shrinks a rectangle's width by a multiplicative factor and takes one argument, **scaleFactor**.

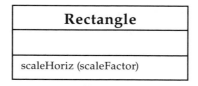

*Fig. 10.8:* **Rectangle.scaleHoriz**.

Let's assume that the rectangle has sides **w1**, **h1**, **w2**, and **h2**.[8] Its class invariant will be

$$w1 = w2 \textbf{ and } h1 = h2$$

A precondition on **scaleHoriz** will be

$$maxAllowedWidth \geq w1 * scaleFactor$$

The obvious postcondition will be

$$w1 = \textbf{old } w1 * scaleFactor$$

Taking everything together gives

$$w1 = w2 \textbf{ and } h1 = h2 \textbf{ and } maxAllowedWidth \geq w1 * scaleFactor$$
//complete precondition

   scaleHoriz (scaleFactor)       // the operation

$$w1 = w2 \textbf{ and } h1 = h2 \textbf{ and } w1 = \textbf{old } w1 * scaleFactor$$
//complete postcondition

Needless to say, few people actually write out the class invariant as part of every operation pre- and postcondition; that would be tedious and redundant. Nevertheless, the class invariant is there implicitly and you should honor it when you design either an operation or the method implementing the operation.

---

[8] You may wonder why my **Rectangle** class has all *four* sides of a rectangle, when just **width** and **height** would do. I do so to provide a simple example of a class invariant. In Sections 13.1 and 13.2, I look in detail at several designs for **Rectangle**.

## 10.6 Summary

This chapter introduced the properties of a class: state-space and allowed behavior. The state-space of a class **A** is the ensemble of the states permitted to an object of class **A**. The dimensions of a state-space are the coordinates needed to specify an object's state. The allowed behavior of **A** is the set of transitions in **A**'s state-space that an object is legally able to make.

If **B** is a subclass of **A**, then **B**'s state-space must be entirely confined within **A**'s. However, **B**'s state-space may extend from **A**'s, which means that it has dimensions that **A**'s state-space lacks. Similarly, **B**'s behavior may be both a confinement and an extension of **A**'s behavior.

Every object of a given class must satisfy the class's invariant. This invariant acts as a constraint, limiting the size of the class's state-space. A subclass both inherits the class invariant(s) of its superclass(es) and adds a further restriction of its own.

Each operation of a class has a precondition and a postcondition, which together form a contract between the operation and a client of that operation. The precondition states what must be true for the operation to execute. The postcondition states what will be true when the operation has completed execution. Formally speaking, the class invariant is part of every operation's pre- and postconditions. (Practically speaking, however, no one actually writes the class invariant as part of pre- and postconditions.)

Class invariants, together with operation preconditions and postconditions, form a framework for the design approach known as "design by contract," which guarantees that a target object's operation will generate the correct response to a message provided that the client object has obeyed that operation's precondition.

In the next chapter, we'll use state-spaces, behavior, class invariants, preconditions, and postconditions to build the important design principles of conformance and closed behavior and to assess the quality of our class hierarchies.

## 10.7 Exercises

1.  Assume a class **MonsterCardAccount** with two dimensions (among others) named **currentBalance** and **creditLimit**. Why don't we simply name the dimension **currentBalance** after its class, **Money**?

2.  What is the dimensionality of the class **Rectangle**'s state-space? In other words, how many dimensions does **Rectangle** have? Before you answer, "Two! Height and width. That's easy!" let me point out that the question is undefined until you have a good idea of what abstraction **Rectangle** actually represents. So let me define **Rectangle** to be a class whose objects are rectangles that may rotate, stretch in height and width, and wander around the plane.

    So, how many dimensions does the class **Rectangle**, with the above definition, have? In other words, how many degrees of freedom does each **Rectangle** object have? If you were to design the internal implementation of **Rectangle**, how many degrees of freedom would your internal design permit? Could this number be different from your first answer? If so, why?

3.  How can the behavior of a subclass be considered more constrained (with respect to its superclass) if a subclass may have extra dimensions in its state-space that its superclasses do not?

4.  The class invariants for the classes **RightTriangle**, **IsoscelesTriangle**, and **RightIsoscelesTriangle** were complex and also similar to one another. Could you factor out the similarities in some way and thereby also simplify the expression of the invariants?

## 10.8 Answers

1.  Although **currentBalance** may be of class **Money**, naming the dimension **currentBalance** as **Money** would lead to ambiguity. For example, since at least two dimensions of **MonsterCardAccount**'s state-space are monetary, how would we know which dimension was the **currentBalance** and which was the **creditLimit**?

    Incidentally, we may choose to give **currentBalance** a more sophisticated class, say **MonsterCardBalance** (which is based on the more fundamental class **Money**). This may be an extravagant solution, because it would give us another class in our library to maintain. It would be worth doing only if **Monster-CardBalance** had important or complicated business properties.

2.  I'll answer the questions in this exercise in reverse order. First, let's explore three possible approaches to the internal design of **Rectangle** and assess the dimensionality (or degrees of freedom) of each. Each design approach—I'll call them A, B, and C—will apparently yield a different dimensionality! After examining each approach, I'll resolve this apparent conflict through the class-invariant concept in order to come up with the true dimensionality of **Rectangle**.

    > *Approach A:* Consider each **Rectangle** object to be represented by four points in a plane. Because each point has two dimensions (**x** and **y**), **Rectangle**'s state-space will have eight (that is, 4 times 2) dimensions.

    > *Approach B:* Consider a **Rectangle** object to be just two points: a **topLeft** point and a **bottomRight** point. Although this would appear to give the state-space just four dimensions, it's not quite enough. Two points will work for horizontal rectangles, but they're ambiguous for rectangles that can turn. (Try it with pencil and paper.) We therefore need to know the rectangle's angle of orientation, too. This makes five (that is, 2 plus 2 plus 1) dimensions.

    > *Approach C:* We can also specify a **Rectangle** object by stating its **center**, its **height**, its **width**, and its **orientation**. This also yields a five-dimensional state-space (that is, 2 plus 1 plus 1 plus 1).

So which answer should it be? Does **Rectangle** have an eight-dimensional state-space or a five-dimensional one? The answer is, the minimum of all those values—in other words, five dimensions.

But why the *minimum*? To answer that question, let's take another look at each of the three design approaches to see how the class invariant reduces the degrees of freedom in an internal design of **Rectangle** that appears to have more than five dimensions.

*Approach A:* Although four points on a plane can certainly specify a rectangle, they can also specify lots of shapes that aren't rectangular, such as trapezoids and parallelograms. Thus, if we choose four points to be the instance variables that define a rectangle, then we'll have to establish a class invariant for **Rectangle** that will forbid non-rectangular shapes. The following calculation tells us how much work we have to do to impose such a constraint.

Four points have eight degrees of freedom, but rectangles (as we've seen) can be designed to have only five. Therefore, if we choose Approach A as our internal **Rectangle** design, we'll need to write and enforce a class invariant to bring the dimensionality of the class effectively back to five. This class invariant must contain three (8 minus 5) constraints. Your subject-matter expertise about rectangles will inspire you with various ways to write this invariant.

For example, you may join the points by lines and check that three intersections are right angles. Or, you may check that one intersection is a right angle and that the lines form two pairs of equal lengths. Or, you may eliminate one of your points entirely and check that the remaining three points meet the Pythagorean condition. When you see the work needed to write the class invariant for Approach A, you might ask whether you could find a simpler core representation, one whose dimensionality would be closer to five and which would therefore simplify the class invariant.

*Approaches B and C:* Class invariants will be simple for these internal designs, because **Rectangle**'s instance variables altogether have five dimensions (degrees of freedom)—exactly the same number as we saw above for rectangles as a whole. For example, in Approach C, a **center**, **height**, **width**, and **orientation** can hardly *not* represent a legal rectangle! No matter what values you put into these variables, you'll get a rectangle. (Of course, you must ensure that **height** and **width** are nonnegative.)

Since they're independent of one another, the above four variables (**center**, **height**, **width**, and **orientation**) give the state-space of **Rectangle** five fundamental dimensions (2 plus 1 plus 1 plus 1). All other sets of instance variables representing rectangles also yield at least five fundamental dimensions. (Try some!)

So, what's really going on here? The answer is that **Rectangle** has two dimensionalities, an external one and an internal one. **Rectangle**'s *external dimensionality* is its dimensionality *as a type*, and is always five. **Rectangle**'s *internal dimensionality* is its dimensionality *as a class* (an implementation of a type). This dimensionality must be at least five. The difference between the internal dimensionality and external dimensionality equals the number of constraints that we must apply via the class invariant to ensure that the class's design fulfills the type and nothing but the type. (In Chapter 13, we return to **Rectangle** to explore both its external design and internal design further.)

Finally, note that you can group simple dimensions into higher-complexity dimensions in several different ways, without changing dimensionality. For example, in Approach B, we saw **Rectangle**'s five dimensions grouped into three: two points and an angle. Two of these three dimensions (the points) are of class **Point**, which has two fundamental dimensions (both of class **Real**). Forming higher-level abstractions (such as **Point**, rather than merely two **Real**s) is usually good object-oriented design practice (as I indicated in Section 9.2.2, on encumbrance).

3.  The behavior that a subclass inherits from a superclass must operate within the possibly constrained state-space of the subclass. Therefore, the subclass may need to override the definition of an inherited operation with a less wide-ranging version. However, a subclass is free to add any behavior to the inherited behavior so long as the class invariant is respected.

    As an analogy, consider the tenor Luciano Pavarotti as an object of a superclass and me as an object of a subclass. I can sing too, but my volume, range, and depth of expression are all less than Signor Pavarotti's. Also, assume that I know all the songs that he knows but, unfortunately, my implementation of them is less impressive. In fact, there are some arias that I must refuse to sing at all because their range defeats me. On the other hand, I sing some of his songs with extra twiddly bits of my own invention.

Notwithstanding the above, there are several rockin' numbers that Signor Pavarotti doesn't know, but which have been very lucky for me (for example, "The Ying Tong Song" and the evergreen country favorite, "Baby, I Wanna Drive You Wild, But I Can't Get Out of First Gear"). Thus, although I inherit a set of songs from Signor Pavarotti whose implementation I modify and constrain to my own talents, I also extend his repertoire with some songs that take singing into a whole new dimension.

4.  Complex class invariants often have sub-expressions that can be factored out as Boolean functions. For example, the Pythagorean property of a right triangle cannot be succinctly expressed for two reasons. First, it isn't obvious which of the three sides is the hypotenuse. Second, because of real-number roundings, the Pythagorean constraint can never be expressed as an exact equality. However, you can write a Boolean function

   isPythagorean (a, b, c: Real) Boolean:

   which can be made part of the class invariant of, say, **RightTriangle** and **RightIsoscelesTriangle**, and which will take care of awkward complexities.

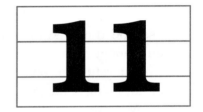

# Type Conformance and Closed Behavior

A robust class hierarchy is heavy-duty and a joy forever: Objects of a class will happily stand in for objects of a superclass, and the hierarchy as a whole will withstand the trials of time. On the other hand, a miserably designed class hierarchy may be an albatross that brings a premature end both to your project and to object orientation in your shop.

*Classes, classes, everywhere.*
*More than you'd ever think.*
*Classes, classes, everywhere.*
*Nor any two would link.*

This chapter introduces a pair of principles that are vital to the construction of healthy, hardy class hierarchies. The principles are type conformance and closed behavior.

In the chapter's first section, I review and contrast the notions of class and type, two terms we've touched on earlier in this book. In the second section, I introduce the principle of type conformance as a way to understand the true nature of subtypes. I recommend that to avoid unpleasant surprises, class hierarchies should be built on sound type hierarchies.

Understanding subtypes in object-oriented systems is complicated by the interaction among object orientation's three major sophistications: level-2 encapsulation, inheritance, and objects used as message arguments. Fortunately, however, we can call upon Chapter 10's ideas of preconditions, postconditions, and class invariants to help clarify the sometimes tricky issues that lurk around subtypes.

The chapter's third section continues the topic of stalwart subclasses with the important principle of closed behavior. In this section, I also show how the two principles of type conformance and closed behavior often constrain or modify the designs of robust class hierarchies.

## 11.1 Class versus Type

The best way to think of a class is as the implementation of a type, which is the abstract or external view of a class. In other words, type includes the purpose of the class, together with its state-space and behavior. (Specifically, the type of a class is defined by the following: the purpose of the class; the class invariant; the attributes of the class; the operations of the class; and the operations' preconditions, postconditions, definitions, and signatures.)

A class *in toto*, however, entails an internal design that implements external characteristics as a type. The internal design, as we saw in Chapter 1, includes the design of the variables of the class and the design of the algorithms for the operations' methods.

Indeed, a single type may be implemented as several classes, with each class having its own particular internal design. For example, you may create several classes of the same type in order to give each class its own efficiency advantage in some special circumstance. Perhaps one design of **OrderedCollection** may have very efficient traversals, while another may have very efficient insertions and deletions. Yet, both versions of **OrderedCollection** can implement the same type with the same attributes and operations. Similarly, you may design a special version of a class to use an algorithm that runs very fast on a particular model of computer.

Figure 11.1 shows UML's notation for a type, which is identical to the class symbol but has the stereotype **«type»** in the name compartment. When types appear in a diagram, you may want to use the stereotype **«class»** in class symbols to emphatically distinguish them from types, as I did in Fig. 11.1.

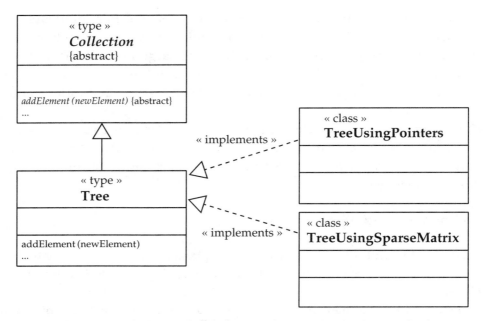

*Fig. 11.1: The type* **Collection** *with its subtype* **Tree**, *which is implemented by the two classes.*

The dotted arrows marked with the **«implements»** stereotype indicate which class is an implementation of which type. As Fig 11.1 shows, a single type may be implemented by multiple classes, each probably with its own efficiency characteristics. (Normally, these classes wouldn't have quite such long names; their implementation techniques would more likely appear in their internal documentation.)

The arrow on the left shows that the type **Tree** is a subtype of **Collection**. The fact that **Collection** is also **{abstract}** means that **Collection** need not be implemented by any classes; only **Collection**'s subtypes will require implementing classes.

Although a type represents the outside view of a class, the concept of subtype is distinct from that of subclass. Even without a formal definition of subtype (which appears in the next section), you can probably tell intuitively that the subclasses of the next paragraph are not valid subtypes of their respective superclasses.

Because you can make any class syntactically a subclass of any other, you could make something like **Elephant** inherit from **Rectangle** or **SalesRep** inherit from **Brick**. These *are* legal class/subclass structures, but semantically they're nonsense because the subclasses have nothing to do with their respective superclasses.

For example, it would make no sense to apply Pythagoras to an elephant in order to find its diagonal! And a **postCommission** operation wouldn't be very happy to get a piece of construction material as an argument when it was expecting a sales representative. (Most customers wouldn't be happy either, although I concede that some sales representatives are indistinguishable from large chunks of building material.)

So, even if **S** is a subclass of **T**, it doesn't automatically follow that **S** is also a subtype of **T**.[1] You have to work at the design of the class **S** if you want to make it a subtype of **T**. The rest of this chapter explains what that work is: the principles that **S** should obey to make it a true subtype of its superclass **T**.

## 11.2 The Principle of Type Conformance

The design principle of type conformance comes from the theory of abstract datatypes, upon which object orientation is founded. This principle, which is extremely important in creating the hierarchies of classes that form your class library, states that

> If **S** is a true subtype of **T**, then **S** must *conform* to **T**. In other words, an object of type **S** can be provided in any context where an object of type **T** is expected, and correctness is still preserved when any accessor operation of the object is executed.[2]

For example, **Circle** is a subtype of **Ellipse**. Any object that's a circle is also an ellipse—albeit a very round ellipse. So, any operation that's expecting to receive an ellipse as an argument in a message should be very happy to get a circle.[3]

---

[1] Incidentally, a subtype needn't be a subclass either: Even in a language without a superclass/subclass inheritance construct, you can still design and implement subtypes by hand (by tediously duplicating code). However, you must obey the principle of type conformance, which is the central topic of the next section.

[2] For more on the principle of type conformance in an object-oriented environment, see [Meyer, 1992] and [LaLonde and Pugh, 1991]. The principle of type conformance is very similar to what authors such as Barbara Liskov term the principle of substitutability [Liskov et al., 1981].

[3] Of course, this doesn't work if the operation tries to stretch the circle! This explains the caveat "when any *accessor* operation is executed" (which implies that no object changes state) in my definition of conformance. Difficulties like this carry a real sting, as I discuss in Section 11.3.

Although we saw in Section 11.1 that subclass and subtype are distinct concepts, I'm now going to turn around and say

> In a sound object-oriented design, the type of each class should conform to the type of its superclass. In other words, the class/subclass inheritance hierarchy should follow the principle of type conformance.

The reason for this is that in order to effortlessly exploit polymorphism, we must be able to pass objects of a subclass in lieu of objects of a superclass. But how do we ensure that the type of each subclass truly and honestly conforms to the type of its superclass? To answer that question, I introduce in the next section two important sub-principles of conformance, contravariance and covariance. These principles use the notions we covered in the previous chapter: class invariants, operation preconditions and postconditions, state-space, and behavior.

### 11.2.1 The principles of contravariance and covariance

> MENTAL HEALTH WARNING: The concepts in this section are important, but counterintuitive on first reading. When I first encountered them, I had to think about them seven times prior to breakfast before they made sense. So be prepared to read this section at least twice.

To ensure type conformance in a subclass, you first need to ensure that the invariant of the subclass is at least as strong as that of the superclass. For example, **Rectangle** has the invariant **w1 = w2 and h1 = h2**. **Square** has the invariant **w1 = w2 and h1 = h2 and w1 = h1**. That's okay, because **Square**'s invariant is stronger than **Rectangle**'s. (In other words, an object that meets **Square**'s invariant is bound to meet Rectangle's invariant; an object that meets **Rectangle**'s invariant may not meet **Square**'s.)

Second, you need to ensure that the following three constraints on your operations are met:

1. Every operation of the superclass has a corresponding operation in the subclass with the same name and signature.

2. Every operation's precondition is no stronger than the corresponding operation in the superclass. This is called the *principle of contravariance,* so named because the strength of operation preconditions in the subclass goes in the *opposite* direction to the strength of the class invariant. That is, the operations' preconditions get, if anything, weaker.

3. Every operation's postcondition is at least as strong as the corresponding operation in the superclass. This is called the *principle of covariance,* so named because the strength of operation postconditions in the subclass goes in the *same* direction as the strength of the class invariant. That is, the operations' postconditions get, if anything, stronger.[4]

These constraints are trivially satisfied if a subclass inherits an operation *as is* from its superclass. In that case, the name and signature and pre- and postconditions are identical in both the superclass and the subclass. More interesting issues arise when the subclass overrides a superclass's operation with an operation of its own, as in the following example.

### 11.2.2 An example of contravariance and covariance

The class **Employee** has a subclass **Manager**. (Yes, managers comprise a subclass of employees!) What must we do to ensure that **Manager** is a valid subtype of **Employee**?

First, let's say that an invariant of **Employee** is **gradeLevel > 0** and an invariant of **Manager** is **gradeLevel > 20**. That makes **Manager**'s class invariant stronger than **Employee**'s, so we're in good shape there.

Second, let's consider **calcBonus**, an operation of **Employee**. This operation takes **perfEval** (performance evaluation) and calculates **bonusPct** (bonus percentage), which is a percentage of the employee's regular salary. The UML of Fig. 11.2 shows **calcBonus**'s signature.

---

[4] The terms "stronger" and "weaker" in the above constraints don't describe quality or robustness in any way. "Stronger" isn't "better" and "weaker" doesn't mean "worse."

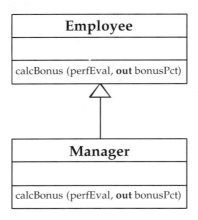

*Fig. 11.2:* **calcBonus** *defined on* **Employee** *and* **Manager**.

We'll say for simplicity that **perfEval** (the input argument passed to **calcBonus**) is an integer between 0 and +5. The output argument, **bonusPct**, is between 0 percent and 10 percent.

The algorithms to compute bonuses may be different for managers and non-managers. Therefore, the class **Manager** may override **calcBonus** with an operation of its own (with the same name and signature).

So let's turn to the operation **calcBonus** as defined on the class **Manager**. Remember that for **Manager** to conform to **Employee**, **Manager.calcBonus** must have a precondition equal to or weaker than **Employee.calcBonus**. This means, in particular, that the range of **Manager.calcBonus**'s input argument **perfEval** must be equal to or larger than the range of **Employee.calcBonus**'s input argument **perfEval**. (To help me remember that "larger range = weaker condition," I think of "larger" as "looser," and "smaller" as "tighter.")

Therefore, each of the following ranges for **Manager.calcBonus**'s input argument **perfEval** would be legal:

    0 to 5     // equal in both classes **Manager** and **Employee**
    0 to 8     // larger (weaker) in **Manager**
    -1 to 9    // larger (weaker) in **Manager** (assuming a negative evaluation
               // makes sense!)

Conversely, the following ranges for **Manager.calcBonus**'s input argument **perfEval** would be illegal:

| | |
|---|---|
| 1 to 5 | // *smaller (stronger) in* **Manager** |
| 2 to 4 | // *even smaller (stronger) in* **Manager** |

Figure 11.3 shows the legal and illegal ranges for **perfEval** in graphic form.

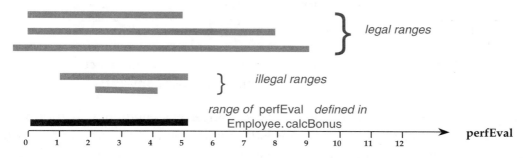

*Fig. 11.3: Contravariance: possible ranges for* **perfEval** *in* **Manager.calcBonus (perfEval, out bonusPct)**.

For **Manager** to conform to **Employee**, **Manager.calcBonus** must have a postcondition equal to or stronger than **Employee.calcBonus**. This means, in particular, that the range of **Manager.calcBonus**'s output argument **bonusPct** must be less than or equal to the range of **Employee.calcBonus**'s output argument **bonusPct**.

Therefore, each of the following ranges for **Manager.calcBonus**'s output argument **bonusPct** would be legal:

| | |
|---|---|
| 0% to 10% | // *equal in both classes* **Manager** *and* **Employee** |
| 0% to  6% | // *smaller (stronger) in* **Manager** |
| 2% to  4% | // *even smaller (stronger) in* **Manager** |

Conversely, each of the following ranges for **Manager.calcBonus**'s output argument **bonusPct** would be illegal:

| | |
|---|---|
| 0% to 12% | // *larger (weaker) in* **Manager** |
| -1% to 13% | // *larger (weaker) in* **Manager** *(assuming a negative* |
| | // *bonus makes sense!)* |

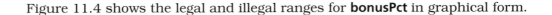

Figure 11.4 shows the legal and illegal ranges for **bonusPct** in graphical form.

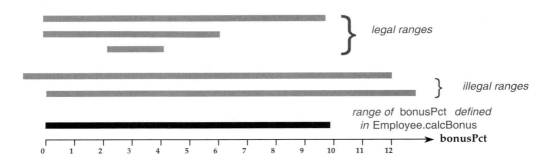

*Fig. 11.4: Covariance: possible ranges for* **bonusPct** *in* **Manager.calcBonus (perfEval, out bonusPct)**.

The principles of weaker preconditions and stronger postconditions in subclasses' operations aren't intuitive (to say the least!). Indeed, when I present them in seminars, I leave my car engine running in case I need to make a quick getaway from infuriated students. So, I think I should explain further *why* these principles will be important to you as an object-oriented designer when you want your class hierarchy to follow a true type hierarchy.

The chief importance of type conformance stems from the demands of second-order design, in which an argument in an object-oriented system, being an object, carries "the entire genetic code of its class" along with it.[5] For example, let's assume that we pass, one at a time, objects representing employees to an operation **conductYearEndReview** (defined, say, on the class **Department**), which conducts a year-end review of each employee. **conductYearEndReview** figures out a value for **perfEval** (the evaluation of the employee's performance), and then sends a message to the object referred to by **emp** to carry out the object's operation **calcBonus**.

---

[5] Second-order design arises when message arguments have level-2 encapsulation—in other words, when message arguments are (references to) objects. In first-order design, software components communicate by passing arguments with level-1 encapsulation (functions or procedures). In zeroth-order design, arguments are simply data. (Structured design is mainly zeroth-order design, with some first-order design occurring where procedures are passed as arguments.)

Textually, this message would be **emp.calcBonus (perfEval, out bonusPct)**.  I show it in UML in Fig. 11.5.[6]

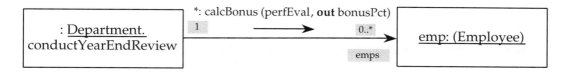

*Fig. 11.5:* **conductYearEndReview** *invoking* **calcBonus** *on each* **emp** *object.  (A given* **emp** *may be either of class* **Employee** *or of its subclass,* **Manager.***)*

When the operation **conductYearEndReview** gets each object (the object referred to by **emp**) from the collection of employees (referred to by **emps**), all this operation knows is that it has hold of some kind of employee, either an ordinary employee or a manager.  But **conductYearEndReview** doesn't worry about what kind of employee it has; the operation knows that, through the miracle of polymorphism, when the **emp** object gets the message **emp.calcBonus (perfEval, out bonusPct)**, the object will respond correctly.

The operation **conductYearEndReview** also knows **calcBonus**'s precondition, the rule for using **calcBonus** correctly:  So long as **perfEval** is between 0 and 5, **calcBonus** will work fine.  But let's assume that we violated type conformance by *strengthening* the acceptable range for **Manager.calcBonus**'s input argument, **perfEval**, to 2 to 4.  Then, if **conductYearEndReview** innocently sends **perfEval = 1** to an object that happens to be a manager, then **calcBonus** would blow up, complaining that the passed **perfEval** was out of range.

If, on the other hand, we followed the type-conformance principle and *weakened* the acceptable range for **Manager.calcBonus**'s input argument, **perfEval**, to 0 to 8, we'd have no problem.  Then, whatever **Manager.calcBonus** received for **perfEval** in the range 0 to 5, it could handle without skipping a beat.

The inverse applies to the postcondition.  Here, if we violated the conformance principle of stronger postconditions, it would be **conductYearEndReview** that would

---

6 A note on the notation:  The message is sent iteratively to each employee in a list of employees for a department.  The parentheses around **Employee** signify that polymorphism is at work and that the sender of the message doesn't know which version of **calcBonus** will be used to satisfy the message each time the message is sent.

suffer. Let's say we weaken the acceptable range for the output argument, **bonus-Pct**, to the range -1 percent to 12 percent. Since the range for employees is supposed to be 0 percent to 10 percent, **conductYearEndReview** would be taken completely by surprise to get a negative number returned to it. It might even be so surprised that it would blow up.[7]

### 11.2.3 A graphic illustration of contravariance and covariance

Since the principles of contravariance and covariance can seem impenetrable to people who only encounter them through textual definitions, I've wondered for a long time how to present the principles in a more graphic and immediate way.

In fact, I wondered that very thing recently while I was watering my garden, at home near Seattle. (Believe it or not, our summers are normally hot and dry.) As I was struggling to stretch the hose to reach the farthest tree, I noticed that my neighbor was also irrigating his parcel of real estate.

"Greetings, fellow hoser!" I announced cordially over our rude common fence.

"What do you want this time?" he replied in his usual neighborly manner. He seemed to already know what I wanted, recalling the last time I accosted him and talked him into lending me his lawnmower. (That had been a real *coup de grace*.)

*My neighbor, the hoser.*

After a short negotiation, I borrowed his hose to extend my meager line to the corner of the garden. Unfortunately, however, his hose had a nonstandard $\frac{5}{8}$-inch diameter, whereas mine was of the regular $\frac{3}{4}$-inch caliber. By luck, though, I had

---

[7] For more ramifications of this employee/manager example, see Exercise 1 at the end of the chapter.

recently purchased from the local HoseHut a set of pipe adapters for foreign travel. After running back from the toolshed, I fitted the hoses together and quickly finished spritzing my carrots.

My horticultural hose-connecting experience inspired me to draw Fig. 11.6:

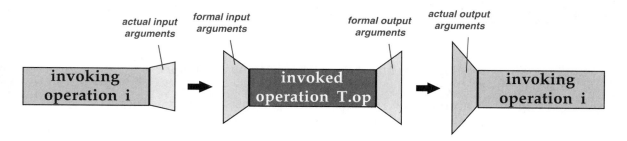

*Fig. 11.6: The invocation of supertype **T**'s operation **op**.*

Using the running hose-connector metaphor, this figure illustrates the connection of an invoking operation **i** to an invoked operation **op** defined on a class **T**. On the left (the input side), we see **i**'s actual input arguments to the invoked operation **op** getting poured into the pipe of **op**'s formal arguments. So long as the range of every actual argument from **i** falls within the range of its corresponding formal argument in **op**, the input arguments will be acceptable to **op**. To symbolize this fact, I've drawn **op**'s formal input argument pipe larger than **i**'s actual input argument pipe.

On the right (the output side), we have the converse situation, as the invoked operation **op** returns its results. (For clarity, I've repeated the name **i** on the far right.) Here, the range of each formal output argument must fall within the acceptable range of the corresponding actual arguments in **i**. To symbolize this, I've drawn **op**'s formal output argument pipe smaller than **i**'s actual output argument pipe.

Now let's look at Fig. 11.7. Here, I show another operation **op**, this time defined on **S**, which is a subclass of **T**. In other words, **S.op** overrides and redefines **T.op**. If **S** is to be a true subtype of **T**, then **S**'s operations, such as **op**, must obey the principles of contravariance and covariance. I've symbolized the principle of contravariance by making **S.op**'s formal input argument pipe (on the left side) even larger than was **T.op**'s formal input argument pipe. So, if **T.op**'s formal input argument pipe was large enough to accept **i**'s actual arguments, then **S.op**'s will certainly be large enough, too.[8]

---

[8] To keep this description straightforward, I've used the concept of a larger range rather than the more general concept of supertype as an illustration of a weaker precondition.

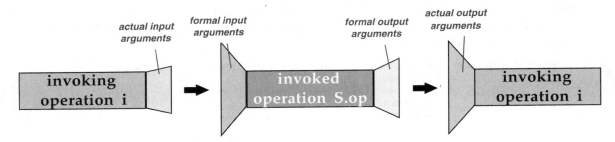

*Fig. 11.7: The invocation of operation* **op** *on subtype* **S**.

On the right (the output side), we again have a converse situation. Here, I've symbolized the principle of covariance by making **S.op**'s formal output argument pipe even smaller than was **T.op**'s formal output argument pipe. So, if **T.op**'s formal output argument pipe was small enough to fit **i**'s actual arguments, then **S.op**'s will certainly be small enough, too.

The two figures above illustrate the commonsense nature of the otherwise obscure principles of contravariance and covariance: For a subtype to conform—that is, to stand in for its supertype—an object of the subtype must be acceptable wherever an object of the supertype would have been.

### 11.2.4 A summary of the requirements for type conformance

The principle of type conformance demands that for a subclass **S** to be a true subtype of a class **T**, the following six constraints must hold. (The first two apply to whole classes; the last four apply to individual operations.)

1.  The state-space of **S** must have the same dimensions as **T**. (But **S** may have additional dimensions that extend from **T**'s state-space.)

2.  In the dimensions that **S** and **T** share, the state-space of **S** must either be equal to or lie within the state-space of **T**. (Another way to say this is, The class invariant of **S** must be equal to or stronger than that of **T**.)

For each operation of **T** (say, **T.op**) that **S** overrides and redefines with **S.op**:

3.  **S.op** must have the same name as **T.op**.

4. The argument list of **S.op**'s formal signature must correspond to the argument list of **T.op**'s formal signature.

5. The precondition of **S.op** must be equal to or weaker than **T.op**'s precondition. In particular, each formal input argument to **S.op** must be a supertype of (or the same type as) the corresponding formal input argument to **T.op**. (This is the principle of contravariance.)

6. The postcondition of **S.op** must be equal to or stronger than **T.op**'s postcondition. In particular, each formal output argument from **S.op** must be a subtype of (or the same type as) the corresponding formal output argument from **T.op**. (This is the principle of covariance.)

## 11.3 The Principle of Closed Behavior

In the preceding sections, we looked at the principle of type conformance. Although respecting type conformance is necessary for us to be able to design sound class hierarchies, type conformance isn't enough. Informally speaking, type conformance alone leads to sound designs only in read-only situations, that is, only when accessor operations are executed. (Perhaps you recall the fine print, "when any accessor operation of the object is executed," in Section 11.2's definition of type conformance.)

To handle situations in which modifier operations are executed, we also need the *principle of closed behavior*. This principle requires that the behavior inherited by a subclass from a superclass should respect the invariant of the subclass. Without this principle, we may design subclasses with modifier operations that have error-prone behavior.

> In an inheritance hierarchy based on a type/subtype hierarchy, the execution of any operation on an object of class **C**—including any operation inherited from **C**'s superclass(es)—should obey **C**'s class invariant. This is the *principle of closed behavior*.

As an example of the principle of closed behavior, let's look at how behavior defined on a superclass **Polygon** might affect objects of a subclass **Triangle.** It's important to remember, as we go through this example, that in each of the two cases below, the object concerned is of class **Triangle** but the behavior is defined by an operation of **Polygon**.

> *Case 1:*  For this, we'll take the object **tri1** to be the left triangle of Fig. 11.8, and the operation to be **Polygon**'s operation **move**, which causes an object to move to the right by a centimeter, say.

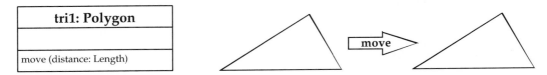

*Fig. 11.8:* **Polygon.move**, *as applied to the triangle* **tri1**, *preserves its "triangle-ness."*

After the move, **tri1** is still a triangle. This piece of **Polygon**'s behavior leaves an object that was in the state-space of **Triangle** still in that same state-space. We say that the subclass **Triangle** is *closed* under the behavior defined by the super-class's operation **move**.

> *Case 2:*  Again we'll take **tri1** to be a triangle. However, this time we'll consider an operation **addVertex** (inherited from **Polygon**) that adds a vertex to a polygon. (See Fig. 11.9.) After this transition, **tri1** won't be a triangle; it will be a quadrilateral. **Triangle** is *not* closed under the behavior defined by **Polygon**'s operation **addVertex**.

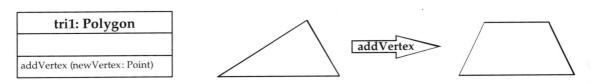

*Fig. 11.9:* **Polygon.addVertex**, *(wrongly!) applied to the triangle* **tri1**, *destroys its triangular property.*

Closure of a subclass under its superclasses' behavior doesn't happen automatically, as we saw in the example of Case 2. You have to "design it in." Therefore, as the designer of a subclass, you must often deliberately and explicitly override operations of the superclass that would otherwise violate the invariant of the subclass.

In this example, as the designer of **Triangle**, you must take one of the following three corrective actions:

- Avoid inheriting **addVertex**, or
- Override **addVertex** so that it has no effect (possibly also raising an exception), or
- Be prepared (in the operation **addVertex**) to reclassify the **Triangle** object as **Rectangle**, if that behavior, which *doesn't* preserve **Triangle**'s closure, is acceptable to the application.[9]

In general, the designer of a class has the duty to ensure the class's closure of behavior. Designers of other classes shouldn't have to worry about maintaining the invariant of the class.

However, it never hurts to check. If you're designing a class that sends a message to an object to invoke a modifier operation, you should check for closure of behavior on the target's class. If you send the message assuming the general (superclass) case, you must be prepared for the object to refuse the message or simply to return without any action. If this is a problem, then before you send the message you need to do one of the following:

- Check the run-time class of the target, or
- Restrict polymorphism on the variable that points to the target, or
- Design the message on the assumption that the target is of the most specific, lowest class in the relevant hierarchy—that is, the class with the greatest constraint on its behavior.

In the next chapter, we use the concepts and principles of this chapter and Chapter 10 to examine specific problems that arise from inheritance, polymorphism, and genericity (alias parameterized classes).

---

[9] Exercise 4 at the end of the chapter follows up this last point and suggests a more drastic—but also more robust—modification to the inheritance design.

## 11.4 Summary

This chapter introduced the principles of type conformance and closed behavior, which help us identify potential problems in our class-hierarchy designs.

The principle of type conformance says that class **B** is a subtype of class **A** only if an object of class **B** will be acceptable in any context in which an object of class **A** is expected and no modifier operation will be executed. A sound super-class/subclass hierarchy will follow this principle: If class **B** is a subclass of class **A**, then **B** will conform to **A**.

To achieve this property, you must ensure the following: The invariant of each subclass is at least as strong as that of its superclass; each superclass operation has a corresponding operation in the subclass with the same name and signature; each subclass operation's precondition is no stronger than the corresponding operation in the superclass; and each subclass operation's postcondition is at least as strong as the corresponding operation in the superclass. These last two principles are termed, respectively, the principle of contravariance and the principle of covariance; they are very important in determining the correct classes for arguments of subclass operations.

Each class in a sound class hierarchy will also obey the principle of closed behavior. This requires that the behavior that a subclass inherits from super-class(es) must respect the subclass's invariant. A subclass designer may achieve this by: not allowing inheritance of conflicting behavior; overriding inherited operations that have conflicting behavior; or migrating to another class an object that has violated its class invariant.

Although you may have found some of the topics in this chapter to be difficult or abstruse, you'll find that they soon become second nature if you refer to them continually as you build class hierarchies and design object-oriented code. Fortunately, you'll also find that ninety percent of the object-oriented design situations you face are straightforward and don't call for deep design knowledge. But when you do run into that awkward ten percent, knowing the principles of this chapter will set you apart from the object-oriented herd.

## 11.5 Exercises

1.  What if, in Section 11.2.2's example of the **Employee** class with the subclass **Manager**, you couldn't make **calcBonus**'s precondition at least as weak and its postcondition at least as strong in the subclass? (For example, the users' business demands may drown out the cries of your design conscience.) Since that would mean that **Manager** isn't a true subtype of **Employee**, should you then revamp your class structure accordingly?

2.  Given that an abstract operation can, by definition, never be invoked, does it make any sense for such an operation to have a precondition and a postcondition? (Hint: Consider the preconditions and postconditions of the concrete operations in the subclasses that override the abstract operation.)

3.  Take the class **Rectangle** and consider one of its operations, **rotate**, which rotates a rectangle in its plane by some angle:

    rotate (rotationAngle)

    Consider also **Square**, a subclass of **Rectangle**, which inherits the operation **rotate**. After **rotate** executes on a square or a rectangle, a square is still a square and a rectangle is still a rectangle. Their fundamental invariants apply, as they did before **rotate** executed. No problem!

    But now take another operation of **Rectangle**, **scaleHoriz**, which stretches a rectangle in one dimension:

    scaleHoriz (scaleFactor)

    A stretched rectangle is still a rectangle. But a stretched square is no longer a square! The class invariant **w1 = h1** is broken. The behavior prescribed by **scaleHoriz** keeps a rectangle within the state-space of its class, but it doesn't keep a square within its state-space. **Rectangle** is therefore closed under **scaleHoriz**, but **Square** is not. If you're not allowed to modify the overall class hierarchy, what are some of your options in the design of **Square** to preserve its closure under **scaleHoriz**?

4.  As we saw in Section 11.3, adding a vertex to a triangle, rectangle, or hexagon violates the principle of closed behavior. If you *are* allowed to modify the overall class hierarchy, what class would you insert between **Polygon** and **Triangle**, **Rectangle**, and **Hexagon** to preserve closed behavior?

## 11.6 Answers

1.  Here's one solution: If the discrepancy in **calcBonus** is **Manager**'s *only* depar-ture from being a true subtype, then you probably wouldn't disturb the class-inheritance hierarchy. But you must document the discrepancy well—in both the overall class description and the specific offending operation. Look carefully for this type of problem in design walkthroughs; if it slips through, it will sooner or later cause a polymorphic blowup.

    But beware, because this solution is like toying with fire. You would be wise to revamp the class hierarchy, as shown in Fig. 11.10, and to cope with the problem once and for all, even if some existing applications will need modification to use the new class name **NonManager**.

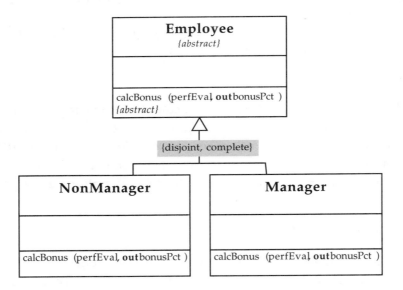

*Fig. 11.10: The class hierarchy with a **NonManager** class factored out of **Employee**.*

Notice that non-managers now have their own class, alongside the managers' class. Since the partitioning between the two classes is complete, we need never create an object of class **Employee**, and **Employee** can thus reasonably be made abstract. Presumably, the operation **calcBonus** should also be abstract, because based on the description of personnel policy in this chapter, a common algorithm for calculating managers' and non-managers' bonuses doesn't appear to exist.

Thanks to the structure used in Fig. 11.10, there isn't any contra- or covariance problem between **NonManager.calcBonus** and **Manager.calcBonus**, because **Manager** isn't a subclass of **NonManager**.

2. Assume that an abstract operation **C.op** with precondition **pre** and postcondition **post** is overridden by the concrete operations **op$_1$**, **op$_2$**, ..., **op$_n$** in the respective subclasses of **C**. The following statements are then true:

$$\text{pre} = \text{pre}_1 \text{ and } \text{pre}_2 \ldots \text{ and } \text{pre}_n$$
(where **pre$_1$** is the precondition of **op$_1$**)

$$\text{post} = \text{post}_1 \text{ or } \text{post}_2 \ldots \text{ or } \text{post}_n$$
(where **post$_1$** is the postcondition of **op$_1$**)

The first expression guarantees contravariance, because any **pre$_i$** must be weaker than **pre** (since **pre** implies **pre$_i$**). The second expression guarantees covariance, because any **post$_i$** must be stronger than post (since **post$_i$** implies **post**).

Since you cannot invoke an abstract operation, the above discussion of an abstract operation's pre- and postconditions may seem academic. But it is relevant when you consider a typical piece of object-oriented design (similar to what we saw in Section 11.2.2 for **calcBonus**): A sender object (say **sendobj**) iterates through a collection of objects of various classes (subclasses of a common parent), sending the same message to each object and invoking through polymorphism the version of an operation that suits the respective object's subclass.

The message-sending object **sendobj** may as well be invoking the common operation—the abstract operation on the superclass—since it has no idea which object belongs to which subclass. In other words, for **sendobj** to fulfill its "contract" with the target objects, **sendobj** should be using the precondition **pre** and the postcondition **post** to ensure the messages' correctness.

But I've seen situations where **sendobj** cannot guarantee, for instance, the satisfaction of **pre** when it sends a message. (For an extreme example, imagine that the preconditions **pre$_1$**, **pre$_2$**, ..., **pre$_n$** are incompatible with one another, so that the Boolean combination **pre$_1$ and pre$_2$ ... and pre$_n$** evaluates to **false**. Then **sendobj** can *never* satisfy **pre**!) If **sendobj** cannot guarantee **pre**, then you should back off from polymorphism and have **sendobj** test for the class (say $C_i$) of each object as it goes. Then **sendobj** should make sure that it meets each specific precondition **pre$_i$** before sending a message to that particular object.

3.   The problem is that we can't simply let **Square** inherit **scaleHoriz** as is. So, without modifying the class hierarchy, we have four options in the design of **Square**:

   a.   Raise an exception when a square violates its class invariant.

   b.   Override **scaleHoriz** so that it does nothing for squares.

   c.   Override **scaleHoriz** with some different behavior that preserves **Square**'s class invariant. (Perhaps invoke **scaleVert** with an equal **scaleFactor** so that a square stretches equally in both dimensions.)

   d.   Take the more drastic approach of letting a square get stretched. Then, change its class—in other words, "migrate" it—from **Square** to **Rectangle**.

All four of the above design options preserve the class invariant of the object's class. Admittedly, though, the last one does so rather trickily by changing the object's class to suit its new state. The option that you choose involves looking at how **Square** will be used in your current application as well as how it might be reused in future applications.

4.   **Polygon** should have two subclasses, **FixedSidedPolygon** and **VariableSided-Polygon**. **Triangle** (and similar classes) should be a subclass of **FixedSided-Polygon**. This approach allows a designer to place the **addVertex** operation in **VariableSidedPolygon** and removes the need to override **addVertex** in classes representing fixed-sided polygons. (If **VariableSidedPolygon** has subclasses, then you should name them **MutableTriangle**, **MutableRectangle**, and so forth, if vertices could be added or removed.)

   Note that this solution, with its factored-out subclasses, resembles the one in Fig. 11.10, on page 296.

# The Perils of Inheritance and Polymorphism

Inheritance and polymorphism set object orientation apart from traditional ways of building software. However, although the inheritance construct is very powerful, it's also perhaps the most overused software construct since the **goto** statement. Object-oriented debutants feel that they must design with inheritance at every possible opportunity in order to show that they've "arrived" in the world of object orientation. The result: problems being perverted to fit an "inheritance design" to the extent that some designs are utterly unimplementable.

The first section of this chapter covers four of the ways that people force inheritance into their object-oriented designs, together with my suggested alternatives to inheritance in those design situations. The second section of this chapter explores polymorphism's danger.

## 12.1 Abuses of Inheritance

I've taken the four examples in this section from real projects in real shops, where real people were applying object orientation, in many cases for the first time. Some of the perverse designs that I cite were secretly and gruesomely coded; others caused disputes that were lengthy, bloody, and—in one case—team-destroying.

The aims of this section are to examine different patterns of inheritance and to prevent loss of time and morale on *your* next project by pointing out where inheritance is and isn't appropriate. Throughout the chapter, the examples proceed from outrageous misuse to more subtle and questionable uses of inheritance. By the way, I've changed the names of the classes in the examples to protect the guilty perpetrators.

### 12.1.1 Mistaken aggregates

The upper class-inheritance diagram of Fig. 12.1 shows the class **Airplane** with its four supposed subclasses: **Wing**, **Tail**, **Engine**, and **Fuselage**. This "design" can never be expressed as code, because there's no sensible way to program the subclasses to meet the needs of the application. The designer has obviously mixed up the concepts of class inheritance and object composition. If we read the diagram as it is, we would assume that a tail "is a kind of airplane" and also that a wing "is a kind of airplane."

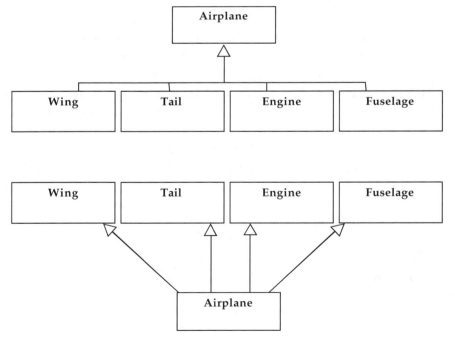

*Fig. 12.1: Two "designs" for the class* **Airplane**—*what's wrong with this picture?*

The lower diagram shows multiple inheritance as another putative design solution to object composition. The designer of this second **Airplane** read his diagram as, "An airplane is a wing, a tail, an engine, and a fuselage." That sounds almost correct. However, the true way to interpret the diagram is, "An airplane is simultaneously a kind of wing, a kind of tail, a kind of engine, and a kind of fuselage." And that certainly is wrong!

The designer was sublimely programming from this ineffable **Airplane** "design" when I met him. He brought the design to my attention only when he began to have trouble programming the fact that an airplane has two wings.

Yet his problems ran even deeper than this individual design: The designer was a novice to object orientation; he'd read but a single book; he'd received no training; he'd been brainwashed by a colleague into thinking that multiple inheritance was the greatest thing since multiple personality; and he worked in a shop where peer reviews were discouraged because they interfered with work. Apart from that, as they say, everything was fine![1]

### 12.1.2 Inverted hierarchy

The example of inheritance in Fig. 12.2 barely warrants a second glance, because its structure exactly corresponds to a normal organization chart. An employee reports to a manager and a manager reports to a board member. But there's a problem. What the diagram actually says is, "An employee is a *kind of* manager, and a manager is a *kind of* board member."

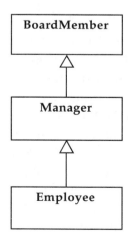

*Fig. 12.2: Looks right—but is it?*

---

[1] This example is very similar to the object-composition **Glider** example in Section 4.3.1, which you may want to review.

I assume that the reality is the other way up, that is, "A board member is a kind of manager, and a manager is a kind of employee." (For simplicity, let's assume that board members are employees.) To depict that, we would simply invert Fig. 12.2 and put **Employee**, which is the most general class, at the top. (As we saw in Exercise 1 of the previous chapter, this is just the start. Next, we may want to factor out further subclasses.)

### 12.1.3 Confusing class and instance

The example of multiple inheritance in Fig. 12.3 is infuriatingly subtle. When I met it in a walkthrough, I *knew* in my bones that it was wrong, but I had tremendous difficulty in explaining why. My difficulty was compounded because the actual application was an obscure, technical one that my walkthrough peers opined I was unqualified to judge.

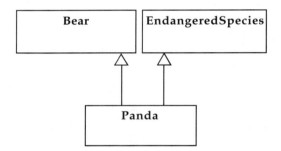

*Fig. 12.3: What does **Panda** really mean?*

The path to understanding this problem is through the question, What are the *instances* of the three classes in Fig. 12.3? The instances of **Panda** are, for example, An-An, Chu-Chu, Ling-Ling, Miou-Miou, Hee-Hee, and Oh-Oh. The instances of **Bear** are, for example, Yogi, Teddy, Winnie, Paddington, and Fred. However, the instances of **EndangeredSpecies** are entire species, such as the snub-nosed muskrat, the lesser-spotted tree-gripper, the reasonably large rat of Sumatra, the unreasonably large rat of Borneo, the American codhurr, the Latvian yodeling-flea, and the net-gilled nodenik, for example.

In other words, two of the classes (**Panda** and **Bear**) have individual animals as instances, whereas the third (**EndangeredSpecies**) has *whole species* as instances. It would be entirely correct to say, "Ling-Ling is an instance of panda" or "Ling-

Ling, as a panda, is also an instance of bear." However, it's *not* correct to say, "Ling-Ling is an instance of endangered species." Thus, the class **Panda** could inherit from **Bear** but not from **EndangeredSpecies**.[2]

So, how should we design the fact that some species are endangered? Figure 12.4 illustrates the answer.

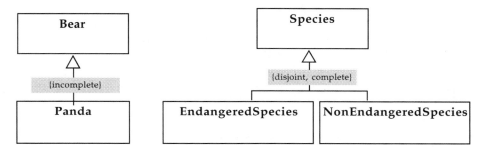

*Fig. 12.4: The corrected inheritance hierarchies.*

The diagram on the left shows the class **Panda** inheriting from **Bear**: A panda is a kind of bear, but as **{incomplete}** tells us, not the *only* kind of bear. The diagram on the right shows **EndangeredSpecies** and **NonEndangeredSpecies** inheriting from **Species**: The two classes represent mutually exclusive subsets of the complete set of species.

The two classes on the left deal with animals, while the class hierarchy on the right deals solely with species. But how do we link the two sides? How do we design the fact that pandas and some other species are endangered?

One design would add an instance attribute, **isEndangered: Boolean**, in **Bear** (or in its superclass, **Animal**). Although this would work, it's overkill, because it affords too much generality. For example, we'd be able to record that Yogi was endangered, whereas Paddington was not. I don't think that's the intent of this application.

Instead, as Fig. 12.5 shows, we should give the class **Animal** the attribute **species** (and the internal variable **species**) to link it to a **Species** object. Each subclass of **Animal** represents a species (such as **Bear**, **Panda**, **Toad**, and so on), and **species** holds the appropriate fixed value for objects of that subclass. For example, each **Bear** object could be given a value when it is instantiated, or each **Bear** object could retrieve the value of its **species** attribute from a class constant **ourSpecies: Species = bear** in the class as a whole.

---

[2] All right, I know that a panda is a kind of raccoon, but please bear with me.

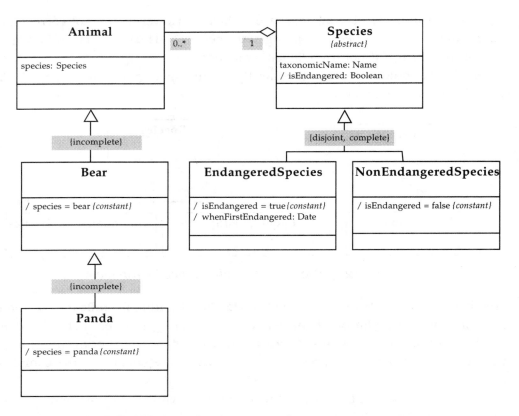

*Fig. 12.5: The corrected inheritance hierarchies, in more detail.*

Whichever way **Bear.species** gets its value, objects of class **Bear** could look up their species—and the associated properties of their species—at run-time with code such as

    **self**.species.isEndangered;
    **self**.species.maxWeight;

**maxWeight: Weight**, for example, would be an instance attribute of **Species**. **isEndangered: Boolean** would be an instance attribute (actually a constant) in both **EndangeredSpecies** and **NonEndangeredSpecies**, set to **true** and **false**, respectively.[3]

---

[3] **isEndangered** could instead be made an instance attribute of **Species**, rather than of **Endangered-Species** and **NonEndangeredSpecies**. See Exercise 1 at the end of this chapter.

People who see this panda example often say to me, "Gosh, that was a remarkably poignant example of inheritance misuse. It brought tears to my eyes. But it's absolutely useless for my shop, which deals in manufacturing applications, not in dwindling racoons." Since I couldn't resist a *cri de coeur* like that, here's Fig. 12.6.

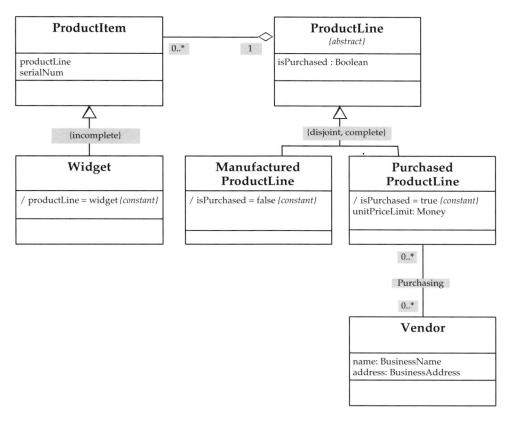

*Fig. 12.6: An analogous business-system structure.*

Although the two applications are from the disparate worlds of wildlife and manufacturing, there's a strong structural resemblance between Figs. 12.5 and 12.6: The former is based around the aggregation of **Animal** into **Species**, the latter around the aggregation of **ProductItem** into **ProductLine**. **Widget**, analogous to **Bear** in Fig. 12.5, is a subclass of **ProductItem**. (Although **Widget** is the only subclass I've shown, others such as **Gadget**, **Gizmo**, and **Whatsit** could exist.)

On the right side of Fig. 12.6, the classes **ManufacturedProductLine** and **PurchasedProductLine** inherit from **ProductLine**. These two classes, which are mutually exclusive, form a complete partitioning of **ProductLine**.[4] The association at the bottom right records the vendors of a product line. (Some purchased product lines haven't yet been assigned a vendor—hence the **0** in the lower multiplicity.)

### 12.1.4 Misapplying is a

In our next example, which again is a version of a real application design, we need to remember the length, width, and height of rooms—perhaps hotel rooms—which in our application are treated as cuboids. We also need to know the volume of each room. Since we already have the class **Cuboid** in our class library, we design a class **Room** that simply inherits from **Cuboid**, as shown in Fig. 12.7.

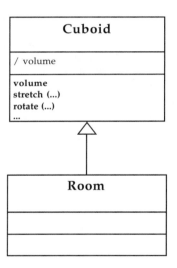

*Fig. 12.7:* **Room** *is designed simply to inherit from* **Cuboid**.

So far, this looks great. An object of class **Room** can return its volume simply by executing the get operation **volume** (implemented as a function) that **Room** inherits from **Cuboid**; no new code is needed. Furthermore, since a room is a cuboid, the *is a* requirement of valid inheritance is satisfied. However, this is where the design begins to fall apart.

The first problem is the behavior that **Room** inherits from **Cuboid**. This behavior comes from **Cuboid**'s operations, such as **stretch**, **rotate**, and so on. Since

---

[4] Exercise 2 at the end of this chapter addresses the possibility of an overlap between **Manufactured-ProductLine** and **PurchasedProductLine**.

such behavior is illegal for **Room** (outside of Wonderland, at least), we should override it—that is, cancel it—in **Room**. On the other hand, we *could* leave the operations in as part of the official behavior of **Room**. Then we'd have to trust people to use them judiciously, because rotating a room in three-dimensional space has curious effects indeed!

But bigger problems arise when we have to deal with rooms of other shapes. Let's say that some rooms are cylindrical. Inheritance, which worked so well for cuboids, should also work for cylinders. So now, as the left diagram of Fig. 12.8 shows, **Room** inherits multiply from both **Cuboid** and **Cylinder**.

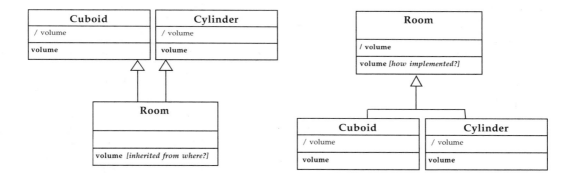

Fig. 12.8: Two attempts to introduce cylindrical rooms.

But what does this mean? The multiple inheritance implies that a given room is both a cylinder *and* a cuboid. That would yield a strangely shaped room, and it certainly wasn't what the designer intended. When I asked the designer about this multiple inheritance, he told me that the diagram indicated that a room could be a cylinder *or* a cuboid. Another designer said, "Then you've got the diagram upside-down," and proceeded to expound the virtues of the diagram on the right side of Fig. 12.8.

We're getting nowhere fast here, although the hierarchy in which **Cuboid** and **Cylinder** inherit from **Room** will at least work—after a fashion. If we instantiate an object of either **Cuboid** or **Cylinder**, then that object will inherit all the necessary properties of **Room**. However, we still have the problem of the extraneous behavior (such as **stretch** and **rotate**), which we now have no chance to override.

The second design in Fig. 12.8 has even deeper problems. We know from Chapter 9 that we shouldn't encumber a class from a low domain (**Cuboid** or **Cylin-**

der) with one from a higher domain (**Room**). If we did so, our geometry library would need the **Room** class in order to work. Also, since not all cuboids are rooms, the class **Cuboid** would have mixed-instance cohesion, as well as mixed-domain cohesion.

The root of the problem is in my original statement, "A room is a cuboid," which I tossed out to justify inheritance. This was sleight of hand. A more precise statement is, "A room has the attribute of shape. The shape of all the rooms in this application is that of a cuboid," which makes quite a difference. A new design for **Room** appears in Fig. 12.9.

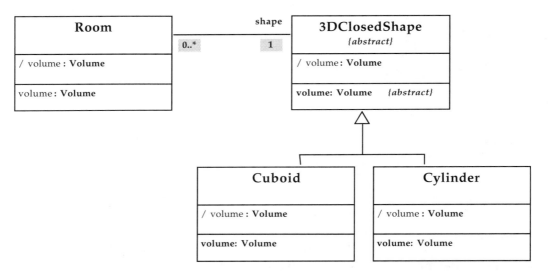

*Fig. 12.9:* **Room** *has a shape, of class* **3DClosedShape**, *and requests its volume from* **shape**.

This time, **Room** has an instance variable **shape** that points to an object of class **3DClosedShape** (or of one of its subclasses, such as **Cuboid**, **Cylinder**, or **Tetrahedron**). In other words, **Room** contains the declaration:

    **var** shape: 3DClosedShape;

At the initialization of a particular room, the variable **shape** is assigned to an object of the correct shape and size for the given room. The operation **Room.volume** now works by asking the object pointed to by the variable **shape** to compute **volume**, as shown in Fig. 12.9. The particular formula actually evaluated (either the cuboid-volume or cylinder-volume formula) will depend on the actual shape of the room—polymorphism, again.

This technique of accessing the code in another class is called *message forwarding*. An object of class **Room** forwards the volume message to another object of class **Cuboid** (or whatever). The design approach of message forwarding, which is an alternative to inheritance, doesn't automatically grant you access to all of another class's facilities. Instead, you have to target that access, message by message, to the attributes and operations of the other class that you seek. You may want to review the headaches that the original, inheritance-based designs caused and check that this message-forwarding design has cured them.[5]

## 12.2 The Danger of Polymorphism

Polymorphism promotes conciseness in object-oriented programming by allowing an operation to be defined with the same name on more than one class and by allowing a variable to refer to an object of more than one class. Polymorphism thus enables the operating environment to choose automatically the correct operation to execute as the result of a message, without the need for a complicated **case** statement.

So, both operations and variables may exhibit polymorphism. In a good design, these two facets of polymorphism work in harmony. In an imperfect design, however, polymorphism brings danger: An object may receive a message that it doesn't understand and may consequently raise a fatal run-time exception.

Sections 12.2.1 and 12.2.2 introduce the polymorphism of operations and variables, respectively. Section 12.2.3 explores polymorphic design problems in terms of general messages to objects. Section 12.2.4 explores a special case, the danger of polymorphism in the design of parameterized classes.

### 12.2.1 Polymorphism of operations

To explain the risk of sending an object a message that it doesn't understand—and how to avoid that risk—I need to introduce some new terms.

---

[5] Some authors use the term *delegation* for message forwarding. However, I've steered clear of this term, because it's more commonly used for an object-oriented concept that's beyond the scope of this book. (Nevertheless, I do define "delegation" in the Glossary.)

> The *scope of polymorphism of an operation* **op** is the set of classes upon which **op** is defined. A scope of polymorphism (SOP) that forms a branch of the inheritance hierarchy—that is, a class **A** together with all of its subclasses—is termed a *cone of polymorphism*, with **A** as the *apex of polymorphism*.

Figure 12.10 depicts a class-inheritance tree. If an operation **op** is defined on each of the shaded classes, then those shaded classes form **op**'s cone of polymorphism (COP). It's a cone in that the shaded classes form a complete branch; the class **A** is the apex of polymorphism (AOP).[6]

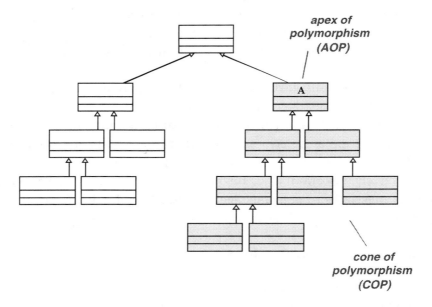

*Fig. 12.10: The structure of a COP.*

As a more concrete example, if the get operation **area** (or **getArea**, if you prefer) is defined on **Polygon** and on all the subclasses of **Polygon**—either locally or via inheritance—then **area**'s SOP forms a cone, with **Polygon** at the apex. See Fig. 12.11.

---

[6] One of my students refers to **A** as the "conehead of polymorphism." Don't let me catch *you* using this term!

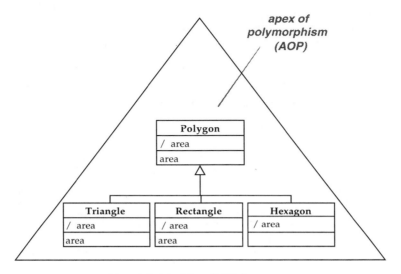

*Fig. 12.11: The COP for* **area.**

Figure 12.12 depicts another class-inheritance tree, where the operation **op** is defined on all the shaded classes. This figure shows a *ragged* SOP in that the shaded classes don't form a neat cone comprising a complete branch of the tree.

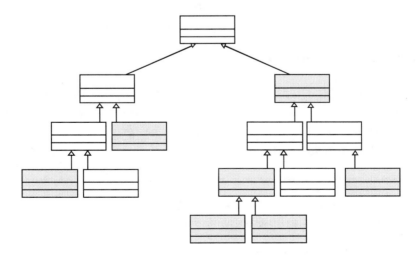

*Fig. 12.12: The structure of a (ragged) SOP.*

A simple, concrete example of a ragged SOP for an operation is a little harder to find.  However, the familiar operation **print** (which sends information about the target object to a **PrinterDriver** object) often has a raggle-taggle bunch of classes in its SOP.  If **print** is defined on **Spreadsheet**, **TextDoc**, and **EMailMsg**, then its SOP isn't a cone, because classes like **Elephant** and even the "top" class, **Object**, have no operation **print** defined on them.[7]  See Fig. 12.13.

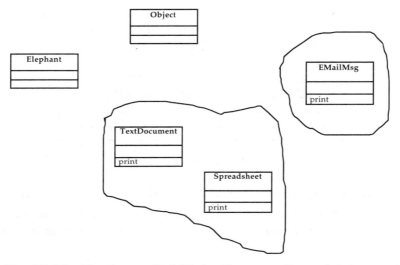

*Fig. 12.13: The (ragged) SOP for the operation* **print** *(assuming that* **Elephant** *and* **Object** *have no operation* **print***).*

## 12.2.2 Polymorphism of variables

As I mentioned earlier, the term polymorphism also applies to variables, which at various times can point to objects belonging to different classes.  So now I define *scope of polymorphism* again, this time applying the terms to a *variable* that holds an object's handle, rather than to an operation.

> The *scope of polymorphism of a variable* **v** is the set of classes to which objects pointed to by **v** (during **v**'s entire lifetime) may belong.

---

[7] I assume here that **Spreadsheet**, **Textdoc**, and **EMailMsg** don't have a common superclass, such as **PrintableDoc**.  I also assume, for this example, that **print** is an acceptable operation for these classes and doesn't cause any cohesion problems.

The scope of polymorphism for a variable is similar to the scope of polymorphism for an operation: They both comprise a group of classes. The classes in the SOP for a variable, however, are those of all the objects to which the variable may refer at any time during the system's execution. We can also use the terms *cone of polymorphism* and *apex of polymorphism* for a variable, in the same way that we use the terms for an operation.

Here are three examples to illustrate the scope of polymorphism of a variable:

1.  Let's say that the declaration **var t: Triangle** allows the variable **t** to point to any object of class **Triangle** or of **Triangle**'s descendants. (This is a natural situation in Java, Eiffel, or C++, in which polymorphism of a variable is usually restricted to descendants of a given class.) In this example, therefore, the variable's SOP forms a cone, with the class **Triangle** as the apex.

2.  Let's say that a variable **v** is allowed, at various times, to point to an object of class **Horse**, **Circle**, or **Customer**. (This may easily occur in Smalltalk, in which polymorphism of variables is typically unrestricted; in other languages, you may have to declare **v** to be of the most-general class, **Object**.) In this example, then, the variable's SOP isn't a cone in that the classes **Horse**, **Circle**, and **Customer** don't have a common immediate superclass to form an AOP. At least, we *presume* that they don't have a common superclass. Although you could introduce a nonsense class as a superclass of **Horse**, **Circle**, and **Customer** to provide an artificial AOP for a variable, I know you wouldn't do that.[8]

3.  In this third example, let's say that (again, as in Smalltalk) we have a declaration **var x: Object**, where the class **Object** is the top of the class hierarchy. In other words, the variable **x** may point to any object whatsoever (because all classes are descendants of **Object**). This time, the variable's SOP does form a cone. Indeed, this cone is the largest one of all, because its apex is the top class in the inheritance hierarchy.

Now let's consider the risk of sending a message to an object that doesn't understand it and discuss how to avoid that risk.

---

[8] As we'll see later, some object-oriented programming languages (such as Eiffel) will enforce a COP on a variable if you so instruct the compiler.

### 12.2.3 Polymorphism in messages

A message is composed of a variable that points to the target object and an operation name that states the operation to be invoked. As we saw above, both the variable and the operation have an SOP. The relationship between these two SOPs has a significant impact on system reliability—or lack thereof. As I discuss this below, I'll assume that the SOPs of the operation and of the variable are COPs—that is, that they form neat cones.

I'll call our sample message **targobj.targop**, where **targobj** is the variable pointing to the target object and **targop** is the operation to be invoked on the target object. There are two possible relationships between **targobj**'s COP and **targop**'s COP:

> *Case 1:* **targobj**'s COP lies within **targop**'s COP. In other words, the variable's COP lies within the operation's COP. See Fig. 12.14.

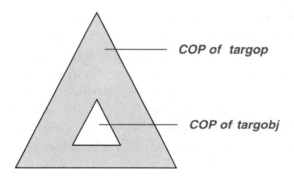

> *Fig. 12.14: The COP of the variable **targobj** lies within the*
> *COP of the operation **targop**.*

> *Case 2:* Part or all of **targobj**'s COP falls outside **targop**'s COP. In other words, some of the variable's COP falls outside the operation's COP. See Fig. 12.15.

In the first case, all is well with the design. No matter what object **targobj** points to, that object will be of a class that "understands" the message **targop**. The second case, however, represents a miserable, non-robust design. This designer is dicing with the devil, because it's quite possible that at run-time **targobj** will point to an object upon whose class **targop** is not defined. If this happens, then the program will probably blow up with a run-time error.

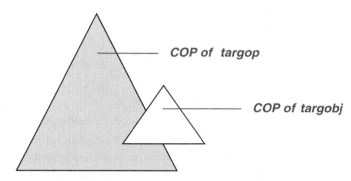

*Fig. 12.15: Part of the COP of the variable* **targobj** *falls out-side the COP of the operation* **targop.**

For a specific example of the possible relationships between a variable's SOP and an operation's SOP, consider the message **factoryDevice.switchOn**. As above, there are two cases:

> *Case 1:* **factoryDevice** always points to an object of class **Tap**, **Motor**, or **Light**, all of which can switch on. Then, **factoryDevice**'s SOP is within **switchOn**'s SOP and everything's fine. However, I'd suggest changing the variable's name to **operableDevice** or **switchableDevice** to indicate that it refers to a device that can be operated or switched. I use a prefix like **switchable** in my variable names as a codeword meaning "anything that can execute **switchOn**."

> *Case 2:* **factoryDevice** refers to any piece of hardware in the factory, including objects of class **Tap**, **Motor**, **Light**, **Pipe**, **Tank**, **Door**, **Lever**, and so on. Not all of these kinds of devices "know how to switch on." This time, therefore, much of **factoryDevice**'s SOP falls outside **switchOn**'s SOP and there's a significant chance of a run-time problem, when, for instance, a plain old door is told to switch on.

Whenever you indulge in the luxury of polymorphic messaging, make sure that you assess the SOP of the message's operation and the SOP of the message's target variable. You need to be especially diligent if either the target variable or the operation has a ragged SOP.

### 12.2.4 Polymorphism and genericity

A parameterized class (termed a template class in C++) is a class that takes a class name as an argument whenever one of its objects is instantiated, as I discussed in Section 1.9. Designers often use parameterized classes to construct containers such as lists, stacks, and sorted trees.

But, like the polymorphic messages that we saw in Section 12.2.3, parameterized classes may create run-time problems because of scope-of-polymorphism conflicts. To illustrate this, let me introduce a parameterized class **SortedTree <NodeClass>** (rather like the binary tree example we saw in Section 1.9).

The following statement instantiates a specific sorted tree:

> realNumTree := SortedTree <Real>.New;

which creates a new object, a sorted tree pointed to by **realNumTree**, that will hold real numbers in its nodes. We could also write

> custTree := SortedTree <Customer>.New;

which would hold objects of class **Customer** in its nodes. Inside the class **SortedTree**, we would write statements such as

> node := NodeClass.New;

The above statement creates a new node of class **Real** (for the first **SortedTree** object above) or of class **Customer** (for the second **SortedTree** object above). Also, in the code of **SortedTree** (say, within the operation **printTree**), we might see

> node.print

which would send a message to the object pointed to by the node to "print itself." Elsewhere in the code within **SortedTree**, we might see the following comparison:[9]

> **if** newItem.lessThan (currNode)
>> // **newItem** *and* **currNode** *each points to a* **NodeClass** *object*
> **then** ...

---

[9] In some languages, the syntax for this comparison would be simply **if newItem < currNode then ....**

The problem with the above comparison is this: The designer of **SortedTree** doesn't have the foggiest idea which actual class will be passed as an argument at run-time. For example, someone could write **SortedTree <Fuselage>.New**, **SortedTree <Complex>.New**, or **SortedTree <Animal>.New**.

The first of these three classes may not understand **print**, and the second may not understand **lessThan**, while the third may understand neither **print** nor **lessThan**. Thus, there's a tremendous risk of a run-time failure when an object held in the tree, of class **Animal** for example, is told to "print itself."

The problem occurs because the scope of **NodeClass** is unlimited: At run-time, *any* class could be provided to **SortedTree** to play the part of **NodeClass**. Thus, the scope of polymorphism of **node: NodeClass** is huge, as big as could be. On the other hand, the scope of polymorphism of the operations within **SortedTree** is actually very small: It's the intersection of the SOPs of the individual operations (such as **print**, **lessThan**, and so on).

Therefore, **SortedTree**'s design violates the principle that I outlined in Section 12.2.3, which ensures that an operation with a smaller SOP is not applied to a variable with a larger SOP. Some of the variables in **SortedTree** have SOPs that potentially lie well outside the SOPs of the operations used in **SortedTree**.

There are two solutions to this design problem: The first is for every user of a parameterized class to be responsible enough to ensure that the actual run-time class provided (say, **ProvidedClass**) is within the SOP intersection described above. In other words, objects belonging to **ProvidedClass** must be able to understand *every* message that the parameterized class's internal code could send to them.

So, when you program or document a parameterized class, you should list at the start of the class all the operations that any class provided as an actual run-time argument should possess. For example, if your parameterized class is **SortedTree**, you would state that any provided classes (such as **Customer** or **Product**) should have the operations **lessThan**, **greaterThan**, **equalTo**, or whatever, defined on them. This will help people who use your parameterized class to check that they're providing an actual class with the right set of operations defined on it.

The second solution is to provide some kind of guard at the beginning of the parameterized class's code. The guard checks that the actual class supplied can understand the required messages. Unfortunately, in most mainstream object-oriented languages, this is difficult to do. Eiffel, however, has an ingenious way to form such a guard.

In Eiffel, you can insist that the actual class supplied to a parameterized class at run-time must be within a specific cone of polymorphism. You do this by specifying the class that's the apex of polymorphism.

For example, you would first write at the top of a parameterized class **Node-Class -> Printable**, where **Printable** is the AOP. This means that the parameterized class will only accept the class **Printable** or one of its descendants as a supplied run-time class.

Next, you would design a class called **Printable** with an operation **print** (which should be an abstract operation—or deferred, to use Eiffel's terminology—because its implementation will be defined in descendants of **Printable**). Now, since everyone who supplies a class to **SortedTree** *has to* supply a descendant class of **Printable**, the supplied class is guaranteed to have the operation **print** defined on it.

Notice that the class name **Printable** implies that "this class has printable objects," which means in turn that "this class must have the operation **print** defined on it." Similarly, the class **Comparable** might be one with the operations **lessThan**, **greaterThan**, and **equalTo** defined on it. This "-able" convention for the class names of operations' AOPs is similar to the convention for variable names I described in Section 12.2.3 (regarding **switchable**).

Printability, comparability, and so on are examples of class capabilities. The class **Printable** in the above Eiffel solution is, in effect, an embodiment of printability—the "print capability."

## 12.3 Summary

Inheritance and polymorphism bring power and conciseness to object-oriented software. They also bring dangers. The chief danger of inheritance lies in its overuse or—more precisely—in its misapplication in situations where other object-oriented constructs would be better.

In this chapter, we looked at four common abuses of inheritance. The first is the use of inheritance where aggregation is called for. This is an elementary mistake, rarely committed by experienced object-oriented designers. The second abuse is the inversion of the class-inheritance hierarchy, often caused by the lure of a misleading real-world structure.

The third misuse of inheritance is the confusion of class with instance. This tends to occur in designs that have to cope both with groups (such as species or companies) and with individuals (such as animals or employees). Since the problem is usually subtle, a designer may initially overlook it. However, when the faulty design is transformed into code, it becomes obvious that the code cannot work as intended. The fourth misuse involves using inheritance where message-forwarding would provide a more appropriate design construct.

The term polymorphism applies both to operations and to variables. A polymorphic operation is defined on several different classes. A polymorphic variable may at various times point to objects belonging to different classes. The scope of polymorphism (SOP) of an operation is the set of classes upon which the operation is defined.

The scope of polymorphism of a variable is the set of classes of the objects to which the variable may point at various times during the system's execution. A scope of polymorphism that forms a complete branch of a class-inheritance hierarchy is called a cone of polymorphism (COP); the class at the top of the cone is the apex of polymorphism (AOP).

For the safe use of polymorphism in operations, the SOP of the variable pointing to the target object must lie within the SOP of the operation named in the message. If a designer transgresses this guideline, then a run-time error will probably occur.

A parameterized class is one that takes a class name as an actual argument when its objects are instantiated at run-time. The designer of the code within a parameterized class generally doesn't know what the actual class supplied to it will be. Therefore, the SOP of any variables referring to objects of the supplied class is very large. So, too, is the chance that the guideline of the previous paragraph will be violated. Some languages (such as Eiffel) enforce restrictions on the actual classes that may be supplied and thereby minimize the run-time errors caused by rampant polymorphism.

## 12.4 Exercises

1. In the **Panda** example of Section 12.1.3, I suggested that you could make **isEndangered: Boolean** an instance attribute (a constant) in both **NonEndangeredSpecies** and **EndangeredSpecies**. But are these subclasses needed? Couldn't we get by with just **Species**, as I suggested in a footnote in Section 12.1.3?

2. What modifications would you have to make to Fig. 12.6 if the two classes **ManufacturedProductLine** and **PurchasedProductLine** were overlapping, rather than disjoint, subclasses of **ProductLine**? (In other words, some product lines are both manufactured in-house *and* purchased from outside vendors.)

3. As you probably know, a last-in, first-out stack is a structure that supports a collection of objects, only one of which may be accessed (read) or removed (popped) at a time. That object is said to be the head of the stack; it is the one that was most recently added to (pushed on) the stack.

   A list is a structure with almost identical properties. Comment on the design of the class **Stack** that inherits from **List**, as shown in Fig. 12.16. (In this example, **List** is a class that supports a singly linked list, accessible at only one end.)

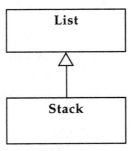

*Fig. 12.16:* **Stack** *is designed to inherit its implementation from* **List***.*

4. Are any of the object-oriented design principles we saw in earlier chapters germane to the inheritance problems we covered in this chapter? If so, which ones?

5. In Section 12.2.1, when I defined the scope of polymorphism of an operation, I implicitly dealt only with single-inheritance class hierarchies. What additional issues, if any, would arise with an operation's SOP if multiple inheritance were present?

6. Assume that an operation **op** is an abstract operation of a class **C** (which is an abstract class). Assume further that **op** is concretely defined on all subclasses of **C**, which are not abstract. Could you consider **C** to be **op**'s apex of polymorphism, even though **C.op** isn't actually implemented?

7. Assume that an operation **op** is defined on a class **A** and is inherited by all of **A**'s descendants. Normally, this would mean that **A** and its descendants form a *cone* of polymorphism for **op**, with **A** at the apex. But, in what situation could this group of classes form a ragged SOP, rather than a complete cone?

8. Imagine that you could close your eyes and wish for an automated tool to help you evaluate your object-oriented design or program. What facilities might your tool provide to assess whether a variable's SOP lay within an operation's SOP?

## 12.5 Answers

1.  We could possibly remove the class **NonEndangeredSpecies**. However, the class **EndangeredSpecies** is necessary if we want to record, say, **dateOfFirstEndangerment**, **responsibleConservationOrg**, and so on. (Otherwise, if these attributes are defined only for some instances of **Species**, then **Species** would have mixed-instance cohesion.) If these attributes aren't relevant, we may get by with **Species** alone. Then, we could make **isEndangered** an attribute of **Species**.

    The value of **isEndangered** would not be constant, because species move into and out of endangerment. However, a species' movement into and out of endangerment becomes a little more difficult to design if **Species** has the subclasses **NonEndangeredSpecies** and **EndangeredSpecies**. One design approach is this: Delete an object of one subclass (say, **NonEndangeredSpecies**) after saving its information; then instantiate an object of the other class (**EndangeredSpecies**), copying across any relevant information about the species.

2.  If the two classes **ManufacturedProductLine** and **PurchasedProductLine** overlapped, then the attribute **isPurchased** with its mutually exclusive **true** and **false** values would no longer make sense. Instead, we'd need *two* Boolean attributes: **isPurchased** and **isManufactured**. We should also add another class, named **ManufacturedAndPurchasedProductLine** (or something less cumbersome), that inherits multiply from **ManufacturedProductLine** and **PurchasedProductLine**. This new class would generate objects representing product lines that were both manufactured and purchased.

    The migration issue of Answer 1 (above) presents itself here, too: What if a particular product line changes, for example, from purchased to manufactured? Again, as above, we could delete the object from its subclass and reinstantiate it in another subclass. But this time I'd like to present an alternative solution, which often goes under the dramatic term *object slicing*.

    Figure 12.17 shows **ProductLine** with its two new parts, **manufacturedAspect** (of class **ManufacturedProductLine**) and **purchasedAspect** (of class **PurchasedProductLine**). Each of these parts holds special information about its respective kind of product line (manufactured and/or purchased). For example, **PurchasedProductLine** maintains a **Purchasing** association with **Vendor**.

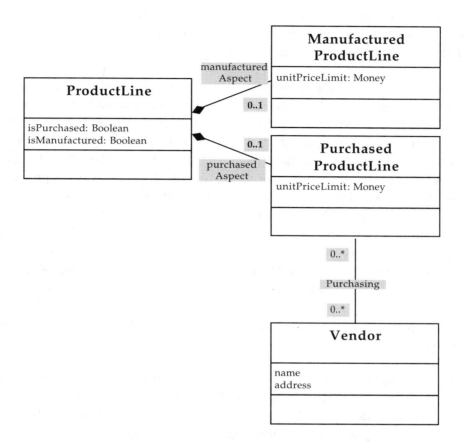

*Fig. 12.17: The class* **ProductLine** *with its two optional aspects as parts.*

Under this design, an object of class **ProductLine** accesses this special information by querying an attribute of the appropriate aspect. For example, to check **unit-PriceLimit** of a product line (the maximum that management wants to pay to buy a unit of a product line), an object would use the following code:

```
if self.isPurchased
then maxPrice := self.purchasedAspect.unitPriceLimit
    ...
```

This design approach relies again on message forwarding, which we also used as an alternative to inheritance in Section 12.1.4's **Room** and **Cuboid**. And that leads us nicely to the next answer.

3. Inheritance may not be the best approach here because **List** may have behavior that isn't appropriate for **Stack**—for example, an operation called **insertIn-Middle**, which isn't allowed for a stack. The *names* of operations inherited by **Stack** may not be quite right, either. Perhaps the operation that **Stack** would term **push** would be termed **append** by the class **List**. (The Eiffel language allows you to rename inherited operations to avoid just this kind of problem.)

But, for me, the biggest problem of having **Stack** inherit from **List** is my annoyance at seeing **Stack** under **List** when I browse through the class hierarchy. After all, in object orientation, implementation is supposed to be hidden from the casual observer.

Message forwarding (from a **Stack** object to a **List** object) would be a better approach to designing **Stack**. As we saw in Section 12.1.4, message forwarding tends to disturb the class hierarchy less than inheritance does (especially if, for example, you later change the design of your **Stack** class to use **Array** rather than **List**).

4. Yes. The principle of type conformance, covered in Chapter 11, is especially important. Even the subtle **Panda** problem, for example, could be assessed via type conformance. Informally, we could ask: Can a **Panda** subtype be provided both in a context in which a **Bear** type is expected and one in which a **Species** type is expected? (Of course, the answer, as we saw in this chapter, is no.) Another design criterion, valuable for assessing the problem with the room and the cuboid, is class cohesion, covered in Chapter 9.

5. An environment with multiple inheritance may have some subtle domain-of-definition problems. The most common example is so-called name clash, which occurs when two operations with the same name (but from two distinct classes) have overlapping scopes of polymorphism. See Fig. 12.18.

A class inheriting both operations will be utterly confused. Language designers have come up with several solutions for determining which operation gets inherited; the best of these is to make the inheriting class rename the inherited operations unambiguously.[10]

---

[10] [Meyer, 1992] treats this topic in detail.

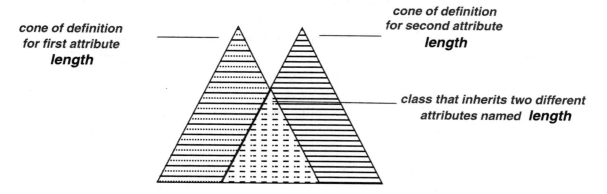

*Fig. 12.18: Two operations with the same name and over-
lapping cones of polymorphism.*

In Section 8.2.2, we saw an example of multiple inheritance that caused a
name clash in a video-rental application. The class **ProgramRentalItem** inherits operations from both **PhysicalInventoryItem** and **RecordingMedium**, each of
which had a get operation for an attribute named **length**. (The former means
length of the cassette in inches, while the latter means playing time in minutes.) Thus, any reference to **length** in **ProgramRentalItem** is ambiguous.

As I hinted in Chapter 8, the best solution is to rename the get operation
**length** (the one that's inherited from **RecordingMedium**) as **duration**. The
operation name **duration** not only removes the ambiguity of **length**, but also
better captures the idea of playing time.

6.  Yes, I do consider **op**'s scope of polymorphism to form a cone, with **C** at the
apex. It doesn't matter that **C.op** has no concrete implementation, since **C** is
an abstract class and will never have any instantiated objects, anyway.

The answer would be the same even if **op** weren't defined *at all* on **C**, so
long as **C** were abstract and **op** were defined on all of **C**'s nonabstract subclasses. For example, if the get operation **area** were defined on all of **Polygon**'s subclasses but not on **Polygon** itself, then the AOP of the **area** would
still be **Polygon**, so long as **Polygon** were an abstract class from which no
objects could be instantiated.

7.   The seemingly complete COP for **op** would be a ragged SOP if some of **A**'s descendants overrode **op**—let's say **NaughtyClass**, for example—either by canceling it out or by giving it a completely different definition or signature from those in **A.op**.  In other words, although in a literal sense **NaughtyClass.op** can be invoked polymorphically, I consider this practice to be such a violation of the spirit of polymorphism that I would cast **NaughtyClass** out beyond the pale of **op**'s SOP.  This practice would also violate type conformance.

   Overriding an operation with an utterly different operation definition is therefore a risky practice:  It may create the illusion that a variable's SOP lies within an operation's SOP, even though—because of the gaps in the operation's SOP—it doesn't.  Indeed, in the words of the object-oriented expert Lynwood Wilson:  "Anyone who overloads an operation name by giving it a completely different definition will never enter the Kingdom of Heaven."

8.   Such a tool might provide two lists of classes.  The first list would contain the classes to whose objects the variable might point, and the second would contain the classes on which the operation was defined.  The tool might also provide an error list of classes that appeared on the first list but not on the second.  Of course, there's a limit to what automation can provide.  For example, as we saw in Answer 7 above, human deviousness can always defeat the guileless mechanisms of a software-engineering tool.

# 13

# Techniques for Organizing Operations

This chapter presents several design techniques for organizing the attributes and operations of a class's interface. These structures go a long way toward increasing the robustness, reliability, extensibility, reusability, and maintainability of your classes.

The first section covers a very useful object-oriented design technique: the use of mix-in classes to add capabilities to a class without compromising the class's cohesion. The use of mix-in classes also increases the chance that classes developed for one application will be readily reusable in another application.

The second section shows how you can organize operations into concentric rings to create an interface within an interface and to further strengthen encapsulation, the chief characteristic of object orientation. This chapter applies several design principles that we covered in previous chapters and uses samples of object-oriented code to illuminate new design concepts.

## 13.1 Mix-In Classes

In this section, I use two examples, one from business and one from graphics, to illustrate the concept of mix-ins.

### 13.1.1 A business example

In order to show what mix-in classes are and how they can be useful, let me describe an object-oriented design problem from an accounts-receivable application at Grabbitt and Runne Enterprises, Inc. (The business could actually be any business that uses a simple invoice to bill for the sale of various items.) The aggregate class **Invoice**, and its constituent class **InvoiceItem**, appear in Fig. 13.1.

*Fig. 13.1: An **Invoice** object is an aggregate of **InvoiceItem** objects.*

The requirement is this: Messrs. Grabbitt and Runne want to send each customer's invoice to that customer in the manner that the customer prefers. Some customers like their invoices faxed, some like them e-mailed, and some of the more-nostalgic customers like their invoices delivered in a bouncy little mail truck.

At first, this requirement doesn't seem to be a design problem at all. We might add, for example, a **fax** operation to **Invoice** that allows an invoice to "fax itself" to the appropriate customer. But that design would create mixed-domain cohesion in **Invoice** (because it would probably encumber **Invoice** with at least some details of faxing protocol, which belong in the architecture domain). Practically speaking, the design would limit **Invoice**'s reusability and, worse, possibly limit the reusability of the **fax** operation.

Confronted by the problems of the previous paragraph, we could create the design of Fig. 13.2. Here, we've factored out operations such as **eMailInvoice** and **faxInvoice** into their own class, **SendableInvoice**, which inherits from the original **Invoice**. Now **Invoice** can revert to its pristine form, with ideal cohesion. To create a new invoice, we instantiate a **SendableInvoice** object, rather than an **Invoice** object. The operation **faxInvoice** will know how to run the fax-modem and will have access to the **Invoice** information (via inheritance) for use in the fax.

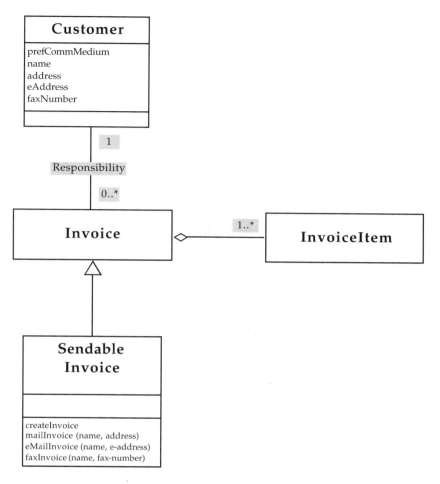

*Fig. 13.2: The class **SendableInvoice** preserves the
cohesion of **Invoice**.*

Incidentally, I should say a word or two about the class **Customer**, which is related
via a **Responsibility** association to the class **Invoice**. This association records
which customer is responsible for which invoices. The attributes defined on **Customer** include **prefCommMedium** (which records a customer's choice of communication medium) and **eAddress** (a customer's e-mail address).

That's all well and good, but the design of Fig. 13.2 still limits the reusability
of the **fax** operation, which we've even *named* **faxInvoice**. What a shame to have
all that fax-modem expertise tucked away and unavailable to us when we want to
fax things other than invoices: acknowledgments, greetings, threats, and so on.

This is where a mix-in class comes to the rescue, as Fig. 13.3 shows.

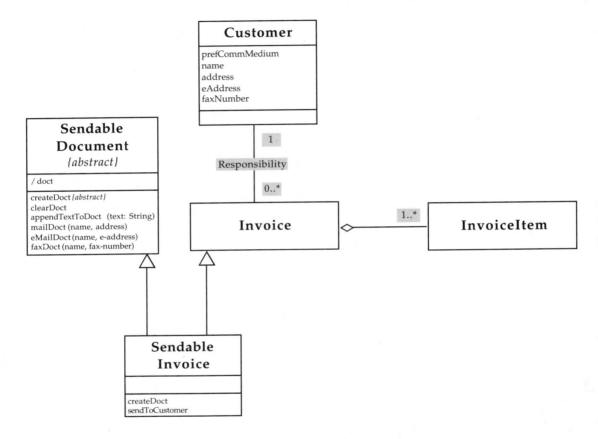

*Fig. 13.3:* **SendableInvoice** *now inherits multiply from* **Invoice** *and the mix-in class* **SendableDocument**.

Although Fig. 13.3 is only subtly different from Fig. 13.2, the difference is important. In this design, we've "factored up" a mix-in class, **SendableDocument**, which has all the smarts to carry out faxing and e-mailing. Importantly, however, **SendableDocument** has no knowledge about invoices; it's a general class, capable of faxing or e-mailing any document. So now let's follow, blow by blow, how the whole design works.

When we want to create an object to represent a new invoice, we invoke **SendableInvoice.New**. We initialize this object—let's refer to it as **sendableInv**—by giving it invoice items (and any header information) and by linking it to the responsible **Customer** object. All of the above happens via inheritance, using the machinery of **Invoice** since **sendableInv** belongs to a subclass of **Invoice**.

Via inheritance, **sendableInv** also has available the communication capabilities of **SendableDocument**. So, when we want to send the invoice represented by **sendableInv**, we do so in two steps:

1. We invoke **sendableInv.createDoct**. This operation creates a standard text document (composed of pages and lines) that can be faxed, e-mailed, or printed. However, the attribute that represents this text document (and the variable that implements it) is defined on **SendableDocument**, *not* on **SendableInvoice**.[1] The operations that build the document (**clearDoct** and **appendTextToDoct**) are also defined on **SendableDocument**. The pseudocode for **SendableInvoice.createDoct** looks something like this:[2]

```
public operation createDoct
begin
    self.clearDoct;                   //set text area to empty — SD
    get the invoice header;                      //— I
    convert it to the text form headerText;
    self.appendTextToDoct (headerText)           //— SD

    repeat
        get the next invoice line;               //— I
    until no more invoice lines
        convert it to the text form lineText;
        self.appendTextToDoct (lineText)         //— SD
    endrepeat

    end createDoct;
```

---

[1] You can use the read-only attribute **doct** to access this text document.

[2] Key: The comment "— **SD**" means "via inheritance from **SendableDocument**"; the comment "— **I**" means "via inheritance from **Invoice**."

2.   Now that we've filled **doct** with the invoice information, we need to send it, using the operation **SendableInvoice.sendToCustomer**, whose code looks something like this:

```
public operation sendToCustomer
begin
  cust:Customer := self.responsibleCust;                        //— I

  case cust.prefCommMedium
     "MAIL":     self.mailDoct (cust.name, cust.address);    //— SD
     "E-MAIL":  self.eMailDoct (cust.name, cust.eAddress);  //— SD
     "FAX":      self.faxDoct (cust.name, cust.faxNumber);  //— SD
  else ...;                                                 // error!
  endcase;

end sendToCustomer;
```

**SendableDocument** is an example of a mix-in class.  A *mix-in class* typically supports an abstraction or mechanism that could be useful in several other classes, but which doesn't belong in any particular one of those classes.  Parceling away distinct abstractions and mechanisms as mix-in classes enhances the reusability of those abstractions and mechanisms.

   Normally, you don't instantiate objects from mix-in classes; that's why **SendableDocument** is marked as **{abstract}**.  Instead, other classes (like **SendableInvoice**, in this example) inherit a mix-in class's capabilities.  **SendableInvoice** also inherits from the class **Invoice**, from which an object of class **SendableInvoice** gets specific information for carrying out its business capabilities.  So, since a mix-in class needs to inherit from at least two superclasses, mix-in classes work best when your language supports multiple inheritance.

### *13.1.2 A graphics example*

In case you hate business-related examples, I've included this next example of mix-in classes just for you.

Figure 13.4 depicts a rectangle that's free to move and rotate so long as it remains within its enclosing frame. (I indicate the limits of its current extent on the screen with lines marked **top**, **bottom**, **left**, **right**.)

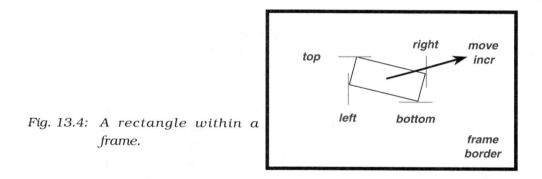

*Fig. 13.4: A rectangle within a frame.*

Figure 13.5 shows part of the design of **RectangleInFrame**, which inherits from the two classes **Rectangle** and **ShapeInFrame**.

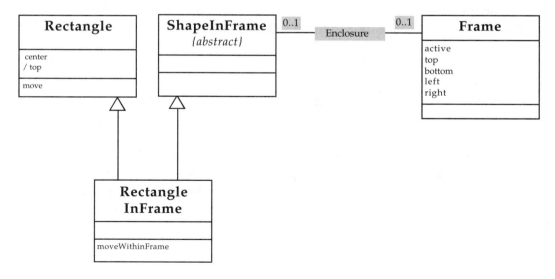

*Fig. 13.5: The inheritance hierarchy for **RectangleInFrame**.*

The class **Rectangle** is the ordinary class that supports the manipulation (such as the moving, rotating, or stretching) of rectangles. It's a class you may purchase as part of a class library. **ShapeInFrame** is a less conventional class that records the relationship between a rectangle and its enclosing frame. **ShapeInFrame** is another example of a mix-in class.

In the rectangle example shown in Fig. 13.4, the mix-in class **ShapeInFrame** offers a design solution to a problem presented by the rectangle and frame: We need to record the frame in which a given rectangle is enclosed. If we modify the class **Rectangle** by giving it a variable to hold this information, then we'll reduce the reusability of **Rectangle** in other applications. (To use the terms that I presented in Chapter 9, we would encumber **Rectangle** with **Frame** and give it mixed-role cohesion.) Anyway, the vendor of **Rectangle** might not give us the source code to modify!

A more reasonable place to record a rectangle's relationship with its frame is the class **RectangleInFrame**, which is all about rectangles and frames. That would be fine, except that **EllipseInFrame** and **TriangleInFrame** also need access to the same kind of machinery. That's why the mix-in class **ShapeInFrame** is so useful. **ShapeInFrame** can be mixed in with **Rectangle** to yield **RectangleInFrame**. In another part of the system, it could be mixed in with **Ellipse** to form **Ellipse-InFrame**, and so on.

Now, let's look at some code for the three classes, **Rectangle**, **ShapeInFrame**, and **RectangleInFrame**. See the box on page 335.

The internal representation of **Rectangle** objects rests on four variables:

- **center** records the center-point of a rectangle
- **height** and **width** are self-explanatory
- **orientation** records how much a rectangle is tilted (counterclockwise from the horizontal)

These are the *core representational variables* of the class; they're the pillars that internally support the external abstraction of a rectangle. Since the information that these variables provides is part of the abstraction that **Rectangle** supports, the variables are also public attributes of **Rectangle**.

```
class Rectangle;

   var center: Point;
   var height, width: Length;
   var orientation: Angle;
      ...
   public read center, height, width, orientation;
      ...
   public operation v1 ( ): Point;        // an attribute that returns a vertex
   begin
      var vertex: Point := Point.New;
      vertex.x := center.x + (height * sin (orientation) + width * cos (orientation)) / 2;
      vertex.y := center.y + (height * cos (orientation) + width * sin (orientation)) / 2;
      return (vertex);
   end v1;
      ...


   public operation top ( ): Length;      // an attribute that returns the top
   begin
      return (max (self.v1.y, self.v2.y, self.v3.y, self.v4.y));
   end top;
      ...


   public operation move (moveIncr: 2DVector);        // an operation that
                                                      // moves the rectangle
   begin
      center.x plus moveIncr.x;                       // the operator plus increments
                                                      // the variable on the left

      center.y plus moveIncr.y;
   end move;
      ...
endclass Rectangle;
```

The class **ShapeInFrame**, like many mix-ins, is simple. It contains little beyond a pointer to the frame that's to enclose the shape, and a Boolean switch recording whether the frame is active (constraining the rectangle) or not.

```
class ShapeInFrame;

    var enclosingFrame: Frame;          // assume for simplicity frame
                                        // is always horizontal

    var isActive: Boolean
    ...
    public read, update enclosingFrame;  // the frame doing the
                                         // enclosing can be changed

    ...
endclass ShapeInFrame;
```

Notice that **RectangleInFrame** in some sense conforms to **ShapeInFrame**. That is, a rectangle in a frame *is a* shape in a frame. However, type conformance isn't usually an issue with true mix-in classes. This is because a mix-in class, say **M**, doesn't have instantiated objects of its own. Therefore, one never has to ask, Can I provide an object of class **SuchAndSuch** in the context that an object of class **M** is expected?

Although a mix-in class rarely has objects of its own, it does capture some aspect that offers a particular capability. Using multiple inheritance, a designer may combine the aspects from mix-in classes into one class, from which objects may be instantiated. Our first example of a capability, printability, appeared in Section 12.2.4. In this section, we saw another example: the capability of moving around within a frame. We return to this topic in the final exercise of the next chapter, when we consider dog ownership (and its attendant capabilities) as part of being a person.

## 13.2 Rings of Operations

In this section, we investigate the structure of operations within a single class and see how to make the most of encapsulation by designing operations in inner and outer rings. For an example, I again pick **RectangleInFrame** (as shown in Fig. 13.5), the class that both creates rectangles within frames and defines the behavior that keeps a rectangle within its enclosing frame. Here's the code for one of its operations, **moveWithinFrame**:

```
class RectangleInFrame;
  inherits from ShapeInFrame, Rectangle;
    ...
  public operation moveWithinFrame (moveIncr: 2DVector);
  begin
    var allwdMoveIncr: 2DVector := 2DVector.New;        // will hold the actual
                                                        // allowed move
    if self.enclosingFrame.isActive          // enclosingFrame is inherited
                                             // from ShapeInFrame
    then
        if moveIncr.x > 0                    // to the right in this convention
        then allwdMoveIncr.x := min (moveIncr.x, self.enclosingFrame.right - self.right);
        else allwdMoveIncr.x := max (moveIncr.x, self.enclosingFrame.left - self.left);
        endif;

        if moveIncr.y > 0                    // upward in this convention
        then allwdMoveIncr.y := min (moveIncr.y, self.enclosingFrame.top - self.top);
        else allwdMoveIncr.y :=
            max (moveIncr.y, self.enclosingFrame.bottom - self.bottom);
        endif;
    else    allwdMoveIncr := moveIncr;       // there's no active frame at present
    endif;

  self.move (allwdMoveIncr);                 // move is the operation inherited
                                             // from Rectangle

  end moveWithinFrame;
    ...
endclass RectangleInFrame;
```

**moveWithinFrame** is one of several operations that this class could contain. (Another would be **rotateWithinFrame**.) The chief job of **moveWithinFrame** is to make sure that the rectangle doesn't go outside its enclosing frame when it's moved in some direction. To do this job, the operation computes the allowed move for the rectangle, which is the smaller of the requested move and the distance to the frame border (in each of the **x** and **y** dimensions), and then sends a message to **self**. This message invokes the operation **move**, as inherited from the class **Rectangle**.

Notice how the designer uses a message to invoke **move**, rather than directly tweaking the value of the variable **center**. But why *didn't* the designer just tweak **center** directly by coding, for example,

> center.x **plus** allwdMoveIncr.x;
> center.y **plus** allwdMoveIncr.y;

instead of invoking **move**? After all, that would do exactly the same thing and would probably be more efficient. And, although the variable **center** is declared within **Rectangle**, it's also available to **RectangleInFrame**, which is a subclass of **Rectangle**.

The answer is encapsulation—or, more specifically, implementation hiding. Invoking another operation (typically a get operation) of the same object, rather than simply "grabbing" a variable directly, is beneficial for three reasons:

1. It may avoid duplication of code in the two operations.

2. It limits the knowledge of some variables' representations to fewer operations.

3. If one of the operations is in a subclass, then sending a message—rather than directly manipulating the superclass's variables—decreases the connascence between the two classes. For example, the subclass doesn't need to know as many of the superclass's variable names (as we saw in the second example in Section 8.2.5).

Figure 13.6 shows how the operation structure might appear when you use this approach of operations invoking operations within the same object. Operations appear in two rings.[3]

---

[3] For clarity, I've limited my explanation to *two* rings, but in practice there could be several rings of operations.

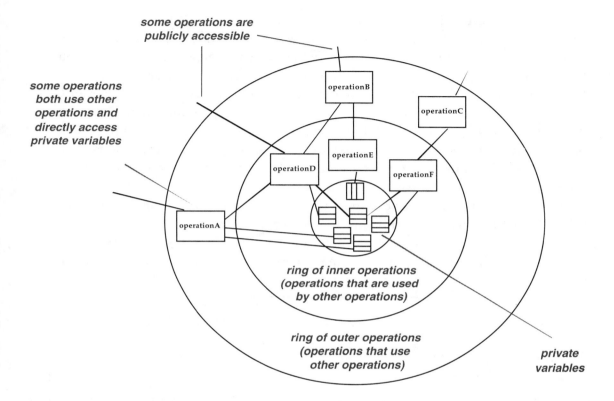

*Fig. 13.6: Inner and outer rings of operations.*

The outer ring comprises operations that use other operations of the same object. **operationB** and **operationC** belong in the outer ring because they send messages that invoke **operationD**, **operationE**, and **operationF**. Notice, however, that the methods of many outer operations access at least one variable directly, as does **operationA**.

Inner rings comprise operations used by other operations' methods. For example, **operationF** resides in the inner ring and is invoked by **operationC**'s method with the message **self.operationF (..., out ...)** to read and update variables.

Other objects may use operations in both the outer ring and the inner ring. In other words, *outer* doesn't mean *public* and *inner* doesn't mean *private*. For example, although **operationD** is located in the inner ring, it's both publicly accessible and used by **operationA** and **operationB** in the outer ring.

The class **Rectangle** offers an example of operations organized in rings. The get operation **top** invokes the get operations **v1**, **v2**, **v3**, and **v4** instead of doing all its calculations directly from the core variables (**center**, **height**, **width**, and **orientation**). The designer's reasons were both to save code and to localize the knowledge of representation of variables. (These match the first two reasons listed above.)

We now also have a fuller answer to the earlier question, Why didn't the designer of the operation **moveWithinFrame** (in the class **RectangleInFrame**) update the variable **center** directly? The reason is the danger of having operations of the subclass **RectangleInFrame** messing around with variables of the superclass **Rectangle**. (This is the third reason listed above.)

Consider what would have happened if the designer of the operation **moveWithinFrame** *did* directly manipulate the center of the rectangle, and if our class vendor had then sent us a new version of the class **Rectangle**, a version that stores (rather than computes) the four vertices of the rectangle, as shown in the code below.

```
class Rectangle;                  // the new, improved-speed version!

  var center: Point;
  var height, width: Length;
  var orientation: Angle;         // these are the core representational variables
  var v1, v2, v3, v4: Point;      // the four vertices of the rectangle, held
                                  // redundantly for efficiency
  ...
public read center, height, width, top, bottom, left, right, v1, v2, v3, v4, orientation;
  ...
public operation move (moveIncr: 2DVector);
begin
  center.x plus moveIncr.x;  center.y plus moveIncr.y;
  v1.x plus moveIncr.x; v1.y plus moveIncr.y;   // move the vertices
                                                // with the center
  v2.x plus moveIncr.x; v2.y plus moveIncr.y;
  v3.x plus moveIncr.x; v3.y plus moveIncr.y;
  v4.x plus moveIncr.x; v4.y plus moveIncr.y;
  end move;
  ...
endclass Rectangle;
```

Notice that the operation **move** is now more complicated, because it must maintain the redundant information held by **v1**, **v2**, **v3**, and **v4**. (The information is redundant because the four vertices can be computed from the core representational variables, **center**, **height**, **width**, and **orientation**.) If the system had simply been recompiled and relinked, then the operation **moveWithinFrame** would exhibit a defect: It would divorce the corners of a rectangle from its center.

The fix would be to rewrite the corner-moving code. Better yet, we should reinstate the first design by invoking the operation **move** defined on **Rectangle**. In other words, we should arrange **Rectangle**'s operations in rings.[4]

---

[4] I return to this example and the issue of design for efficiency in Exercise 4 at the end of this chapter.

## 13.3 Summary

This chapter covered the placement and design of operations. The first design approach that we explored used mix-in classes to rid other classes of abstractions that don't belong in their interfaces. We saw that a mix-in class is a relatively simple construct that is normally abstract. Instead, a designer uses the abstraction or mechanism that the mix-in class embodies, via inheritance, to create a new combination class. This new class, with its multiple avenues of inheritance, may then possess both general (say, business-domain) abstractions and more special (say, architecture-domain) abstractions.

By relocating restrictive abstractions from a business class into a mix-in class, a designer enhances the business class's cohesion, encumbrance, and reusability. Since the same mix-in class may be useful in several design situations, superfluous code can be eliminated from applications and class libraries. The reusability of the mix-in class's capabilities is also improved.

The second design approach in this chapter addressed the organization of operations into rings to create layers of encapsulation within a single class. This approach uses information and implementation hiding in the "inner-ring" operations to shield "outer-ring" operations from unnecessary knowledge of the way variables are implemented. Then, if the designer should change, say, the names, classes, or other details of certain variables, fewer operations will need to be rewritten.

## 13.4 Exercises

1.  In the design of Fig. 13.3, the class **SendableInvoice** has mixed-domain cohesion, because it knows about invoices (the business domain) and about communication (the architecture domain).  Is this mixed-domain cohesion a problem with this design?

2.  In the design of **RectangleInFrame** shown in Fig. 13.5, why didn't the designer simply have **RectangleInFrame** inherit multiply from **Frame** and **Rectangle**, rather than introduce the class **ShapeInFrame**?

3.  Look again at the design of **Room** (in Section 12.1.4, at Fig. 12.9), which used message forwarding, and the design of **RectangleInFrame** (in Section 13.1.2, at Fig. 13.5), which used multiple inheritance.  What would happen if you swapped the approaches used to design these two classes?   In other words, how might you approach the design of the "room volume" problem using multiple inheritance?

4.  Conversely, how would you design a solution to the "rectangles in frames" problem using message forwarding?

5.  Why might the design of the class **Rectangle** (first version, in Section 13.1.2) lead to run-time inefficiencies?  (Hint:  Consider the local declaration **var vertex := Point.New;** within the operation **v1**, and note that **v1** returns **vertex** as its result.)

## 13.5 Answers

1.  **SendableInvoice**'s mixed-domain cohesion isn't really a problem, because we don't expect reusability from **SendableInvoice**. That class is a sacrificial goat, whose job is to enhance the reusability of **SendableDocument** and **Invoice**.

2.  The reason is straightforward: A rectangle is *not* a frame. (Coincidentally, though, the frames in this application *were* rectangles.) If we were to allow **Rectangle** to inherit from **Frame**, then we'd violate the principle of type conformance that was covered in Chapter 11.

3.  Figure 13.7 shows **CuboidRoom** designed so that it inherits multiply from the classes **Cuboid** and **Room**.

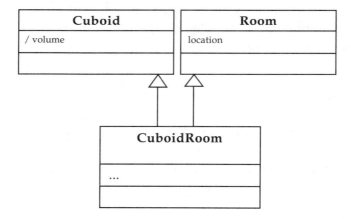

*Fig. 13.7:* **CuboidRoom** *inheriting multiply from* **Cuboid** *and* **Room**.

This design will work in the sense that objects of class **CuboidRoom** will understand the message **volume** (or **getVolume**, if you prefer that naming style). They will execute the **volume** operation defined on **Cuboid** (where, presumably, **length**, **width**, and **height** also reside). However, as we saw in Chapter 12, such a design has the problem that **CuboidRoom** will inherit unneeded behavior from **Cuboid** (**rotate**, for example). To prevent someone from using **rotate** on a cuboid room, **CuboidRoom**'s designer must override the operation (and any others that aren't needed or are dangerous).

Another problem with this design is that you can't replace the class **Cuboid** with **3DShape**, whose subclasses include **Cuboid**, **Cylinder**, and so on. The best way to understand why not is to imagine that the designer of **3DShape** had made **volume** an abstract operation, which would be very likely. Now, a subclass such as **3DShapedRoom** would inherit a **volume** operation with no implementation. Not very useful!

Of course, the problem of having **CuboidRoom** inherit from **Cuboid** is a violation of the principle of type conformance. You could avoid all the above difficulties by having a class like **3DRoom** inherit from something like **3DFixedShape** and **Room**.[5] In turn, the class **3DFixedShape** would have a variable that referred to an object of class **3DShape**. This is exactly analogous to the design of **RectangleInFrame** of Fig. 13.5, but that's overly elaborate compared to the design of **Room** in Fig. 12.9.

4.  Shown below is the code for one of **RectangleInFrame**'s operations, **moveWithinFrame**, which now moves the rectangle within the enclosing frame by means of message forwarding to a **Rectangle** object referred to as **rectangle**, rather than via inheritance from **Rectangle** (as in the design shown in Fig. 13.5).

---

[5] **3DFixedShape** is a class that resembles **3DShape** but lacks (for instance) a **scale** operation.

```
class RectangleInFrame;

   ...
  var rectangle: Rectangle;       // will be initialized to point to the movable rectangle
  var enclosingFrame: Frame;  // will be initialized to point to the enclosing frame
   ...
  public operation moveWithinFrame (moveIncr: 2DVector);
  begin
    var allwdMoveIncr: 2DVector := 2DVector.New;       // will hold the actual
                                                       // allowed move

    if enclosingFrame.isActive
    then
      if moveIncr.x > 0                 // to the right in this convention
      then allwdMoveIncr.x := min (moveIncr.x, enclosingFrame.right - self.right);
      else allwdMoveIncr.x := max (moveIncr.x, enclosingFrame.left - self.left);
      endif;

      if moveIncr.y > 0                 // upward in this convention
      then allwdMoveIncr.y := min (moveIncr.y, enclosingFrame.top - self.top);
      else allwdMoveIncr.y := max (moveIncr.y, enclosingFrame.bottom - self.bottom);
      endif;
    else allwdMoveIncr := moveIncr;        // there's no active frame at present
    endif;

    rectangle.move (allwdMoveIncr);        // message forwarding
  end moveWithinFrame;
   ...
endclass RectangleInFrame;
```

This design has many similarities to the design of **RectangleInFrame** shown in Fig. 13.5 (and, as code, in Section 13.2). The crucial difference, of course, is that now **RectangleInFrame** doesn't inherit from the classes **ShapeInFrame** and **Rectangle**. Instead, we have two variables (**rectangle** and **enclosingFrame**) that point to the movable rectangle and its enclosing frame, respectively.

This design retains the major advantage of the design shown in Fig. 13.5, in that the class **Rectangle** isn't encumbered with the class **Frame**. However, in this design, the operations of **Rectangle** aren't automatically available to objects of class **RectangleInFrame**. The designer of **RectangleInFrame** must explicitly duplicate several operations of **Rectangle** (such as **rotate**) in **RectangleInFrame**. Although the implementation of these operations will be trivial (because each one will be a single forwarded message to the **rectangle** object in the form **rectangle.rotate**, for example), this chore will be tedious. Furthermore, the design of **RectangleInFrame** may need to be changed whenever a new operation is added to **Rectangle**.

5.  To answer this question in a specific way, I'll assume that local variables—that is, variables declared within an operation's method, the way **vertex** was declared within **v1**'s method in Section 13.1.2—are placed on the computer's stack and are removed when the operation ends. This normally means that objects pointed to *only* by local variables are swept away by the garbage collector when the operation ends. (Section 1.4 mentioned garbage collection of no-longer-accessible objects.) Thus, objects pointed to only within a single operation don't consume memory for long; they live but an ephemeral life.

    However, in the first design of **Rectangle** (see the code in Section 13.1.2), the object pointed to by **vertex** cannot simply vanish when the get operation **v1** terminates. Indeed, that object *must* be preserved when the operation ends, because a pointer to that object is precisely what **v1** returns. Unfortunately then, if **v1** is invoked, say, 100 times, memory will fill up with about 60 objects. (Some objects *may* have been garbage-collected in the meantime.) This could be a very inefficient use of space and could also be a little slow.

    The second design of **Rectangle** (see the code at the start of Section 13.2) avoids the repeated local creation of an object within an operation by keeping **v1** as an instance variable of the entire object itself. However, this design must make sure that **v1** was always up to date by obsessively updating it every time a rectangle moves. This creates quite a lot of extra code. A good compromise design would be midway between the two designs: Update **v1** only when someone asks for it and then return a pointer to **v1**, rather than a pointer to some new memory-filling object.

    Remember that since languages, compilers, and run-time environments vary quite a lot, the code in your shop's language may behave differently from my description here. However, the general point is still apt: During design, it sometimes pays to consider what will actually happen in the machine. By doing that, you may keep your design clean *and* your code efficient. That's what I aimed for in this third (compromise) design.

Nevertheless, don't build your design efficiencies around some quirk of Version 2.3.1.2.6 of your compiler, because when Version 2.3.1.2.7 comes out, you may be ruined. For most code, portability is more important than efficiency.

# Class Cohesion and Support of States and Behavior

In this chapter, I discuss the quality of a class's interface—the complexion of its "outside face." This quality depends not only on the class's cohesion, which we looked at in Chapter 9, but also on the placement and design of its operations. In essence, this chapter answers two questions: What makes a class a good realization of an abstract data-type? and, What causes a class to fall short of this ideal?

Part of the answer to these questions involves the design of a class's state-space and behavior, which we examined in Chapter 10. I return to these concepts to distinguish the various ways that a class's state-space and behavior may be accessed via the class's interface, and to demonstrate how the design of individual operations can affect the quality of a class's entire interface.

The chapter's first section discusses how an interface may support a class's state-space. The second section discusses how an interface may support a class's behavior. The final section addresses the cohesion of individual operations in an interface. Throughout this chapter, I use as examples the **Rectangle** class from Chapter 13 and a **CustomerOrder** class from an order-entry application at Grabbit and Runne Enterprises, Inc.

This chapter completes our tour through the design factors that determine the quality of an object-oriented application: its robustness, reliability, extensibility, reusability, and maintainability. The exercises at the end of the chapter also tie together many of the design ideas that we've explored in previous chapters.

## 14.1 State Support in a Class Interface

As we saw in Chapter 10, during its lifetime an object moves from state to state within the state-space of its class. Messages that the object receives drive it from state to state.

You'd expect that an object could be driven to only the legal states of its class's state-space. While this is true in a *good* class-interface design, I'm afraid that it's not true in *all* designs. In this section, I address four types of class-interface design and point out the deficiencies (if any) of each one in supporting a class's state-space.

### 1. Illegal states

A class interface that allows *illegal states* enables an object to reach states that violate that object's class invariant. For example, consider an operation **movePoint** defined on **Rectangle** that allows a single corner of a rectangle to be moved independently of the other corners. This is likely to distort a rectangle into a trapezoid. In other words, a rectangle could become a non-rectangle, which would violate its class invariant.

An interface that permits an object to reach illegal states represents poor design. It usually occurs when a designer reveals some of the class's internal implementation. (I once heard someone describe such an interface as "letting the implementation leak out.") In this example, we'd guess that **Rectangle** is implemented internally by four variables, pointing to the four corners of a rectangle. However, by exposing these corners without constraints, the designer has allowed a **Rectangle** object to fall into illegal states.

In the worst kind of design, an object may be allowed to reach *all the states possible* for the implementation, many of which could be illegal. For example, a rectangle implemented by lines for its sides, with each of these lines directly manipulable from outside the object, could wind up as four unconnected lines.

## 2. Incomplete states

In a class-interface design with *incomplete states*, there are legal states in **Rectangle**'s state-space that an object cannot reach. For example, let's imagine that because of a poor design of **Rectangle**, all rectangles must be wider than they are high. In other words, no square rectangles or "tall" rectangles could be created.

In my experience, this kind of interface-design flaw occurs less often than does the illegal-states flaw. But note that an interface may have a double problem: It may support illegal states *and* incomplete states.

## 3. Inappropriate states

A class-interface design with *inappropriate states* typically offers the outside users of an object some states that are not formally part of the object's class abstraction. For example, imagine that a designer has created a **Stack** ("last in, first out") class. He has implemented the stack by means of an array and an array-pointer. So far, so good. But what if he now makes the array-pointer publicly visible? Then he's created an interface with inappropriate states, for an array-pointer is not part of a stack abstraction. (Users of a stack should see only the last element and whether the stack is empty or full.) As another example of this interface sin, the designer may let users of a stack look at, say, the 17th element of the stack.

(I'm assuming here that the designer doesn't let users of the stack actually *change* the array-pointer or the 17th element. If that were allowed, then the designer would have created an interface that supported illegal states. For example, a user could set the array-pointer to a negative or to some ridiculously large number.)

However, the question of inappropriate states becomes a thorny one on many projects. For example, is the *depth* of a stack appropriate information to be made public? Most people who study the concept of stacks would answer, "No. Only the top of a stack is relevant." However, consider the **Queue** ("first in, first out") class. Here, many designers would consider the current length of a queue to be highly relevant to a user of a queue.

As you see from the above examples, you're probably still in for some heated discussions in your next project about what's appropriate and what's inappropriate. However, I hope that by contemplating the issue of inappropriate states, you can avoid some of the interface designs that I've seen recently, in which random, potentially changeable pieces of classes' internal implementations were inappropriately revealed to the world.

### 4. Ideal states

A class interface with *ideal states*, as the name suggests, is the best design for a class interface. An object of a class may reach any state legal for that class, but *only* states legal for the class. Obviously, knowing which states are legal and which are illegal depends on having a good understanding of the purpose of the class and a definition of its class invariant (a topic to which I return below, in the section on behavior).

## 14.2 Behavior Support in a Class Interface

An object carries out some behavior when it moves from its current state to another state (or, sometimes, to the same state) as the result of receiving a message. The interface to a class may be badly designed so that either illegal behavior is supported or legal behavior is not supported. Below, I list and explain the seven ways in which a designer may build a class interface to support—or not support—behavior correctly. Most of these have specific deficiencies, which I also describe.

### 1. Illegal behavior

A class interface that supports *illegal behavior* has an operation that allows an object to make illegal transitions from one state to another. For example, let's say that a customer order must be approved before it can be filled. If an object of class **CustomerOrder** can go directly from a state of **unapproved** to **filled** by means of some operation provided on the interface, then the interface supports illegal behavior.

Notice that it's the *behavior* here that's illegal—not the two states involved, each of which is a legal state for a customer order. The designer of this class has not supported the required state-transition model for **CustomerOrder**, probably because he's allowed **CustomerOrder.fulfillmentStatus** to be directly manipulated through the interface.

There are many other, often more subtle, examples of interfaces that support illegal behavior. I recently saw a design of the class **Stack** in which a user of a stack object could pull out an element from the middle of the stack (say, the 19th element) and then "shove together" the two disjointed stack fragments to make the stack whole again. Percival, the designer, had let the stack abstraction break down, which would make me nervous if I were contemplating using such a **Stack** from a library.[1]

You might be able to guess from Exercise 3 at the end of Chapter 12 why the designer had supported such illegal behavior in his **Stack** interface. The answer is that he allowed **Stack** to inherit from **List**, which legitimately allows the removal of a middle element, and had not overridden the offending behavior within **Stack**. In fact, he should probably have named his class **PercivalsList**, which would be more honest than **Stack**.

Again, as with inappropriate states, deciding which behavior is illegal and which legal for a given class may involve some project discussion. However, you should always seek out and eliminate chance cases of illegal behavior that result from overzealous use of inheritance.

## 2.  Dangerous behavior

When a class has an interface with *dangerous behavior*, multiple messages are needed to carry out a single piece of an object's behavior and at least one of the messages takes the object to an *illegal* state. (Thus, a class interface with dangerous behavior must also permit an object to reach illegal states, which was the first poor interface design described in Section 14.1.)

Many interfaces with dangerous behavior that I've seen were bizarre. Here's an example: Let's say that a customer's order is currently approved, but it turns out that all the product lines requested on the order are out of stock. (I'm assuming they're *all* out of stock for simplicity.) Thus, we need to give the order a state of **backOrdered**.

If the interface to **CustomerOrder** is designed with dangerous behavior, then changing an order's state might not be easy. For example, perhaps the only way to make the transition from **approved** to **backOrdered** is this:

- First, send a message to an order that sets the number of items ordered to a negative number. This is the bizarre illegal state.

---

[1] Percival actually had a perfectly good **Stack** available in the shop's library. He declined to use it, however, because it (rightly) didn't support the kind of high jinks he thought he needed.

- Second, send a message telling the order to fill itself. The code within **CustomerOrder.fill** then sets the number of items ordered back to positive and sets the state to **backOrdered**.

This interface therefore requires two messages to achieve one result, the first of which puts the object in an illegal state.

**Rectangle** may provide another example of this kind of interface, one that's just as gruesome as the above but not quite so weird. Let's say that we want to move a rectangle to the right. In order to do that for a certain horrid **Rectangle** design, we have to send four messages to the rectangle object because each message moves one corner. As the rectangle staggers to the right, it winds up in two or three intermediate illegal states. (This, of course, was also the example of an interface with illegal states that I used in Section 14.1.)

An interface supporting dangerous behavior breathes an evil life into an illegal-states interface because it encourages—nay, obliges—people to put an object into illegal states. Not only does it further expose an implementation that may change, but it also increases the risk of an object's being *left* in some illegal state. Notice, too, how a dangerous-behavior interface also promotes connascence of algorithm across class boundaries because users of **Rectangle** need to know the algorithm by which a rectangle is moved (namely, one corner at a time).

### 3. Irrelevant behavior

*Irrelevant behavior* in a class interface is behavior that simply doesn't belong to that class and its objects. For example, if **CustomerOrder** contained an operation named **computeLoanRepayment**, then **CustomerOrder** would have irrelevant behavior. The behavior isn't relevant to the class, because it has nothing to do with customer orders: It updates no **CustomerOrder** object and doesn't even access any variables of **CustomerOrder**.

No, you haven't misunderstood; including irrelevant behavior in an interface is idiotic design. Fortunately for the object-oriented world, it very seldom occurs. The arch exponent of irrelevant behavior is an egregiously shoddy fellow named Genghis the Perverse, who works at a large company nowhere near yours (I hope). Genghis will happily put an operation **compute-DateDifference** in the interface to **Customer** and **determineBestTransportation-**

**Route** in **Product**'s interface. Don't ask me why. It makes no sense to me, either. Go ask Genghis—I think he'll know!

**4.  Incomplete behavior**

A class interface with *incomplete behavior* doesn't allow all behavior needed by objects of that class to be carried out. For example, let's assume that a customer order has the state **approved**, but the customer suddenly goes bankrupt. It's entirely reasonable for the accounting department's users to change the order's state back to **unapproved**. But in a system I was reviewing recently, I saw **CustomerOrder** designed so that once an order had achieved **approved** state, there was *no possible way* to return it to **unapproved** state. (The designer had simply ignored one of the analysis requirements.)

With incomplete behavior, we don't have a case of an interface supporting behavior awkwardly or via illegal states. An interface of this type actually *forbids* some legal behavior, because not all legal transitions among those states are supported. Notice, however, that a class with an interface that supports incomplete behavior may still support ideal states, because (in the example above) an order might somehow be able to reach an **unapproved** state; the problem is that it just can't get there from an **approved** state.

**5.  Awkward behavior**

An object whose class has an interface with *awkward behavior* may require two or more messages to carry out a single piece of legal behavior. Awkward behavior resembles dangerous behavior (described above) in that multiple messages are needed to effect a single piece of an object's behavior. However, with awkward behavior, none of the messages takes the object to an illegal state.

For example, let's say that a customer order with a state of **approved** can become **filled** when it has stock and a shipment date assigned to it. It's perfectly reasonable that a filled order could have its shipment date changed. However, an interface may be designed so that the only way to do this is to set the state of the order back to **approved** and then reset it to **filled** with the new shipment date. You'll therefore need to send two messages in order to change a shipment date.

Notice that the object goes through a bogus, albeit legal, state. The state is bogus because it doesn't correspond to reality: The order in question is now filled and is no longer merely approved. The designer has failed to support the required behavior of changing the shipment date. Or, to be fair to the designer, he may have failed to support the required behavior because he was handed an incomplete specification for **CustomerOrder**.

However, designing an interface with awkward behavior is not a capital offense. Indeed, it may not always be clear whether an object *should* be able to move from one state to another in a single step. For example, should we be able to move a rectangle to the right *and* rotate it by 30 degrees with a single message, or should that be considered two pieces of behavior? Or, if we can rescale a rectangle with its center held in the same place, should **Rectangle**'s interface also support rescaling with a corner held in place? (After all, that could be done by invoking **rescaleAboutCenter** and then **move**.)

The best way to answer these questions is to study the needs of the problem and see how the class is intended to be used. If you can predict the future infallibly, you'll always get the answers absolutely correct. (But if you can predict the future infallibly, what are you doing in the software business?)

My general recommendation is this: *Don't* provide an operation to support a speculative piece of behavior if that behavior can already be supported by executing two or three operations. Wait until the need for the behavior actually arises before you consider adding another operation to the interface. (This topic crops up again in this list, under replicated behavior, below.)

Although I've just mentioned "the needs of the problem," I haven't defined this phrase explicitly. This is deliberate, for appreciating all possible uses for a class is a matter of human judgment. It's why your experience as an object-oriented designer will always be valuable. It's also why the walkthrough (or any form of peer-group review) is vital in object-oriented design, for a solitary person can seldom appreciate all the subtleties of—and potential future changes to—a given application or class.

## 6.  Replicated behavior

An interface to a class has *replicated behavior* if the same piece of behavior in an object may be carried out via the object's interface in more than one way. Class designs that I've seen contain countless examples of replicated behavior. Let me give you a representative sample to illustrate the various causes of, and reasons for, replicated behavior.

Recall the class **Hominoid** of Chapter 1.  This class has two operations, **turnLeft** and **turnRight**, which turn a hominoid 90 degrees to the left or to the right, respectively.  Now, let's say that we need to veer a hominoid by, say, 30 degrees clockwise (toward the right, as seen from above).  To do so, we write another operation, **turn**, which takes an argument of **turnAngle**.  By adding this operation, we've created replicated behavior in **Hominoid**'s interface in that we can now turn a hominoid by 90 degrees in two distinct ways:

```
turnRight;                      // first way
turnClockwise(rightAngle);      // second way
```

This piece of replicated behavior arose for historical reasons, specifically because we generalized **Hominoid**'s original interface.  If we'd foreseen the need for arbitrary turns originally, we might never have written **turnLeft** and **turnRight**.  But now that we have these two operations, what shall we do?  We can't just remove them in a cavalier way, because code in dozens of other classes may be referring to them.

Two possible solutions arise:

- Leave them alone and live with **Hominoid**'s replicated behavior and its resulting more complex interface.
- Remove the two operations after, say, a year, during which time the other software can be modified to use **turnClockwise(rightAngle)** instead.

Ironically, a class may sometimes evolve conversely to the way I described above, as its designer may deliberately introduce replicated behavior into its interface.  For example, let's say that **Hominoid** currently has only the general **turnClockwise** as an operation for turning.  However, let's also assume that 99 percent of applications needing to turn a hominoid need to turn that hominoid by a right angle. The designer might then add **turnLeft** and **turnRight** as a convenience to the many (who then won't have to remember whether it's left or right that has a negative angle or a counterclockwise motion). Of course, he'll have to leave **turnClockwise** in the interface for the 1 percent, which will create the replicated behavior.[2]

A variation on the theme of the above paragraph occurs in the following (simplified) example: Imagine that we have the class **EquityAccount** in a stockbroking application. One of its operations is **sellEquityPosition (equity, amtToSell, out saleOK)**, which sells a given amount of a customer's position in a given equity. Another operation is **sellAllEquityPositions (out saleOK)**, which sells all of the customer's positions in equities (in that account). This latter operation is superfluous, because the first operation would achieve the same if you looped through each equity in the account, put into **amtToSell** the entire amount that the customer held in that equity, and then sent the message **sellEquityPosition (equity, amtToSell, out saleOK)**.

However, that looping code, which is nontrivial, must be written wherever the application needs to sell all equity positions. This may occur in dozens of places. To avoid such duplicated effort and the accompanying connascence of algorithm, **EquityAccount**'s designer has created **sellAllEquityPositions**, which is a legitimate, though superfluous, operation.[3]

Incidentally, the operation **sellAllEquityPositions** could be designed as a stand-alone function outside **EquityAccount**. But the operation belongs so much with maintaining equity accounts that to separate this operation from its class would introduce additional connascence in the overall design of the application.

As you can imagine from the above examples, replicated behavior raises lots of arguments about class design. Replicated behavior may make a class's interface more complex and more difficult to learn. Nevertheless, as we saw above, a designer may choose to postpone (or even eschew) removing replicated behavior from an interface, because of existing usage. Indeed, a designer may even *introduce* replicated behavior in order to provide a special-

---

[2] In a walkthrough of this issue, one colleague suggested adding yet another replicated operation—**turnCounterclockwise**—on the grounds that invoking **turnClockwise** with a negative angle was unnatural. What do you think?

[3] If you think that **sellAllEquityPositions** is too dramatic an operation to be useful, then you can apply the same argument using the operation **sellEntireEquityPosition**, which simply sells all shares owned in a single company.

ized operation that's more useful than the general operations already in the interface.

Although there's rarely a clear-cut answer to the question of whether replicated behavior is called for, class designers must consciously address the question whenever they add an operation to a class. Otherwise, unwarranted and baroque replicated behavior will grow into a class's interface by accretion, or from the whims of an argumentative designer with a forceful personality, or from arbitrary, poorly-thought-out demands from users of the class. Such a class will be more difficult than necessary to learn and to modify.

## 7. Ideal behavior

An interface to a class supports *ideal behavior* if it enforces the following three properties:

- An object in a legal state can move *only* to another legal state.
- An object can move to another state *only* in a legal way—that is, in a way that's part of the prescribed behavior for the object's class.
- There is only one way to use the interface in order to carry out a piece of behavior.

Again, knowing which behavior is legal and which is illegal depends on having a good understanding of the purpose of the class and a complete specification of its required behavior, in the sense that I discussed previously.

An example of an interface with ideal behavior is provided by the class **Stack<Widget>**, which is a class whose objects are stacks of widgets.[4] Its interface contains these operations:

| | |
|---|---|
| top: Widget; | *// returns the top element of the stack* |
| pop; | *// removes the top element of the stack* |
| push (newElem: Widget); | *// places a new element on the top of the stack* |
| isEmpty: Boolean; | *// returns whether the stack is empty* |
| isFull: Boolean; | *// returns whether the stack is full* |

The above interface is ideal, because its five operations encompass the entire range of behavior of a normal stack and there is only one way to carry out any

---

[4] This is derived from the generic class **Stack <C>**, where the formal class parameter **C** has been bound to the actual class parameter **Widget** in this example.

particular operation on a stack. (Note, however, that the **Stack.pop** operation traditionally returns the top element of the stack, too. This definition of **pop** would add a little replicated behavior to the **Stack** interface.)

## 14.3 Operation Cohesion in a Class Interface

The third way to spruce up your class's interface (after achieving ideal states and behavior) is to strengthen the cohesion of individual operations.

For decades in structured design (SD), module cohesion has been a standard criterion for assessing a procedural module's quality. In object orientation, operations should have good cohesion in the same way that individual procedural modules in SD should have good cohesion.[5]

In SD, cohesion highlights the designer's purpose in creating a particular module—whether the designer saw a strong, application-based reason for the module or whether he just stuffed a few random lines of code into a procedure. For example, **determineInventoryReorderPoint** is likely to have high cohesion, whereas **doSomeMiscFrunkStuff** probably has low cohesion.

Poor operation cohesion results from the misguided combination of operations that should have been kept apart. The two versions of such misbegotten combinations yield alternate cohesion and multiple cohesion, respectively, both of which I describe below. I then conclude this section on a more positive note, by describing functional—or ideal—cohesion, which is achieved by keeping distinct operations cleanly separated.

### 1. Alternate cohesion

*Alternate cohesion* arises when a designer combines several pieces of behavior into a single operation that, on receipt of a message, applies only *one* piece of behavior to the object.[6] In other words, someone sending a message to invoke the operation must supply a flag (or switch) telling the operation which piece of behavior to execute this time.

---

[5] In structured design, Larry Constantine ranked the seven possible levels of module cohesion into approximate order of design quality, from best to worst: functional, sequential, communicational, procedural, temporal, logical, and coincidental. See [Yourdon and Constantine, 1979] or [Page-Jones, 1988], for example.

[6] Alternate cohesion is equivalent to logical cohesion of SD. It could also cover SD's coincidental cohesion if part of the code of an operation with alternate cohesion was completely irrelevant to the object on which the operation was executing. Again, only a dedicated Genghis would commit such a crime.

For example, **Rectangle** might have an operation

scaleOrRotate (scaleFactor: Real, rotateAngle: Angle, whichToDo: Boolean)

**scaleOrRotate** either changes the size of a rectangle or rotates it, depending on whether **whichToDo** is set to **true** or **false**. Notice that in each case only one of the first two arguments is used; the other one is a useless dummy. With a little more scheming, however, a depraved designer could make the operation's interface still worse—like this:

scaleOrRotate (amount: Real, whichToDo: Boolean)

Here, the **amount** argument is confusingly doing double-duty: It means a **scaleFactor** in one case, but a **rotationAngle** in the other.

This was a mild example. I'm sure you can picture a grotesque operation with 23 pieces of behavior crammed into it and 15 arguments needed in every message, over a dozen of which are usually dummies. This kind of operation design makes a mockery of object orientation. Let's draw a shroud over it and move on to a kinder, gentler cohesion.

## 2. Multiple cohesion

*Multiple cohesion* is similar to alternate cohesion in that a designer has stuffed several pieces of behavior into a single operation. However, when an operation with multiple cohesion executes, it applies all (rather than one) of the pieces of behavior to the object.[7] For example, an operation **Person.changeAddressAndPhoneNum**, which changes both a person's address and telephone number, has multiple cohesion.

Often, such an operation yields a class interface with incomplete behavior (that is, one that lacks some legal behavior) because the operation carries out several steps and may therefore skip over some legal states. In SD, this wasn't a big problem, because such a module could always be factored into two modules, **changeAddress** and **changePhoneNum**, each of which could be called

---

[7] Multiple cohesion includes both sequential and communicational cohesion of SD. Procedural and temporal cohesion of an operation are rare, since all the code in an operation is working on the same object. That fact boosts its cohesion level. However, I suppose that Genghis *could* create a procedurally cohesive operation, part of whose code was irrelevant to the object on which the operation was executing.

individually. In object-oriented design, you can do the same thing so long as you ensure that the two operations are publicly available in the interface. (But then, you rightly wonder, if the operations are separately available, why retain the replicated behavior that the combined **changeAddressAndPhoneNum** introduced? The only reason is that other code may be using it, but it should probably be scrapped as soon as possible.)

In a **Person** class that I saw recently, the designer hadn't factored this operation into two. He boasted to me that he didn't need to factor, because his **changeAddressAndPhoneNum** "could do everything" and supported all legal behavior. He further claimed, "If a person changes address but not telephone number, then you merely invoke the operation with a null phone number and the operation is smart enough to avoid changing **phoneNum**." Although that may be true, this design creates a cumbersome interface whereby some messages need to pass dummy arguments. It's actually a thinly veiled alternate cohesion, in which null is serving as a covert flag.

Another form of multiple cohesion occurs when a designer inserts into an operation some function that makes extraneous computations that should be performed outside the class. For example, let's say that **area** is a get operation of **Rectangle**. Now let's introduce another operation, **biggerAreaThan (someArea: Area): Boolean**, which tells us whether the rectangle is bigger than some other area. It would be used like this:

```
ourRectIsBigger: Boolean := rect.biggerAreaThan (someArea);
if ourRectIsBigger
then ...
```

The operation **biggerAreaThan** therefore carries out two functions. The first determines the rectangle's area; the second compares this area to some fixed amount that was passed to it as an input argument. However, the determination of which area is bigger should be made by the object sending the message and not by the **Rectangle** object. The code in the sender object would simply look like this:

```
if rect.area > someArea
then ...
```

The reason for moving the comparison out of the class **Rectangle** is that it isn't part of the **Rectangle** abstraction. And dedicating an entire operation to each extraneous computation that should occur outside a given class is extravagant. However, you may have noticed a resemblance between the operation **biggerAreaThan** and the operation **sellAllEquityPositions** of Section 14.2, which I suggested could remain part of the class interface.

The issue is this: Make sure that your class provides operations that don't engage in extracurricular activities. This is easier said than done—after all, what does "extracurricular" actually *mean* for a given class? Although the answer will always be a judgment call, if you have doubt about an operation, then it probably doesn't belong in the class. However, you may wish to look at whether including the operation will increase or decrease connascence.

Finally, if your criterion for including an operation will spawn a proliferation of operations, then your operation probably doesn't belong. For example, if you allow the operation **biggerAreaThan**, then why not allow **smallerAreaThan** and **equalAreaTo** as well?

## 3. Functional cohesion

*Functional cohesion* is a term taken directly from SD, where it represents the ideal level of cohesion for a module. A functionally cohesive operation is one that is dedicated to a single piece of behavior, as defined by the needs of the problem. Functional cohesion is also known as *ideal cohesion*.

The name of an operation gives the clue to its cohesion: An "and" name implies multiple cohesion, while an "or" name implies alternate cohesion. However, a strong name with neither "and" nor "or" in it implies an operation with functional cohesion.

For example, **Tank.fill**, **Rectangle.area**, **ProductItem.weight**, **CustomerOrder.dispatch**, **Customer.setCreditLimit**, **Airplane.turn**, **Account.makeDeposit**, and **Customer.phoneNum** would be functionally cohesive operations. Each operation carries out a single piece of behavior that's appropriate for its class; each operation also has a strong name. Conversely, you know that an operation with a feeble name such as **Customer.doSomeStuff** isn't much good.

## 14.4 Summary

This chapter covered the quality of a class's external interface in terms of how well the class's operations support the class's state-space, behavior, and cohesion.

A class's interface may support the class's state-space in four ways: *illegal states*, in which the interface allows an object to reach states that are illegal for its class (that is, states that violate the class invariant); *incomplete states*, in which the interface does not allow an object to reach some states that are legal for its class; *inappropriate states*, in which the interface manifests some states that are not germane to the class's abstraction; and *ideal states*, in which the interface allows an object to reach all states that are legal for its class and only states that are legal for its class. A class's designer should aim for a class interface that supports ideal states.

A class's interface may support the class's behavior in seven ways: *illegal behavior*, in which the interface allows an object to carry out state transitions that are illegal for its class; *dangerous behavior*, in which the interface requires an object to carry out some state transitions via multiple messages that take the object through intermediate (but illegal) states; *irrelevant behavior*, in which the class's interface supports behavior extraneous to the class; *incomplete behavior*, in which the interface does not allow an object to carry out some state transitions that are legal for its class; *awkward behavior*, in which the interface requires an object to carry out some state transitions via multiple messages that take the object through intermediate (but legal) states; *replicated behavior*, in which the interface supports the same behavior in multiple ways; and *ideal behavior*, in which the interface allows an object to carry out in one way state transitions that are legal for its class and only state transitions that are legal for its class. A class's designer should aim for a class interface that supports ideal behavior.

A single operation has three possible cohesions: *alternate cohesion*, in which a designer combines in an operation several pieces of behavior to be executed alternatively, depending on the value of a flag; *multiple cohesion*, in which a designer combines in an operation several pieces of behavior to be executed together; and *functional (or ideal) cohesion*, in which a designer creates an operation dedicated to carrying out a single piece of behavior. The strength and clarity of an operation's name often reveals its likely cohesion. A class's designer should create operations with functional cohesion.

The cohesion of operations is our final criterion for class quality. The ideal class, then, has these properties: It has ideal class cohesion; its interface supports ideal states and ideal behavior; each of its operations is functionally (ideally) cohesive; it has no unnecessary encumbrance; it has an encumbrance appropriate to its domain; it has no unnecessary connascence; and it has no connascence that crosses boundaries into other classes. In addition, it obeys the principles of type conformance and of closed behavior.

A class with these exemplary design qualities is a worthy implementation of an abstract data-type. It will be as robust, reliable, extensible, reusable, and maintainable as a class can ever be. All who behold it will weep with happiness. More importantly though, if you build your object-oriented systems from such well-designed classes, you'll derive the maximum value that object orientation can deliver to your organization.

## 14.5 Exercises

1.  In Section 14.2, where I discussed interfaces with replicated behavior, I suggested that sometimes a designer might deliberately introduce replicated behavior into a class interface, adding specialized operations for the convenience of users. How might you use rings of operations, which we saw in Chapter 13, for this purpose? How might the idea of overloading, discussed in Section 1.8, also help?

2.  Many structured-design principles still apply in object-oriented design. Choose a structured-design principle and briefly explain how it might apply to object-oriented design.

3.  Imagine a shipping application in which the users ship crates of packages to customers. Figure 14.1 shows the aggregation structure of an object of class **ShipmentUnit**. The structure comprises a set of packages (the actual contents of the shipment) and a containing crate that holds the packages.

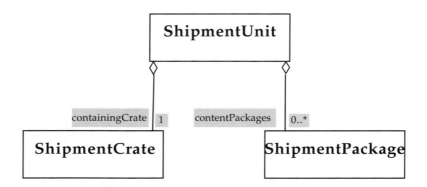

*Fig. 14.1: A shipment unit is an aggregation of a containing crate and a set of content packages.*

The total weight of the ensemble is the sum of the weight of the containing crate and the weights of all the content packages. Figure 14.2 shows one possible design of **ShipmentUnit.weight**.

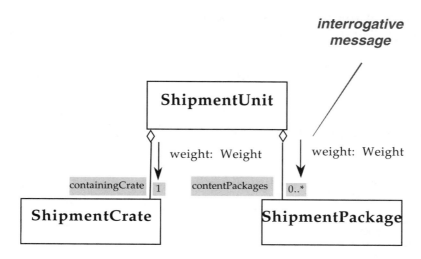

*Fig. 14.2: A shipment unit finds its weight by interrogating its constituents.*

In the design shown in Fig. 14.2, the method implementing the operation **ShipmentUnit.weight** sends an interrogative message (that is, a get message, as mentioned in Chapter 1) first to the containing crate to obtain *its* weight and then, iteratively, to all the content packages to obtain *their* weights. The method adds each of these weights to a running total, which it returns as the total weight of the shipment unit.

Is it possible to design a method for **ShipmentUnit.weight** so that the constituent objects take the initiative in sending information to the aggregate object? How would that change the nature of the interface between **Shipment-Unit** and, say, **ShipmentPackage**? Would that design have any advantages or disadvantages?

4. Imagine we have a dog-tracking application that has, as one of its requirements, the need to record which person owns which dogs. (We saw this example in Section 9.3.3, and you may wish to review some of the issues that were raised there.) Let's say that we also need to know, for a given person, how many dogs that person owns.

Figures 14.3 through 14.6 show four (of several) possible designs. Using the design principles and terminology that you've encountered in this book, comment on the pros and cons of each design approach. You may find it helpful to read the following brief synopsis of each design before you begin.

*Design A* (see Fig. 14.3): The designer has created two classes, **Person** and **Dog**, and the navigability arrow suggests that the class **Person** maintains the link between a person and his dogs, perhaps with a variable **ownedDogs: Set <Dog>**. A read-only attribute of **Person** is named **numOfDogsOwned**.

*Fig. 14.3: Design A for "person owns dog."*

*Design B* (see Fig. 14.4): The designer has created three classes. The middle one, **PersonDogOwnership**, is dedicated to maintaining the relationship between **Person** and **Dog**. Each instance of **PersonDogOwnership** associates one dog-owning person with a (nonempty) set of dogs. The get operation **NumOfDogsOwned** is a class operation of **PersonDogOwnership**, to which you pass a **Person** object as an argument. The operation finds the appropriate instance of **PersonDogOwnership** for that person (if any) and then returns the size of the "dog-set" for that instance.

*Fig. 14.4: Design B for "person owns dog."*

*Design C* (see Fig. 14.5): The designer has created an abstract mix-in class, **DogOwner**, which maintains the link to dogs and returns **NumOfDogsOwned**, like **Dog** in Design A. The class **DogOwningPerson**, which inherits multiply from **Person** and **DogOwner**, is the class from which you instantiate objects that represent dog owners.

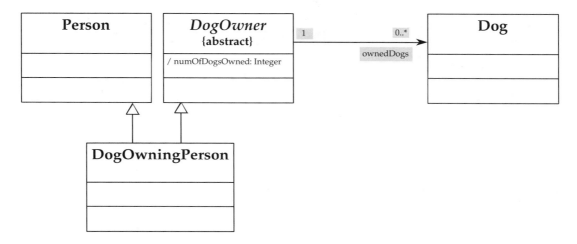

*Fig. 14.5: Design C for "person owns dog."*

*Design D* (see Fig. 14.6): The designer has created a class **Owner**, which unlike **DogOwningPerson** in Design C acquires its properties not through inheritance but by referring to two objects, one of class **Person** and the other of class **DogOwner**. (Note that the latter is a concrete class, in contrast to its counterpart in Design C.) This design takes the approach of slicing a single real-world thing (a dog-owning person) into multiple aspects, an approach that I covered in Exercise 2 of Chapter 12. Incidentally, since a reference to a **DogOwner** object is not always present—note the multiplicity of **0..1**—the designer should perhaps rename **Owner** as **PotentialOwner**. (The **isDogOwner** attribute will be set to **true** if a potential owner actually *is* a dog owner.)

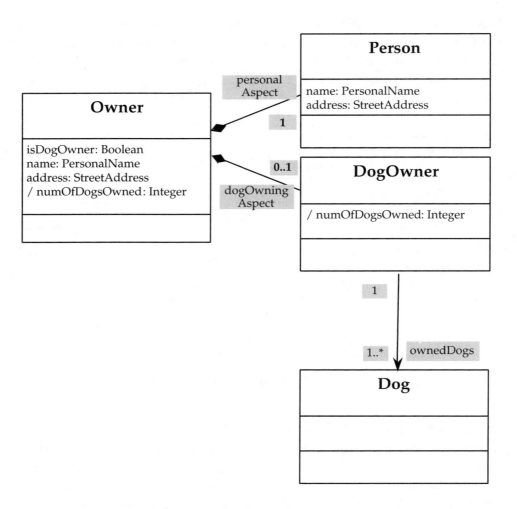

*Fig. 14.6: Design D for "person owns dog."*

## 14.5 Answers

1. A designer could place the more specialized operations in the outer ring and the more general operations in the inner ring. The outer operations would then be implemented by means of messages to use the inner operations.

   Overloading allows different operations in the same interface to have the same name. This can be useful for implementing replicated behavior where a general operation in the interface has more arguments than a similar, specialized one. However, it's often better in this situation to use different names for operations. For example, the name **sellAllEquities** is more meaningful (and safer!) than a mere **sell** with no arguments.

   I have also occasionally built an adjunct "ring operation" class, separate from a "core class," to provide useful but seldom-needed operations related to the operations on the core class. For example, to solve the proliferation of operations such as **biggerAreaThan** (which could cause multiple cohesion, as we saw in Section 14.3), you could design the class **RectangleUtilities** (perhaps as a utility package), which would have such operations as **biggerAreaThan**, **smallerAreaThan**, and so on. Although **RectangleUtilities**, for example, may need such operations, the core class **Rectangle** would remain free from these marginal operations, whose inclusion would perhaps make **Rectangle** more difficult for typical users to understand. To summarize, this design approach takes a set of operations that might comprise an "outer ring" of a class and places them in a separate class.

2. One example of a structured-design criterion is fan-out. High fan-out from an SD module often hints at a missing level in the structure-chart hierarchy. Similarly, in object-oriented design, high fan-out (say, seven or more) in a superclass/subclass hierarchy may imply classes, or even whole levels, missing from the structure. Also, if you find many messages emanating from a method, you may want to factor out a function or procedure to reduce the method's complexity. This factored-out element may also be useful to methods implementing other operations of the class, or even to methods of other classes' operations.

3. The design I showed is based on "pulling information from objects" when it is needed. Although this design is clean and easy to understand, it may not execute very rapidly when you need a shipment unit's weight. A message to

**ShipmentUnit.weight** may generate hundreds of messages to the objects that represent packages. To improve **weight**'s execution time, we could modify the design in Fig. 14.2 so that the class **ShipmentUnit** has a variable (say, **totalWeight**) that always holds the current weight of the shipment unit. Then, **ShipmentUnit.weight** would simply return the value of that variable. Its method would execute in a twinkling of the eye.

However, to do this we must ensure that the constituent objects keep **totalWeight** up to date: Whenever a constituent object is added or changes its weight, it must send a message to the shipment-unit object to inform it of the change. This would be an informative message, a message that "pushes information" into the objects that need it.

This second design, although possibly more efficient, is also more complex. Now all the constituent objects need to be aware of the aggregate object, which may prejudice their reusability (because they're encumbered with the machinery of another class). Also, the aggregate object needs at least another operation to capture the information passed in the informative message. Finally, if changes to package weights are frequent and messages invoking **ShipmentUnit.weight** are infrequent, then there may be little or no improvement in overall run-time efficiency.

Therefore, unless you have strong reasons to the contrary, you should design aggregate objects to obtain their information from constituents via interrogative ("pull") messages, rather than via informative ("push") messages emanating from the constituents.[8]

4.   Here are my comments on the four designs:

*Design A:* This design has the merit of extreme simplicity. It has the fewest classes of the four designs and is very easy to use. By this, I mean that if you have an object of class **Person**, say **fred**, then in order to find out how many dogs Fred has, you simply write

   fredsOwnedDogs := fred.numOfDogsOwned

---

[8] Incidentally, this pair of designs illustrates the difference between an attribute and a variable. Both designs implement the attribute **weight**. However, the first design has no variable corresponding to **weight**, and **weight**'s value is computed by its get operation "on the fly." The second design has an explicit variable corresponding to **weight**, named **totalWeight** in this example.

However, the major disadvantage of this design lies in the fact that the class **Person** is encumbered with the class **Dog**. (As we saw in Section 9.3.3, this gives **Person** mixed-role cohesion.) In practical terms, this means that **Person** needs many "dog operations" in its interface to handle, for example, acquiring dogs and losing dogs. Imagine that we wish to place **Person** in our class library and later reuse it in a personnel application. The reusers of **Person** would be very surprised to find all the references to **Dog** in **Person**. Indeed, there might even be a problem getting the class **Person** to compile or link in an application that didn't also have **Dog**!

I would therefore recommend Design A only in situations where you have no intention of reusing **Person** in other applications.

*Design B:* Design B solves the mixed-role cohesion problem of **Person** in Design A by creating a class (**PersonDogOwnership**) to link a person and that person's dogs. Each object of that class links one **Person** object with one object of class **Set <Dog>**. It's OK for **PersonDogOwnership** to be encumbered with **Person** and **Dog**, since "person-ness" and "dog-ness" are intrinsic to the notion of dog ownership. Also, intuitively speaking, **numOfDogsOwned** is better placed as an attribute of the relationship between persons and dogs than as an attribute of person.

However, when I show Design B to a typical object-oriented programmer, his reaction is often: "This design is weird!" The reason for this response is that to find the required number of dogs, we can no longer simply invoke an instance operation on an object by writing **fred.numOfDogsOwned**. Instead, we must invoke a class operation on a class by writing **PersonDogOwnership.NumOfDogsOwned (fred)**. The method for this operation scans a table (a class variable within **PersonDogOwnership** that holds pointers to all the class's objects) to find the object pointed to by **fred** and the number of dogs in the associated set. For programmers only used to instance operations, this approach may seem unnatural.

Another objection arises from the word "scans" in the previous paragraph. A programmer might exclaim in anguish: "You mean that the method has to scan an entire table? Boy, that's inefficient!" This objection may be valid; it depends on how cleverly you've designed the internals of **PersonDogOwnership**. (Note: You may wish to try designing this class to minimize such efficiency problems.)

Design B is a design that promotes reusability by removing unnecessary encumbrances from **Person**. However, it may suffer in terms of efficiency. It also may suffer from (what some people consider) cumbersome message syntax: the syntax of class messages, rather than of instance messages.

(A follow-on exercise: Could the class **PersonDogOwnership** be generalized so that it supports binary relationships, including many-to-many relationships, other than those between persons and dogs? If so, would the concept of genericity—that is, of parameterized classes—prove useful?)

*Design C:* This design, which uses the mix-in class **DogOwner** to implement the machinery for dog ownership, has the merit of flexibility. For example, we could easily create the class **DogOwningCorporation** by having this class inherit from both **DogOwner** and **Corporation**. This design also allows us to send a message directly to **fred** (now of class **DogOwningPerson**) to find out how many dogs this person owns. (Note that the object **fred** will execute the get operation **numOfDogsOwned** via inheritance from **DogOwner**.) Another advantage of this design is that since neither **Person** nor **Dog** has mixed-role cohesion, the classes are likely to be easily reusable.

But what if Fred buys a boat, a car, and a cat? To deal with dog, cat, boat, and car ownership under this design, we may have to create up to 15 classes! (Examples include **DogCatOwningPerson** and **DogCarBoatOwningPerson**.)[9]

Also, when we instantiate the object known as **fred**, we must instantiate it from the class **DogOwningPerson**. This implies that we know that (in the real world) Fred is a dog owner and that Fred is unlikely to forsake this role. However, here we re-encounter the dynamic partitioning issue we first met in Section 4.1.3: Fred may belong to the venerable company of dog owners right now, but next year he may become an "ex-dog-owner."

---

[9] The basic problem here, in my opinion, is that all current mainstream object-oriented languages contain a fundamental flaw: They don't support an object's ability to acquire or lose class membership or to hold multiple class membership (apart from that implied by the inheritance hierarchy) at one time. A design approach that provides such abilities is a work-around for an object-oriented language flaw. I hope that mainstream object-oriented languages will soon provide class-migration facilities, as some object-oriented database languages are already doing. (The Iris object-oriented database has such a facility.) However, I concede that general class migration is not a trivial issue. To follow up this research topic, see, for example, [Bertino and Martino, 1993] and [Zdonik, 1990].

So, if Fred later ceases to be a dog owner, then we must delete the object **fred** to facilitate the class migration that dynamic partitioning demands, making sure first that we copy the "person" information contained in **fred**. Then, we must re-instantiate **fred** as an object simply of class **Person**, using the copied information to initialize the object.[10] The disadvantage of this, of course, is that the new "fred object" has a different handle from the old one, which could become a severe problem if there are existing references to the old object throughout the system.

Thus, Design C is at its best in situations where partitioning is static and combinatorial explosions of classes, such as the one above, are unlikely. (A follow-on exercise: You may want to experiment with a variation on Design C that subsumes dogs, cats, boats, and cars under the more general term "possession" and avoids the above explosive flaw.)

*Design D:* The distinguishing feature of this design is that when a single real-world dog owner like Fred comes along, we'll have to instantiate *three* objects in the system:

1. an object of the class **Person** to hold the aspect of Fred's personal information (such as the attributes **name** and **address**),

2. an object of the class **DogOwner** to hold Fred's dog-owning aspect (such as the attribute **numOfDogsOwned**), and

3. an object of the composite class **Owner**, which will refer to the former two objects as components, and thus tie all the "Fred stuff" together. The get operations on the class **Owner** (as shown in Fig. 14.6) obtain their values by forwarding messages to the similarly named attributes on the appropriate component objects.

Design D has an advantage over Design C in its design treatment of dynamic partitioning. By this I mean that should Fred cease to be a dog owner, then we can simply delete the object of class **DogOwner**, while leaving the object of class **Owner** intact. Furthermore, we can introduce cats, boats, cars, and so on without a combinatorial explosion—just one additional class for each kind of possession—and allow Fred to move in and out of these roles with little design or programming difficulty.

---

[10] We also encountered this migration problem with an animal species moving in and out of endangerment. (See Exercise 1 of Chapter 12.)

Design D works well where a real-world thing has multiple aspects derived from multiple roles and moves into and out of these roles. However, this design approach suffers from the drawback that a single thing in the real world becomes multiple objects in the system. Moreover, the ease of inheritance is replaced by the tedium of message forwarding.[11]

Note: The four design approaches in this exercise are independent of persons and dogs. In other words, they would be useful for "person owns frog" and "corporation owns boat" (as well as many other associations not involving legal possession). They therefore provide examples of patterns, set pieces that can be put to use in application after application, since they're not dependent on the specific semantics of any one application.

Therefore this exercise is typical of object-oriented design: A single analysis requirement may be designed in many legitimate ways. All four of the above designs are valid, in the sense that they can be coded, they'll run, and they'll meet the analysis requirements. Thus, your choice of which design to deploy depends on factors beyond the stark requirement itself—factors such as simplicity, flexibility, generality, or efficiency.

In object-oriented design, rarely does The One Right Answer make itself known. Instead, as a designer, you must trade off the pluses and minuses of several possible designs. This book has set forth some design principles by which you can judge, and terms with which you can discuss, the merits of one design approach over another.

Only you and your design team can prevent maintenance fires. Ultimately, you must decide which design is most suitable for *your* application. Have fun designing your next system!

---

[11] Slicing an object into aspects (as in Design D) is an excellent design approach for handling "migrating subtypes." For example, consider **CustomerOrder**, an instance of which migrates from **TentativeOrder** to **ApprovedOrder**, to **FilledOrder**, and so on. The composite class **CustomerOrder** could refer to any or all of the component classes **TentativeOrder**, **ApprovedOrder**, and so on. See [Odell and Martin, 1995] for more on this example.

# Designing a Software Component

This chapter isn't about the simple component objects of Chapter 4, which represent parts of real-world composites, but about larger software components, the next great enrichment to our lives after plain old objects. As usual with terms in the software industry, there's plenty of debate about exactly what *component* means. So, to clarify matters, the first section proposes a list of characteristics that, I believe, capture the cardinal properties of components.

The second section compares and contrasts component characteristics with those of object-oriented software, exploring characteristics that components have in common with objects and/or classes.

The third section dives into an example of a component. This example makes no attempt to adhere to any one of the competing—and less-than-compatible—current standards for component technology. Neither does it deal with issues such as distributed-transaction monitors, which are outside the scope of this text. Instead, in keeping with the spirit of this book, I try to rise above the level of volatile technology to examine some of the design principles involved in creating software components.[1]

---

[1] For an excellent review of component technology and other component issues, see [Szyperski, 1998].

The fourth section looks at the internal object-oriented design of a component in considerable detail by studying the interactions between a component's interfaces and the classes and objects inside the component. The fifth section addresses the issues that determine a basic choice in component architecture: whether to create lightweight or heavyweight components.

The final section explores the advantages and disadvantages of using components, especially those purchased from external vendors. As this section shows, the decision whether to "go with components" will involve pondering the weight of several competing factors in order to determine whether the balance at your shop comes down in favor of components or against them.

## 15.1 What Is a Component?

Just when you thought it was safe to ignore the terminologically challenged gurus of Part I (the ones who wrestled over the definition of *object orientation*), forget them not . . . for they're back! This time they're struggling over the meaning of *component*.

At a recent conference called "Object and Component Stuff," I stopped a posse of experts passing in the hallway and accosted them with a simple request: "Er, excuse me, could you tell me what a component is, please?"

With a hurried backward glance, many of them scurried quickly away, as nervous as if I'd panhandled them for some spare airline upgrade coupons. Here, though, are the answers of those component connoisseurs who didn't immediately skitter off:

- Components are bigger than objects.
- A component could be an object, but on the other hand, it could be bigger. It could be a DLL [dynamically linked library].
- Components are definitely not objects. They're bigger, more complex, and more reusable.
- Components are like objects, because their complexity and functionality are supported through an interface.
- Anything that supports IDL [interface-definition language] is a component. It could be an object, I suppose.
- A component is binary code; it doesn't need to be compiled.
- Objects get instantiated. A component cannot be instantiated.

- Components are self-contained units of code that provide specific functionality. (This statement was from an employee of BloatoSoft, Inc. When I pursued him about what, specifically, was *excluded* from this definition, he fled.)

My frustration was finally assuaged by a competent component connoisseur, who gave me an eight-part definition (and also some first-class upgrade coupons). According to this expert, a software component

1. has an external interface that is distinct from the component's internal implementation of the operations declared by that interface

2. has an interface that is defined in a contractual manner: Each of the component's operations is defined in terms of its signature (its types of input and output arguments), its precondition, and its postcondition

3. is *not* instantiated into multiple copies, where each copy has its own unique state[2]

4. demands a certain set of operations (often termed *context dependencies*) from the environment in which it is deployed

5. provides a certain set of operations demanded by the environment in which it is deployed

6. can interact with other components (that follow compatible standards) in the same environment, in order to form software units of arbitrary capability

7. is sold (or given away) in executable (binary) form, rather than in compilable (source) form

8. may offer publication (at run-time or development-time) of the operations that it supports, for other components to discover and use

---

[2] Note that some component technologies don't insist on this property: Some allow instantiations of components, each instantiation with its own persistent state.

## 15.2 Similarities and Differences Between Components and Objects

After expressing my gratitude to the component connoisseur, I wandered slowly away, wondering what the differences were (if any) between a component and an object. Or, I wondered further, What are the differences between a component and a class?

Each of the above eight characteristics of a component offers its own partial resolution to these questions:

1.  The strong distinction between a component's interface and its implementation promotes encapsulation, the cornerstone of object orientation that I introduced in Section 1.1. In fact, a typical component encapsulates many run-time objects and thus exhibits level-3 encapsulation. (See page 211 for a discussion of levels of encapsulation.) Thus, like a good class interface, a good component interface limits connascence across encapsulation boundaries, as I discussed in Section 8.2.3.

2.  Again, the contractual property of operations in components' interfaces is identical to the property of operations of classes that I discussed in Section 10.5.

3.  Classes can be instantiated into objects that each has its own, mutable state. Components, on the other hand, tend to avoid maintaining persistent state. This means that multiple copies of a component (unlike multiple objects of a class) will be identical in internal values as well as in structure. (A slight exception to this is when a component is preset with certain default values, as I discuss below.)

    A component that cannot be instantiated is thus more like the utility that I discussed in Section 3.8, rather than like a classical class. As you may recall, you can consider a utility to be a class without objects, whose operations are all class operations. Since many component technologies forbid inheritance among components, the correspondence between components and utilities (which also normally shun inheritance) is still greater.

4.  Object orientation, as such, has no sense of "environment" around an object. In other words, standard object-oriented design is inclined neither toward designing classes to be used in an existing environment nor toward designing classes for a "green field" situation. Component designers, however, must consider the environment in which the component will function (often termed

the *container).* As we'll see below, a component designer may need or take advantage of services offered by the component's environment to reduce the complexity of the component.

5.  Although language (or shop and project) standards may require a set of basic operations for every class, object orientation per se doesn't demand that a class meet the expectations of a run-time environment. A component, on the other hand, runs only in its designated environment and must normally provide a set of operations mandated by that environment.

    This mandate may be technical or business (or both). An example of a technical mandate: Every component must support a count of references to it, so that it can be removed from memory when it's no longer referenced. An example of a business mandate: A component dealing with physical products in a Web-based e-commerce business must support operations to handle customers' product reviews and operations to present products' pictures as JPEG images.

6.  Component-based software shares an important goal with object-oriented software: reusability. Object-oriented design combines and recombines objects of various classes, each with limited functionality, into grander structures with more sophisticated ability than any individual class.

    Component design does the same with components, but the standardization of a given component environment permits a designer to incorporate existing (or readily purchasable) components into a design. This is an advantage in that it avoids a great deal of programming to implement the design. Obviously, object-oriented design could reap the same happy benefit if preexisting classes could be found that would readily operate together in the way that environmental standards force components to interoperate.

7.  Since components are normally distributed as run-time executables, they correspond more to objects (which are run-time software units) than to classes (which are development-time software units). Furthermore, component standards are typically standards about binary, executable code. Adherence to a binary standard allows components to interconnect via their interfaces, without being troubled by source-language idiosyncrasies. It also potentially allows components written in different source languages to interoperate. Thus, two components written in different languages and/or com-

piled using different compilers can still work together, so long as the compiled code follows the binary standard.

Reality may fall short of this ideal, however. I recently saw an example in which one vendor's C++ compiler would automatically generate executable code that obeyed the environmental standard, whereas another vendor's compiled code needed tweaking before it would obey.

8. Some component standards allow another piece of software to query a component at run-time about the operations that it implements. In practice, a component will respond with the *interfaces* that it supports, a component interface being (as for a class) a family of related operations.

Incidentally, some components come with preset operations—operations that can be invoked at development-time to establish run-time defaults within the component. For example, an argument to a preset operation may cause the e-commerce product component mentioned above to provide an image in JPEG format. Alternatively, a developer may preset the image format to GIF or TIFF. Of course, if you don't have access to the component at development-time, then you won't be able to invoke its preset operations.

## 15.3 Example of a Component

The example in this section is **ResourceManager**, a business component for managing resources. To be more concrete, **ResourceManager** could be used to set up a meeting, which is the confluence of resources including employees, a meeting room, and an overhead projector. However, since the component is neutral about the kinds of resources involved, you could equally well use it to set up a van pool, where the resources are employees and vans.[3]

As the UML component diagram of Fig. 15.1 shows, **ResourceManager** supports four business interfaces (**ResourceTypeServices**, **ResourceInstanceServices**, **ResourceGroupingServices**, and **CalendarServices**), as well as one technical interface (**StandardServices**).

---

[3] As usual with an example in a book, the need to be concise has forced me to omit some business details. For example, I don't deal with the important issue of meeting-room or van capacity. In those timeless words, I leave such enhancements to the reader. See Exercise 5, at the end of this chapter.

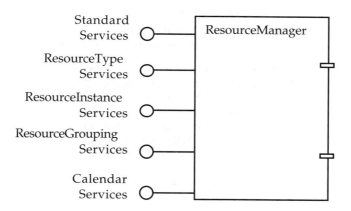

*Fig. 15.1: The* **ResourceManager** *component.*

Now I'll briefly describe the purpose of each interface, together with some of its most significant attributes and operations, as shown in the UML interface diagrams of Figs. 15.2 through 15.6.

The stereotype **«interface»** is a keyword on a "class symbol" denoting that the symbol actually represents an interface, rather than a class. Since an interface has operations but no attributes, the normal attribute compartment is absent. The operations that the interface supports are listed in the operation compartment. However, the assumption in UML is that the methods implementing these operations reside elsewhere. Hence, the stereotype **«interface»** is similar to the stereotype **«type»** that I introduced in Section 11.1, in that it represents an abstraction rather than an implementation. A symbol that is stereotyped with **«type»**, however, may support attributes.

The interface **ResourceTypeServices** (see Fig. 15.2) provides operations that pertain to the whole group of resource types, a group that might include **Employee**, **Room**, and **Van**. Examples include **getTotalNumber** (the number of resource types in the entire group) and **getNumberOfInstances**, which gives, for example, the number of employees. (Note that since **ResourceTypeServices** works with an entire group of resource types, **getNumberOfInstances** requires an **id** input argument to specify *which* resource type must be counted for instances.

```
                    « interface »
                ResourceTypeServices

    getTotalNumber (): Integer
    getNumberOfInstances (id: ResourceTypeID): Integer
    getName (id: ResourceTypeID, out name: String): Boolean
    setName (id: ResourceTypeID, name: String): Boolean
    isPresent (name: String): Boolean
    getID (name: String, out id: ResourceTypeID): Boolean
    getIsHuman (id: ResourceTypeID): Boolean
    setIsHuman (id: ResourceTypeID, isHuman: Boolean)
    add (name: String, out id: ResourceTypeID): Boolean
    remove (id: ResourceTypeID): Boolean
    ...
```

*Fig. 15.2: The operations of* **ResourceTypeServices**.

The reason that each resource type has an ID (like 1) as well as a name (like **Employee**) is to facilitate changing the resource type's name. The two operations **getID** and **getName** allow translations between ID and name. If the operation **getIsHuman** returns **true**, then instances of that resource type can communicate and make decisions (no Dilbertian cynicism, please).

The operation **add** allows new resource types to be added and initialized. It does nothing and returns a value of **false** if, for example, the resource type already exists. Setting up the component **ResourceManager** for first use involves repeatedly invoking **add** until all the required resource types are present.[4]

The operation **remove** allows an unneeded resource type to be deleted. It does nothing and returns a value of **false** if there are still instances of that resource type present. (To avoid that problem, you could first invoke **removeAllOfType**, which I describe below.) Incidentally, **remove** affords us a good opportunity to examine the contractual nature of an operation in a component interface, the second characteristic of a component that I listed above.

ResourceManager::ResourceTypeServices.remove (id: ResourceTypeID): Boolean
Precondition:      getNumberOfInstances (id: ResourceTypeID) = 0
Postcondition:     remove = **true**;
                   getTotalNumber = **old** getTotalNumber – 1;

---

[4] Note that I show just one input argument to **add**, namely **name: String**. In practice, others will be needed, such as **isHuman: Boolean**.

First, above, is the fully qualified name of the operation, together with its signature. Next comes its precondition—what must be true for the operation to actually agree to operate. In this case, there must be no instances of the resource type. Finally, the postcondition states that the functional-style operation returns the value **true** and that the total number of resource types has diminished by one.

The interface **ResourceInstanceServices** (see Fig. 15.3) is similar in some ways to **ResourceTypeServices**, except that it provides operations that pertain to the group of resource instances, rather than to types. (Resource instances may include: Room-101, Room-12A, The Mafeking Room, Overhead Projector #94, Hugh Jampton, Daisy Weale, Loomis Ganderbody, Barney Schutt, Mustapha Bobortu, and so on.) Again, to facilitate name changes, each instance has an ID as well as a name.

---

« interface »
**ResourceInstanceServices**

---

getTotalNumber (): Integer
getName (id: ResourceInstID, **out** name: String): Boolean
setName (id: ResourceInstID, name: String): Boolean
getType (id: ResourceInstID, **out** type: ResourceTypeID): Boolean
setType (id: ResourceInstID, type: ResourceTypeID): Boolean
getID (name: String, **out** id: ResourceInstID): Boolean
getEMailAddress (id: ResourceInstID): String
setEMailAddress (id: ResourceInstID, eMailAddr: String)
getIsAvailable
  (id: ResourceInstID , time: DateTime): Availability
setIsAvailable
  (id: ResourceInstID , time: DateTime, avail: Availability)
add (...): Boolean
remove (id: ResourceInstID): Boolean
removeAll ()
removeAllOfType (id :ResourceTypeID)
...

---

*Fig. 15.3: The operations of* **ResourceInstanceServices**.

The operation **getType** returns the resource type (in the form of the resource type's ID) of the resource instance. **getEMailAddress** returns the e-mail address of any resource instance that has one (including some, but not all, of the human resources). **getIsAvailable** returns an **Availability** value (**available**, **unavailable**, **unknown**) for a given resource instance at a given date/time.

The operations **add** and **remove** work much like their counterparts in **ResourceTypeServices**, except, of course, at the instance level. To set up **Resource-Manager** for use, you must repeatedly invoke **ResourceTypeServices.add**, once for each resource instance that you need.

**removeAll** is a dramatic operation that removes every resource instance at once. A milder version is **removeAllOfType**, which gets rid of the instance population of just one resource type. (For example, invoking **removeAllOfType** with the Employee resource type ID as an argument would eliminate Jim Spriggs, Brunhilde Schreck, Angus Podgorny, along with the instances of **Employee** listed above.)

The next interface to explore is **ResourceGroupingServices** (see Fig. 15.4). This interface could almost be called **MeetingServices**, except that we want the **ResourceManager** component to be more general—to manage resources other than those for meetings. (However, if it helps, you may think of a resource grouping as a meeting.)

---

« interface »
**ResourceGroupingServices**

---

getTotalNumber (): Integer
getName (groupID: ResourceGroupID, **out** name: String): Boolean
setName (groupID: ResourceGroupID, name: String): Boolean
getID (name: String, **out** id: ResourceGroupID): Boolean
getScheduleStatus (groupID: ResourceGroupID): ResourceGroupStatus
getTime (groupID: ResourceGroupID, time: DateTime): Boolean
create: ResourceGroupID
cancel (groupID: ResourceGroupID)
addResource
  (groupID: ResourceGroupID, instID: ResourceInstID,
  mandatory: Boolean): Boolean
releaseResource
  (groupID: ResourceGroupID, instID: ResourceInstID): Boolean
getPossibleTimes
  (groupID: ResourceGroupID, start, end: DateTime): TimeList
schedule
  (groupID: ResourceGroupID, time: DateTime): ResourceGroupStatus
unschedule (groupID: ResourceGroupID)
...

---

*Fig. 15.4: The operations of* **ResourceGroupingServices**.

The operation **getScheduleStatus** returns the current scheduling status of the resource grouping as a value of **ResourceGroupStatus**, as either: **scheduledAll** (scheduled, with all resource instances available); **scheduledOnlyMandatory** (scheduled, with some non-mandatory resource instances unavailable); or **unscheduled** (no time currently scheduled). The operation **getTime** returns the date and time of the resource grouping (if it's currently scheduled).

The operation **create** sets up a new resource grouping. (The term *create* sounds more natural than *add* for this operation.) It returns a value of **Resource-GroupID** (such as 142857), which will serve as the unique identifier for the resource grouping being established. **create** does nothing else; other operations further build and manipulate the resource grouping.

**cancel** gets rid of a resource grouping (and makes any tied-up resource instances available again). In "meeting parlance," **cancel** cancels the meeting.

To specify which resource instances you need for the resource grouping, you call the operation **addResource** multiple times, once for each instance you need. You must specify whether or not a resource instance is mandatory (which means that the grouping cannot be scheduled at a time when that instance is unavailable). **addResource** returns **false** if the instance is already part of the grouping. The operation **releaseResource** removes a resource instance from a grouping and returns **false** if the instance is not currently part of the grouping.

The operation **getPossibleTimes** returns a list of all the dates/times when every resource instance in a grouping is available. The list spans only the range specified by the two dates/times, **start** and **end**. (In practice, each date/time on the list would be marked with a status, noting whether *all* the resources are available or just the mandatory ones; I haven't done that here.)

The operation **schedule** schedules a date/time for the instances in the resource grouping to come together. It returns a value of **ResourceGroupStatus**, which indicates that at the given date/time, all resource instances are available; only mandatory ones are available; or some mandatory ones are unavailable. **unschedule** puts a resource grouping on hold (deletes its scheduled date/time) and releases the involved resource instances from their commitment at that date/time.

The fourth business interface of **ResourceManager** is **CalendarServices** (see Fig. 15.5), which handles general date and time issues. For example, the operation **getSmallestTimeIncr** returns the value of the smallest increment of time that the component will recognize. (You may preset this to a default—perhaps the famous

15 minutes—at development-time, although you could still change this default at run-time via **setSmallestTimeIncr.**)

```
┌─────────────────────────────────────────────────────┐
│                    « interface »                      │
│                  CalendarServices                     │
├─────────────────────────────────────────────────────┤
│  getSmallestTimeIncr (): Integer                      │
│  setSmallestTimeIncr (timeIncr: Integer)              │
│  setDefaultAvailability (date: Date, status: Availablility) │
│  ...                                                  │
│                                                       │
│                                                       │
└─────────────────────────────────────────────────────┘
```

*Fig. 15.5: The operations of* **CalendarServices**.

The operation **setDefaultAvailability** offers a means to establish "holidays" in the calendar. You provide it with a date and it will mark the initial availability of all resource instances on that date as, say, **unavailable**. **CalendarServices** no doubt has many other operations—I mention some of them in Exercise 3, below—but, in the interest of brevity, let's move on to the final interface of **ResourceManager**.

The interface **StandardServices** (see Fig. 15.6) provides operations that all components must have for technical (rather than business) reasons. Each component technology has a different set of these operations; the next few paragraphs describe a typical set.

```
┌─────────────────────────────────────────────────────┐
│                    « interface »                      │
│                  StandardServices                     │
├─────────────────────────────────────────────────────┤
│  getReferenceCount (): Integer                        │
│  getHandle                                            │
│    (client: Client, name: InterfaceName,              │
│     out handle: InterfaceHandle): Boolean             │
│  connect (client: Client, handle: InterfaceHandle): Boolean │
│  disconnect (client: Client, handle: InterfaceHandle): Boolean │
│  ...                                                  │
│                                                       │
└─────────────────────────────────────────────────────┘
```

*Fig. 15.6: The operations of* **StandardServices**.

The operation **getReferenceCount** returns the number of references that other software has made to this component. (In many technologies, separate reference counts are kept for each *interface* of the component.) When the component is being used—and therefore, **getReferenceCount** returns a nonzero positive value— the component must be retained as an executable in main memory.[5] When nobody's using the component—and therefore, **getReferenceCount** returns zero— the component may be deleted.

A component's client may obtain the handle for a component interface by invoking **getHandle**. This returns a pointer to the interface, which is much like the handle of a standard object in that it's the number "you need in all future correspondence" with the interface (such as to invoke an operation of that interface).

However, some clients may not be privileged enough to access a given interface of a component. For example, only very privileged clients of **ResourceManager** may be allowed to use the interface **ResourceTypeServices**. Other clients, if they asked for a handle to this interface, would be given nothing; **getHandle** would return a value of **false**. (On the other hand, the interface **ResourceGroupingServices** may be available to all clients, regardless of their rank.)

The operation **connect** tells a component that another piece of software is now using an interface. (This operation may increase the component's reference count by one; alternatively, **getHandle** could do that job.) **connect** returns **false** if, for example, the supplied **handle** is incorrect or an underprivileged client has somehow gotten a valid value for **handle**. The operation **disconnect** is the inverse; it reduces the component's reference count by one.

Now, having looked at **ResourceManager**'s external interfaces, let's investigate this component's internal design.

## 15.4 Internal Design of a Component

As I pointed out in Characteristic 3 of Section 15.1, a component doesn't normally appear in multiple "stateful" instantiations, so you're not obliged to use object orientation to design your components. For instance, you could design each operation of each interface as a simple, stand-alone procedure and design the internal pieces of the component in the same way. That, of course, would be structured design.

---

[5] Or, as more philosophical components put it, *Me utuntur, ergo exto.* (I'm being used, therefore I exist.)

However, assuming you want to garner the advantages of object orientation that I discussed in Chapters 1 and 2, I'll approach the internal design of **Resource-Manager** in an object-oriented way.

First, let's examine the overall package architecture for **ResourceManager** and its attendant software, as shown in Fig. 15.7.[6] (I'll examine the contents of each package in further detail below.)

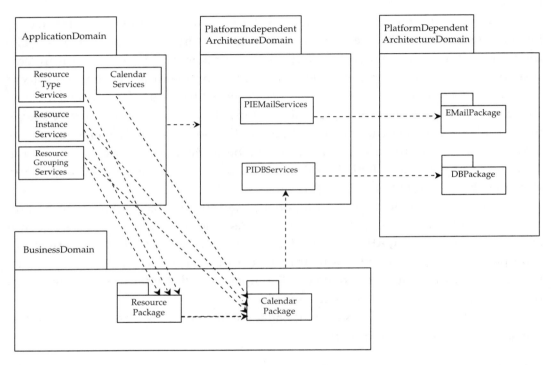

*Fig. 15.7: A UML package diagram for the resource-management software.*

At the highest level, we see the domain structure that Section 9.1 addressed: The application domain includes the four interfaces of Section 15.3. I left off the stereotype **«interface»** in the diagram to reduce clutter.[7] I also omitted **Standard-**

---

[6] I introduced UML package notation in Section 7.1.1.

[7] In practice, you would probably develop a "shadow" class for each interface, which would reside in the application domain. For example, you could create a class **ResourceTypeServices** that would provide the methods to implement the operations in the interface **ResourceTypeServices**. With this approach, each of the boxes in the application domain of Fig. 15.7 would, in effect, represent both an interface and the class that implements it.

**Services** entirely because, since this interface is present in every component, it adds no value to this particular example.

The business domain contains two packages: one for the resource subdomain and one for the calendar subdomain. Each of these packages contains several classes, which we'll examine below.

I've divided the architecture domain into two parts. The platform-dependent architecture domain includes utilities (probably purchased from a vendor) that are written specifically for a single platform (a hardware and software combination). The platform-independent architecture domain includes a version of the same utilities that (from the point of view of the utilities' clients) is not platform-specific. In other words, the platform-independent architecture domain is a layer of software that protects the utilities' clients from the quirks of the actual e-mail and database software operations provided with the platform.

The platform-dependent and -independent architecture domains contain two packages each: one for the e-mail utility library and one for the database utility library.

Now let's return to the business domain to examine the contents of **Resource-Package**.

Figure 15.8 shows the chief classes and associations within **ResourcePackage**. You may have noticed that Fig. 15.8 follows the same pattern as two previous class diagrams: Fig. 11.6 (for **Species** and **Animal**) and Fig. 11.7 (for **ProductLine** and **ProductItem**). This is no coincidence; all three class diagrams deal with types, each of which aggregates a bunch of instances.

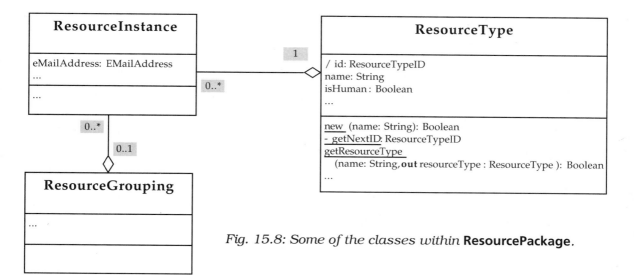

*Fig. 15.8: Some of the classes within* **ResourcePackage**.

We need to generate one object of class **ResourceType** for each of the resource types in the enterprise. For example, if the resource types were **Employee**, **Room**, and **Whiteboard**, then we'd have to create three objects of class **ResourceType** (via the operation **add** in the **ResourceTypeServices** interface of **ResourceManager**).

Methods implementing operations in a component's interfaces do much of their work by manipulating classes in the business domain. To highlight this by example, here's the code within **ResourceManager::ResourceTypeServices.add** that creates a new resource type (by sending messages to invoke operations of the class **ResourceType**). Note that many of **ResourceType**'s operations are class operations; that's why they're underlined in Fig. 15.8.

> **operation** ResourceTypeServices.add (name: String, **out** id: ResourceTypeID): Boolean
>
> **begin method**
>
>     newResourceType: ResourceType;
>
>             // this will hold the handle of the created object
>
>     id := **null**;
>
>     **if**        ResourceType.isPresent (name)
>
>                       //checks whether **name** is present
>
>     **then**    **return false**;    // **name** is already in use
>
>     **else**    newResourceType := ResourceType.new (name);
>
>             id := newResourceType.id;
>
>             **return true**;
>
>     **endif**
>
> **end method**

A few explanatory notes are in order: The **if** statement checks whether the name of the new resource type is already in existence. If so, the **add** operation returns unsuccessfully. If all is well, then the operation appeals to the class operation **new** in the class **ResourceType** to create a new object. The returned handle of this object gets stored in the variable **newResourceType**.

When **new** creates an object, it also carries out two further actions: It gets a unique ID for the object (by appealing to the private class operation **getNextID**); and it stores all the attributes of the fresh **ResourceType** object as a row in a relational table. (Although I haven't shown this connection between **new** and a database explicitly anywhere, it's implicit in Fig. 15.7 as the vertical reference from the entire **BusinessDomain** to **PIDBServices**. The **new** operations of other classes will avail themselves of **PIDBServices**, too.)

Finally, the method for the **add** operation finds and returns the ID of the freshly created **ResourceType** object by appealing to **id**, an accessor instance operation of the object itself.

If I were not a merciful soul and I were to harangue you further with details of how the interface operations of **ResourceManager** interact with the underlying classes in **BusinessDomain**, as shown in Fig. 15.7, I would cover the following:

- the remaining operations of **ResourceTypeServices**, which interact mostly with the class **ResourceType**[8]
- the operations of the other "resource" business interfaces (**ResourceInstanceServices** and **ResourceGroupingServices**), each of which interacts with several of the classes in **ResourcePackage**
- the operations of **CalendarServices**, each of which interacts with classes in **CalendarPackage**
- details of attributes and operations in other **BusinessDomain** classes, many of which are similar in nature to the sample attributes and operations that I showed for the class **ResourceType** in Fig. 15.8
- other interactions between classes in **BusinessDomain** and **PIDBServices**

Although I'll spare you all that, there's one remaining aspect of **ResourceManager** that I must cover. This aspect is the interaction between the interface **ResourceGroupingServices** and the utility **PIEMailServices**, an interaction that's needed to contact human resources (people!) to ask whether they're interested in attending a meeting. This e-mail communication has significant implications for the component interface itself.

*Sending* an e-mail is straightforward. You just package up the message text with a suitable header—including sender's address, recipient's address (found from the attribute **eMailAddress** of the object **recipient: ResourceInstance**), and some kind of message title—and send it off to an appropriate operation of **PIEMailServices**, say **sendEMail**. The message title may include the name and time

---

[8] To be pedantically precise, it's the methods that implement operations in the interface that interact with class operations of **ResourceType** and instance operations of objects of class **ResourceType**.

of the grouping; the message text may include the same information, followed by a more detailed description and a place to "mark an X" if the recipient will be able to attend.

However, the problem comes when the recipient responds. When the e-mail response arrives at the e-mail server (or wherever), how does the **ResourceGroupingServices** interface that sent the original message learn whether the response to the meeting is thumbs-up or thumbs-down? The answer involves events and callbacks.

As we saw in Section 5.3.2 (when we explored the callback mechanism), a subscriber object interested in hearing about occurrences of a certain event type may register that interest with a listener object that is deputized to listen for those occurrences. The listener object then "calls back" the subscriber object when an occurrence takes place.

The design of the callback structure between **ResourceGroupingServices** and **PIEMailServices** requires the following:

1. A subscriber that's interested in a particular type of event. In this example, it's the interface **ResourceGroupingServices** that's interested in receiving e-mail responses about the availability of resource instances.

2. A listener that's able to detect each occurrence of that type of event. In this example, it's the package **PIEMailServices**, which isn't just a layer of software to furnish nicer names or tidier argument sequences for operations provided in the vendor's **EMailPackage** software. Rather, it can check each incoming e-mail message to see whether it satisfies the criteria (such as sender name, recipient name, title, and so on) for any registered event type.

3. The means for the listener to accept event-type registration from the subscriber.

4. The means for the listener to inform the subscriber within a reasonable time about each event occurrence (the callback).

5. The means for the subscriber to get hold of the complete text of the e-mail message that triggered the event occurrence.

Let me amplify some of the above requirements.

To satisfy Requirement 2, we need a link between **PIEMailServices** and **EMail-Package** so that the former can review each e-mail message to determine whether it meets the criteria (such as having the right recipient) for any event type. This can be done if **EMailPackage** itself provides some kind of callback mechanism. Otherwise, **PIEMailServices** needs to scan all messages of interest to it (or rather, to its subscribers) in order to detect relevant event occurrences. It could do this by having the authorization to retrieve messages for certain recipients, which it would then peruse and file in a database.

Requirement 3 simply requires an operation on the listener's interface that will accept the registration of an "e-mail" event type, including all the relevant criteria for assessing whether or not an e-mail receipt constitutes an occurrence of that event type. (The interface needs another operation, too—one for "de-registering.")

There are at least three design approaches to meeting Requirement 4:

- The first approach follows the literal callback design we saw in Section 5.3.2, in which **PIEMailServices** would invoke an operation on an interface of **ResourceManager**, perhaps named **eMailReceived**. We could add this operation, which so far is missing from any of **ResourceManager**'s interfaces, to the interface **ResourceGroupingServices**. Unlike the other operations of **ResourceGroupingServices** (such as **addResource** or **schedule**, in Fig. 15.4), this kind of operation doesn't provide a service to a component's clients; it's an event-notification operation needed by the component itself.[9]

- The second design approach is a variation on the first, in which the *environment* wherein the subscriber and listener operate may mediate the callback by maintaining the list of subscribers registered for an event type. In this approach, when a listener detects an event occurrence, it informs the environment—perhaps a service of the operating system. In turn, the environment notifies registered subscribers that the event has occurred.

- The third design approach to Requirement 4 is to have **PIEMailServices** record in a table every event occurrence that it detects. Subscribers would then periodically check (that is, poll) this table for

---

[9] As you may recall from Section 1.5.4, a message that invokes an operation to inform an object—or, here, an interface—that something that has happened is termed an *informative message*.

their events of interest. The advantage of this design is that it doesn't require an event-notification operation in the subscriber's interface. The disadvantage is that the subscriber wastes a lot of time checking for events (if it polls frequently) or it may wait a long time to hear about an event occurrence (if it polls infrequently).

There are two approaches to designing Requirement 5:

- In one approach, the listener passes to the subscriber *all* the details on the event occurrence (in this case, an entire e-mail message).
- In the other approach, the listener simply informs the subscriber that an event has happened; the subscriber has the job of retrieving the details of the specific occurrence, presumably from a table where the listener has deposited them.

As a graphical summary of this section, Fig. 15.9 illustrates that a component provides services to other components and also requires services from other components. Furthermore, a component may detect events for other components and may also require notification on events from other components.

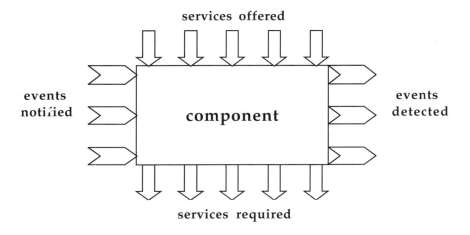

Fig. 15.9: What a component provides and requires.

## 15.5 Lightweight and Heavyweight Components

In the previous section, I treated **PIEMailServices** as a package: a group of related classes. However, there are good reasons to elevate **PIEMailServices** to a component in its own right. For example, a package typically makes visible several classes, each with several operations, although clients of the package may need to see only a small number of those operations. (To use simplistic arithmetic as an illustration: The package may contain 5 classes, each with 10 operations, whereas only 20 of these 50 operations are useful to clients.) Also, the best organization of operations in a component's interface(s) may differ from the way that operations are arranged in the classes themselves.

We could make a similar argument for elevating **PIDBServices** to a component. If we do so, we get the component structure shown in Fig. 15.10, where each bold box encloses a single component.

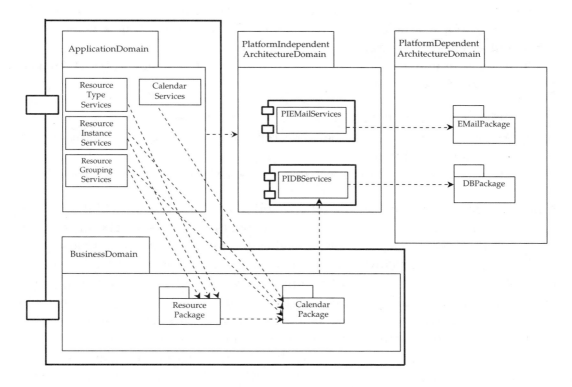

*Fig. 15.10: A UML package diagram showing component boundaries as bold lines.*

We also need to address another question: Why not combine **PIEMailServices** and **ResourceManager** into one component? If we look only at **PIEMailServices**, the answer is clear. Burying such a useful component inside another would be like locking a pearl inside an oyster; anyone wanting to use **PIEMailServices** would also have to buy (and load into their machine) the larger and much less reusable software of **ResourceManager**.

However, from **ResourceManager**'s point of view, the answer isn't nearly so obvious. Because we've designed **ResourceManager** to use the component **PIEMailServices** as an e-mail service (and an "event listener"), we can't sell the former component without the latter also being available to the buyer. If we buried **PIEMailServices** inside **ResourceManager**, then we'd *guarantee* that **PIEMailServices**'s capabilities would be available to **ResourceManager**.

The general question is this: Should we make **ResourceManager** a *lightweight* or a *heavyweight* component? A lightweight component contains only the software for the "job in hand" (in our example, gathering resources for meetings, and so on). It assumes that any ancillary services it needs are provided either by the environment (for example, the platform's database or operating system) or by other components (in our example, **PIEMailServices**).

If these assumptions are valid, then the lightweight component, being smaller, has a number of advantages:

- It will be cheaper to build (and so should sell for less).
- Being simpler, it should be more reliable, both initially and after subsequent maintenance.
- It won't tax the platform's memory with possibly unneeded software.

A heavyweight component, on the other hand, doesn't trust the capabilities of its operating environment or of its fellow components. To be self-reliant, it packs into itself all the secondary software it might need to achieve its primary job.

Discussions about lightweight and heavyweight components often put me in mind of the dozen or so little black transformers that adorn the electrical-power outlets of my house. Each one exists to provide low-voltage (usually DC) power to one or other modern hardware component—appliances such as my answering machine and buzzing toothbrush—without which I'm told I cannot function.

In a perfect world, I'd have no little black transformers in my house, because my house would be wired with low-voltage DC outlets at, say, 12v. If appliance manufacturers could make such an assumption about the operating environment, then they could all standardize their voltage requirements at 12v and sell lightweight components without voltage converters, at a slightly lower price.

Since manufacturers cannot make that assumption, they have the option of creating heavyweight components with the transformers built into the appliances, though that would make the appliances bulkier, heavier, and hotter. Instead, the little black boxes around my walls represent an interesting compromise: Manufacturers sell the primary appliance component as a lightweight, but bundle an ancillary transformer component into the purchase to ensure that the appliance has the voltage it needs.

We have the same option in software. If we were selling **ResourceManager**, we could bundle in **PIEMailServices** as an ancillary component. But **PIEMailServices** must be offered in several versions, because it has to bridge its platform-neutral operations to platform-dependent operations of **EMailPackage**. We would offer the version of **PIEMailServices** most appropriate for the customer's platform.[10]

The concept of an indirect class-reference set (see Section 9.2.1, on encumbrance) gives us another way to think about the issue of lightweight and heavyweight components. Informally speaking, a component's indirect class-reference set is the set of "machinery" (classes or other components) that the component needs in order to work. This machinery can be shown in tree form, as in Fig. 15.11.

In the figure, each ancillary component is labeled $C_x$, with services provided by the platform labeled $P_x$. The lightweight component incorporates just $C_1$, $C_2$, and $C_3$, whereas the heavyweight one also incorporates $C_4$, $C_5$, $C_6$, $C_7$, and $C_8$.

Ideally, components should be lightweight, with single-domain cohesion. In other words, each component should implement nodes in the tree from a single domain, for example, the architecture domain.[11] Then a component for the application domain will use components from the architecture domain to support its work, rather than *include* architectural fragments itself. Creating arbitrarily complex applications for various platforms would then involve a mix-and-match of preexisting single-minded components.

---

[10] For a household analogy to multiple platforms, imagine that some houses have 110v outlets with round pins, some have 220v outlets with square pins, and others have 163v outlets with hexagonal pins. Appliance sellers would then have to offer three different versions of their transformers for each appliance they sold.

[11] Some deviation from this is possible, such as components that straddle application and business domains. Also, every component will include something from the fundamental domain.

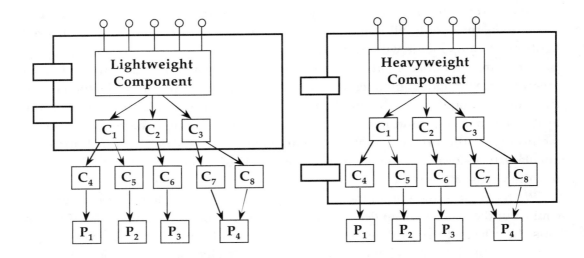

Fig. 15.11: The "contents" of a lightweight and a heavyweight component.

## 15.6 Advantages and Disadvantages of Using Components

However fashionable and potentially useful components may be, it isn't easy to decide whether to use components purchased from external vendors in your next application. Here are some of the advantages (denoted by **+**) and disadvantages (**–**) of using purchased components:

**+    They're cheap.**

And you can't beat that! A component to check customer credit, for example, may be 100 times cheaper to purchase from a vendor than it would be to develop in-house. A well-capitalized vendor can take advantage of market scale to offer components that are far less expensive than those you develop solely for your own use.

**+    They're available.**

Even if you were to spend the money to develop your own set of components, you may never complete the job. Some shops have a less-than-stellar record of software development, with a project-cancellation record of more than 50 percent. In-house component development, therefore, carries the risk that the components you need may never become available.

**+  They're available now.**

Even if you have a good record of completing software projects, you can't carry out a component-development project in zero time. You may have to wait twelve or eighteen months to take delivery of your custom-built componentware.

**−  They may be *almost* available now.**

Your friendly component vendor may take you to one side, put his hand on your shoulder, and assure you that the killer component for your business is almost ready for delivery—and would you mind very much beta-testing it for them? But beware: Components not yet in the marketplace are subject to the same vaporware and betaware problems that any other vendor software may suffer.

If you let assumptions about the promised availability, functionality and straightforward beta-testing of this much-proclaimed component determine your next application's success, then the component could indeed be a killer. Before you can deliver the application to the users, the homicide squad may show up to draw a chalk outline around your entire project.

To avoid this risk, you need to keep close tabs on your vendor to ensure that you're kept apprised of any problems with the component. Alternatively, you should develop stand-in software that can take the place of a late or incapacitated component.

**+  They're mature.**

Components from major vendors are often tested and debugged by literally thousands of users. Therefore, a component that you purchase may enjoy a level of correctness and stability that would be months away for your home-grown software.

**+ They may incorporate "best of breed" ideas.**

A component vendor that has culled requirements from dozens of major customers may create components with a set of features that you wouldn't have dreamed of, or that you would have found too expensive to implement.

**– They're also available to competitors.**

Your competitors probably shop in the same component marketplace as you. If you're seeking competitive advantage from your software applications, then you may have to eschew readily available street-ready components—at least for crucial parts of your applications—in favor of customized software that you develop in-house.

**– They may be too complex for straightforward needs.**

If you buy a business component for vehicle/route/freight management, you may find that it handles trains, trucks, cars, cargo ships, tankers, planes, and rickshaws carrying both solid and liquid freight on all international routes. If your company just carries bricks on trucks around Podunk, then you may not want to deal with the business complexity of the component.

A heavyweight component may also be too big or complex. For example, it may feature network and distributed database capability that you neither need nor want to pay for.

**– Customizability may be tough or impossible.**

Ideally, you'd like to tailor a purchased component to match the needs of your business.[12] For example, if you only carry bricks on trucks around Podunk, then you would probably like to lower the sophistication of your purchased component by eliminating references to cargo ships, space shuttles, oil tankers, and trans-Pacific ocean voyages. However, if that proves difficult or impossible, you may have to put up with an irritating interface that makes irrelevant references to exotic vehicles and faraway ports of which you know little.

---

[12] As we saw with the component **ResourceManager**, a vendor can make a component general enough for each of the component's customers to tailor it to specific business needs.

–  **An intransigent component may require changes to your business.**

If you purchase, say, customer-account and billing componentware, you may find that it doesn't allow certain corporate hierarchies (for example, a hierarchy in which one of your customers is a corporation that owns another of your corporate customers).  Also, since it may allow only three accounts per customer and the Wallace Co. just opened its fourth account with you (for the Gromit branch), you have to treat the Gromit branch office as a new customer with the name Wallace-Gromit.

–  **Business components may not be available for niche industries.**

If your company is the world leader in a vast trillion-dollar industry, you might expect that groveling component hawkers would be lined up around the block to proffer their wares to your esteemed management.  However, if your company is a laggard in the Mongolian camel-hair rug industry, will component vendors come when you call for them?  Probably not.  I fear that when you peer eagerly from your window anticipating a jostling throng of ardent component-mongers, only disappointment will await you.

+  **They're maintained by someone else.**

Many an organization spends the majority of its software budget on maintaining its compendium of existing applications.  The good news is that component vendors have such economy of scale in their software-maintenance operations that their cost per customer for updating a component is much less than your in-house cost would be to update equivalent software.

–  **Revised versions may arrive too slowly.**

And the bad news is that component vendors may be sluggish to make important fixes to their components.  Also, when the revised component finally does arrive, the changes may differ from the ones that *you* would have made if you'd had complete control over the component.

– **Revised versions may arrive too quickly.**

The opposite problem is that a vendor may bombard you with Version 1.3.1.2.4 of a component just a few weeks after Version 1.3.1.2.3 showed up. You may find yourself spending so much time installing the latest version of components that your application incorporating the components never stabilizes. Alternatively, if you install every *third* upgrade, your vendor may refuse to speak to you when you call for support because you "don't have the latest version."

+ **Components follow standards.**

Although component standards are still emerging (at the time of this writing), vendors will eventually follow one of a small set of standards in the components they provide. This will encourage interoperability among different vendors' components.

We're unlikely ever to arrive at a single, global, set of component standards. Nevertheless, we can hope that major vendors will continue to provide bridgeware that allows their sundry sets of component standards to interoperate.

– **They may involve multiple vendors.**

Despite the above fond hope, the world of multiple-vendor support isn't always a happy one. Bridgeware may be imperfect and leave you drowning in a river of component incompatibility. More subtly, inter-vendor compatibility may depend on your having the right versions of the appropriate components. For example, your billing component (Version 2.3.1.2) from PlutoSoft, Inc., may happily sing with an accounting component (Version 1.4.6.3) from MegaModules Co. But when you upgrade to Version 1.4.6.4 of MegaModules' accounting component, great disharmony may bruit forth.

In such a situation, although you probably feel like banging the two component vendors' heads together, in practice you may be stuck with using the old version of MegaModules' accounting component until PlutoSoft trots out Version 2.3.1.3 of *its* masterpiece. Meanwhile, if you can even reach the two vendors on the phone (Press 1 to wait indefinitely on hold, Press 2 to wait indefinitely for a return call, and so on), all you'll hear is the verbal equivalent of mutual finger-pointing between the two software hucksters.

— **The component vendor may go out of business.**

Although in the light of the previous paragraph such a demise may seem a consummate cessation devoutly to be wished, in reality the disappearance of a component's vendor will be a major nuisance. After the vendor vanishes, you "own" the vendor's components, but this de facto ownership is hollow: You probably have the components in compiled (binary) form, but the source code has gone with the vendor. You'll be locked in time with the crock of components you possessed when their developer shuffled off the corporate scene, and you'll have to endure the components' annoyances, defects, and deficiencies in perpetuity.

Nevertheless, you should weigh the risk that smaller vendors may go out of business with the fact that such vendors may produce components that are more innovative and imaginative than those of their larger, more established counterparts.

## 15.7 Summary

A software component is a unit of software with most or all of the following characteristics: It has an external interface that is distinct from the component's internal implementation; it has an interface that is defined in a contractual manner; it is not instantiated into multiple stateful copies; it demands a set of operations from the environment in which it is deployed; it provides a set of operations demanded by the environment in which it is deployed; it can interact with other components in the same environment in order to form software units of arbitrary capability; it is distributed to customers in executable form; it offers publication of the operations that it supports.

In some of these characteristics, components resemble classes or objects; in others, components diverge from traditional classes and objects.

A component provides to its clients one or more interfaces, each of which provides one or more operations. At least one of these interfaces supports operations demanded by the environment (also known as the container) in which the component operates. The other interfaces provide business-oriented operations. In addition to providing services via operations, a component may listen for event occurrences and notify one or more other components about them.

A component may be depicted by a UML component symbol. Each of the component's interfaces, with its operations, may be depicted by a UML interface symbol.

A component may be built as a lightweight component, which means that it relies on software that is external to itself (such as ancillary components or platform services) to accomplish its primary tasks. A heavyweight component includes all the services it needs to operate in a given environment. Lightweight components have several advantages, so long as the ancillary software is available to the component.

A typical component to support business functions has interfaces that belong to the application domain, although other software within the component (especially if it's a heavyweight) may belong to the business domain, the architecture domain, and the foundation domain. (This internal software and its structure may be depicted using a UML package diagram.) Components are often designed in an object-oriented way, although this is not compulsory. Each of the operations in a component's interface interacts with classes in the business, architecture, and foundation domains in order to meet its contractual duty.

Purchased components have several advantages over in-house, home-grown software, but also several disadvantages. Deciding whether or not to adopt components in your project involves weighing a number of important considerations, such as the competitive differentiation that your software should provide and the reputations of the components' vendors.

## 15.8 Exercises

1.  In Section 15.3, I noted that setting up the component **ResourceManager** for first use involves repeatedly invoking **add** until all the required resource types are present. So, why not sell **ResourceManager** with all its resource types already loaded in, perhaps via preset operations? Then developers deploying **ResourceManager** won't have to include code to establish Employee, Meeting Room, Overhead Projector, and so on as resource types.

2.  The operation **getEMailAddress** in the **ResourceInstanceServices** interface (see Fig. 15.3) returns the e-mail address of any resource instance that has one (including some, but not all, of the human resources). Presumably, it returns a null string for the many resource instances without such an address. Comment on the design of this accessor operation, and also on that of its "partner," the modifier operation **setEMailAddress**.

3.  As I said in Section 15.3, the operation **setDefaultAvailability** marks the initial availability of all resource instances on a given date. What other facilities of this kind might you add to **CalendarServices**?

4.  In my Section 15.2 musings on Characteristic 3 of components, I noted that components do not retain state in the way that objects do. If this is the case, then how does a component like **ResourceManager** remember instances of resources (such as Jim Spriggs and Room-101) over days and weeks?

5.  If you were a user of **ResourceManager**, what enhancements might you request for the next version of this component?

## 15.9 Answers

1. This epitomizes a dilemma facing all component builders: whether to make a component very general, which will require customization by the deployer (typically complicating the component's initialization), or to make the component restrictive (which will make it simpler to use, but which may restrict its market). In other words, should this component be a resource-management component or a meeting-scheduler component? The answer to that question is not solely technical: Ultimately, it's a marketing decision.

2. The operation **getEMailAddress** should return an explicit **Boolean** argument, set to **false** for those instances without e-mail, rather than relying on a null string to convey this fact implicitly:

   getEMailAddress (id: ResourceInstID, **out** eMailAddr: String): Boolean

   The operation **setEMailAddress** should probably check whether an instance is human before allowing it to acquire an e-mail address (although cognoscenti tell me that we'll soon be sending e-mail to our faithful office and household devices to turn them on and off again).

3. You should probably be able to set times (as well as dates) of default availability, such as "unavailable during the night." You could go further and allow users to put in patterns of dates, such as those generated by weekends. And, if you want to be even bolder, you could allow, say, the first Monday of every September or—one that's always mystified me—the first Tuesday after the first Monday in November. (However, perhaps that kind of calendrical prestidigitation fits better in a purpose-built **ShopCalendar** component, which could then be used by several other components, including ours.)

   Finally, you could apply availability defaults to specific resource types or instances, rather than as a blanket across all resources at once.

4. Although the component per se doesn't record this information, *something* must. This "something" is normally a database, such as the one accessed via **DBPackage** in Fig. 15.7. (You could imagine that to use a component you would have to specify which database to open or which new database to create.)

If a component is designed using object orientation, then objects created inside a component will have state while they're alive. However, between component uses (invocations of interface operations), a component doesn't rely on internal objects to maintain state; those objects may, for example, get deleted between component uses, having first recorded their attribute values for posterity in a database.

5. One enhancement would be the ability to give certain resource types (such as vans, rooms, and so on) a capacity. This would be needed to ensure that a resource instance was sufficient for a given grouping. Another enhancement might be to allow a resource instance to be chosen arbitrarily from a collection of suitable candidates. (For example, for a meeting of ten people, *any* sufficiently large meeting room will probably work.)

# Appendix A: Checklist for an Object-Oriented Design Walkthrough

This appendix contains a list of questions that will help you to smoke out common design problems during a walkthrough or inspection. You may choose to have everyone on the design team ask all the questions, or you may assign a subset of the questions to each person.

In this appendix, I haven't suggested cures for any design problems, because the purpose of the walkthrough is to *identify*, rather than to fix, problems. However, the appendix that follows this one, *The Object-Oriented Design Owner's Manual*, suggests cures for several object-oriented design problems. If you'd like to review the basic concept of reviews (including walkthroughs and inspections), see [Freedman and Weinberg, 1990].

The questions below will expose many common object-oriented design flaws. Each question addresses the design of a single class, or a group of cooperating classes, or a section of a specific application. (The last six questions, in particular, address the design of an application.)

Although having a checklist will save you time in finding lurking design flaws, no checklist can be exhaustive. You should, therefore, continue to add questions to this list as you discover further recurrent design problems.

## Questions

1. Should the class under review (and others like it) be built, or should it be purchased from an outside vendor? (This question is especially germane for foundation classes and many architectural classes.)

2. Does a new class really need to be built, or could an existing class in the library be modified, extended, or generalized?

3. Does the class make as much use as possible of existing classes in the library?

4. Is any connascence (including contranascence) present that's not readily apparent from the code? Where is that connascence documented?

5. Is the class too large or complicated to assess the connascence that exists within it?

6. Does any connascence violate the encapsulation boundaries of object orientation?

7. Does the class rely on any assumptions in order to work correctly? Do any other classes also rely on the same assumptions? How likely are those assumptions to change? Where are the assumptions documented?

8. Does the class have a degree of reusability that's appropriate to its domain?

9. Is the encumbrance of the class appropriate for its domain?

10. Is the class's context of applicability—the types of systems or situations in which it's intended to be usable—documented? Should that context be broadened by generalizing the class, or reduced by making the class more restrictive?

11. Does the class have mixed-instance, mixed-domain, or mixed-role cohesion? If so, why?

12. Is any part of the class's design dependent on a coding language or operating environment? If so, can that part be factored out? If not, is the dependence documented?

13. Is the class's invariant documented?

14. Is the class's invariant so complex that it suggests another set of core representational variables would be a better basis for the internal class design?

15. Does each of the class's operations have a documented pre- and postcondition?

16. If the class inherits from a superclass, does its type conform to the type of its superclass? That is, is its invariant at least as strong as its superclass's? For each of its operations, does the operation have the same formal signature as the corresponding operation in the superclass and does the operation obey the principles of contravariance and covariance? If the answer to any of these questions is "No," then why not? Is that reason documented?

17. If the class inherits from a superclass, is the principle of closed behavior followed? That is, do all operations of the superclass respect the class invariant of the subclass? If not, then what countermeasures has the designer of the subclass taken?

18. Does the class inherit any features of a superclass that should be private to the superclass? (In some languages, all features of a superclass are visible to a subclass.) If so, why? If so, what configuration-management practices will ensure that a change to the superclass's internal design will be reflected in the subclass?

19. (This question is especially germane if the above question yielded a "Yes.") Does the subclass really capture a more specialized version of the concept that the superclass captures? In other words, does the subclass pass the *is a* test? If not, why not?

20. (This question is especially germane if the above question yielded a "No" or if the subclass cancels several inherited operations through overriding.) Is inheritance appropriate? Or would message forwarding (from the subclass to the superclass) yield a sounder class-reuse structure?

21. Is any part of the class hierarchy (superclass/subclass inheritance structure) too deep? ("Too deep" is obviously subjective, but five or more levels beneath a root class should trigger a warning.) If so, should message forwarding, rather than inheritance, be used anywhere in the hierarchy?

22. Do subclasses of a common superclass contain similar or identical features that should be moved to the superclass?

23. If the design exploits multiple inheritance, do the inherited class invariants conflict in any way in the inheriting subclass? Do any inherited names clash? Is the principle of closed behavior respected by all superclasses, or

handled by the subclass?  Is type conformance between superclasses and subclass obeyed (with the possible exception of abstract superclasses, such as mix-in classes)?

24. If message forwarding is used, is it appropriate?  Or would inheritance yield a more efficient or maintainable class-reuse structure?

25. Does any operation used by the class (or defined on the class) have a ragged SOP?  If so, should other classes be extended to include that operation or should the operation be defined and implemented higher in the class hierarchy in order to give the operation a complete COP?

26. For each operation exploiting polymorphism, does the SOP of the variable (pointing to the target object) lie within the SOP of the operation?

27. Does any message apparently need to be encased in a complicated **if**, **case**, **inspect**, or **switch** structure?  If so, is this because of a poor use of object orientation (specifically, underuse of polymorphism) or because an operation has a ragged SOP?

28. If the class is a parameterized class, is it suitably constrained (or, at least, has its constraints documented) so that, for each message within the class, the SOP of the message's variable lies within the SOP of the operation?

29. If the class represents composite (or aggregate) objects, are the messages between the composite object and its components of the correct form?  In other words, have interrogative (pull) and informative (push) messages been used appropriately?

30. Do any asynchronous messages cause timing conflicts?  (This question is especially important if the timing algorithm is distributed across multiple classes, or even multiple run-time objects of the same class?)  Also, is the concurrency of the system so complicated that the question is difficult to answer?

31. If a broadcast message is used, is the correct subset of objects broadcast to?  Is a broadcast message appropriate, or should the sender object send the message iteratively to a set of explicit objects?

32. Should the operations of the class be designed in rings in order to reduce connascence between operations and private variables?

33. Does the class's interface support illegal, incomplete, or inappropriate states?  If so, why?

34. Does the class's interface support illegal, dangerous, or irrelevant behavior? If so, why?

35. Does the class's interface support incomplete behavior? If so, will that create an immediate problem, or can the incomplete behavior be tolerated for the near future?

36. Does the class's interface support awkward behavior? If so, should further behavior be added to the interface, even if that results in replicated behavior?

37. Does the class's interface support replicated behavior? If so, is that for the convenience of diverse users of the class, or has it happened by accident? If the latter, should the replicated behavior be eliminated?

38. If the class's interface *doesn't* support replicated behavior, should it? In other words, should replicated behavior (for example, restrictive operations with few arguments, as well as general operations with several arguments) be added to the interface for the convenience of users?

39. Do any operations of the class have alternate or multiple cohesion? If so, why? Should any operation be replaced by two or more operations?

40. Is the class too restrictive for its current purposes, that is, the applications in which it's likely to be used?

41. Is the class too general or broad for its current purposes? In other words, does the class contain a lot of "unnecessary baggage" based on fantasy rather than firm requirements?

42. Is the design of the class difficult to generalize to meet the class's predicted purposes, that is, the applications in which it's likely to be used during the coming two years? (This question may cause long wrangles that can be resolved only by a crystal ball. Truncate such wrangles.)

43. Does the design of the class meet shop-library standards (for example, with respect to naming, sequence of arguments, and so on)?

44. Is the class documented according to shop-library standards? Does the class have (in addition to the documentation highlighted in the above questions) user documentation stating: the class's purpose and context of applicability, the use of each of its operations, the meaning of each operation's argument, known inefficiencies, known defects, known oddities, and any known lack of generality?

45. Does the class have necessary auxiliary documentation, such as: the class's administration history (designer, programmer, modifiers, dates, metrics, and so on), its status (such as the fact that it's obsolete and has been replaced by another class), its physical history (location of its design, source code, compiled code, development tools used, and so on), its test history (tests carried out and results, location of test suite for current version, and so on), and the applications in which it's known to be used?

46. Consider the part of the requirements specification (produced during analysis) that the design portion under review is intended to fulfill. Does the design fulfill the spec, the whole spec, and nothing but the spec? If not, why not?

47. Are there other designs that would also fulfill the requirements specification? If so, were they considered and rejected because of maintainability, extensibility, reusability, efficiency, or some other reason? Or were they simply not considered?

48. What are the most likely changes that the users will make to the system requirements? (Again, avoid crystal-ball wrangles here.) How much impact would each one make on the design? Would it cost a great deal to carry out any of the more minor changes?

49. Does the application's human interface follow shop standards? Do the windows-navigation diagrams indicate that the system dialogue corresponds to the users' units of work? Can any changes be made to the interface to improve users' productivity?

50. If the application is distributed across processors, is the distribution appropriate? Given the system statistics (for example, rate of update, population of objects, and so on), where are the performance bottlenecks likely to arise? (This may require benchmarking to nail down precisely.) Does the design allow the partitioning to be changed after the system is deployed?

51. Do larger software groupings, such as the packages addressed in Chapter 7, include classes from several subdomains or even several domains? If so, how should the classes be regrouped to achieve better domain separation?

52. Finally, a couple of important questions: Can the design actually be coded? Will it work?

# Appendix B: The Object-Oriented Design Owner's Manual

Below, I summarize many of the design issues that this book has covered, in the form of a table. The first column identifies the symptom of an object-oriented design problem, and the second column covers the most likely causes of that problem. The third column identifies possible cures to eliminate each cause, while the last column points out potential dangers or ill effects that might result from the cure. (Obviously, you don't want to apply a cure that's worse than the disease!)

| Problem symptom | Likely cause | Possible cure | Potential danger |
|---|---|---|---|
| Connascence that crosses encapsulation boundaries | Class(es) whose implementation is not properly encapsulated | Redesign class(es), paying careful attention to the classes' external interfaces | |
| | | Avoid any reliance on a class's "accidents of implementation" | |
| | Use of C++ friend construct | Remove friends, replacing with connections to classes' external interfaces | |
| Implicit connascence | The proliferation of the same design decision across several classes | Isolate design decision into a single class, possibly creating a new class | |
| | Connascence that cannot easily be made explicit | Document the implicit connascence | Documentation may be inadequate or may become obsolete or lost |
| Large amount of potential connascence (including contranascence) that's difficult to evaluate | Class that is far too large | Break class into smaller classes | Class that no longer represents an entire abstraction |
| | Class hierarchy in which subclasses extensively inherit implementation details of superclasses | Use inheritance only to inherit externally visible interface of classes | May require rewriting entire library if this is a widespread problem |
| Poor reusability of foundation class | Design of class too restrictive | Generalize class design | Greater effort and expense of design |
| | Classes developed in-house | Purchase foundation-class library | May not be entirely compatible with shop's requirements, language, or architecture |
| | | | Vendor reliability |
| Poor reusability of architectural class | Design of class too restrictive | Generalize class design | Greater effort and expense of design |
| | Class has mixed-instance, mixed-domain, or mixed-role cohesion | Split the class into classes with ideal class cohesion | |
| | Shop has motley technology | Standardize shop's technology | Expense of hardware and porting software |

| Problem symptom | Likely cause | Possible cure | Potential danger |
| --- | --- | --- | --- |
| Poor reusability of business class | Design of class too restrictive | Generalize class design | Greater effort and expense of design |
| | Class has mixed-instance, mixed-domain, or mixed-role cohesion | Split the class into classes with ideal class cohesion | |
| | Analysis of the class based on too-narrow segment of company | Reanalyze class in broader business context | Greater effort and expense of both analysis and design |
| | | | A class design so general that it's cumbersome to understand and maintain |
| | | | Irreconcilable business / policy differences between different segments of company |
| | Perception of poor reusability, because class's intended reusability unclear | Document explicitly the class's intended reusability | |
| Class from low domain has high encumbrance | Inappropriate operation allocation, resulting in mixed-domain cohesion | Reallocate operation(s) with high encumbrance to class(es) in higher domains | |
| | Class has mixed-domain cohesion | Split class into two (or more), each with ideal class cohesion | |
| | Class contains unnecessary references | Redesign class, paying attention to the Law of Demeter | |
| Class from high domain has low encumbrance | Class has been designed from "too fundamental" a set of classes | Use classes from library to design the class. (If such classes don't exist, design and build them too.) | Library may need to be reorganized, possibly disturbing current users of library classes |
| Class has mixed-instance, mixed-domain, or mixed-role cohesion | Class represents more than one fundamental concept | Split the class into classes with ideal class cohesion | Increase in number of classes may be deemed excessive |
| | | Use mix-in class to create classes with ideal class cohesion | |

| Problem symptom | Likely cause | Possible cure | Potential danger |
|---|---|---|---|
| Subclass is not true subtype of superclass | Subclass fails to obey the principle of type conformance | Redesign subclass to obey type conformance, particularly the principles of contravariance and covariance | Hierarchy of classes in the "real world" may not fully obey the principle of type conformance |
| Behavior inherited from a superclass violates the invariant of a subclass | Subclass fails to obey the principle of closed behavior | Do not inherit violating operations in the subclass | Loss of some of the power of inheritance |
| | | Override violating inherited operations in the subclass | |
| | | Have senders of messages to objects of the subclass check for violations of closed behavior | Requires other classes to contain knowledge of the subclass, which creates extra code and connascence problems |
| | | Factor superclass into two classes (**Closed** and **Open**) and have subclass inherit from **Closed** | Added complexity in class hierarchy |
| | | Redo class hierarchy so that subclass inherits only closed behavior | Introduction of additional classes may affect existing code |
| | | Migrate an object of the subclass to another class, whose invariant will not be violated | Class migration may not be appropriate in the application |
| | | | Class migration isn't well supported in most mainstream languages |
| Class invariant complex and unwieldy | Core representational variables inside class allow too many degrees of freedom | Choose another internal class design with fewer degrees of freedom | May increase algorithmic complexity or preclude elegant internal class design |
| Subclass inheriting inappropriate operations from superclass | Inheritance used where message forwarding would be more appropriate | Forward messages from an object of the former subclass to an object of the former superclass | Design loses ability of subclass automatically to inherit new operations added later to superclass |
| | | | Possibly less efficient |

| Problem symptom | Likely cause | Possible cure | Potential danger |
|---|---|---|---|
| Operation has ragged SOP | Class hierarchy doesn't follow type hierarchy | Redesign the hierarchy following the principle of type conformance | May require rewriting entire library if this is a widespread problem |
| | Similar operation (for example, **print**) is defined on widely different classes | (Not always a problem per se, but may cause mixed-domain cohesion or the problem below) | |
| In a message, SOP of variable denoting target object not within SOP of operation | Variable of too high a class in hierarchy | Declare variable to be of lower class in hierarchy | Variable's SOP may no longer cover all the possible objects relevant to the application |
| | Within a parameterized class, the class of some objects may not be known at design time | Document at the start of a parameterized class the operations that a supplied class must support | Documentation alone won't *guarantee* that suitable classes will be supplied |
| | | Constrain the supplied classes that a parameterized class will accept | |
| | Operation defined too low in the class hierarchy | Define and implement operation higher in hierarchy | |
| | SOP of operation ragged | Introduce **if** statements to avoid "falling into the holes" in the operation's SOP | Code may become complex and ugly and may lose power of object orientation |
| Class interface supports illegal states | Class design reveals internal implementation | Redesign class with better encapsulation | |
| Class interface supports incomplete states | Poor choice of core representational variables or other poor internal design decision | Redesign class internals | |
| Class interface supports inappropriate states | Class designer has failed to understand the true abstraction that the class represents | Redesign the class from a solid, documented abstraction, supporting only states appropriate for that abstraction | Hackers using the class may get upset that they can no longer write tricky code exploiting the availability of inappropriate states |

| Problem symptom | Likely cause | Possible cure | Potential danger |
|---|---|---|---|
| Class interface supports illegal or dangerous behavior | Class design reveals internal implementation | Redesign class with better encapsulation | |
| Class supports irrelevant behavior | Behavior that doesn't belong in the class | Move behavior to another class | |
| | | Factor behavior into a procedural module that can be called by an operation of any class | Design may be criticized for not being "object oriented enough" |
| Class supports incomplete behavior | Some legal behavior not supported | Generalize existing operations or add operations to support all legal behavior | |
| | An operation has multiple cohesion | (See below) | |
| Class supports awkward behavior | Some legal behavior supported via multiple messages | Generalize existing operations or add operations to support all legal behavior via a single message | |
| Class supports replicated behavior | Some behavior supported in several different ways | Replace multiple operations, supporting replicated behavior with single, more general operation | May create compatibility problems for existing users of the class |
| | | | Replicated behavior may actually be convenient, if it allows messages with fewer arguments |
| Large amount of connascence between operations and private variables | Implementation of core representational variables and other private variables visible to all operations | Design operations in rings | Possible slight reduction in efficiency |
| Operation has alternate or multiple cohesion | Combined functionality within the operation | Split the operation into two or more operations, each with ideal (functional) cohesion | |

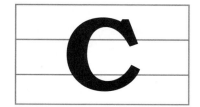

# Appendix C: The Blitz Guide to Object-Oriented Terminology

The following table shows the approximate translations of terms that I use in this book into the terminology of some popular object-oriented languages. Since words never translate exactly across languages and since this table is necessarily concise, I don't guarantee that all cases represent an exact semantic match. Terms in parentheses are those not commonly employed by aficionados of that particular language, but which you will find in some texts on the language.

For the exact nuance of terms in a particular language, consult the manual of the language in which you're interested. Alternatively, consult [Firesmith and Eykholt, 1995], which provides an excellent, comprehensive list of object-oriented terms, together with their assorted definitions. In any case, please don't blame me if you go to a C++ conference and accidentally utter the object-oriented equivalent of "Your father was a hamster."

| This book | C++ | Eiffel | Smalltalk |
|---|---|---|---|
| Class | Class | Class | Class |
| Object | Object | Object | Object |
| Instantiation | Construction | Creation | Instantiation |
| Self | This | Current | Self |
| Operation (instance) | Member function | Feature | Method (instance) |
| Operation (class) | Static member function | — | Method (class) |
| Variable (instance) | Member variable | Entity | Variable (instance) |
| Variable (class) | Static member variable | — | Variable (class) |
| Private | Private | (Private) | Private |
| Protected | Protected | (Restricted export) | — |
| Public | Public | Exported | (Public) |
| Message | Call | Call | Message |
| Sender | (Caller) | Client (simple) | Sender |
| Target | (Called) | Supplier (simple) | Receiver |
| Signature | Argument list | Signature | Argument list |
| Superclass | Base class | Ancestor class | Superclass |
| Subclass | Derived class | Descendant class | Subclass |
| Overloading | Overloading | — | — |
| Overriding | Virtual/redefinition | Redefinition | Overriding |
| Deferred class | Abstract class | Deferred class | Abstract class |
| Parameterized class | Template class | Generic class | — |

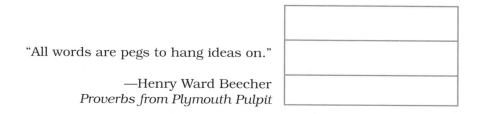

"All words are pegs to hang ideas on."

—Henry Ward Beecher
*Proverbs from Plymouth Pulpit*

# $G$lossary

***abstract class*** (or ***deferred class****)*  A class from which objects cannot be instantiated (normally, because the class has one or more abstract operations).  An abstract class is usually used as a source for descendant classes to inherit its concrete (nonabstract) operations.

***abstract data-type***  A data-type that provides a set of values and a set of interrelated operations, and whose external definition (as seen by outside users of that data-type) is independent of their internal representation or implementation.  (A class is a particular implementation of an abstract data-type.)

***abstract operation*** (or ***deferred operation****)*  An operation lacking a workable implementation (a method).  Normally, a descendant class will override this inherited abstract operation with its own concrete operation (one having a working method).

***accessor operation***  See ***query operation***.

***action message***  An outbound message from an object resulting from the object's transition from one state to another (usually applied only to transitions represented on a state diagram for that object's class).

***actual argument***  An argument of the target operation of a message, as defined and used by the sender object.

***aggregate object***  An object that represents a group of other objects known as constituent objects.

**alternate cohesion**  The cohesion of an operation containing several pieces of behavior that are executed alternatively (depending on the value of a flag).

**ancestor class**  Of a class **C**, a direct superclass of **C** or an ancestor of a superclass of **C**.

**apex of polymorphism (AOP)**  The highest class in a cone of polymorphism.

**application domain**  The group of classes (which are sometimes actually simple procedures) whose applicability and reusability are restricted to a single application (or to a small suite of applications).

**architecture**  A system's organization of hardware and software elements.

**architecture domain**  The group of classes whose applicability and reusability are restricted to a single combination of hardware and software implementation technology (or to a small range of such technology).

**architecture model**  A model that represents the mapping of an essential, non-technological model onto a chosen hardware and software implementation technology.

**argument**  Information passed in a message either into (as an input or **in** argument) or out from (as an output or **out** argument) the target operation of the message. (Although the argument is usually a reference to an object, it may also be data or a reference to data.)

**aspect**  A major part of a class's abstraction that allows it (and its objects) to be used in a certain context. (For example, the class **Customer** may have a financial aspect.) A class may have several aspects.

**asynchronous message**  A message whose sender object may continue to execute while the message is being processed by the target object.

**attribute**  A part of the interface to a class (and to its objects) that represents an element of information (comprising a defined set of values) belonging to the class's abstraction.

**awkward behavior**  The property of a class interface that requires an object to carry out some state transitions via multiple messages that take the object through intermediate (but legal) states.

**behavior**  The set of permitted transitions among states in the state-space of a class.

**broadcast message**  A message whose sender object specifies as target objects a group of objects that fulfill a particular criterion, rather than specifying one object by means of its handle. Often, a broadcast message takes *every* object as its target.

**business domain**  The group of classes whose applicability and reusability are restricted to a single business or industry. In the extreme case, this may be a single corporation or a single division within a corporation.

**callback**  A mechanism by which the target object of a message (often a listener) returns the result of the message (or notification of an event occurrence) by initiating a second message, whose target object is the sender of the original message (often a subscriber).

***capability*** The ability of a class or its objects to carry out a particular operation or set of operations. (For example, a capability of the class **Document** may be printability.)

***class*** A design/programming construct that defines the features (that is, attributes and operations) of the objects—the instances of that class—that will actually be created at run-time.

***class based*** Pertaining to a software environment having only object-oriented encapsulation, state retention, object identity, and classes.

***class cohesion*** The measure of interrelatedness of the features (the attributes and operations) in the external interface of a class.

***class constant*** A constant defined on a class as a whole, not on a single object instantiated from that class.

***class coupling*** The set of connections (normally, explicit references) from one class to another class.

***class diagram*** A diagram that depicts a collection of static elements (chiefly classes), together with their associations, superclass/subclass structure, and other static interrelationships. Optionally, such a diagram includes, for each class, its attributes, operations, and the signatures of the operations.

***class-inheritance hierarchy*** An organization of subclasses and superclasses that are related through inheritance.

***class interface*** The external view of a class, specifically the following: the class's name and invariant; the name, formal signature, preconditions, and postconditions of each of the class's operations; and the externally observable state-space and behavior defined by the class.

***class invariant*** Of a class **C**, a condition that every object of **C** must satisfy at all times when the object is in equilibrium.

***class library*** A collection of classes and frameworks intended for reuse in several systems. Each class is carefully tested and is accompanied in the library by its test suite and user documentation. Some classes are grouped into frameworks that work together to accomplish a higher-level purpose.

***class message*** A message that invokes a class operation (rather than an instance operation).

***class migration*** From class **A** to class **B** by object **obj**, **obj**'s simultaneous loss of membership of class **A** and its acquisition of membership of class **B**. (Most object-oriented languages do not support class migration directly.)

**class operation**  An operation defined on a class as a whole, rather than being defined on a single object instantiated from that class.

**class variable**  A variable defined on a class as a whole, rather than being defined on a single object instantiated from that class.

**cohesion**  The relatedness of elements that constitute an encapsulated unit.

**collaboration diagram** (or **object-collaboration diagram**)  A diagram that shows the messages passed between objects (and occasionally classes) at run-time, together with the links between the objects.

**component**  (1) One of the objects contained in the structure represented by a composite object; (2) a unit of software (a **software component**) with most or all of the following characteristics:  It has an external interface that is distinct from the component's internal implementation; it has an interface that is defined in a contractual manner; it is not instantiated into multiple stateful copies; it demands a set of operations from the environment in which it is deployed; it provides a set of operations demanded by the environment in which it is deployed; it can interact with other components in the same environment in order to form software units of arbitrary capability; it is distributed to customers in executable form; it offers publication of the operations that it supports.

**composite object**  An object that represents a structure of other objects known as component objects.

**concrete class** (or **nonabstract** or **effective class**)  A class from which objects can be instantiated.

**concrete operation** (or **nonabstract** or **effective operation**)  An operation that has a working implementation (a method).

**concurrency** (or **system-level concurrency**)  The ability of a system to support several loci of execution.  (Note that although true concurrency requires several physical processors, concurrency may be simulated on a single processor.  The latter is termed *pseudo-concurrency*.)

**cone of polymorphism (COP)**  A scope of polymorphism that forms a complete branch in the superclass/subclass inheritance hierarchy.

**confinement of behavior**  Of subclass **S**'s behavior within class **C**'s behavior, the situation in which every legal transition among **S**'s states is also a legal transition among **C**'s states.

**confinement of state-space**  Of subclass **S**'s state-space within class **C**'s state-space, the situation in which every state of **S** is also a state of **C**.  (**S**'s state-space is also said to be a subspace of **C**'s state-space.)

**connascence**  Between software elements **A** and **B**, the property by which there is at least one change to **A** that would necessitate a change to **B** in order to preserve overall correctness.

**constant**  A reference to an object or data value (or occasionally to some other kind of element) that is immutable and therefore cannot change.

**constituent**  One of the objects that compose the group represented by an aggregate object.

**container**  Of a component, the environment in which a component is designed to operate; by implication, the set of services that the environment provides to the component.

**context dependency**  Of a component, a set of operations that a component requires from the environment in which it is deployed.

**continuously variable attribute**  An attribute that (in principle, at least) has an infinite set of possible values, rather than a finite set of discrete values.

**contranascence**  Between software elements **A** and **B**, a form of connascence in which there is some property of **A** that must be held different from the corresponding property of **B**.

**core representational variables**  Variables (usually, instance variables) used in the internal design of a class to support the class's external abstraction.

**coupling**  The dependence of one software element upon another (or the degree thereof).

**dangerous behavior**  The property of a class interface that requires an object to carry out some state transitions via multiple messages that take the object through intermediate but illegal states.

**delegation**  A mechanism whereby an object (known as a prototype or exemplar object) permits other objects to share part or all of its state-space or behavior.  Delegation is a mechanism for sharing object properties that does not require classes and inheritance.  (Confusingly, some authors use *delegation* to mean *message forwarding*.)

**deployment diagram**  A diagram depicting the configuration of run-time processing artifacts and the software constructs that they host.

**descendant class** (or **derived class** or **descendant**)  Of a class **C**, a direct subclass of **C** or a descendant of a subclass of **C**.

**design**  The act of representing a chosen implementation for a set of requirements (or the resulting product thereof).  Each design will possess a certain quality vector.

**dimensionality** (or **degrees of freedom**)  Of the state-space of a class **C**, the number of dimensions of the state-space of **C**.

**dimensions**  Of the state-space of a class **C**, the set of coordinates needed to specify the state of an object of class **C**.

***direct class-reference set*** Of a class **C**, the set of classes to which **C** refers directly. **C** refers to a class by: inheriting from it; having an attribute or variable of that class; receiving a message with an argument of that class; sending a message that returns an argument of that class; having a method with a local variable of that class; or having a "friend" of that class.

***direct encumbrance*** The size of a class's direct class-reference set.

***disnascence*** Between software elements **A** and **B**, the absence of any connascence (or contranascence) between **A** and **B**.

***domain*** Of a class, the category of that class determined by the range of applicability (or reusability) of the class. More generally, a domain is an area of knowledge or practice governed by distinct concepts and terminology.

***dynamic binding*** The run-time identification of the actual software element indicated by a reference. The term is normally used to describe the run-time identification of the exact method (operation implementation) that should be invoked as a result of a message.

***dynamic classification*** The ability of an object to acquire, lose, or change its class(es) during its lifetime, without changing its handle (OID).

***dynamic connascence*** Connascence that is defined by the execution pattern of a running system.

***encapsulation*** The grouping of related ideas or constructs into one unit, which can thenceforth be referred to by a single name. In object orientation, encapsulation usually means the grouping of operations and attributes into an object or class structure, whereby the operations provide the sole facility for the access or modification of the attributes' values.

***encumbrance*** See ***direct encumbrance*** or ***indirect encumbrance***.

***essential model*** A model of a system that depicts system requirements in a manner free of the characteristics of any particular implementation or technology. Informally, the essential model is said to assume perfect technology.

***event model*** An analysis model, not covered in detail in this book, that organizes and classifies event types and defines their associated recognizer and activity-manager constructs and other characteristics.

***event type*** A type of occurrence that requires some action by a system.

***explicit connascence*** Connascence that is readily apparent from a document such as a code listing.

***extensibility*** The property of a piece of software that allows it to be augmented or generalized by adding new software and without extensively changing the original software.

***extension of behavior*** By a subclass **S** from a class **C**, the presence of additional behavior in **S**, usually needed to navigate the portion of **S**'s state-space that extends from **C**'s state-space.

***extension of state-space*** By a subclass **S** from a class **C**, the presence of dimensions in **S**'s state-space that are not present in **C**'s state-space.

***external dimensionality*** The number of dimensions (or degrees of freedom) of a class's state-space, as revealed by the class interface. It is equivalent to the dimensionality of the class, considered as an abstract data-type.

***external state*** The ensemble of values (or, more formally, object references) that an object possesses at a given time and that are accessible outside the object (typically, via query operations).

***extrinsic*** **B** is extrinsic to **A** if **A** can be defined with no notion of **B**.

***fan-out*** Of an element **E**, the number of references that **E** makes to other elements. (Normally, the other elements are of the same kind as one another.) Typically used in structured design for the number of modules called by a given module.

***feature*** An attribute or an operation.

***first-order design*** (or ***higher-order design***) A design paradigm in which arguments accompanying invocations have level-1 encapsulation (such as pointers to functions passed as arguments in module calls).

***formal argument*** An argument of the target operation of a message, as defined by the operation header in the target object's class.

***foundation domain*** The group of classes whose applicability and reusability are unrestricted by any application, business, or technology. In other words, a foundation class has the widest possible applicability.

***framework*** A set of collaborating classes, arranged to be able to carry out some meaningful portion of an application. (A framework is more sophisticated than a single class, but normally less sophisticated than a subsystem. Typically, a single class in the framework has limited reusability on its own.)

***friend function*** (or ***friend class***) A C++ term for a software function (or class) that, although formally defined to be external to a class **C**, has access to **C**'s internals.

***frozen operation*** An operation that, if inherited, cannot be overridden.

***functional cohesion*** (or ***ideal operation cohesion***) The cohesion of an operation dedicated to carrying out a single piece of behavior. (A class's designer should aim to create operations with functional cohesion.)

***function-style operation*** An operation that returns an argument in its own name. It's normally (but not always) used for a get operation.

**garbage collector**  The portion of the run-time operating environment that detects objects that are no longer referenced and removes them from memory.

**generic class**  See **parameterized class**.

**get operation**  An operation that returns the value of an attribute.  It is normally a query operation; most query operations are also get operations.

**graphical user interface (GUI)**  An interface between a human and an automated system in which possible actions by the human and responses by the system are presented in the form of visual cues (such as icons).

**guarded state transition** (or **guarded transition**)  A transition on a state diagram that may occur only if its attendant guard evaluates to **true** for the object concerned.  A guard is an expression that's a Boolean combination of input arguments to the object, output arguments of outbound message(s) from the object, and attributes of the object.

**hacking**  As used in this book, programming without prior, formal, communicable, identifiable, or documented analysis and design.

**handle** (or **object identifier** or **OID**)  An object's identifier, whose value (in an ideal object-oriented environment) is unique to that object in that no other object has, had, or will have a handle with that value.  An object's handle is constant and is independent of the object's state.

**heavyweight**  Of a component, containing not only the software necessary to carry out the specific functionality of the component, but also software that provides services necessary to the operation of the component.

**horizontal partitioning**  Partitioning of a population of objects across system artifacts (typically, processors or databases) so that some objects live on one artifact and some on another.  The term is usually applied to a population of objects belonging to the same class.

**human-interface model**  A model defining the mapping of the essential information crossing the human-machine boundary into (typically) windows, defining also the layout of the windows, the activities carried out by the windows, the application-specific navigation among the windows, and the information passed among windows.

**ideal behavior**  The property of a class interface that allows an object to carry out in one way state transitions that are legal for its class and only state transitions that are legal for its class.  (A class's designer should aim to create an interface with ideal behavior.)

**ideal class cohesion**  The property of a class that has no mixed-instance, mixed-domain, or mixed-role cohesion.  (A class's designer should aim to create classes with ideal cohesion.)

***ideal operation cohesion*** See ***functional cohesion***.

***ideal states*** The property of a class interface that allows an object to reach all states that are legal for its class and only states that are legal for its class. (A class's designer should aim to create an interface with ideal states.)

***illegal behavior*** The property of a class interface that allows an object to carry out state transitions that are illegal for its class.

***illegal states*** The property of a class interface that allows an object to reach states illegal for its class (that is, states that violate the class invariant).

***immutable class*** A class whose objects are immutable objects.

***immutable object*** An object whose state cannot change.

***imperative message*** A message to an object that requests it to carry out some action, typically to set some object (perhaps itself) or the environment to a prescribed value or state. (Such a message invokes a non-query operation and may also cause information to be sent to the environment to change its state.) It is a "future-oriented" message, in that it asks the object to make some change in the immediate future.

***implementation hiding*** An encapsulation technique whereby the encapsulated unit's externally visible interface suppresses the unit's internal details of representation, algorithm, or technology.

***implicit connascence*** Connascence that is not readily apparent from a document (such as a code listing).

***inappropriate states*** The property of a class interface that presents some states that are not germane to the class's abstraction.

***incomplete behavior*** The property of a class interface that does not allow an object to carry out some state transitions that are legal for its class.

***incomplete states*** The property of a class interface that does not allow an object to reach some states that are legal for its class.

***indirect class-reference set*** Of a class **C**, the transitive closure of the direct class-reference set of **C**.

***indirect encumbrance*** Of a class **C**, the size of the class's indirect class-reference set. Less formally, it's the number of classes that **C** requires in order to compile, link, and run successfully.

***information hiding*** An encapsulation technique whereby the encapsulated unit's externally visible interface suppresses certain information available within the unit.

***informative message*** A message to an object that informs it of the state of some object—or perhaps of the environment. (Such a message typically invokes a set operation.)

It is a "past-oriented" message, in that it informs an object of what has already taken place elsewhere.

**inheritance** By subclass **S** from class **C**, the facility by which a subclass **S** has implicitly defined upon it each of the attributes and operations of **C** as if those attributes and operations had been defined upon **S**.

**instance** Of a class **C**, an object instantiated from **C** (or one that has in some other way acquired membership of **C**).

**instance constant** A constant that is (in principle) instantiated for each object of a given class.

**instance message** A message sent to an object (as opposed to a class).

**instance operation** An operation that is instantiated (in principle) for each object of a given class.

**instance variable** A variable that is instantiated for each object of a given class.

**instantiation** The act (normally carried out at run-time) of creating an object from a class.

**interaction diagram** (or **object interaction diagram**) A diagram that shows the messages passed between objects (and occasionally classes) at run-time. It has two forms in UML: the collaboration diagram and the sequence diagram.

**internal dimensionality** The number of dimensions (or degrees of freedom) of a class's state-space, as determined by the total dimensionality of the core representational variables in the class's internal design. It is normally reduced by class invariants to the same value as the class's external dimensionality.

**internal state** The ensemble of internal values that an object possesses at a given time (or, more formally, the object references held by an object's internal variables).

**interrogative message** A message to an object requesting that it reveal its current state. (Such a message usually invokes a get operation.) It is a "present-oriented" operation, in that it asks an object for a current state or value.

**intrinsic** **B** is intrinsic to **A** if **B** captures some characteristic inherent to **A**.

**irrelevant behavior** The property of a class interface that supports behavior extraneous to the class.

**iterated message** A message that is repeatedly issued, normally to several constituents of an aggregate object.

**iterator** An operator that repeatedly issues a message (normally to several constituents of an aggregate object).

**Law of Demeter**  A guiding principle for limiting the encumbrance of a class by constraining the size of its direct reference set.

**level-0 encapsulation**  Lines of code (including data declarations) without any encapsulation.

**level-1 encapsulation**  Encapsulation of lines of code (including data declarations) into (usually invocable) procedural modules. This is the chief level of encapsulation used in structured design.

**level-2 encapsulation**  Encapsulation of operations (themselves encapsulations of methods) into a class or object. The operations provide (among other capabilities) access to attributes (which are themselves, in effect, encapsulations of variables). This is the level of encapsulation used in object orientation.

**lightweight**  Of a component, containing only the software necessary to carry out the specific functionality of the component, with other necessary services being provided by ancillary software, such as other components or services of the container.

**listener**  An object (or component) deputized to detect occurrences of a given event type and normally also to notify another object (or component)—the *subscriber*—about the event occurrence.

**literal class**  A class (such as **Integer** or **Date**) whose objects are literal objects. All the objects of a literal class are considered to be already instantiated and are not instantiated at run-time.

**literal object**  A rudimentary object represented merely by its value (such as 67) and denoted by a literal (such as "67"). It has no object handle and is invariably an immutable object.

**message**  A request by a sender object **sendobj** to a target object **targobj** that **targobj** apply one of its operations. **sendobj** and **targobj** are normally distinct, although they may be the same object. (If the target of the message is a class, rather than an object, the message is termed a class message.)

**message forwarding**  The routing of a message by the object initially receiving it to another object that is better able to process it.

**message queue**  In a system with concurrency, a storage area for each message that an object is unable to process at the time the object receives the message.

**metaclass**  Used chiefly in languages like Smalltalk, a class whose instances are themselves classes.

**method**  An implementation of an operation.

**mixed-domain cohesion**  Of a class **C**, the presence of an element within **C** that encumbers **C** with an extrinsic class from a different domain.

**mixed-instance cohesion**  Of a class **C**, the presence of an element within **C** that is undefined for at least one instance of **C**.

**mixed-role cohesion**  Of a class **C**, the presence of an element within **C** that encumbers **C** with an extrinsic class of the same domain as **C**.

**mix-in class**  A class from which objects are not normally instantiated, but which is designed to have its capabilities inherited by ("mixed in" with) other classes.

**model**  An intentional arrangement of a portion of reality (the medium) to represent another portion of reality (the subject) such that the model represents some facets of, and behaves in some ways like, the subject.  The parts, the sets of details and the abstractions of the subject that the model encompasses, constitute the *viewpoint* of the model; the ways in which the model behaves like the subject is called the *purpose* of the model.  An object-oriented design model often takes the form of a diagram, each of whose graphic elements is defined textually.

**multiple classification**  The ability of an object to belong to several classes simultaneously.  (The term is normally not used for properties obtained through the standard class-inheritance mechanism.)

**multiple cohesion**  The cohesion of an operation containing several pieces of behavior that are executed together.

**multiple inheritance**  Inheritance whereby a class may have several direct superclasses.

**mutable class**  A class whose instantiated objects are mutable.

**mutable object**  An object whose state can change.

**name clash**  A situation whereby a class or object has access to more than one element with the same name (typically, through multiple inheritance).  The actual reference intended by the name must be discovered via some resolution mechanism.  More generally, a name clash occurs when two identical symbols with different meanings are present in the same symbol space.

**non-inheritable operation**  An operation defined on a class **C** that is not available to descendants of **C**.

**non-query operation** (or **modifier operation**)  An operation whose execution changes the state of at least one object in the system (typically, the object upon which the operation is executed) or changes the state of the environment.

**object**  A unit with level-2 encapsulation that has a unique identity separate from its state; an instance of a class.

**object-action paradigm**  A term usually applied to a type of human/system interface in which the user first identifies an object and then determines which action to apply to that object.

**object based** Pertaining to a software environment that has only object-oriented encapsulation, state retention, and object identity. (In other words, an object-based environment lacks inheritance and the distinction between classes and objects.)

**object identifier (OID)** See **handle**.

**object identity** The property by which each object (regardless of its class or current state) can be identified and treated as a distinct software entity.

**object-level concurrency** Concurrency such that a single object, by supporting several loci of execution, can process multiple messages simultaneously.

**object oriented** A software environment having "most of" the following properties: level-2 encapsulation, implementation hiding, information hiding, object identity, messages, classes, inheritance, polymorphism, and parameterized class (together with possible further refinements on these properties).

**object structured** Pertaining to a software environment that has only object-oriented encapsulation and state retention.

**OID** See **handle**.

**operation** A procedural feature of an object, whose procedure (known as the operation's method) is executed upon the object's receipt of a message that specifies that operation.

**operation-level concurrency** Concurrency such that a single operation of an object, by supporting several loci of execution, can process multiple messages simultaneously.

**overloading** The use of the same name for multiple operations of the same class. Resolution of the ambiguity is usually by means of the signature of the operations (specifically, the number and classes of their arguments).

**overriding** The local redefinition of the implementation of an inherited operation or type of an attribute, which then takes precedence over the inherited definition.

**package** A general-purpose construct for organizing software constructs. Packages may be grouped hierarchically; in other words, packages may be grouped within packages.

**parameterized class** A class C, where one or more of the classes that C uses internally is supplied only at run-time (at the time that an object of class C is instantiated).

**perfect technology** A hypothetical form of technology without any deficiencies or flaws (in which, for example, all processors are infinitely fast, all networks have infinite speed and bandwidth, all storage media are infinitely large, and everything is infinitely reliable).

**platform** The entire mechanism on which software may be run, including both hardware (processor, volatile memory, persistent memory, network, and so on) and system software (operating system, database management system, communications software, and so on).

**pointer** A variable that contains an object handle.

**polymorphism of an operation** The facility by which a single operation name may be defined upon more than one class and may denote different implementations (methods) in each of those classes.

**polymorphism of a variable** The property whereby a variable may point to (hold the handle of) objects of different classes at different times.

**postcondition** Of an operation, a condition that must be true when an operation successfully ends its execution.

**precondition** Of an operation, a condition that must be true for an operation to begin execution and to execute successfully.

**preset operation** An operation on a component that can be executed at development-time, typically to set a default value within the component.

**principle of closed behavior** For a subtype **S** of a type **T**, the principle whereby the behavior of **S**—including that derived from **T**—does not violate the class invariant of any class of type **S**.

**principle of contravariance** Part of the principle of type conformance, the principle whereby, for each operation of a subtype **S** corresponding to an operation in a type **T**, the precondition of **S.op** must be equal to or weaker than that of **T.op**. In particular, all the input arguments to **S.op** must either be of the same type as or be supertypes of the corresponding input arguments to **T.op**.

**principle of covariance** Part of the principle of type conformance, the principle whereby, for each operation of a subtype **S** corresponding to an operation in a type **T**, the postcondition of **S.op** must be equal to or stronger than that of **T.op**. In particular, all the output arguments from **S.op** must either be of the same type as or be subtypes of the corresponding output arguments from **T.op**.

**principle of type conformance** (or **substitutability**) For a subtype **S** of a type **T**, the situation whereby correctness is always preserved when an object of type **S** is provided in a context where an object of type **T** is expected.

**procedure-style operation** An operation that does not return a value in its name. (It is often used as a non-query operation.)

**process** A program with its own data and code space that runs independently of (and usually concurrently with) other processes, in the sense that processes do not have access to one another's data and code spaces. A process may be single-threaded or multi-threaded.

***quality vector*** A set of system qualities (such as flexibility, usability, or efficiency), each with a particular management or user priority. Each design alternative for a system (or subsystem) will possess a particular quality vector. (The chosen design is normally the one with the most appropriate quality vector for the needs of the business.)

***query operation*** (or ***accessor operation***) An operation that does not change the state of the system by its execution.

***redefinition*** A mechanism for carrying out overriding.

***reliability*** The property of a piece of software that can be repeatedly depended upon to execute consistently with its specification.

***repeated inheritance*** Inheritance in which a class may be a descendant of the same superclass by more than one path.

***replicated behavior*** The property of a class interface that supports the same behavior in multiple ways.

***reusability*** The property of a piece of software that allows it to be employed in more than one context (subsystem, application, organization, and so on).

***ring of operations*** An informal term denoting a way to design the internals of a class so that not all operations access variables directly. Instead, some operations (inner operations) shield other operations (outer operations) from knowledge of variables' details.

***robustness*** The property of a piece of software that permits it to recover without catastrophe from some modes of failure.

***scope of polymorphism (SOP) of an operation*** The set of classes upon which the operation is defined (either directly or via inheritance).

***scope of polymorphism (SOP) of a variable*** The set of classes to which objects pointed to by a variable (during its entire lifetime) may belong.

***second-order design*** A design paradigm in which arguments accompanying invocations have level-2 encapsulation (such as pointers to objects passed as message arguments in object-oriented design). Object-oriented design is an example of second-order design.

***self*** (or ***this***, as in C++, or ***Current***, as in Eiffel) An instance constant that holds the handle of the present object (that is, the object in which **self** is mentioned).

***sender object*** An object that sends a message to another object (or to itself).

***sequence diagram*** (or ***message sequence diagram***) A grid-like diagram that shows time on its vertical access and objects (or sometimes other system elements, such as processors) on its horizontal axis. Vertical bars within the grid represent the exe-

cution times of the elements' operations.  Horizontal arrows show elements' interactions via messages, ordered vertically in chronological sequence.

***set operation***  An operation that changes the value of an attribute.  (It is a simple non-
query operation.)

***signature***  Of an operation **op**, the name of **op**, the list of formal input arguments to **op**,
and the list of formal output arguments from **op**.  (Some authors would also
include the pre- and postconditions of **op**.)

***single inheritance***  Inheritance in which a class has at most one direct superclass.

***state***  The collection of values (or, more formally, object references) that an object possesses at a given time.

***state attribute***  An attribute, each of whose values represents (or could represent) a state
on a state diagram.

***state diagram*** (or ***statechart diagram***)  A diagram that depicts states (discrete values of
some attribute(s)) and the permitted transitions between those states.  The state
diagram may also show events (such as inbound messages to an object) that cause
transitions and outbound messages caused by transitions.  In object-oriented
design, the state diagram is often used as part of the definition of an object class.

***state retention***  The property by which an object can retain its current state indefinitely
and, in particular, between activation of its operations.

***state-space***  Of a class, the ensemble of all the permitted states of any object of that class.

***state transition*** (or simply ***transition***)  A change by an object from one state to another
state (or, possibly, to the same state).

***static binding***  The compile-time (or link-time) identification of the actual element indicated by a reference.  (The term is normally used to describe the compile-time
identification of the exact method—the operation implementation—that should be
invoked as a result of a message.)

***static connascence***  Connascence that is defined by the lexical representation of a system
(such as its source code).

***stereotype***  A novel modeling element, but one that is based on an existing class of elements in a meta-model.

***Structured Design Notation (SDN)***  A notation (developed by Larry Constantine and others) for depicting a software design that chiefly comprises a hierarchy of procedural
modules.

***subclass***  Of a class **C**, a class that inherits from **C**.

***subdomain***  A more specialized area within a domain (or another subdomain).  For example, a **business** domain may include (at a particular company) **transportation** and

**accounting** subdomains. The latter may itself include further subdomains, such as **payables** and **receivables**.

***subscriber*** An object (or component) that registers interest with another object (or component)—the *listener*—in learning of occurrences of a given event type.

***subtype*** Of a type **T**, a type that conforms to **T**.

***superclass*** Of a class **C**, a class from which **C** inherits.

***supertype*** Of a type **T**, a type to which **T** conforms.

***synchronous message*** A message whose sender object must suspend execution while the message is being processed by the target object.

***Synthesis*** An approach to analyzing and designing object-oriented systems, developed and used at Wayland Systems, Inc., but not covered in this book. See **www.waysys.com**, for example.

***target object*** An object that receives a message.

***target operation*** The operation specified by a message.

***task*** A collection of computations that work together, implemented either as a process or a thread. An operating environment may provide single-tasking or multi-tasking.

***thread*** A separate path of execution through a process. A thread has its own local stack, but shares code and global data with other threads in the same process.

***trigger message*** Informal term signifying an inbound message to an object that causes a transition from one state to another (usually applied only to transitions represented on a state-transition diagram for that object's class).

***type*** See ***abstract data-type***.

***Unified Modeling Language (UML)*** A set of concepts, constructs, terminology, and notation for modeling systems—governed by a defining meta-model.

***use case*** A defined, purposeful, interaction between a system and a human or non-human actor that is playing a specific role outside the system.

***variable*** An implementation (that is, programming) construct declared within a class and instantiated for the class's objects, used to hold pointers to objects or data, or often to implement attributes.

***vertical partitioning*** Partitioning of a population of objects across system elements (typically, processors or databases) so that some aspect(s) of each object live on one element and some aspect(s) on another. Each object is therefore physically split into parts. The term is usually applied to a population of objects belonging to the same class.

***virtual function*** See ***abstract operation***.

**window-layout diagram**   A diagram that shows the fields, buttons, menus, and other "widgets" on a window. It is supported by a document that defines the properties (such as field-validation criteria and command-button-enablement conditions) of these window widgets.

**window-navigation diagram**   A diagram depicting how the users of an application may traverse from window to window through application-specific paths (usually implemented by menus and command buttons).

**yo-yo messaging**   An informal term for a design structure in which a pair of objects repeatedly exchange messages in order to accomplish some piece of an application.

**zeroth-order design**   A design paradigm in which arguments accompanying invocations comprise unencapsulated data.

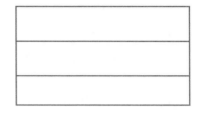

# Bibliography

I refer to most of the following works in the text of the book. However, I've included other works in this Bibliography that I consider to be valuable reading on object orientation.

[Ambler, 1998]

Ambler, S. *Process Patterns.* Cambridge, England: Cambridge University Press, 1998.

[Atkinson, 1991]

Atkinson, C. *Object-Oriented Reuse, Concurrency and Distribution.* Reading, Mass.: Addison-Wesley, 1991.

[Bertino and Martino, 1993]

Bertino, E., and L. Martino. *Object-Oriented Database Systems.* Reading, Mass.: Addison-Wesley, 1993.

[Booch, 1994]

Booch, G. *Object-Oriented Analysis and Design with Applications.* Reading, Mass.: Addison-Wesley, 1994.

[*Chambers'*, 1972]

*Chambers' Twentieth Century Dictionary*, ed. A.M. MacDonald. London: W. & R. Chambers, 1972.

[Chidamber and Kemerer, 1991]

Chidamber, S.R., and C.F. Kemerer. "Towards a Metrics Suite for Object-Oriented Design," *OOPSLA '91 Conference Proceedings*, pp. 197-211. New York: Association for Computing Machinery, 1991.

[Coleman et al., 1994]

Coleman, D., et al. *Object-Oriented Development: The Fusion Method*. Englewood Cliffs, N.J.: Prentice-Hall, 1994.

[Constantine, 1968]

Constantine, L.L. "Control of Sequence and Parallelism in Modular Programs," *AFIPS Proceedings of the 1968 Spring Joint Computer Conference*, Vol. 32 (1968), pp. 409ff.

[Constantine and Lockwood, 1999]

_____, and L. Lockwood. *Software for Use: A Practical Guide to the Models and Methods of Usage-Centered Design*. Reading, Mass.: Addison-Wesley (ACM Press Series), 1999.

[Cook and Daniels, 1994]

Cook, S., and J. Daniels. *Designing Object Systems*. Englewood Cliffs, N.J.: Prentice-Hall, 1994.

[Cox, 1986]

Cox, B. *Object-Oriented Programming: An Evolutionary Approach*. Reading, Mass.: Addison-Wesley, 1986.

[Dahl and Nygaard, 1966]

Dahl, O.-J., and K. Nygaard. "SIMULA—An Algol-Based Simulation Language." *Communications of the ACM*, Vol. 9, No. 9 (September 1966), pp. 23-42.

[DeMarco, 1978]

DeMarco, T. *Structured Analysis and System Specification*. Englewood Cliffs, N.J.: Prentice-Hall, 1978.

[Dijkstra, 1982]

Dijkstra, E. *Selected Writings on Computing: A Personal Perspective.* New York: Springer-Verlag, 1982.

[Embley et al., 1992]

Embley, D.W., B.D. Kurtz, and S.N. Woodfield. *Object-Oriented Systems Analysis: A Model-Driven Approach.* Englewood Cliffs, N.J.: Prentice-Hall, 1992.

[Firesmith, 1993]

Firesmith, D.G. *Object-Oriented Requirements Analysis and Logical Design.* New York: John Wiley & Sons, 1993.

[Firesmith and Eykholt, 1995]

_____, and E. Eykholt. *The Dictionary of Object Terminology.* New York: SIGS Books, 1995.

[Fowler and Scott, 1997]

Fowler, M., and K. Scott. *UML Distilled.* Reading, Mass.: Addison-Wesley, 1997.

[Freedman and Weinberg, 1990]

Freedman, D.P., and G.M. Weinberg. *Handbook of Walkthroughs, Inspections, and Technical Reviews,* 3rd ed. New York: Dorset House Publishing, 1990.

[Goldberg and Robson, 1989]

Goldberg, A., and D. Robson. *Smalltalk-80: The Language.* Reading, Mass.: Addison-Wesley, 1989.

[Graham, 1991]

Graham, I. *Object-Oriented Methods.* Wokingham, England: Addison-Wesley, 1991.

[Grehan et al., 1998]

Grehan, R., R. Moote, and I. Cyliax. *Real-Time Programming.* Reading, Mass.: Addison-Wesley, 1998.

[Harel, 1987]

Harel, D. "Statecharts: A Visual Formalism for Complex Systems." *Science of Computer Programming*, Vol. 8 (1987), pp. 231-74.

[Hatley and Pirbhai, 1988]

Hatley, D.J., and I.A. Pirbhai. *Strategies for Real-Time System Specification*, 2nd ed. New York: Dorset House Publishing, 1988.

[Hatley et al., 2000]

_____, and P. Hruschka. *Process for System Architecture and Requirements Engineering.* New York: Dorset House Publishing, 2000.

[Henderson-Sellers and Edwards, 1994]

Henderson-Sellers, B., and J. Edwards. *The Working Object.* Englewood Cliffs, N.J.: Prentice-Hall, 1994.

[Jacobson et al., 1992]

Jacobson, I., M. Christerson, P. Jonsson, and G. Övergaard. *Object-Oriented Software Engineering.* Wokingham, England: Addison-Wesley, 1992.

[Kay, 1969]

Kay, A. *The Reactive Engine.* University of Utah, Department of Computer Science, August 1969.

[Kuhn, 1970]

Kuhn, T. *The Structure of Scientific Revolutions.* Chicago: University of Chicago Press, 1970.

[LaLonde and Pugh, 1991]

LaLonde, W., and J. Pugh. "Subclassing Not= Subtyping Not= Is-a." *Journal of Object-Oriented Programming*, Vol. 3, No. 5 (January 1991), pp. 57-62.

[Lampson and Redell, 1980]

Lampson, B.W., and D.D. Redell. "Experience with Processes and Monitors in Mesa." *Communications of the ACM*, Vol. 23, No. 2 (February 1980), pp. 105-17.

[Larman, 1997]

Larman, C. *Applying UML and Patterns.* Englewood Cliffs, N.J.: Prentice Hall, 1997.

[Lieberherr and Holland, 1989]

Lieberherr, K.J., and I.M. Holland. "Assuring Good Style for Object-Oriented Programs." *IEEE Software,* Vol. 6, No. 9 (September 1989), pp. 38-48.

[Liskov et al., 1981]

Liskov, B., et al. *CLU Reference Manual.* New York: Springer-Verlag, 1981.

[Love, 1993]

Love, T. *Object Lessons.* New York: SIGS Books, 1993.

[Lurch, 1972]

Lurch, E.J. *A Legion of Disasters.* Colchester, England: Wyvern Press, 1972.

[Martin and Odell, 1995]

Martin, J., and J. Odell. *Object-Oriented Methods: A Foundation.* Englewood Cliffs, N.J.: Prentice-Hall, 1995.

[McConnell, 1993]

McConnell, S. *Code Complete.* Redmond, Wash.: Microsoft Press, 1993.

[Meyer, 1988]

Meyer, B. *Object-Oriented Software Construction.* Englewood Cliffs, N.J.: Prentice-Hall, 1988.

[Meyer, 1992]

_____. *Eiffel: The Language.* Englewood Cliffs, N.J.: Prentice-Hall, 1992.

[Mowbray and Zahavi, 1995]

Mowbray, T.J., and R. Zahavi. *The Essential CORBA.* New York: John Wiley & Sons, 1995.

[Muller, 1997]

Muller, P.-A. *Instant UML.* Birmingham, England: Wrox Press, 1997.

[Orfali et al., 1996]

Orfali, R., D. Harkey, and J. Edwards. *The Essential Distributed Objects Survival Guide*. New York: John Wiley & Sons, 1996.

[Page-Jones, 1988]

Page-Jones, M. *The Practical Guide to Structured Systems Design*, 2nd ed. Englewood Cliffs, N.J.: Prentice-Hall, 1988.

[Page-Jones, 1991]

_____. "Object Orientation: Stop, Look and Listen!" *Hotline on Object Orientation*, Vol. 2, No. 3 (January 1991), pp. 1-7.

[Page-Jones et al., 1990]

_____, L.L. Constantine, and S. Weiss. "The Uniform Object Notation." *Computer Language*, Vol. 7, No. 10 (October 1990), pp. 69-87.

[Parnas, 1972]

Parnas, D. "Information Distributing Aspects of Design Methodology," *Proceedings of the 1971 IFIP Congress*. Booklet TA-3. Amsterdam: North-Holland, 1972.

[Porter, 1992]

Porter, H.H. "Separating the Subtype Hierarchy from the Inheritance of Implementation." *Journal of Object-Oriented Programming*, Vol. 4, No. 9 (February 1992), pp. 20-29.

[Richards and Whitby-Strevens, 1980]

Richards, M., and C. Whitby-Strevens. *BCPL—The Language and Its Compiler.* Cambridge, England: Cambridge University Press, 1980.

[Rosenberg and Scott, 1999]

Rosenberg, D., and K. Scott. *Use Case Driven Object Modeling with UML*. Reading, Mass.: Addison-Wesley, 1999.

[Ross and Schoman, 1977]

Ross, D.T., and K.E. Schoman. "Structured Analysis for Requirements Definition." *IEEE Transactions on Software Engineering*, Vol. 3, No. 1 (January 1977), pp. 23-37.

[Rumbaugh et al., 1999]

Rumbaugh, J., I. Jacobson, and G. Booch. *The Unified Modeling Language Reference Manual.* Reading, Mass.: Addison-Wesley, 1999.

[Sha et al., 1990]

Sha, L., R. Rajkumar, and J.P. Lehoczky. "Priority Inheritance Protocols: An Approach to Real-Time Synchronization." *IEEE Transactions on Computers,* Vol. 39, No. 9 (September 1990), pp. 1175-85.

[Sharble and Cohen, 1993]

Sharble, R.C., and S.S. Cohen. "The Object-Oriented Brewery: A Comparison of Two Object-Oriented Development Methods." *ACM Software Engineering Notes,* Vol. 18, No. 2 (April 1993), pp. 60-73.

[Shlaer and Mellor, 1992]

Shlaer, S., and S. Mellor. *Object Lifecycles: Modeling the World in States.* Englewood Cliffs, N.J.: Prentice-Hall, 1992.

[Skolnik, 1980]

Skolnik, M. *Introduction to Radar Systems.* New York: McGraw-Hill, 1980.

[Stroustrup, 1997]

Stroustrup, B. *The C++ Programming Language,* 2nd ed. Reading, Mass.: Addison-Wesley, 1997.

[Szyperski, 1998]

Szyperski, C. *Component Software: Beyond Object-Oriented Programming.* Reading, Mass.: Addison-Wesley, 1998.

[Ward and Mellor, 1985]

Ward, P., and S. Mellor. *Structured Development for Real-Time Systems.* Englewood Cliffs, N.J.: Prentice-Hall, 1985.

[*Webster's,* 1981]

*Webster's Third New International Dictionary,* ed. P.B. Gove. Chicago: G. & C. Merriam Co., 1981.

[Wegner, 1990]

Wegner, P. "Concepts and Paradigms of Object-Oriented Programming." *ACM SIGPLAN OOPS Messenger,* Vol. 1, No. 1 (August 1990), pp. 7-87.

[Wiener, 1995]

Wiener, R. *Software Development Using Eiffel.* Englewood Cliffs, N.J.: Prentice-Hall, 1995.

[Wilkes et al., 1951]

Wilkes, M.V., D.J. Wheeler, and S. Gill. *The Preparation of Programs for an Electronic Digital Computer.* Reading, Mass.: Addison-Wesley, 1951.

[Yourdon, 1989]

Yourdon, E. *Modern Structured Analysis.* Englewood Cliffs, N.J.: Prentice-Hall, 1989.

[Yourdon and Constantine, 1979]

_____, and L.L. Constantine. *Structured Design,* 2nd ed. Englewood Cliffs, N.J.: Prentice-Hall, 1979.

[Zdonik, 1990]

Zdonik, S. "Object-Oriented Type Evolution." *Advances in Database Programming Languages,* ed. F. Banchillon and P. Buneman. Reading, Mass.: Addison-Wesley, 1990.

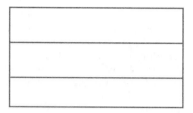

# **I**ndex